# *Advance Praise for* Achieving College Dreams

"If we are to solve the manifold problems of public schools, higher education can no longer hold itself aloof and just skim off the top. *Achieving College Dreams* tells the story of Cal Berkeley's efforts to partner and help, asking the hard questions, assessing what works and doesn't, and learning along the way, in the best spirit of public service. Let's hope more of higher education is inspired by this to roll up its sleeves."

**—Anthony Marx, President, New York Public Library; former President of Amherst College**

"Weinstein and Worrell take us inside the development and evolution of CAL Prep by focusing on expanding the opportunities for the education and socio-emotional development of low-income, under-represented secondary school students. They weave together diverse voices, data sets, theory and research into a volume that is compelling and engaging. The volume is of vital interest to practitioners, academics, policy makers, and laymen alike."

**—Edward Seidman, Professor of Applied Psychology, Steinhardt School of Culture, Education and Development, New York University**

"*Achieving College Dreams* is an honest and powerful story of a university committed to creating a high school that embodies equity and excellence. It tells a sometimes heartwarming, sometimes painful story of the trials and triumphs of a school in the making. The book's value comes in part from the authors' willingness to share, along with their success, what did not work and the lessons learned. I recommend it to anyone interested in connecting research and theory to practice, university-community partnerships, designing new schools, or school reform more generally."

**—Deborah Stipek, Judy Koch Professor of Education, Graduate School of Education, Stanford University**

"*Achieving College Dreams* presents a clarion call to colleges and universities to engage their local schools and communities for mutual benefit, along with a roster of strategies for overcoming the daunting obstacles and challenges for creating an excellent and equitable educational environment for poorly served students."

**—Hugh Mehan, Professor Emeritus of Sociology, The Center for Research on Educational Equity, Access, and Teaching Excellence (CREATE), University of California, San Diego**

"The story of the California College Preparatory Academy captures the commitment of a great university, a handful of dedicated professors and educators, and a charter school organization to pave the road to college for underserved youth. I am left to wonder why other universities have failed to follow suit and use their intellectual and material resources to promote college readiness."

—**Daniel L. Duke, Professor, Curry School of Education,**
**University of Virginia**

Achieving College Dreams

# Achieving College Dreams

HOW A UNIVERSITY–CHARTER DISTRICT
PARTNERSHIP CREATED AN EARLY COLLEGE
HIGH SCHOOL

*Edited by*

**RHONA S. WEINSTEIN**

**FRANK C. WORRELL**

OXFORD
UNIVERSITY PRESS

**OXFORD**
UNIVERSITY PRESS

Oxford University Press is a department of the University of Oxford. It furthers
the University's objective of excellence in research, scholarship, and education
by publishing worldwide. Oxford is a registered trade mark of Oxford University
Press in the UK and certain other countries.

Published in the United States of America by Oxford University Press
198 Madison Avenue, New York, NY 10016, United States of America.

© Oxford University Press 2016

Library of Congress Cataloging-in-Publication Data
Names: Weinstein, Rhona S., editor of compilation. | Worrell, Frank C.,
editor of compilation.
Title: Achieving college dreams: how a university-charter district
partnership created an early college high school / edited by Rhona S.
Weinstein, Frank C. Worrell.
Description: New York: Oxford University Press, [2016] | Includes index.
Identifiers: LCCN 2015037543
Subjects: LCSH: Preparatory schools—California—Case studies. | Charter
schools—California—Case studies. | California College Preparatory
Academy (Oakland, Calif.) | University of California, Berkeley. |
Educational equalization—California.
Classification: LCC LC58.5.C35 A44 20106 | DDC 373.22/2—dc23 LC record available
at http://lccn.loc.gov/2015037543
ISBN 978–0–19–026090–3

9 8 7 6 5 4 3 2 1
Printed by Sheridan, USA

*To the youth who bloom with rich educational opportunities,*
*To a world where unequal schools become a social ill of the past.*

# CONTENTS

## FOR THE FUTURE...

I t's one thing to have voices in your head, but it's twice as hard to have anxiety attacks when every single voice is repeating, "I'm slipping, I'm falling, I can't get up . . ."

When you fight the fatigue that crept up on you every single night after heating this pencil trying to figure something out, or pull something out of your head because most of your life you heard others, and trained yourself to believe . . . there's nothing there . . .

And you question yourself, was this your fault, or were you trained to believe that too, because I don't know about you, but I know there was at least one person in my life who tried to control my every move, and it took me the longest to get myself together to say, respect the nature of my growth—

Everyone knows, the more you pull on a plant in soil, the more complications arise in its process of development, be patient . . .

Time management, self-preservation, patience, yeah I thought without those three things I could make it, but I also found myself face first inside the same crater of failure . . . and I figured, this would be the only mark that I would leave on this Earth, until I noticed the beautiful works of life filling it in.

You heard others say "you're not half empty, you're half full," but what you needed to hear was "release all the waste of fear, and allow your self to be filled up with fearlessness,"

So here I am, there you are,

and hopefully you as well as them may know one day that my words move with **LOGIC**, and what I am full of right now is my **HEART**!

So now, I can tell myself as well as I tell you,

That this is the process of your conscience killing those horrific ghosts in your soul and waking up your dome,

This is the light sparking under your frozen feet after others had you tied you down to the ground of this cold world,

This, this is the **AFTERMATH** from not killing every **BRAIN CELL** for **ONE INTEGRAL**,

This is for the peace that you may find in your life during a new level of a beautiful struggle

This is for your supportive loved ones who you knew you would see physically on this day, but who ended up blowing in the wind,

This is for the voice of yours that was overshadowed by ignorance and disbelief

This is for the gun shots that missed us, and therefore gave us more strength to reach this day

And this is for the adolescent in you who, who went from saying seven more years, to time's up . . .

Shyra Gums, Class of 2013
California College Preparatory Academy
Graduation Exercises, June 8, 2013
Alfred Hertz Memorial Concert Hall
University of California, Berkeley

# FOREWORD

I n the fall of 2005, the University of California (UC) Berkeley, in partnership with Aspire Public Schools, opened the California College Preparatory Academy (CAL Prep), a new charter school designed to immerse students in a culture of high academic expectations and improve their college readiness. The partners wanted to develop a model for preparing students for success in competitive college settings. As then chancellor of UC Berkeley, I spoke to the 85 children attending the inaugural classes of sixth and seventh grade of this new public charter school in Oakland. They came almost entirely from low-income families, many were underrepresented minorities, and all hoped to be the first in their families to attend college. One of the seventh grade students who led us on a tour of the facility told me that her goal was to go to UC Berkeley. Six years later, I experienced the great joy of speaking at the high school graduation of the first cohort of CAL Prep students, every one of whom was accepted to a 4-year college. Gratifyingly, I had the privilege of welcoming this outstanding young woman to UC Berkeley.

*Achieving College Dreams* speaks to this deep and long-term partnership between a public university (UC Berkeley) and a charter school management organization (Aspire) to create a new secondary school, blending expertise drawn from practice and research. The project was initially funded with grants from the Bill & Melinda Gates Foundation and support from UC Berkeley. To be frank, there was some disagreement within the Berkeley leadership team as to the suitability of this enterprise for UC Berkeley. But it was clear to me that we must do whatever we can to address the challenges faced by the K–12 system, most especially for students from low-income and minority backgrounds. The CAL Prep mission to eliminate disparities in K–12 and to increase access to higher education is consonant with the mission of a great public university such as UC Berkeley. And CAL Prep has attracted the passion of many dedicated faculty. CAL Prep has turned out to be one of the very best investments that I made as chancellor.

It is not uncommon to find that many university leaders come from disadvantaged backgrounds. One reason these individuals may have chosen education as a career is because it is the most effective leveling mechanism in society. As I told the excited students of that first CAL Prep class, I knew personally what their lives would be like without education. My family lived in a tenement, infected by rodents and insects, and one was expected to quit school and find a job when one turned 15½, as my older brother and sister did. Not a single person in my eighth grade class finished high school. I was fortunate to be bused out of my neighborhood to an elite Catholic boys' secondary school; my local church paid the tuition. Having the privilege of a great secondary school education that led to an excellent 4-year college was critical to changing my life prospects. Ultimately, it proved even more important than what I chose as an undergraduate major and my PhD work.

My transition from the community I came from to the community I was joining was not easy for me as a teenager. While attending high school, family and local challenges did not go away. Fortunately, my teachers provided the personal attention needed to deal with these challenges so that I could continue to achieve academically. Importantly, my high school offered the beyond-the-classroom support that is as necessary as the in-classroom support for students from ultra–low-income families. CAL Prep is committed to the success of students from disenfranchised backgrounds, to prepare them to attend and succeed in institutions such as UC Berkeley, by providing intense academic support as well as emotional and social support, including engaging their families in preparedness for college education.

Coming to UC Berkeley as chancellor from Yale (where I completed my PhD) and from the Massachusetts Institute of Technology (where I spent the majority of my career) was both a great privilege and an enormous responsibility. As a public institution that is also one of the world's preeminent universities, UC Berkeley attracts excellent faculty who offer large numbers of students from all demographic backgrounds a rigorous education comparable to that provided by the nation's best private universities. My priority as chancellor was to ensure that UC Berkeley maintained its public character as expressed in our motto of "Access and Excellence." Overall, we have done well in maintaining accessibility for students from low-income families, with some 35% to 39% of our students coming from families with incomes under $45,000 during my tenure (2004–2013).

Regrettably, at UC Berkeley, we have had less success in improving the representation of minority groups. The impetus for CAL Prep came in part from the demise of affirmative action in California because of Proposition 209 and the concomitant shrinking minority student representation at the university. CAL Prep represents a prospective vehicle for increasing diversity in the undergraduate and graduate population and, ultimately, the professoriate. The year I became the chancellor of Berkeley, there was not a single African American student in the freshman engineering class! This was simply shocking to me. It was impossible to believe that among the more than two million African Americans in California, there was not a single one who was qualified to enter UC Berkeley as a freshman in engineering.

The shortfall in underrepresented minority students at UC Berkeley showed how important it was to have an impact at the secondary school level. We believed that it must be possible to be more effective in educating underrepresented minority students from disadvantaged backgrounds. The conception for CAL Prep was not just to have an impact on students but also to improve significantly college preparatory education methodologies for those coming from challenging backgrounds. CAL Prep's importance goes beyond individual students to advancing higher education in communities where tertiary education has not traditionally been part of the culture.

It is the mission of public universities to serve the whole population and not just those from privileged backgrounds. This ideal has been put at risk by the recent economic crisis and the unprecedented withdrawal of state funding from public universities. Currently, I am co-leading the Lincoln Project, an initiative of the American Academy of Arts and Sciences to seek new models of support for public research and teaching universities through public–private partnerships of universities, businesses, governments, foundations, and philanthropists. Without new funding models, both access and excellence in higher education cannot be preserved.

CAL Prep serves as a model of the important role that public universities should play in community partnerships, especially in educational reform, and of what can be achieved through innovative public–private partnerships to the benefit of our communities, our state, and our nation. Unique to this journey is the deep and sustained partnership between tertiary and secondary education (a research university and a charter district), which has enabled an increase in resources (visionary, fiscal, and personnel), a testing ground or urban field station for innovative practice, and ultimately, *mutual* learning with benefits for both sides.

A final note about that young woman from CAL Prep who is now at Berkeley—I ran into her on campus the other day and she tells me that she aspires one day to become chancellor of this great university. Do not count her out!

Robert J. Birgeneau
Arnold and Barbara Silverman Distinguished Professor
Physics, Materials Science and Engineering, and Public Policy
Ninth Chancellor of the University of California,
Berkeley (2004–2013)

# CONTRIBUTOR LIST

**Gibor Basri**
Department of Astronomy
University of California, Berkeley
Berkeley, California

**Lionel H. Bialis-White**
Schoolzilla
Oakland, California

**Robert J. Birgeneau**
Department of Physics
University of California, Berkeley
Berkeley, California

**Michelle Y. Cortez**
Aspire Lionel Wilson
Preparatory Academy
Oakland, California

**Elise Darwish**
Aspire Public Schools
Oakland, California

**Tatiana Epanchin-Troyan**
Teach For America
Seattle, Washington

**Marjorie (Susie) Goodin**
Berkeley, California

**Ryan Grow**
Aspire Richmond California
College Preparatory Academy
Richmond, California

**Shyra Gums**
California State University,
East Bay
Hayward, California

**Robert E. Jorgensen**
San Luis Obispo, California

**Gail Kaufman**
Center for Educational Partnerships
University of California, Berkeley
Berkeley, California

**Tatiana Lim-Breitbart**
Aspire Richmond California
College Preparatory Academy
Richmond, California

**Justin F. Martin**
Department of Psychology
Whitworth University
Spokane, Washington

**Zena R. Mello**
Department of Psychology
San Francisco State University
San Francisco, California

**Genaro M. Padilla**
Department of English
University of California, Berkeley
Berkeley, California

**P. David Pearson**
Graduate School of Education
University of California, Berkeley
Berkeley, California

**Megan Reed**
Achievement Network (ANet)
Boston, Massachusetts

**Sarah Salazar**
Aspire Richmond California
College Preparatory Academy
Richmond, California

**Nilofar Sami**
Youth and Family Services
Fremont, California

**Angelica Stacy**
College of Chemistry
University of California, Berkeley
Berkeley, California

**Stacy Thomas**
Aspire Golden State College
Preparatory Academy
Oakland, California

**Rhona S. Weinstein**
Department of Psychology
University of California, Berkeley
Berkeley, California

**Frank C. Worrell**
Graduate School of Education
University of California, Berkeley
Berkeley, California

# I | Beginnings

# 1 | Introduction—A University's Role in Secondary School Reform

**RHONA S. WEINSTEIN AND FRANK C. WORRELL**

*"This class will always be the one that broke all the barriers . . . We have to set a model not just for younger students, but for our brothers, sisters, and cousins. We need them to believe that if we can make it, they can make it. We have the responsibility to continue to make college not a dream, but a reality for others."* (Jorgé Lopez, Graduation Speaker, California College Preparatory Academy, June 2011)

*"Our work is not only to make students college-ready but also to prepare universities to become student-ready."* (P. David Pearson, Dean, Graduate School of Education, University of California, Berkeley, 2001–2010)

THIS BOOK TELLS THE STORY of a more than 10-year partnership between a public research university (University of California [UC] Berkeley) and a charter management organization (CMO; Aspire Public Schools) to create and nurture a nonselective, early college, and regional high school for low-income students who are the first in their family to attend college. Our goal was to address glaring inequities in educational opportunity by designing a school setting that would move underserved students *upward*— from low expectations and academic failure toward a college-preparatory education that would ready them for college eligibility and success. All of us on both sides of the partnership became immersed in a deliberate process of co-construction of the secondary school and in community-engaged scholarship to improve the school as well as contribute to knowledge.

*Achieving College Dreams* takes us inside the workings of the partnership, the development of the school over time, and the spillover of effects across district and university—as seen through diverse lenses of method (theory, research, and practice) and voice (stakeholders from students to superintendents). Our focus is on the process of this work over time, rather than the results at the finish line. Honest about the struggles, we are also hopeful about the outcomes. Our wish is to broaden the debate of what is possible and how to get there—in redesigned high schools that prepare their diverse students to be ready for college and be successful there—and in student-ready universities that can better serve the needs of this population. Not only has college readiness for all become a hot-button issue in the United States, but it has also captured the attention of countries across the globe. Importantly, case studies of new-start schools and of partnerships across secondary–tertiary education systems are sorely lacking, especially involving high schools and especially under-served students.

In this chapter, we begin with an overview of our journey. Next we describe the context in 2002–2003 that made a campuswide role in comprehensive secondary school reform a vital imperative for UC Berkeley. Finally, we turn to the need for a book such as this one and its overarching plan—the gaps in understanding and questions to be addressed, our theoretical perspectives and methods, and the organization of the chapters therein.

## Breaking Down Barriers: Bird's Eye View

The California College Preparatory Academy, or CAL Prep, as it is affectionately called, first opened its doors in 2005, although planning had begun in 2002. Faced with glaring achievement gaps in high school graduation rates and in access to and success in college, the demise of affirmative action as a remedy, and a shrinking number of students of color at the university, UC Berkeley took a bold step to directly address the academic underpreparedness of low-income and minority youth. We responded to an initiative from the Bill & Melinda Gates Foundation to start an early-college secondary school and to do so in partnership with Aspire Public Schools. Launched by the Gates Foundation in 2002, early college secondary schools required collaboration across the secondary–tertiary divide and were envisioned to accelerate the academic preparation of low-income and underserved students (Webb, 2014). By design, such schools use a standards-based, college-preparatory program infused with college-credit courses, ensuring a more successful transition to and through higher education. Now 15 years later, this network of partnered early college secondary schools has grown to 280 such schools across 32 states in the United States, with growing evidence of impact on student college-going rates and college success.

The decision to start a new secondary school led us down a new and challenging path, not the university laboratory school of old for largely privileged students but rather a 21st-century urban field station that targeted underserved students and issues of educational equity (Cucciara, 2010; Lytle, 2010). Within the UC system, CAL Prep (founded in 2005) at UC Berkeley followed in the footsteps of the Preuss School (1999) at UC San Diego and was later joined by West Sacramento College Prep (2007) at UC Davis and the UCLA Community School (2009). These efforts in creating new secondary schools reflected our shared concern about ensuring diversity across the nine UC campuses with undergraduates and illuminating the conditions for both equity and excellence.

We found ourselves in complex waters, working across the K–12 and higher education divide and engaged in partnerships with private philanthropy and a CMO. Our venture also required the respectful coordination of two different cultures—one primed for action and the other for reflection—toward shared goals. We began with hopes for a Grade 6–12 secondary school, but reality on the ground narrowed the vision to a Grade 9–12 high school—a part of the story that lengthened the start-up history but did not reduce its challenges.

We, the editors of this volume, served as founding co-directors for research and development for our new-start secondary school, playing a leadership role in both the vision for the school and the evidence provided here. I (Weinstein), a faculty member in psychology and a community psychologist by training, study the dynamics of how low expectations, especially for poor and ethnic minority youth, become self-fulfilling prophecies in schooling. For too many years, I carried searing images of African American and Latino youth languishing in many classrooms I visited—heads on desks, stuck in low-track classes and disciplinary actions, failing in great numbers, and opting out of the academic enterprise. I also worked on the ground, using research findings to promote more equitable classrooms and schools with raised expectations. These projects included collaborations to detrack a high school and to turn around a low-performing elementary school at risk for closure. Such efforts to reform schools proved frustrating at every turn—stymied by politics and institutional resistance, frequent changes of principals and superintendents, and a narrow vision of what was needed or what was possible.

One poignant encounter, which I never forgot, was with an articulate third grader, who was crying softly in the front office. When I asked why, she reported that she was being punished for not doing her homework, and she was even held back a grade for the same reason. I learned that she was homeless and although she carried her assignments with her, she never found a quiet space or time in which to work. No effort on my part could unite social services and the school to develop an effective plan for housing or to secure a caring context at the school for this student to grow academically. I held on to my hope by a thread that one day all children, no matter their circumstances at home, could attend schools that fostered their capacity to achieve at the highest level. The call to join this collaboration met my lifelong interest in creating a new setting—an exemplary school, which would offer both rigor and support for children and youth ill-served by the current educational system.

I (Worrell), a faculty member in the Graduate School of Education and a school psychologist, came to the United States from Trinidad and Tobago to obtain my doctoral degree. In Trinidad, I attended and then taught at one of the most selective schools in the country. I also served as principal of a small private school—similar to continuation schools in the United States—for students who had flunked out of or been expelled from the public school system. Moving from being a member of a majority group in Trinidad to a member of a minority group in the United States, I was confronted with how critical social context is for the positive integration of academic and ethnic identities. Conflict between these two identities (where being a scholar is perceived by some minority group members in the United States as acting White) can undermine achievement.

I became interested in students at both ends of the spectrum—those at risk for school failure (who appear to be pushed out, rather than dropping out of school) and those who are identified as academically talented (whose paths are smoothed as they are groomed to succeed). Low-income and ethnic minorities such as African Americans and Latinos are disproportionately present in the at-risk pool and absent from the talented pool. As faculty director of the Academic Talent Development Program at UC Berkeley, a program geared to developing rather than merely selecting talent, I saw firsthand what collegelike seminars within a supportive summer program could awaken in students with limited opportunities at the elementary and secondary level. This type of academic challenge, with a range of supports, proved life-changing. Thus, the chance at CAL Prep—to create such an intellectual environment for all students and to foster the positive integration of academic and ethnic identities—galvanized my participation.

CAL Prep enrolls underserved students on the San Francisco–East Bay corridor, setting no academic or motivational requirements for admission. Its students are largely low-income, ethnic minority (African American and Latino), and the first in their families to complete college. At entry, many of these students are academically behind, accustomed to failure, unsure of their capacity to succeed, and prone to avoid effort. In the poem at the beginning of this book, high school graduate Shyra Gums captures the experience of early failure in previous schools, recalling the pain of negative messages that eradicated any belief that she could succeed. In her words, "Most of your life you heard others, and trained yourself to believe . . . there's nothing there." She tells us this school enabled her to "release all the waste of fear" and to find joy in achievement, which she eloquently describes as "the light sparkling under your frozen feet" and the liberated "voice of yours that [earlier] was overshadowed by ignorance and disbelief."

The earliest days of this school are etched in our brains—visions of students lining the halls outside of classrooms, disciplinary infractions, violent incidents, and attrition of both teachers and students—challenges that occurred despite or perhaps because of our very high expectations. And student transformation proved incremental and uneven, taking far more time than education policy would typically allow. As history teacher Ryan Grow stated (UC Berkeley–CAL Prep faculty dinner, October 17, 2008),

> Transformation, for me, is epitomized by one student . . . we'll call him T. The first year, T. set the record for the number of times I had to send a student out of the class for detention, but 3 years later T. is one of the class leaders in academic focus and achievement. In T.'s first year, he acted out daily, turned out the classroom lights whenever he was sent to detention, and almost never turned in his work. At the end of his first year, although he faced the principal and teachers with bravado, it was clear that his biggest fear was that he would be expelled from CAL Prep. Instead, he repeated the grade and slowly his behavior changed. As far as I know, his family situation and living situation are the same now as it was 3 years ago. The only change is T.'s recognition that any teacher or adult at CAL Prep will help him . . . there is always an adult role model who asks only and always the best from him. T. is not perfect, but T. is transformed. And there are 150 other students at CAL Prep who are also transformed.

Against tremendous odds, the first graduates of CAL Prep were accepted into college—each and every one of them. The harsh reality of strict high school graduation requirements left one of these students behind as a fifth-year senior. In a loving display of community, this student was chosen to be one of the class speakers. His speech, honest about wrong turns taken and inspiring about his burning intent to graduate, brought the house down in the Pauley Ballroom at UC Berkeley, where a crowd of more than 600 gathered to honor this special moment. For this student, it was the support of teachers and peers that turned his pledge into reality—high school graduation and a college path 1 year later.

Although the ride was rough, the attainment results of our first graduating class and the ones that followed were gratifying. For this first class, 100% of seniors gained college admission (with an average of 4 college classes and 12 units under their belt). And 94% of these graduates enrolled in college, 73% in 4-year institutions. Furthermore, 33% of these graduates were enrolled in the highly selective UC campuses, more than two times the state eligibility rate of 13.4% and more than four times the state rate for African American and Latino students (6.3% and 6.9%, respectively), the population we serve.

How and why did we embark on this journey? What kind of high school did we jointly create and how did we move from chaos to student transformation? What were the opportunities as well as challenges for this university and charter district partnership? Blending the perspectives of researchers and practitioners, we tell this story in the pages that follow.

## The Context

### The Demise of Affirmative Action in College Admissions

The interdependence between secondary and tertiary education is felt most keenly in public universities. As Timar and colleagues (2002, p. 11) have underscored, "Throughout its history, UC's capacity to realize its mission as a selective, yet public, land-grant institution has been closely connected to the quality of graduates coming from the state's high schools." In its earliest years, education historian Geraldine Clifford (1995) noted that the boundaries between the UC system and secondary schools were porous, with university professors teaching both secondary and college students. This was a time where "*preparatory school appendages* were still common in American higher education" (Clifford, 1995, p. 22). In the face of unprepared students and insufficient numbers of secondary schools, the creation of a secondary academy at Berkeley was one way to develop a supply of qualified students for admission. Clifford described two university-run schools in UC Berkeley's early history, no longer in existence or institutionally remembered: University High School (founded in 1914) and University Elementary School (founded in 1921).

UC was founded in 1868 as a public land-grant institution—funded under the 1862 Morrill Act by President Abraham Lincoln to educate the full diversity of citizens as well as to advance research in disciplines of great societal need. At the start, the UC system embraced criteria of both *diversity* and *selectivity* in its student body. To reflect diversity, admissions were to be nonsectarian, nonpolitical, not based on income, from across the state, and without gender bias. Reflecting universal access as well as selectivity, the California Master Plan for Higher Education, adopted in 1960 under Clark Kerr, became a world model for higher education (Marginson, 2014). This three-tiered system included (1) 10 University of California campuses, specializing in research, of which 9 campuses admit the top 12.5% of high school graduates; (2) 23 California State University campuses, which enroll the top third of high school graduates; and (3) 112 California community colleges, which accept all students into 2-year programs, with transfer opportunities into the UCs or CSUs to complete an undergraduate degree.

In 1974, a more exacting principle for enrollment was added through legislation and was approved by the UC Regents: undergraduate admissions should "reflect the general ethnic, sexual, and economic composition of California high school graduates" (Timar, Ogawa, & Orillion, 2002, p. 11). Despite the historic commitment to a diverse student body and extensive outreach efforts, achieving diversity in student admissions—in the face of intractable achievement gaps—proved difficult without the help of affirmative action policies. Yet in public universities across the country, the use of affirmative action as a tool for admissions had become a divisive issue that had been under legal challenge in the courts since the 1970s.

In 1995, the UC Regents adopted SP-1, a resolution which outlawed the use of race, religion, and gender as criteria for university admission. This decision was followed by voter approval of Proposition 209 in 1996, which in effect ended affirmative action in all California state government actions. The result was a severe drop in the enrollment of African American and Latino students on highly selective UC campuses such as UC Berkeley (Grodsky & Kurlaender, 2010; Orfield & Miller, 1998). Reflective of impact along the pipeline, a study of affirmative action bans in four states (California, Florida, Texas, and Washington) documented great reductions in the enrollment of underrepresented students of color in six different graduate fields of study, placing scientific and technological advances at enormous peril (Garces, 2013).

The Regents, however, reaffirmed their commitment to diversity in the student body, underscoring that it would be achieved "through the preparation and empowerment of students in this state to succeed rather than through a system of artificial preferences" (Timar et al., 2002, p. 3, citing Regents of the University of California, 1995). The postaffirmative action era came with far greater financial investment in educational outreach, sharply cut during the economic recession of the late 1990s, and a greater commitment to school-centered reform—a commitment that was hotly debated. Timar and colleagues (2002) described skepticism in the President's Office about engagement in school reform—concerns that such efforts that might be beyond university capacity and might incur an unrealistic accountability for improving the most difficult schools. Ultimately, school-centered approaches became only one of four components of the new UC outreach strategy. Although the Early Academic Outreach Program continued to bring resources to underrepresented students in order to strengthen eligibility, they were now to be delivered through partnerships with 150 of the most underperforming K–12 schools in California.

It was this context that fueled the creation of the four UC secondary schools targeting low-income and first-generation college students (at UC San Diego, UC Berkeley, UC Davis, and UC Los Angeles), preparing them for college eligibility and providing models of what can be achieved with underserved students (Mehan, Kaufman, Lytle, Quartz, & Weinstein, 2010). Importantly, the existence of these four schools moved the engagement of the UC system beyond disparate college-preparatory programs toward a deeper partnership around comprehensive secondary school reform. Consistent with UC's land-grant heritage, this new schools effort advanced service, research, and training around a societal problem of great need—to provide an excellent college-preparatory education with equity for all students.

## Unequal Schools, Unequal Outcomes

We face a complex set of achievement gaps—implicating both K–12 and higher education. These gaps are nested in unequal schools, in a country with shifting demographics (more ethnic minorities, greater income inequality, an aging population) but fewer supports (a shrinking safety net), and in a global world of ever-rising academic expectations. Just during the course of our journey, discussions shifted from college-*eligible* students to college-*ready* ones to college-*successful* ones. In a knowledge-based and rapidly changing global economy, an undergraduate degree has become a requirement *for all* in order to ensure a more secure economic future (Bowen, Chingos, & McPherson, 2009).

Long called the bellwether state, California has the largest population in the United States, with the most linguistic and income diversity, and among the lowest per-pupil expenditure (EdSource Report, September 2010). A report by the California Assembly Select Committee on the Status of Boys and Men of Color (2012) illustrates the time bomb at hand. As argued, in the face of a growing proportion of adults older than 65 and a declining birthrate, "a greater share of the population will depend on fewer working adults" (p. 1). As of 2010, more than 70% of Californians younger than age 25 were of color, with the numbers growing. Moreover, these students (African American, Latino, Native American, and Southeast Asian) were *disproportionately* disadvantaged by poverty, unsafe neighborhoods, and inferior schools. Although the current high school graduation rate of 56.6% for males of color would yield $8.1 billion for the economy, a 100% graduation rate would produce more than four times the amount at $37.2 billion. The report emphasizes that the state's "prosperity and health depend upon all Californians [having] a fair chance to thrive and succeed" (p. 1).

As many have argued, the costs of this lost talent are enormous to both individuals in lifetime salary and to society in missed taxes, declines in global competitiveness, and added costs in government assistance, imprisonment, and healthcare (e.g., Levin & Rouse, 2012). From subject-matter proficiency to high school dropout and graduation rates, from college readiness to college graduation, the pipeline to and through college remains a leaky and inequitable one, with a loss of talent at every turn, especially so for certain ethnic minority groups and low-income students. Although attention is focused on the US position in the middle on international rankings of student achievement in 2012, the larger story lies beneath the averages, for example, with the mathematics (math) scores of Black (421) and Hispanic (455) students greatly trailing those of White (506) and Asian (549) students (National Center for Education Statistics, n.d., p. 22).

Using data from the US Department of Education, Greene and Forster (2003) showed that although high schools lose 30% of their ninth-grade cohort by graduation (a 70% graduation rate), they lose disproportionately

more Black (49%) and Hispanic (48%) students. Moreover, at graduation, only 32% of these high school graduates (20% of Blacks and 16%
of Hispanics) are eligible for college. Once in college, only 58.3% of the
2004 cohort entering 4-year institutions completed a bachelor's degree
in 2010, with completion rates diverging by more than 20 percentage
points across racial ethnic groups (Aud et al., 2012): African American
(39.5%), Asian American (68.7%), European American (61.5%), Hispanic
American (50.1%), and Native American (39.4%). High school and college completion rates for students of low socioeconomic status parallel
those of underperforming racial and ethnic minorities, but at even lower
levels (Chapman, Laird, Ifill, & KewalRamani, 2011). As Reardon (2011)
has also demonstrated, this income-achievement gap is now 30% to 40%
higher than it was 25 years earlier and it is more than twice as large as the
Black–White gap.

The research evidence remains clear that unequal opportunities both
*between* and *within* schools are at the heart of these seemingly intractable
achievement gaps (Carter & Welner, 2013; Weinstein, 1996). Although
disparities in academic skills are evident in the prekindergarten years by
income level and race/ethnicity (Child Trends, 2012), such disparities are
compounded yearly by an uneven playing field. As a result of residential
segregation by income and race and unequal school funding, low-income
and underrepresented minority students are more likely to attend schools
with the fewest resources. Children in underresourced schools have less
experienced teachers, less learning time, fewer college-preparatory classes
and counselors, and the lowest levels of school safety (Aud et al., 2010,
2012; Darling-Hammond & Sykes, 2003; Oakes et al., 2006; Rogers, Mirra,
Seltzer, & Jun, 2014). Furthermore, regardless of the amount of school
resources, the dynamics of institutionalized expectancy effects are at work,
where, in the face of achievement differences or behavioral infractions,
expectations are lowered and practices exclude rather than support struggling students (Weinstein, 2002). Troubling racial disparities exist within
schools, with African American and Latino students overrepresented in
less challenging classes (Kalogrides & Loeb, 2013) and in suspensions
and expulsions (Aud et al., 2010; Gregory, Skiba, & Noguera, 2010).

Such disparities in educational opportunity and performance varia-
tions by ethnic group and income level are also evident on the global stage
(e.g., Heath & Brinbaum, 2015). As Wilkinson and Pickett (2009) have
shown, the greater the income inequality in countries or even between
states in a country (such as the United States), the lower the average educational attainment. And a casebook edited by Julia Clark (2014) speaks

to reform efforts across the globe directed toward closing the pervasive achievement gap in math and science. As described in *The Economist* (Reforming education, 2011), the world is engaged in "the great schools revolution" with the goal of increasing opportunity by "bringing their worst schools up to the standard of their best."

## Rethinking Secondary Schools for Equity and Excellence

The great schools revolution for excellence with equity is hard to find on a national scale in our high schools. The large comprehensive high school (e.g., Conant, 1959), in place for more than a century, has been notoriously difficult to change, despite new visions and years of restructuring efforts. In a national survey of 820 secondary schools, Lee (2001) found surprisingly few high schools (from 9% to 30%) with *restructuring* reforms known to promote higher achievement *equitably* for all students (such as mixed-ability classes, longer school periods, more sustained teacher–student contact, interactive or constructivist instruction, and teacher collaboration). Even fewer schools reported use of several features. Similarly, Warren Little and DoRPH (1998) found only partial success of the California 5 School Restructuring Demonstration Program, with uneven positive efforts, fewest in high schools and greater benefits for higher rather than lower achieving students. Much of the innovation is found at the elementary school level and most efforts are teacher- or subject-centered rather than school-level focused. We have far to go to move from exemplary practices to exemplary and equitable schools, especially at the secondary level.

All of us on the UC Berkeley side of the partnership wanted to think critically about school design, not only about single programs or practices but also about how the features we envisioned could together create new social regularities between students and teachers in schools. With the sorting of students for different pathways as an entrenched feature of comprehensive high schools, profound change required the detracking of curricular and disciplinary systems in favor of a *single but accommodative* pathway (e.g., Alvarez & Mehan, 2006). The challenge lay in providing a college-preparatory curriculum *for all students*, with both acceleration through college courses and remediation ensured. This outcome could be achieved only when we improved our capacity—organizationally and pedagogically—to interweave rigor and support in engaging a diverse population in learning and in the development of a scholar identity (Weinstein, 2002; Whiting, 2006). To do so would entail a different kind of student learning (fueling curiosity, inquiry, and motivation), programmatic coherence (reducing disjunctions between grades, secondary and postsecondary levels, and between school design and the needs of students), and equal opportunities (trained teachers, effective college counseling, enrichment, and supports). Such directions for reform have been spelled out in a number of reports (e.g., Conley, 2010; Eccles & Grootman, 2002; National Research Council and Institute of Medicine, 2004; Oakes et al., 2006).

It was apparent that the federal reform—No Child Left Behind (NCLB, 2002)—would fail to reduce the achievement gap. Schools were held publicly accountable on high-stake tests for moving a rising number of students within each demographic group toward subject-matter proficiency, with threat of increasing punishment such as school closure. Despite warnings from the academic community, NCLB embraced an accountability *prior to* providing equity in the opportunity to learn—and a punitive one at that. Additionally, an entire industry emerged in the service of school turnaround, upon judged failure: the consequences included transforming schools with newly assigned teachers and principals, converting schools to charters, and creating new-start schools. However, these newly constituted schools had many of the same problems as their predecessors and they often focused narrowly on test scores to avoid being reconstituted once more.

Although newer federal initiatives have pushed for adoption of the Common Core Standards (Porter, McMaken, Hwang, & Yang, 2011), which emphasize critical thinking skills more reflective of college readiness, standards alone will not address the problem of disparities in educational opportunity. The Equity and Excellence Commission (2013, p. 15) concluded that "we cannot continue to leave the *structure* of the schools, systems, and spending unexamined." With the pending and much delayed reauthorization of NCLB, both the scholarly community and the public have become deeply divided over federal versus state rights, the role of standards, testing, and teacher accountability in the reform of schools— even the priority of an equity goal.

Yet NCLB has also had some positive consequences. Fleischman and Heppen (2009, p. 107) have argued that NCLB exposed the failure of a school system to "provide all children with acceptable levels of education;" it pressed districts to adopt reforms "supported by scientifically-based research," and it drove "the search for more effective programs and practices for low-performing schools." Their review of promising high school reform models included charters and educational management organizations, early college high schools, small learning communities, and comprehensive school reform programs. With a boost from NCLB, more than two decades after charter school authorization became available in 1991, 6,700 charter schools now serve 3 million students (The National Alliance for Public Charter Schools, 2015). Moreover, such schools are taking on the challenge of educating a larger proportion of low-income minority students (Wohlstetter, Smith, & Farrell, 2013). Although research shows that charter school outcomes are no better, on average, than their district counterparts, the findings also highlight that some charter schools, especially those run within CMOs or what we call districts, are exemplary in raising achievement (Center for Research on Education Outcomes, 2009). We need to look beneath these averages, examining exemplars to learn more about the features that promote educational excellence and equity and how these conditions can be disseminated to traditional districts.

Importantly, across both traditional and charter public schools, there exists a rising tide of exemplar college-preparatory high schools for historically underserved students, which provides existence proof that under optimal educational conditions, such students can achieve at the highest level. The Fleischman and Heppen (2009) review suggests that although the reform models vary in innovative features (whether in instruction, structure, and/or governance), they all provide smaller environments (more personalized and positive), improved instruction and support, and preparation for life beyond high school. Fleischman and Heppen (2009) also underscore that while design is easy, implementation is the critical challenge.

In recent years, a series of lottery-based experimental studies of many of these model schools offers more rigorous evidence of substantial school impacts, such as improved academic preparedness, graduation rates, and college-going of their students. These include evaluations of early college high schools (Berger et al., 2013, 2014), the Preuss 6–12 School (Bohren & McClure, 2011), career academies (Visher & Stern, 2015), KIPP middle schools (Tuttle et al., 2013), and New York City Small Schools of Choice (Bloom & Unterman, 2013; Unterman, 2014). Although these impact findings are promising, questions remain about the levers that might mediate such impressive outcomes. How do we successfully move a population of greatly underprepared students towards achievement at the level of college-readiness standards? How do we translate these critical features into coordinated practice, bringing it all together at a school level over time? Our knowledge about implementation and school development is decidedly limited.

These models also reflect new pathways and players, such as cross-sector partnerships, private philanthropy, and university-run schools, raising questions about collaboration challenges across the divide with implication for different types of outcomes. Research–practice partnerships offer innovative opportunities for cross-disciplinary knowledge and translational research of more immediate use to schools and districts. Yet they are complex to implement, as Coburn, Penuel, and Geil (2013, p. 24) have argued, pointing to the need for "a more robust dialogue . . . about the strategic trade-offs partnerships face and the resources that are required for success." The Domina and Ruzek (2012) study of K–16 partnerships in California has shown that such alliances take time to show effects and not all are equal. Among their findings, the more comprehensive and policy-focused partnerships, rather than the more narrowly programmatic ones, showed greater positive effects on high school graduation rates and university enrollment rates, but neither type of partnership appeared to improve student access to the highly selective UCs, an issue of interest to us.

Another example can be found in the P-16 movement, which knits together systems from preschool through higher education to spur reform. Davis and Hoffman (2008) suggested that this type of partnership most typically shines a spotlight on the attainment crisis in K–12 but rarely examines this same crisis in higher education, where changes are also urgently needed. Mutual learning across the divide includes confronting the necessary but often ignored reforms in our own house, as David Pearson put it, to become "student-ready" for a greater diversity of students and we add, readier for different kinds of research and training programs. We need to learn more about partnership mechanisms that may be effective for different outcomes.

Finally, universities are stepping up to the plate of running K–12 schools but with different goals than in the past. Cucciara (2010) described the complex history that began with the earliest colonial colleges (preparing secondary students for college), shifted to Laboratory Schools (experimentation and teacher training often for faculty populations), and evolved into 21st-century models (educating low-income urban students or assisting schools to become hubs for the community). Cucciara also noted the boldness of the universities that take on the tough challenges of creating new schools for underserved students but pointed to mixed outcomes despite extensive resources and to the difficulty of combining dual goals of student preparedness and research. Indeed in moving forward, we feared to replicate headlines such as this one, "When universities run schools . . . into the ground" (Redden, 2008).

New school creation in partnership with a charter district proved exciting to us, with the promise but not necessarily the reality of greater innovation. We were suitably forewarned about the failures of reform to fundamentally change what happens in the classroom between teachers and students (Cuban, 1990, 2013; Sarason, 1972). Given societal blinders as well as institutional complexities within universities and charters, were we doomed to recreate the same roadblocks that have threatened the progress of too many underrepresented youth? Or would new settings and partnerships be freer to address the opportunity gap? Not deterred, we believed that a new-start school, designed by a university-charter district partnership and committed to research and reflection, might provide a more enabling context for new ideas and, ultimately, new knowledge.

## This Book

The birth of CAL Prep occurred in the context of a growing social movement of *shared* responsibility for reducing inequities in access to and success in a college education. A policy change that banned affirmative action led four UC research universities to start new secondary schools, taking deeper responsibility for educating historically underserved students to the highest levels of academic preparedness. This effort fueled our engagement in public scholarship and in an intensive research–practice collaboration. The Gates Foundation Initiative for early college secondary schools also called for an enduring partnership between higher education and school districts. The initiative sought to change practice (access to college courses and greater articulation between educational levels), affect policy (dual enrollment policies for college credit in high school), and bring the early college movement to national scale. Support came from networked improvement communities (Bryk, Gomez, & Grunow, 2010) that here crossed university types, states, and the nation (Venezia & Jaeger, 2013; Webb, 2014).

Like many of the reform models, CAL Prep is a hybrid, adapting to its context and the opportunities provided. It is a charter high school, jointly created and run in a partnership between UC Berkeley and Aspire Public Schools, a CMO or charter district as we refer to it in this book. It is an early college secondary school for low-income and first-generation college students, and the school has no academic or behavioral criteria for admission. And beyond the deeply valued high school seats CAL Prep provides each year, the school, its development driven by data and reflection, continues to be a work in progress.

As noted earlier, although the impact results of newer models of college-preparatory high schools for underserved populations are promising, knowledge about model implementation, partnership, and school development is limited. There is much to learn through rich case studies about how such schools are created, how they achieve these results with greatly underprepared students, and how secondary–tertiary partnerships add value to this effort. Although there is a growing literature about the challenges of new-start schools, viewed largely from a journalist or practitioner perspective, longitudinal case studies of the creation of new secondary schools for first-generation college students—facilitated by research–practice partnerships—are rare indeed with few exceptions (see Lytle, 2010; Mehan, 2012).

## Pivotal Questions

Our interest here is in learning about the challenges of and successes in translating ideas into practice. Whereas many books highlight end results, this book is about the processes of partnership development and school creation—cycles of struggle, revision, and improvement as these unfold over a period of 10 years. A look inside these processes can help foster a mutual exchange of ideas between charter and traditional public schools, an all too infrequent occurrence but a much needed cross-collaboration (Yatsko, Cooley Nelson, & Lake, 2013). Despite the enormous controversy surrounding charter schools, alternatively characterized as saviors and villains in public education, our goal is to look beyond politics, to determine what is possible and whether lessons learned here can be useful for other contexts.

Although we recount a single example, this case study has many features that are worthy of examination. Among these features is the focus on high schools, often thought of as coming too late in an educational career to change trajectories, and on a first-generation college population of low-income and minority youth, often written off as scholars. Importantly, this case is nested in a state that foretells the future demographics of this nation. Also rare is the more than 10-year length of this partnership between a major research university and a leading charter district, both with special characteristics. On the UC Berkeley side, known for its research excellence and social activism, this was a campuswide and multidisciplinary commitment, not localized within a school of education or a research center. On the Aspire side, this was a charter district known for innovative practices and excellent outcomes with low-income populations and students of color, which grew from 12 schools when we began our partnership to 38 schools. Aspire is now the largest CMO in California, with schools also opening in Tennessee. Finally, as a collaborative effort in new school creation and public scholarship, this case study bridges many perspectives rarely brought together in a single book.

We explore three interrelated questions. First, what are the reciprocal dividends and challenges of a sustained partnership between K–12 and higher education that can add value in our efforts to eradicate the achievement gap? Second, what can we learn from the school creation process—in a charter context—that informs our theory of setting (an excellent and equitable high school) and action (how we can get there)? Third, what kind of high school provides a fair chance in an unequal world, enabling underprepared and underserved students to rise to the highest expectations of becoming ready for college and being successful there?

At a time of heightened concern about educational inequality, the book extends our understanding about the workings of high-expectation school environments—linking district, school, and classroom processes, and highlighting ways to overcome stumbling blocks in the actualization of high academic expectations for underserved and underprepared students. At a time of national pressure for new-start schools and scant knowledge, the book also sheds light on processes of school creation from beginnings to maturity—exploring the potential for more novel designs outside the constraints of traditional school districts. Finally, at a time of great interest in partnerships as a vehicle for increasing our capacity to confront critical social problems such as inequality, the book speaks to structures and processes that enabled multilevel collaboration between university and school district. Although this case study is located within US educational structures and policies, these issues are relevant to those countries that seek to better serve low-income and ethnic minority students through improved college-preparatory secondary schools.

## An Ecological Theory and Method

Our deepest commitments at the start were to a collaborative method and community-engaged scholarship as a force for school creation and improvement. We recognized school creation as a systems intervention with many component parts—born with a prehistory, multilayered, set within interlocking contexts, and changing over time (Trickett, 2009). As we saw it, our work was not about the implementation of a single innovation, such as access to college classes in high school, but rather multiple and interactive innovations, embedded within the university–district partnership, the university, surrounding policy environment, and local community. And there was considerable change over time—planned and unplanned as a result of new challenges. The model first framed by UC Berkeley became reframed in partnership with Aspire, and reframed again in a three-way partnership with the school.

Our school design work drew from theories of settings and social change. As examples, Seidman (2012) has delineated the malleable components of social settings. These included resources, their organization and allocation, which together created the social regularities of a setting or "patterns of transactions between two or more groups of people, including norms and practices" (p. 5). Maton (1999) has identified key social forces—cultural challenge, opportunity structures, community-building, and capacity-building—that fuel organizational and societal change. And Schlechty (2005) has described six organizational subsystems (recruitment and induction, goal orientation, knowledge transmission, power/ authority, evaluation, and boundary definition) where invention in each, when coherently aligned, can make deep alterations to the social regularities of school settings.

As one example, providing an elite education to all students is a *new* goal for schools (a culture challenge with differently allocated resources), which demands engagement from students, not compliance. Our failure to change what and how students learn, Schlechty (2005) argued, rests in the structural misfit between inquiry-oriented learning and the authoritarian relationships that are typical in high schools. In pressing for innovation, we voiced many culture challenges, reframed resources and resource allocation, and assessed social regularities on the ground, ever alert for misaligned features that might thwart intended outcomes. As the first step, this partnership opened the school boundaries, providing new opportunities for capacity building that crossed district and university borders.

Thinking ecologically required a contextualist theory of knowledge— which utilizes multimethods, recognizes multiple realities, explores meaning within the local context, and makes room for discovery— this contrasts with a positivist theory where general laws are sought (Lincoln & Guba, 1985). We were never outside evaluators but rather co-developers, involved in what has been called design and development research, community-engaged public scholarship, or participatory action research (e.g., Anderson & Shattuck, 2012; Ozer, Ritterman, & Wanis, 2010; Van de Ven, 2007). Although an insider role may have opened the door to some biases in our understanding, this role also afforded us a rare opportunity for (1) a deep understanding of school creation, (2) research vital to its improvement, and (3) scalability of innovation.

Fueled by a collaborative effort, this is an edited book, by design. It reflects the voices of the many participants who engaged in a sustained process of school creation, and perspectives gleaned across time. It also represents a hybrid of theory, research, and on-the-ground experience—culled from a variety of materials such as literature reviews, meeting records, research studies, observations, interviews, and reflections. Our work occurred within a strong research and development culture, as reflected in the memorandum of understanding signed by UC Berkeley and Aspire Public Schools and in the school handbook, where participation in research was noted as an important activity at CAL Prep. Transparency about our learning and about successful practices has been the hallmark of our collaborative work.

We protected the confidentiality and privacy of individuals in a number of ways. Research studies were reviewed by the Committee for the Protection of Human Subjects at UC Berkeley, with informed consent obtained from parents, students, and teachers as needed. Data from these studies were aggregated across individuals, quotations were either non-identified or identified by a pseudonym, and details were altered for privacy, as noted in relevant chapters. Student permissions were obtained for use of quotations from interviews (nonidentified) and from public settings such as graduation (with consent to identify by name). Permissions were also acquired from named individuals for attitudes or actions attributed to them.

## Organization of the Book

How best to tell this story that unfolded over a decade in a way that vividly conveys our learning and sheds light on the questions we raised? Reflecting an ecological perspective, we interweave knowledge gleaned from research and practice, different levels of settings (classroom, school, district, university), disparate voices (student to superintendent), and different time periods. We recount the story in four parts. These include (1) the prehistory and early days of the collaboration, (2) research studies that informed school improvement as well as tracked student outcomes, (3) reflections of teachers and administrators about the deepening of practices that promoted equity and excellence, and (4) lessons learned across the secondary–tertiary divide. Together these parts frame a progressive story that takes us from planning through the second class of graduates and ends with a brief glimpse into the future. Table 1.1 illustrates the timeline—showing patterns of both stability and change in school location, grade levels, and players, and indicating the place of each chapter.

## Part I: Beginnings

Theory about setting creation underscores the importance of a prehistory and constitution as foundational for the capacity of a setting to innovate and survive. Covering the years from 2002–2006, this first section provides a *real-time* account of events during this early history—within the university, within the university–charter district partnership, and during the school's first year. Drawing material from dated narrative records of project meetings, we identify our processes, the issues debated, and the challenges confronted.

Chapter 2 (Kaufman, Jorgensen, Padilla, & Pearson) reflects the voices of the UC Berkeley staff, representing university outreach, and administrators, the Vice Chancellor for Undergraduate Affairs and Dean of the Graduate School of Education, who spearheaded the Early College Initiative on our campus. Should a research university be actively involved in creating and running a secondary school? Are faculty and staff spread across the university up to this task, and under what conditions? This chapter highlights the players, ensuing controversies, and deliberative actions that built support on the university campus to start an early college secondary school.

Chapter 3 (Weinstein) turns to the early meetings that took place between UC Berkeley and Aspire Public Schools to build a partnership for the co-construction of an early college secondary school. This chapter details structural elements (such as roles, regularized meetings, and a memorandum of understanding) that proved pivotal to a creating a partnership that was both long and deep. This chapter also describes the dizzying array of decisions made and actions taken during this planning period, culminating in our earliest vision for CAL Prep.

Chapter 4 (Weinstein) captures life on the ground during the school's first year. Such reality was a far cry from the rosy educational vision that we had envisioned.

TABLE 1.1 A Look at CAL Prep from Planning through Year 7

| | PREHISTORY 2002–2005 | YEAR 1 2005–2006 | YEAR 2 2006–2007 | YEAR 3 2007–2008 | YEAR 4 2008–2009 | YEAR 5 2009–2010 | YEAR 6 2010–2011 | YEAR 7 2011–2012 |
|---|---|---|---|---|---|---|---|---|
| **Grade Level** | | 6–7 | 6–8 | 6–9 | 7–10 | 8–11 | 9–12 | 9–12 |
| **School Site** | | Golden Gate Oakland | Golden Gate Oakland | Golden Gate Oakland | St. Joseph's Berkeley | St. Joseph's Berkeley | St. Joseph's Berkeley | St. Joseph's Berkeley |
| **Charter** | | Oakland District | Oakland District | Oakland District | Alameda County | Alameda County | Alameda County | Alameda County |
| **Number of Students** | | 82 | 149 | 215 | 198 | 196 | 192 | 209 |
| **Principal** | | Prada | Prada | Liles | Reed | Reed | Reed | Reed |
| **Regional Superintendents** | Darwish/ Kirkpatrick | Darwish | Darwish | Lee | Lee | Lee | Epanchin-Troyan | Epanchin-Troyan |
| **ECI Cochairs** | Stacy/Wilson | Stacy/Wilson | Stacy/Stern | Stacy/Stern | Stacy/Worrell | Stacy/Worrell | Stacy/Worrell | Stacy/ Worrell |
| **Staff Liaisons** | Kaufman/ Jorgensen | Kaufman/ Jorgensen | Kaufman/ Jorgensen | Kaufman/ Jorgensen | Kaufman/ Jorgensen | Kaufman | Kaufman | Kaufman |
| **Faculty Liaisons** | Padilla/ Pearson | Weinstein/ Worrell | Weinstein/ Worrell | Worrell/ Goldsmith | Worrell/ Goldsmith | Worrell | Worrell | Worrell |
| **Book Chapters** | 1–3 | 4 | 5 | 6–7 | 8 | 8 | 8 | 9–17 |

NOTE: Data on student numbers in early October of each school year were obtained for Aspire California College Preparatory Academy from Ed-Data on the California Department of Education website. For 2011–2012, CAL Prep is listed as a K–5/9–12 school due to combined charter status in Alameda County, but the enrollment figure in this table reflects student numbers in the 9–12 classes only. ECI = Early College Initiative.

## Part II: Collaborative Research Informs School Development

The chapters in this section report on a series of research studies designed by UC Berkeley faculty and graduate students in collaboration with CAL Prep school staff and carried out during Years 2 to 7 (2006–2012) of the school's history. These rich opportunities for inquiry grew from our research–practice partnership and met pressing needs expressed by the school, as we moved from the identification of important school features to the challenges of implementation. Adopting a mixed-method approach, we engaged in design/intervention projects as well as descriptive studies and utilized both quantitative and qualitative data.

The findings from these studies reflect real-time work in progress, showcasing struggle as well as success as we partnered to improve programs and practices. The voices of students, teachers, and parents during these early years of CAL Prep ring loud and clear, as they illuminate domains for needed changes. In line with our vision for CAL Prep, these topics illustrate our efforts to strengthen the provision of support—through small-group advisories to better meet adolescent needs and through an investigation of transition effects into this high-challenge school environment—for students, parents, and teachers alike. The topics also speak to our interventions to increase intellectual challenge—in the development of a library to support a deeper literacy for students struggled with reading remediation—and to learn more about how students were faring at CAL Prep.

Chapter 5 (Weinstein, Sami, & Mello) describes the collaboration with teachers during Year 2 to strengthen advisories, a key design feature to personalize relationships for students. This intervention study first assessed student wishes for advisories and teacher needs for support, and second, created an evidence-based advisory curriculum that was implemented and evaluated. Chapter 6 (Sami & Weinstein) reports on a study conducted in Year 3, which examined students' transition into the high-challenge CAL Prep. This study contrasted the experiences of new and continuing students, looking for factors such as a perceived match between needs and environment at school and home that might explain student achievement gains and connection to school. Chapter 7 (Sami, Worrell, & Weinstein) describes an interview study with CAL Prep parents and teachers conducted in Year 3 to examine parent involvement practices, the challenges faced, and the types of help needed—parents from the school and teachers from parents—to better support student learning. Chapter 8 (Goodin & Pearson) highlights a design research project—the development of a library at CAL Prep—implemented in Years 4 to 6. The chapter traces its evolution from need, a common interest in strengthening student literacy, to design and utilization by students. Chapter 9 (Weinstein, Martin, Bialis-White, & Sami) tracks student indicators across Years 1 to 7, from school opening through the second graduating class of seniors. Using school- and individual-level data, this chapter explores shifts in student population, rates and predictors of attrition, and patterns of achievement and attainment, as compared to populations with the same demographics.

## Part III: Equity and Excellence in a High School Setting

From the vantage point of Year 7 and looking back at school development over time, this third section takes a *retrospective* view gleaned from practitioner knowledge. It draws upon the voices of teachers and the principal at CAL Prep to illustrate school features and teaching practices that, in their view, enabled students to reach higher toward college dreams and succeed. Through a series of guided questions, we tapped emerging theories about what fosters equity, excellence, and engagement in the subject matter disciplines of history, math, and chemistry, and in the student support system—and most importantly how they achieved it. This material was elicited in a variety of ways, in essays, as presentations at conferences, and through interviews, which were taped, transcribed, and shaped into chapters. These chapters shed light on the features at CAL Prep and in the partnership that made it possible to move from the early years of tumult to the transformation of students. These chapters also reflect the importance of growth, not just of the students but also of the educators serving those students.

In Chapter 10, history teacher Ryan Grow describes the important role of the history class in enabling equity of theme, access, and experience. When achieved, this pedagogical equity enables a diversity of students to see their historical legacy, deeply engage with the material, and have a stake in the subject matter, seen as relevant to their own lives. Chapter 11, written by math teachers Sarah Salazar and Stacy Thomas, presents their conversation about the nature of their collaborative efforts as a subject-matter team to balance mathematical rigor, basic skill remediation, rich relationships, and life lessons in reaching these students. These teachers are refreshingly frank about their early struggles as well as their growing successes, in part due to a team approach and the opportunity for reflection. In Chapter 12, Professor Angela Stacy and science teacher Tatiana Lim-Breitbart illustrate a long-standing faculty–teacher collaboration around the development of a chemistry curriculum with a student-centered pedagogy that engages students in higher-level thinking skills. Here, greater student success in science was fueled by a stable and committed vertical science team that included professors, staff, and students from UC Berkeley, teachers at CAL Prep, and science coaches from Aspire. Chapter 13, written by principal Megan Reed and supports coordinator Michelle Cortez, describes how a supportive college-preparatory culture was progressively built, allowing the school to combine remediation with acceleration for students who entered high school several years behind academically and faced a quickly looming graduation.

## Part IV: Lessons Learned

In the final section of the book, we look across these chapters to distill what we learned—about cross-sector partnerships, innovation in school creation, and equity and excellence at the secondary school level. We address in some detail what we consider to be among the greatest and often overlooked challenges, the interweaving of rigor and support as a primary lever of change and the development of student identity, as an important educational outcome. We also provide an opportunity for both Aspire and UC Berkeley to reflect on the partnership.

Chapter 14 (Weinstein & Bialis-White) draws from the research literature and experiences on the ground to suggest a SMART Supports framework for integrating rigor and support in high-challenge secondary schools, importantly applied across six domains of youth development. This model proved critical to actualizing the highest of expectations for first-generation college youth. Chapter 15 (Worrell) applies the lens of gifted education to interviews conducted with seniors from the first two graduating classes at CAL Prep. Student voices illustrate the pathway to the development of talent. Through the provision of opportunity and support, students find themselves developing task commitment and integrating academic and ethnocultural identities. Chapter 16, written by two Aspire Bay Area superintendents, Elise Darwish (now Chief Academic Officer for Aspire) and Tatiana Epanchin-Troyan, provides an analysis of the opportunities that were realized and the challenges confronted by the partnership with UC Berkeley, likening our cultural differences to those reflected in the games of Pac-Man and chess. Chapter 17 (Weinstein, Worrell, Kaufman, & Basri) offers the UC Berkeley perspective on the partnership and the school, examining successes, challenges, and benefits on both sides of the divide. We also explore the lessons learned for policy, practice, and research, taking up the generalizability of these findings to other contexts. Finally, we conclude with a brief epilogue (Worrell & Weinstein) that looks into the future.

## Cross-Sector Partnerships to Reduce Disparities

Rampant inequalities in the opportunity to thrive are among the greatest of 21st-century challenges, not only in the United States but also around the world, and we ignore them at our peril (Gamoran, 2013). As we tell this story, we can envision every university partnered in a deep and sustained way with school districts—working collaboratively at a systems level to enhance practice and policy, importantly directed toward reducing entrenched educational inequities. What if, as a result of these collaborations, many more schools were strengthened in their design and capacity to provide a rigorous and supportive college-preparatory education for all its students? What if these collaborations offered unanticipated dividends to universities by reframing fundamental research questions, professional training programs, and the university environment for undergraduate and graduate students, in ways more welcoming to issues of diversity and better aligned with the challenges on the ground? And what if such cross-sector partnerships were established with other human service settings, such as health and welfare, and with the criminal justice system, again framed around reducing inequality at a systemic level?

This book offers new insights on one such collaboration, between a research university and a charter school district, which in spanning the divide between secondary and postsecondary education, enabled us to confront in novel ways the issues of equity and excellence in actualizing high academic expectations for historically underserved students. In the chapters to come, by interweaving multiple voices, multiple methods and levels of analysis, and different points of time, we capture our journey.

## References

Alvarez, D., & Mehan, H. (2006). Whole-school detracking: A strategy for equity and excellence *Theory into Practice, 45*, 82–89. doi:10.1207/s15430421tip4501_11.

Anderson, T., & Shattuck, J. (2012). Design-based research: A decade of progress in education research. *Educational Researcher, 41*, 16–25. doi:10.3102/0013189X11428813

Assembly Select Committee on the Status of Boys and Men of Color in California. (2012). *Claiming the promise of health and success for boys and men of color* in California: Final report and policy platform for state action (2012–2018). Sacramento, CA: Author. Retrieved from https://www.hiponline.org/storage/documents/SELECT_COMMITTEE_REPORT_ACTION_PLAN_FINAL.pdf

Aud, S., Fox, M., & KewalRamani, A. (2010). *Status and trends in the education of racial and ethnic groups* (NCES 2010–2015). U.S. Department of Education, National Center for Education Statistics. Washington, DC: U.S. Government Printing Office.

Aud, S., Hussar, W., Johnson, F., Kena, G., Roth, E., Manning, E, . . . Zhang, J. (2012). *The condition of education 2012* (NCES 012-045). Washington, DC: U.S. Department of Education, National Center for Education Statistics.

Berger, A., Turk-Bicakci, L., Garet, M., Song, M., Knudson, J., Haxton, C., . . . Cassidy, L. (2013). *Early college, early success: Early college high school initiative impact study*. Washington, DC: American Institutes for Research.

Berger, A., Turk-Bicakci, L., Garet, M., Knudson, J., & Hoshen, G. (2014). *Early college, continued success: Early college initiative impact study*. Washington, DC. American Institutes for Research.

Bloom, H. S., & Unterman, R. (2013). *Sustained progress: New findings about the effectiveness and operation of small public high schools of choice in New York City*. New York, NY: MDRC. Retrieved from http://www.mdrc.org/sites/default/files/sustained_progress_FR_0.pdf

Bohren, A., & McClure, L. (2011). *The Preuss School at UCSD: Academic performance of the class of 2010*. San Diego, CA: CREATE. Retrieved from https://create.ucsd.edu/_files/Preuss%20Report%202010%20Dec%201%20Final%20Version%20for%20Distribution.pdf

Bowen, W. G., Chingos, M. M., & McPherson, M. S. (2009). *Crossing the finish line: Completing college at America's public universities*. Princeton, NJ: Princeton University Press.

Bryk A. S., Gomez L. M., & Grunow A. (2010). *Getting ideas into action: Building networked improvement communities in education*. Carnegie Foundation for the Advancement of Teaching, Stanford, CA. Retrieved from http://files.eric.ed.gov/fulltext/ED517575.pdf

Carter, P. L., & Welner, K. F. (2013). *Closing the opportunity gap: What America must do to give every child an even chance*. New York, NY: Oxford University Press.

Center for Research on Education Outcomes. (2009). *Multiple choice: Charter school performance in 16 states*. (2009). Stanford, CA: Author. Retrieved from http://credo.stanford.edu/reports/MULTIPLE_CHOICE_CREDO.pdf

Chapman, C., Laird, J., Ifill, N., & KewalRamani, A. (2011). *Trends in high school dropout and completion rates in the United States: 1972–2009* (NCS 2012-006). Washington, DC: U.S. Department of Education, National Center for Education Statistics.

Child Trends. (2012). *Early school readiness*. Retrieved from www.childtrendsdatabank.org/?q=node/291

Clark, J. V. (Ed.) (2014). *Closing the achievement gap from an international perspective: Transforming STEM for effective education*. New York, NY: Springer.

Coburn, C. E., Penuel, W. R., & Geil, K. (2013). *Research-practice partnerships: A strategy for leveraging research for educational improvement in school districts*. New York, NY: William T. Grant Foundation.

Conant, J. B. (1959). *The American high school today: A first report to interested citizens*. New York, NY: McGraw-Hill.

Clifford, G. J. (1995). *"Equally in view": The University of California, its women, and the schools*. Center for Studies in Higher Education and Institute for Governmental Studies, University of California, Berkeley.

Conley, D. T. (2010). *College and career ready: Helping all students succeed beyond high school*. San Francisco, CA: Jossey-Bass.

Cuban, L. (1990). Reforming again, and again, and again. *Educational Researcher, 19*, 3–13.

Cuban, L. (2013). *Inside the black box of classroom practice: Change without reform in American education*. Cambridge, MA: Harvard Education Press.

Cucciara. M. (2010, Summer). New goals, familiar challenges?: A brief history of university-run schools. *Perspectives on Urban Education*, 96–108. Retrieved from http://www.urbanedjournal.org/sites/urbanedjournal.org/files/pdf_archive/PUE-Summer2010-V7I1-pp96-108.pdf

Darling-Hammond, L., & Sykes, G. (2003). Wanted: A national teacher supply policy for education: The right way to meet the "Highly Qualified Teacher" challenge. *Education Policy Analysis Archives, 11*(33). Retrieved from http://epaa.asu.edu/epaa/v11n33/

Davis, R. P., & Hoffman, J. L. (2008, Fall). Higher education and the P-16 movement: What is to be done? *Thought & Action*, 123–134.

Domina, T., & Ruzek, R. (2012). Paving the way: K–16 partnerships for higher education diversity and high school reform. *Educational Policy, 26*, 243–267.

Eccles, J., & Grootman, J. A. (Eds.). (2002). *Community programs to promote youth development*. Washington, DC: National Academies Press.

EdSource. (2010, September). *How California ranks*. Mountain View, CA: Author. Retrieved from http://edsource.org/wp-content/publications/pub-2010-09-CaliforniaRanks.pdf

Equity and Excellence Commission. (2013). *For each and every child: A strategy for education equity and excellence*. Washington, DC: U.S. Department of Education. Retrieved from http://www.ctbaonline.org/reports/each-and-every-child-strategy-education-equity-and-excellence

Fleischman, S., & Heppen, J. (2009). Improving low-performing high schools: Searching for evidence of promise. *The Future of Children, 19*(1), 105–134.

Gamoran, A. (2013). *Inequality is the problem: Prioritizing research on reducing inequality*. Retrieved from http://cds.web.unc.edu/files/2014/10/Inequality-is-the-Problem.WTGF-Annual-Report-essay-2013.pdf

Garces, L. M. (2013). Understanding the impact of affirmative action bans in different graduate fields of study. *American Educational Research Journal, 50*, 251–284. doi:10.3102/0002831212470483

Greene, J. P., & Forster, G. (2003). *Public high school graduation and college readiness rates in the United States*. New York, NY: Manhattan Institute. Retrieved from http://www.manhattan-institute.org/html/ewp_03.htm

Gregory, A., Skiba, R. J., & Noguera, P. A. (2010). The achievement gap and the discipline gap: Two sides of the same coin? *Educational Researcher, 38*, 59–68. doi:10.3102/0013189X09357621

Grodsky, E., & Kurlaender, M. (Eds.). (2010). *Equal opportunity in higher education: The past and future of California's Proposition 209*. Cambridge, MA: Harvard Education Press.

Heath, A., & Brinbaum, Y. (Eds.). (2015). *Unequal attainments: Ethnic educational inequalities in ten Western countries*. New York, NY: Oxford University Press.

Kalogrides, D., & Loeb, S. (2013). Different teachers, different peers: The magnitude of student sorting within schools. *Educational Researcher, 42*, 304–316. doi:10.3102/0013189X13495087

Lee, V. E. (2001). *Restructuring high schools for equity and excellence: What works?* New York, NY: Teachers College Press.

Levin, H. M., & Rouse, C. E. (2012, January 25). The true costs of high school dropouts. *New York Times*. Retrieved from http://www.nytimes.com/2012/01/26/opinion/the-true-cost-of-high-school-dropouts.html

Lincoln, Y. S., & Guba, E. G. (1985). *Naturalistic inquiry*. New York, NY: Sage.

Lytle, C. (2010). *The burden of excellence: The struggle to establish the Preuss School UCSD and a call for educational field stations*. La Jolla, CA: RELS Press.

Marginson, S. (2014, October 2). *The Californian model of higher education in the world*. 2014 Clark Kerr Lecture, Center for Studies in Higher Education, University of California, Berkeley.

Maton, K. I. (1999). Making a difference: The social ecology of social transformation. *American Journal of Community Psychology, 28*, 25–57. doi:10.1023/A:1005190312887

Mehan, H. (2012). *In college's front door: Creating a college bound culture of learning in high schools*. Boulder, CO: Paradigm Publishers.

Mehan, H., Kaufman, G., Lytle, C., Quartz, K. H., & Weinstein, R. S. (2010). Building educational field stations to promote diversity and access in higher education. In E. Grodsky and M. Kurlaender (Eds.) *Equal opportunity in high education: The past and future of California's Proposition 209* (pp. 173–193). Cambridge, MA: Harvard Education Press.

National Research Council and Institute of Medicine. (2004). *Engaging schools: Fostering high school students' motivation to learn*. Committee on Increasing High School Students' Engagement and Motivation to Learn, Board on Children, Youth, and Families. Washington, DC: National Academies Press.

The National Alliance for Public Charter Schools. (2015). *Estimated number of public charter schools & students, 2014–2015*. Washington, DC: Author. Retrieved from http://www.publiccharters.org/wp-content/uploads/2015/02/open_closed_FINAL.pdf

National Center for Educational Statistics. (n.d.). *Table M12. Average scores of U.S. 15-year-old students on PISA mathematics*. Washington, DC: Author. Retrieved from http://nces.ed.gov/pubs2014/2014024_tables.pdf

No Child Left Behind (NCLB) Act of 2001, Pub. L. No. 107-110, § 115, Stat. 1425 (2002).

Oakes, J., Rogers, J., Silver, D., Valladares, S., Terriquez, V., McDonough, P., . . . Lipton, M. (November 2006). *Removing the roadblocks: Fair college opportunities for all California students.* Los Angeles, CA: UCLA IDEA. Retrieved from http://idea.gseis.ucla.edu/publications/files/RR-ExecutiveSummary.pdf

Orfield, G., & Miller, E. (1998). *Chilling admissions: The affirmative action crisis and the search for alternatives.* Cambridge, MA: Harvard University Press.

Ozer, E. J., Ritterman, M. L., & Wanis, M. G. (2010). Participatory action research (PAR) in middle school: Opportunities, constraints, and key processes. *American Journal of Community Psychology, 48,* 152–166. doi:10.1007/s10464-010-9335-8

Porter, A., McMaken, J., Hwang, J., & Yang, R. (2011). Common Core standards: The new U.S. intended curriculum. *Educational Researcher, 40,* 103–116. doi:10.3102/0013189X11405038

Reardon, S. F. (2011). The widening socioeconomic status achievement gap: New evidence and possible explanations. In R. J. Murnane & G. J. Duncan (Eds.), *Whither opportunity? Rising inequality, schools, and children's life chances* (pp. 91–116). New York, NY: Russell Sage Foundation.

Redden, E. August 7, 2008 "When universities run schools... into the ground." *Inside Higher Ed.* Retrieved from https://www.insidehighered.com/news/2008/08/07/charter.

Reforming education: The great schools revolution. (2011, September 11). *The Economist.* Retrieved from http://www.economist.com/node/21529014

Rogers, J., Mirra, N., Seltzer, M., & Jun, J. (2014). *It's about time: Learning time and educational opportunity in California high schools.* Los Angeles, CA: UCLA IDEA. Retrieved from http://idea.gseis.ucla.edu/projects/its-about-time/Its%20About%20Time.pdf

Sarason, S. B. (1972). *The creation of settings and the future societies.* San Francisco, CA: Jossey-Bass.

Schlechty, P. C. (2005). *Creating great schools: Six systems at the heart of educational innovation.* San Francisco, CA: Jossey-Bass.

Seidman, E. (2012). An emerging action science of social settings. *American Journal of Community Psychology, 50,* 1–16. doi:10.1007/s10464-011-9469-3

Timar, T., Ogawa, R., & Orillion, M. (2002). *New directions for student outreach: The University of California's school-university partnerships* (CSHE.8.02). Berkeley, CA: Center for Studies in Higher Education. Retrieved from http://www.cshe.berkeley.edu/new-directions-student-outreach-university-californias-school-university-partnerships

Trickett, E. J. (2009). Multilevel community-based culturally situated interventions and community impact: An ecological perspective. *American Journal of Community Psychology, 43,* 257–266. doi:10.1007/s10464-009-9227-y

Tuttle, C. C., Gill, B., Gleason, P., Knechtel, V., Nichols-Barrer, I., & Resch, A. (2013). *KIPP middle schools: Impacts on achievement and other outcomes.* Oakland, CA: Mathematica Policy Research. Retrieved from http://www.kipp.org/results/mathematica-study/mathematica-2013-report

Unterman, R. (2014). *Headed to college: The effects of New York City's small high schools of choice on postsecondary enrollment.* New York, NY: MDRC. Retrieved from http://www.mdrc.org/sites/default/files/Headed_to_College_PB.pdf

U.S. Department of Education. (2013). *For each and every child—a strategy for education equity and excellence.* Washington, DC: Author.

Venezia, A., & Jaeger, L. (2013). Transitions from high school to college. *Future of Children, 23,* 117–136.

Van de Ven, A. H. (2007). *Engaged scholarship: A guide for organizational and social research.* New York, NY: Oxford University Press.

Visher, M., & Stern, D. (2015). *New pathways to careers and college: Examples, evidence, and prospects.* New York, NY: MDRC. Retrieved from http://www.mdrc.org/publication/new-pathways-careers-and-college

Warren Little, J., & DoRPH, R. (1998, December). *Lessons about comprehensive school reform: California5 School Restructuring Demonstration Program.* University of California, Berkeley.

Webb, M. (with Gerwin, C.). (2014). *Early college expansion: Propelling students to postsecondary success, at a school near you.* Oakland, CA: Jobs for the Future. Retrieved from http://www.jff.org/publications/early-college-expansion-propelling-students-postsecondary-success-school-near-you

Weinstein, R. S. (1996). High standards in a tracked system of schooling: For which students and with what educational supports? *Educational Researcher, 8,* 16–19. doi:10.3102/0013189X025008016

Weinstein, R. S. (2002). *Reaching higher: The power of expectations in schooling.* Cambridge, MA: Harvard University Press.

Whiting, G. W. (2006). Enhancing culturally diverse males' scholar identity: Suggestions for educators of gifted students. *Gifted Child Today, 29*(3), 46–50.

Wilkinson, R., & Pickett, K. (2009). *The spirit level: Why greater equality makes societies stronger.* New York, NY: Bloomsbury Press.

Wohlstetter, P., Smith, J., & Farrell, C. C. (2013). *Choices and challenges: Charter school performance in perspective.* Cambridge, MA: Harvard Education Press.

Yatsko, S., Cooley Nelson, E., & Lake, R. (2013). *District/charter collaboration compact: Interim report.* Seattle, WA: Center on Reinventing Public Education. Retrieved from http://www.crpe.org/publications/district-charter-collaboration-compact-interim-report

## 2 | The University of California, Berkeley Commits

GAIL KAUFMAN, ROBERT E. JORGENSEN, GENARO M. PADILLA,
AND P. DAVID PEARSON

*"I have remained . . . involved in pre-college preparation
throughout my career. I was very torn by this invitation . . . to
serve on the faculty committee that was contemplating the
creation of a charter school. On the one hand I had seen how
much better it might be to have control of the school culture
to combat many of the problems we had wrestled with in
the I HAD A DREAM project, but on the other hand, I had
gained a real appreciation for how difficult it is to run a good
school. I was skeptical that Berkeley faculty had anything
remotely approaching the bandwidth to take this on."* (Gibor
Basri, Professor of Astronomy and Vice Chancellor for
Equity and Inclusion, University of California, Berkeley)

I T IS AUGUST 20, 2002, and a letter arrives in the Chancellor's office at the
University of California (UC) Berkeley—one of hundreds. Who would
have guessed that as this book goes to press, in response to this letter,
there would be five graduating classes of young people of color on their
path to college success? This chapter chronicles the period from August,
2002 to October, 2003, when, in little more than a year, UC Berkeley took
a bold step and committed to founding a secondary school focused on
serving low-income, first-generation college students and ensuring their
access to and success in higher education. Our records, which included
e-mail exchanges, meetings, memos, and proposals, provide a time-ordered
account of the processes we engaged in to secure this campus commitment.

In this chapter, we first review the specific roles of the Division of Student Affairs and the Graduate School of Education (GSE) in this endeavor and how these two entities came together to champion this initiative. Second, we describe how these two entities collaboratively led the campus effort (1) in its deliberations regarding the use of the California public charter option, and (2) in steps taken to gain broad faculty engagement as well as support from the upper administration. Finally, we document the culmination of these efforts in a funding request to the Woodrow Wilson National Fellowship Foundation (WWNFF). This prehistory provides an example of how a preeminent research university went about making such a bold decision, examining both the role of staff and faculty and the context at a particular point in time that enabled a campuswide inclusive commitment. These were the early seeds planted that shaped the course of what was to become a more than 10-year project, which is still underway.

## Champions of the Initiative

### The Role of Student Affairs

**The Letter.** Every day, bureaucratic missives go back and forth on a regular basis. Many are handled without much thought, and then one appears that ultimately is going to change the course of many young people's lives and how the university engages with the issues of educational disparity. On September 16, 2002, a letter sent by Anthony Marx, a political science professor at Columbia University, representing the WWNFF, landed on the desk of Ms. Kaufman, Director of School/University Partnerships in the Center for Educational Partnerships (CEP) at UC Berkeley. The letter read, "I am writing to begin a conversation, to see if Berkeley would be interested in joining in this major project for public educational improvement through a partnership with higher education." Professor Marx explained that this "Gates (Bill and Melinda Gates Foundation) Initiative will support and help establish small model public high schools in urban areas . . . offering college level credit in the 11th and 12th grade," and added that "getting involved in establishing a public high school is an endeavor not to be taken lightly."

This letter had gone from Chancellor Berdahl to the Vice Chancellor for Student Affairs (Professor Padilla), due to his role in overseeing and coordinating the various academic development and outreach programs operated by the campus in K–12 and community college settings. Padilla told his present Chief of Staff that "we should learn more [and] get Marsha in the loop too." Dr. Marsha Jaeger is the Director of the CEP, the office in which Ms. Kaufman works, and Jaeger asks Kaufman to "check this out." Some checking revealed that the project came with a potential $400,000 grant for the planning and development of a school.

**The Center for Educational Partnerships.** For the CEP, the letter was more than a "conversation starter," for CEP was experiencing deep budget cuts in its outreach work, work dedicated to increasing the numbers of low-income, first-generation university students of color coming to Berkeley and the University of California. When the anti–Affirmative Action Proposition 209 passed in 1996, the data regarding the first classes admitted under the new policy were devastating—the percent of Latino students at Berkeley went from 15% in 1997 to 8% in 1998, and for African American students, enrollment went from 8% in 1997 to 4% in 1998 (West-Faulcon, 2006). In response, the legislature allocated millions of dollars to the UC campuses—doubling the resources and creating new initiatives. Thus, in the late 1990s, the UC Berkeley campus received more than 4 million dollars in funds for its academic development and college-going outreach work. However, by the time the letter from WWNFF arrived in 2002, more than half of that money was no longer allocated and outreach programs were cut back or shut down.

So the letter provided an opportunity for resources coupled with an intriguing idea. Ms. Kaufman wrote Professor Marx an e-mail on September 30, 2002, suggesting he come to campus to meet with staff working in K–12 who had been brainstorming ideas. Basically, the goal was to create small public high schools in partnership with Institutions of Higher Education (IHEs) that would be models of excellence; they would offer college level courses in 11th and 12th grade, integrate university faculty in the curriculum planning and teacher development, and make the university more approachable and manageable (by saving time and money) for a diverse population of students. We were sent more information that described a prescriptive program regarding earning college credit and the engagement of IHEs in issues of secondary education and improvement.

Our first meeting with Professor Marx on November 15, 2002, involved a dynamic group of staff from CEP, Student Affairs, and the UC Office of the President (UCOP), all of whom were involved in outreach efforts and local partnerships with schools. Marx provided additional context, including how the Gates Foundation viewed this project as an opening for engaging faculty and IHEs more deeply in solving the problems of access and success of a diverse student body in higher education. We discussed a variety of options, including a small school (either stand-alone or part of a larger school) in a local district with which we already partnered, as well as the idea of a UC Berkeley College Preparatory School as a new, separate entity.

In retrospect, it seems that a number of simultaneous factors were in play at UC Berkeley, creating a fertile ground for pursuing the idea of a UC Berkeley school separate from the other school work occurring in our partner districts and schools. There was regular communication between staff and faculty working in K–12, including CEP, due to a structure developed by the Vice Chancellor of Student Affairs Padilla. It helped that Ms. Kaufman had previously served as Padilla's Chief of Staff. At the same time, several members of the faculty were ready to participate in a K–12 initiative that could make a difference in schools and students' lives and were eager to demonstrate how research evidence could affect educational disparities. Given the research showing that the change process in an existing school takes a long time, there was interest in starting a school from scratch and building its culture together, and the GSE's new vision included finding "a place" to provide evidence of efficacy of instructional models and practices. All of these forces were at play in a context of pressure from UCOP to be more involved in solving the problems of California's education system. Also, the promise of a grant for planning and implementation, given the budget cuts being experienced throughout the campus, provided a potent driving force. With these forces at work and starting with the mid-November meeting, the course seemed set for CAL Prep's birth.

Before Thanksgiving, CEP staff used an opportunity at a campus reception to tell then Chancellor Berdahl about Professor Marx's visit and to pitch the idea of developing a UC Berkeley school. His response was positive about both the potential impact on students and expanding best practices in education more broadly. We also talked to Dr. Vincent Doby, Vice President for Educational Outreach in the UC Office of the President, who was also very encouraging. Few of us knew very much about charter schools and generally did not have positive views regarding their role in reforming public education. UC San Diego's pioneering work in founding the Preuss School in 1999, a charter school on that campus, was one model we explored.

Professor Marx was pleased with the positive responses from the campus, and directed us to more specific information on the grant, and to other IHEs who were also exploring the idea. UC Berkeley was the only Research I campus (with extensive doctoral and research programs as defined by the Carnegie Classification of Institutions of Higher Education) in the mix for the first group. This situation raised some concerns among faculty, and Marx provided names of other selective IHEs in the pipeline, but ultimately, none of these institutions started a new school. Moreover, although Vice Chancellor Padilla encouraged a team of staff from CEP and Student Affairs to research charter regulations, look at the Preuss School, and create a plan for how to move ahead, he was both skeptical and concerned about the reach of such a project in terms of the culture of Berkeley: how do we ensure that the project is sustained, has ladder-rank faculty on board, and is not yet another project that does not live up to its promise, especially to low-income communities of color?

**Student Affairs.** The Gates Funding Opportunity Team—still made up of mostly CEP and Student Affairs staff—decided that we needed to convert Vice Chancellor Padilla into a champion, because without a campus leader playing that role, we would have little chance of convincing other campus leaders to give us the green light to move ahead. This strategy resulted in a five-page memo spearheaded by Ms. Kaufman to Padilla on January 6, 2003, with impassioned rhetoric about why Berkeley should become involved:

> What could be more important for an institution of Berkeley's stature than to demonstrate that youth who do not excel using traditional educational approaches can be high achievers in an educational environment that is designed and nurtured based on the vast knowledge and expertise of the Berkeley campus? . . . K–12 is at a crossroads, the reform strategies and accountability mandates are on a collision course with the state budget crisis and the fiscal troubles of our partner districts . . . How can we protect public education, and especially the aspirations of our young people, while our programs are being cut? . . .What is UC's responsibility to K–12?

At a meeting on January 9, 2003, Vice Chancellor Padilla said to Ms. Kaufman, "this is the most cockamamie idea you have ever brought to me." Kaufman responded, "Maybe, but it's one of the best." Padilla (see Box 2.1) then raised several questions for the team to consider: (1) what are other models of this type of program excepting the Bard early college model and the Preuss School, (2) what should we avoid, and (3) how do we address the issue of a UC Berkeley charter school being seen as demonstrating a vote of "no confidence" in public schools and abandoning our commitment to public education? In discussing these questions with Professor Marx, he pointed out that there are few models other than

## BOX 2.1 PADILLA

While I was Vice Chancellor for Student Affairs, we underwent a sustained admissions crisis. The number and percentage of low income, first-generation, underrepresented students admissible to the University of California (UC) Berkeley fell by well over 50%. It was clear to many of us that the California public schools were failing many of our children, so when a group of staff members suggested we consider building a charter school that would demonstrate our ability to model a successful learning environment I was intrigued. Of course, I was also initially skeptical. If we were to engage in such a venture we would have to be utterly serious, disciplined in our approach, and committed to the long term, notwithstanding the huge obstacles that so often undermine charter education. I was, to my surprise, deeply impressed by the interest and commitment shown by a core group of faculty and administrators. I felt we had a real chance to make a difference for families and students in the East Bay corridor. I also felt that I must quite simply do all I could to support and further the venture; this was the right thing to do and the right decision to make.

Additionally, as a Chicano and one of the very few faculty of color here at UC Berkeley, I wanted to be part of an enterprise that would resonate with my own social values and my sense of outrage that, with respect to Latinos alone, so few students even had a shot at admission to universities such as UC Berkeley. Even though Latinos constitute more than 50% of the school-age population in California, well under 10% of Latino high school graduates are eligible to even apply to UC Berkeley and the other UC campuses. Just in the East Bay public schools, there are large numbers of African American and Latino students who could never imagine coming up the street to UC Berkeley. Something is deeply wrong with this reality. I actually feel insulted as a Latino, and as a member of the faculty I was (and remain) furious that so few of my students come from underrepresented communities.

My vision of what Berkeley's involvement would look like was simple. A successful school would require full campus support as well as (1) a sustained commitment to funding needs; (2) faculty oversight and coordination (which might also require administrative teaching buyout to provide time for California College Preparatory Academy (CAL Prep) work; (3) full collaboration with the charter school administration/teachers; (4) dedicated UC staff time to work with school personnel; (5) Berkeley student involvement via tutoring/mentoring programs; and (6) equally important to all of the above, parents' and families' involvement with and commitment to the academic success of their children. With respect to funding, we also needed a commitment from the Development Office to include CAL Prep in major fund-raising initiatives.

My hope, stated at the outset of our planning discussions, was that success would be measured when every graduating senior was fully college ready, that all students would be admitted to a 4-year college/university (or that for students going first to community college we would ensure their transfer to a 4-year college), and that a significant percentage of graduating students would be admitted to UC Berkeley or other first-rank universities.

university laboratory schools, which have not had much impact in improving public education. Moreover, it was not yet clear what the pitfalls will be, but he also pointed out that what we are proposing is actually a "ratcheting up" of higher education's commitment to K–12, as universities needed to take seriously their own interest and ties to secondary education in terms of being feeder institutions, diversity, and community relations.

## The Role of the Graduate School of Education

On January 10, 2003, Ms. Kaufman contacted Mr. Jorgensen, Director of School Relations in the GSE, on behalf of Vice Chancellor Padilla, soliciting Dean Pearson's advice and degree of interest. Jorgensen wrote to Dean Pearson describing the situation. In mid-January, Kaufman and Dr. Marsha Jaeger from CEP met with Dean Pearson and Jorgensen to talk over the initiative and provide a full status report, and Pearson wrote an encouraging e-mail to Padilla saying he had would bring up the idea with the Vision Committee of the GSE on January 17. He wanted to ask the committee if it made sense for the campus to submit a grant proposal for the early college high school competition that would encompass the Vision Committee's initiative to be an exemplar of how education schools can be transformed to better serve the goals and practices of education. Dean Pearson also indicated that he was anxious to talk to Professor Marx directly. By January 17, Dean Pearson was scheduled to talk to Marx and Padilla and it was agreed that Kaufman (representing the CEP and Student Affairs) and Jorgensen (representing the GSE) should work together to coordinate the initiative. The strength of the collaboration between Student Affairs and the GSE as co-champions of the Early College Initiative (ECI) ultimately engaged faculty and campus leadership.

**The Early College Initiative and the Graduate School of Education's Vision.** The timing of the request to the GSE was fortuitous because the GSE had been having related discussions in the fall of 2002. In response to the initiative of faculty for needed reforms, especially to foster vital interactions among researchers and practitioners, Dean Pearson, who also was sympathetic to the need for more hands-on sites, appointed a Vision Study Group composed of select senior faculty. This group was charged to report back on the vision's dimensions and how it might be realized.

The Vision Study Group began meeting fall, 2002, but the group's work stalled because the imagined scale required massive resources.

Dean Pearson was first informed of the ECI while he was looking for opportunities to leverage the vision being developed. At the same time, Pearson wanted to elevate the GSE's standing on campus by building reciprocal intellectual relationships with non-GSE faculty, expanding the GSE's ability to collaborate and fund-raise for applied research activities, and securing GSE recognition for creating or fostering urban education improvements. He recognized that these complementary goals would be reinforced if the GSE were to gain access to Gates Foundation planning funds. His first faculty consultations after speaking to Professor Marx revealed sufficient curiosity to invite Marx to present the initiative to the Vision Committee. Dean Pearson became involved in planning for Marx's visit to the campus scheduled for February 27, 2003, in part to engage the GSE faculty, and he specifically invited Professor Rhona Weinstein from Psychology as well, given her long-standing work on the achievement gap and school reform.

The GSE hosted a lunch at the Faculty Club for Professor Marx with an agenda focused on the Vision Committee's interest in rolling out its over-arching initiative to reconceptualize the GSE. Faculty members in atten-dance questioned how much flexibility there would be in working with the Gates Foundation and how sustainable the partnership could be. Marx later reported to Ms. Kaufman that the GSE had a vision for restructur-ing itself that included the establishment of learning places and that these intended reforms might fit into the ECI. A week later, on March 5, Dean Pearson convened the standing GSE Policy Committee to discuss how best to respond to the ECI. The five committee members expressed consider-able interest in the Gates initiative. This interest was tempered by concerns about partnering with a single public school and identifying what kinds of peer-reviewed research, if any, could be conducted there or alternatively, if evidence-proofs of particular theories might be effectively tested. One member expressed discomfort with the thrust to accelerate high school even more by requiring college courses. Pearson summarized the GSE's views as follows after hearing from everyone:

> The GSE wants a learning place in a community setting to enrich its scholarship on teaching and learning. It ought to be possible for the GSE to pursue this in partnership with Gates without compromising its own interests. And while the GSE still needs to reach consensus on whether it is best to work with an existing school or create a new one, it was agreed the student body ought to widely represent the East Bay or Alameda County to protect against any creaming effect in admissions.

## From Idea to Tentative Commitment

Dean Pearson and Vice Chancellor Padilla met in mid-March to discuss how they could work together on the ECI. Pearson came away with the impression that Padilla wanted him to take the lead in building a campus academic commitment for partnering with Gates and creating a school. Mr. Jorgensen's notes to Ms. Kaufman on March 19 suggested that Pearson was now planning to broaden the GSE's Vision discussion and link it to the ECI while recruiting interested faculty inside and outside the GSE. This organizing effort would be followed by a presentation to Executive Vice Chancellor Gray that would demonstrate broad faculty commitment. However, Padilla's unit had always expected to take the lead for the campus in preparing to participate in the ECI. Sensing early that the GSE could both benefit from, and enrich, campus participation, Jorgensen worked collaboratively with Kaufman to organize meetings, report on GSE deliberations, arrange exploratory visits, and work on documents, such as the first draft of a briefing to Gray in mid-March.

By early April (and only a month before the end of the spring semester), Dean Pearson was pushing simultaneously on three levers to sustain momentum. First, he sought senior faculty endorsement, as represented by the GSE's Vision Study Group, for embracing the initiative. To this end, Pearson asked the Vision Study Group to review the briefing document prepared for Executive Vice Chancellor Gray before its submission. This document laid out the issues and opportunities presented by the Gates initiative but said very little about the GSE vision, and it was unclear whether this document was ever endorsed by the Vision Study Group.

Second, Dean Pearson recognized, as did Vice Chancellor Padilla, the need for a broader faculty coalition outside of the GSE that could endorse the initiative and agree to participate. They believed that this was a precondition to the Executive Vice Chancellor Gray's allowing the campus to proceed. Pearson invited faculty from several departments to a meeting on April 18 to seek buy-in for the ECI opportunity and identify emerging champions. At the meeting, Pearson and Professor David Stern (Education) advocated for a school with a diverse enrollment in terms of race, socioeconomic status, and intellectual capability, measured by alignment with the demography of counties close to the campus or perhaps the state itself. Those outside the GSE who attended supported this concept and expressed interest in participating. None, though, was positioned to be a leader. Pearson wrote afterward to Padilla that the turnout was insufficient to demonstrate faculty commitment to Gray.

Third, Dean Pearson recognized the critical value of seed funding to sustain momentum. The Jorgensen–Kaufman briefing outline highlighted a May 27 deadline to submit a letter of intent to apply for a state charter planning grant, with the final grant due on June 27. This grant would precede and complement the upcoming ECI funding pledged by Professor Marx on behalf of the WWNFF. More importantly, it would underwrite a planning process without a precommitment to the Gates initiative and its restrictions. Pearson understood the potential of the planning grant to stimulate buy-in, and he wanted Kaufman and Jorgensen to begin work on it right away, presuming that campus endorsement of the project could be realized by mid-June. A key precursor, however, was to identify leadership for a faculty advisory group that would guide the writing of the state planning grant. At the time, Pearson could not come up with an available candidate from the Vision Study Group due to impending travel plans and other commitments. His note to Vice Chancellor Padilla also identified five GSE faculty who expressed genuine interest in the initiative.

On May 14, Dean Pearson convened the last GSE faculty meeting for the spring semester where the Vision Study Group's deliberations were presented in context of the ECI opportunity. The pros and cons of working with an existing school were discussed. Benefits included deeper immersion for GSE student teachers and the chance to develop and sustain a school and district partnership; costs included inheriting teachers and a culture resistant to change. At meeting's end, Pearson invited all GSE faculty to attend a faculty meeting of interested campus faculty being convened by Vice Chancellor Padilla on May 16. Although Pearson did not have a resounding faculty endorsement for the project, there were no strong naysayers either (see Box 2.2).

To continue to build consensus, Robert Jorgensen sent out notes of the May 16 meeting to GSE faculty who had not attended previously, and he scheduled an early June meeting to brainstorm a vision for the proposed secondary school to include in the state charter planning grant proposal. At that point, Professor Mark Wilson assumed the role of representing the GSE faculty in the school's relationship to the ECI and later in guiding CAL Prep's creation and development. Although there had been no formal poll of the GSE faculty to proceed, the lack of strong resistance gave Dean Pearson the confidence the GSE could partner on the initiative. The clearest commitment was Pearson's willingness to serve as co–principal investigator (PI) for the grant to be submitted to WWNFF in the fall.

## BOX 2.2 PEARSON

Relatively early in my deanship at the Graduate School of Education at the University of California (UC) Berkeley, we were asked to consider sponsoring an early college high school. At that time, there was a network of partnerships between universities and high schools around the country that had committed themselves to the principle that the problem with high school in America, particularly for minority students was too little, not too much, challenge. Thus, if we wanted to increase college participation among students in this population, we would have to raise not lower the standards to which they were held accountable. When this principle was translated into practice at the secondary level, it meant that we would "up the ante" on coursework challenge for academically talented underperforming youth; push credit-bearing college courses down into Grades 9–12; and help these vulnerable students acquire the infrastructure of academic skills, knowledge, and habits of mind that would transform failure into success.

When presented with this opportunity, I jumped at the chance. What could be better for a graduate school of education in a prestigious Research I institution than being a part of an effort to increase academic opportunity for traditionally marginalized students. But I was convinced, from the outset that such a venture could not, indeed should not, reside within the four walls of the School of Education. If it was going to be successful, I thought (and not just me but all of us who were in on the initial conversations), it would have to entail the sponsorship of the whole campus, including the chancellor and the provost, and many departments in the arts and sciences and other professional schools. So like all good academics, we formed a committee of key faculty across campus. Both for the sake of symbolism and for the sake of recruiting the disciplinary talent we would need, it was co-chaired by the Vice Chancellor for Student Affairs, Genaro Padilla, and myself as Dean of the Graduate School of Education (GSE). And the rest, as they say, is history—the history that is reported in this book.

But my motives were as personal as they were institutional. UC Berkeley had been my ticket to academic capital in the early 1960s. I grew up poor in a small farming community in the Sonoma Valley where the percentage of college-going graduates hovered in the low 20s. Going to UC Berkeley changed my life, so I knew it could change the lives of lots of poor kids who might attend the California College Preparatory Academy (CAL Prep) and distinguish themselves to the degree that they would qualify for Cal (UC Berkeley).

CAL Prep, I thought, would be first and foremost a place that privileged the academic and personal welfare of its students above all other goals. It would care about their futures, their families, and their "portfolio" of academic and personal skills—the stuff that would get its students into universities such as UC Berkeley, Stanford, and Harvard. Second, it would be a test bed for new ideas, a place in which scholars from UC Berkeley and teachers at CAL Prep would invent the next generation of curricula and teaching strategies that would define secondary education. We would take risks, but always with the goal of equipping our students with deep knowledge and cutting edge skills in reasoning, creative thinking, and critique. Third, it would be a school in which we would place our small cadre of teacher education candidates so that they could learn from the very best teachers and professors about how to engage students in challenging academic endeavors. Fourth, in implementing this three-part agenda, CAL Prep would become the "go-to" place for teacher professional development; CAL Prep teachers, working side-by-side with UC Professors, would offer dazzling seminars to those Bay Area teachers thirsting for cutting edge knowledge about effective and engaging teaching practices.

## Collaborative Steps Forward

### The Decision to Go "Charter"

Many of the UC Berkeley participants involved in the preliminary discussions regarding this initiative were wary of charter schools. They were concerned with draining resources from districts, "creaming" the best students of diverse and low-income backgrounds, and undermining general public education and reform efforts. A charter school also flew in the face of a desire to share best practices with traditional public school districts. Yet, the idea of using the charter school model kept surfacing. A number of forces pushed that agenda to the forefront. First, preliminary studies on the Gates Foundation's small school initiative pointed to better results from starting a school from scratch versus working with an existing school. Second, charter school regulations seemed to offer flexibility in terms of school structure and curriculum. Third, support for this approach was evident from donors and foundations. Fourth, a charter school would allow UC Berkeley to focus on what it does best (teacher development, curriculum and instruction, developing a climate of high expectations and support, access to rigorous and college-level courses) and not be bogged down in the day-to-day management of the school. Finally, there was a possibility of chartering through the Alameda County of Education, so no specific district's finances would be affected more than others (or so we thought).

As these discussions developed, Mr. Jorgensen and Ms. Kaufman began learning more about charter organizations operating in the Bay Area. Also, in January 2003, a highly respected university-affiliated educator recommended Aspire Public Schools as a potential partner because they were already working with Stanford University in an East Palo Alto high school they had created together. Kaufman and Jorgensen held an initial meeting with Dr. Don Shalvey, the Chief Executive Officer of Aspire Public Schools, in February. Aspire was a widely respected nonprofit California charter management organization (CMO) founded in 1998 by Shalvey, a former Superintendent of the San Carlos School District in California and Reed Hastings, a Silicon Valley entrepreneur. When we began our discussions with Aspire, this CMO had opened seven charter schools serving approximately 2,000 students. At that meeting, Shalvey shared his vast knowledge about charter schools as well as the memorandum of understanding (MOU) between Aspire and Stanford University for the East Palo Alto High School. Although he expressed enthusiasm for meeting and talking to faculty about how a partnership could be developed, he also encouraged UC Berkeley to talk to other charter operators.

Although Mr. Jorgensen and Ms. Kaufman continued to diligently investigate a variety of charter operators, they kept returning to Aspire Public Schools as the most promising potential collaborator. Dr. Shalvey and Aspire Public Schools received rave reviews from stakeholders and respected colleagues for their commitment to low-income, first-generation college students underrepresented in universities; business and political know-how; competent and creative staff; integrity; and flexibility. Initial results in terms of performance of Aspire students were promising, although Aspire did not have extensive experience in secondary education. Aspire had developed schools in the poorest neighborhoods in the Bay Area and in other California communities, and the organization's philosophical tenets were complementary to those of UC Berkeley (e.g., all students can achieve at high levels; students must be challenged and supported simultaneously; students' pursuits should reflect their interests; importance of personalization and community for students, staff, and families; shared purpose among teachers). Aspire also had experience working with other institutions of higher education; a comprehensive student assessment program; a track record of fund-raising, including a strong relationship with the Gates Foundation; and a commitment to evaluation and stakeholder input operationalized with annual surveys of students, staff, and families.

By April, the discussions with Aspire had matured to the point that it became the prime candidate to be Berkeley's charter partner. The partnership potential was tested on the ground as Aspire included other members of its high level staff in sessions with Ms. Kaufman and Mr. Jorgensen to develop a joint State Charter Start-Up Grant, sharing proposals as exemplars, and making plans to visit the Stanford/Aspire school in East Palo Alto. An important element of this relationship was the chemistry between Dr. Shalvey and the two faculty administrators championing this endeavor, Vice Chancellor Padilla and Dean Pearson. Dr. Shalvey understood that there was a great deal of concern and skepticism about this project and especially the growing consensus to partner with a charter organization, and he understood the differences between the cultures of IHEs and K–12 schools (e.g., the speed with which decisions need to be made in K–12 versus the deliberative and lengthy process in which IHEs engage). He gave UC Berkeley room for deliberation and demonstrated his respect for its complex communication and organizational structure. Although he was willing to give the university the space it needed to make decisions, he was always clear on the timeframe and immediacy of the work. Based on the positive assessment of Aspire and its growing relationship with the campus, in mid-May, Padilla and Pearson asked the informal grouping of faculty that had coalesced around the initiative to endorse partnering with Aspire on the planning and development of an early college high school, which they did.

## Campuswide Faculty Engagement

This initiative could have fallen apart at any number of points in this first year; it was fragile, at best. What was needed now was the enthusiastic support of ladder-rank faculty from across the campus representing a diversity of departments and disciplines. The UC Berkeley workgroup (Jaeger, Jorgensen, Kaufman, Padilla, and Pearson) knew that campus leadership would not support the CEP–GSE collaboration moving forward if it did not have a chorus of faculty voices supporting the enterprise. The workgroup decided that face-to-face meetings with Professor Marx were essential to winning support from senior faculty from across the campus. As the emissary from the Gates and Woodrow Wilson Foundations, he was an eloquent spokesperson for the philosophy and ideals of the project and offered sound reasons for why UC Berkeley should sign on. It helped that he was a respected faculty member from Columbia University and spoke the same language as UC Berkeley faculty. In drawing up the lists of which faculty to invite to these meetings, the workgroup began with faculty who had engaged with K–12 in their own work (e.g., National Science Foundation grants, curriculum development, research, and educational outreach). A series of faculty meetings were scheduled in April and May of 2003.

April's meeting drew senior faculty from the GSE and the sciences, primarily. This meeting was pragmatic in tone, with discussions about involving prospective teachers early in the design of the school, the role of the school in UC Berkeley's efforts to increase the numbers of underrepresented students at Berkeley, the admissions process, and UC Berkeley's role in curriculum and professional development, because the school would provide easy access for faculty to K–12 settings without complicated protocols. The idea of a faculty oversight committee was also discussed at this meeting for the first time. The May meeting was envisioned as a larger grouping with several outcomes, including inviting a broader range of faculty to meet Professor Marx, hearing about the nationwide implications of the initiative and seeking advice going forward on critical issues such as the charter partnership and the submission of grants. As noted, a consensus was achieved for the critical decision to develop a partnership with Aspire Public Schools and submit a collaborative California Charter Start-Up Application. Consensus was also reached to start the school with sixth graders (rather than ninth graders) to allow enough time to prepare underperforming students for college level work. Marx met with Chancellor Berdahl in May as well, and Berdahl, while appreciative of the leadership of Student Affairs and the GSE, also expressed concerns about the difficulties in securing a facility close to the campus and whether the faculty would remain involved and engaged.

The last campuswide faculty meeting was held early in June, 2003, and it included a representative from Aspire. A broader representation of faculty, including individuals from Psychology, Engineering, Physics, Environmental Science, Chemistry, Mathematics, and Education participated, and raised many questions from admissions and curriculum to professional development and teacher's salaries. Outcomes included a beginning list of must-haves for UC Berkeley:

- An admissions policy that ensured equitable representation by race, ethnicity, and income
- Berkeley faculty being actively involved in evaluation/research, curriculum, professional development, and hiring school leaders and teachers
- A commitment that allowed faculty and graduate students freedom to explore in the school setting what it takes to create high-quality

instruction to prepare underresourced students for access and success in higher education.

The following week, Dean Pearson, Vice Chancellor Padilla, and Professor Wilson had lunch with Dr. Shalvey. Although some specifics were hashed over, this was also an opportunity to continue the relationship-building process, because this partnership could not move forward if each entity did not assume good intentions on the part of the other.

**Consolidation.** Despite the concern from participating faculty, that neither the departmental culture nor the faculty appraisal policies rewarded the work we set out to do in K–12 reform (see Chapters 3 and 17), we pushed forward. After the three meetings—April, May, and June—the following points represented the consensus that emerged from the faculty:

1. UC Berkeley would guide the intellectual conceptualization of the school and actively participate in forming criteria for admission, student outcome goals, curriculum, assessment measures, and evaluation. A faculty advisory committee would be established as the planning begins.
2. A key mission was to create a research and development test bed. Faculty, graduate students, and undergraduates across the campus would be encouraged to participate in the school's academic design and implementation. An important goal was to learn how to make a school successful for its students in ways that can be widely replicated.
3. The school would be sufficiently freestanding and independent to allow a substantial role for UC Berkeley. It would include Grades 6–12 and be located conveniently to the UC Berkeley campus and public transportation from the East Bay.
4. The student body would reflect the demographics of the East Bay, with an emphasis on underrepresented minority students. Stratified random samples would be the basis for admission lotteries, and steps should be taken to avoid "creaming" high-performing students.
5. School goals would include the creation of a college-going culture and preparation of most students for UC and UC Berkeley eligibility. A curriculum would be developed that bridged high school and college, leading to opportunities for high school students to enroll in college classes.

6. The school would nurture a professional community of teachers who would become part of reciprocal connections with UC Berkeley faculty. It would encourage parent and student voices and proactive participation.
7. A campus organizational structure would be developed to foster UC Berkeley's deep engagement with the school.

These faculty recommendations formed the backbone for Berkeley's negotiations with Aspire and submissions in response to requests for proposals from WWNFF for Gates Foundation funding. They also comprised the primary values put forth in the workgroup's advocacy for endorsement from campus leadership to move forward with this work. By mid-June, a faculty leadership structure began to develop. Dean Pearson and Vice Chancellor Padilla agreed to serve as the PIs for the WWNFF grant and Professor Wilson (Education) and Professor Angelica Stacy (Chemistry) began developing a Faculty Oversight committee.

## Securing Campus Commitment

After Professor Marx's visit to campus on February 24, Dean Pearson broached for the first time a discussion about the initiative with the highest levels of campus leadership at the Dean's Council in February and with Executive Vice Chancellor Gray. Dean Pearson wanted to learn if the Executive Vice Chancellor would consider investing in the ECI, and if so, under what conditions. He wanted to ask early on because this project would not be a strictly academic initiative that could be vetted as part of the cyclical academic budgeting process. He understood that while the ECI might be attractive as a way of showing that UC Berkeley cared about equity and K–12 education, it would be risky to the university's name if the project were not successful. Pearson also needed to know early on if any campus resources would be provided to the GSE if it were to take the lead. Such assurances would deliver a clear signal to GSE faculty as they consider whether to participate.

Likewise, Dean Pearson needed to reassure Executive Vice Chancellor Gray that this unprecedented initiative would be received favorably by faculty, be sustainable without draining campus budgets, involve minimal risk, and avoid a besmirching of UC Berkeley's name. Although Gray recognized the opportunity for Berkeley to be viewed as a leader in improving K–12 education and foresaw the possibility of developing students to attend the campus, he wanted a business plan that would protect the university's interests and allow the weighing of the opportunities projected with the possible costs and risks. Like Gray and Pearson, Vice Chancellor Padilla was also concerned with developing UC Berkeley–ready applicants, and he was anxious to engage more faculty across campus in educational outreach, build alliances with academic units, and be included in grants that would add resources at a critical time.

These efforts culminated in a briefing paper submitted to the Executive Vice Chancellor on May 23. The paper was organized generally as a business plan. Headings included Opportunity for Berkeley, First Findings (including alternative models for developing a school), Longer-term Funding and Resource Issues, Recommended Multistage Strategy, and Timeline. The working assumption throughout was that UC Berkeley would not own or run the school to be developed. After reviewing the paper, the Executive Vice Chancellor recommended identifying Berkeley facilities opportunities with the campus real estate manager, a concrete indication that he supported a campus effort to provide an appropriate facility, most likely off-campus, for a school.

Other efforts were also moving forward in tandem. Professors Wilson and Stacy planned and led a meeting with the Academic Senate leadership in September aimed at securing buy-in. Out of these discussions, the incoming Academic Senate Chair, Professor Gronsky (Engineering), agreed to serve on the advisory committee. In October, when the faculty advisory committee was formally appointed by the Chancellor, Professors Stacy (Chemistry) and Wilson (Education) were asked to serve as founding co-chairs. Other committee members included Vice Chancellor Padilla, GSE Dean Pearson, faculty members from Astronomy (Professor Basri), Engineering (Professor Gronsky), Journalism (Professor Henry), Psychology (Professor Weinstein), and Education (Professors Worrell, Stern, Seyer-Ochi), and a doctoral student in Education (Duckor). Ms. Kaufman and Mr. Jorgensen served as committee staff. Unlike the Preuss School, where the Academic Senate at UC San Diego was asked to vote on establishing the school, as it would become an academic unit of the university, the Academic Senate at UC Berkeley was consulted, but no formal vote was ever taken. The faculty advisory committee became an administrative committee and not an Academic Senate committee.

## The Grant Submission

UC Berkeley's funding request (Padilla & Pearson, 2003) was not submitted to the WWNFF until October 8, 2003, more than a year after Professor

Marx's initial invitation to Chancellor Berdahl to join the ECI. The 3-year, $399,676 request was the most public manifestation of Berkeley's commitment to develop and affiliate with a stand-alone, public secondary school.

The grant proposal was submitted jointly by Vice Chancellor Padilla and Dean Pearson as PIs, with the Student Affairs' Center for Educational Outreach (now the CEP) as the home unit. The required listing of campus leadership for the "California Early College Academy" on p. 2 of the proposal included the PIs as well as Professors Wilson and Stacy and Staff Coordinators Jorgensen and Kaufman. The structure based on parallel representation from the GSE and CEP—and the GSE and faculty across campus—was also incorporated into the organization of the faculty advisory committee. The Executive Vice Chancellor made clear such a committee must be in place to guide the initiative and arrangements were made to have the members appointed directly by the Chancellor. In the grant, the advisory committee was described as playing "a critical ongoing role in nurturing the school and building a strong relationship between it and UC Berkeley" (Padilla & Pearson, 2003, p. 7).

Everyone who participated in organizing a UC Berkeley response to the invitation believed from the outset that the campus could only commit on its own terms. The grant narrative carefully melded key concepts that had arisen as concerns with the ECI model as presented. Careful compromises were hammered out to keep the UC Berkeley stakeholders and the charter operator on board while striving to submit a competitive bid appropriate to UC Berkeley's reputation. The concerns were discussed throughout with Professor Marx and then, with Dr. Robert Baird, as WWNFF Director of School/University Partnerships. The negotiated responses to UC Berkeley concerns, as reflected in the grant proposal, varied considerably from the standard guidelines that WWNFF and the Gates Foundation had established and included the following:

1. Funding an extended 18-month planning period (although tied in the single grant to an 18-month implementation phase for a total of 3 years of funding). Faculty, particularly in the GSE, had wanted a dedicated planning grant at the end of which they would determine whether and how to launch a school.
2. Delaying the school's opening until September 2005 instead of 2004 as WWNFF had expected (and apparently needed to meet its own contractual obligation to the Gates Foundation).

3. Subcontracting the bulk of grant funding to Aspire Public Schools[1] so that they could identify and secure a facility, hire teachers and principal, recruit and enroll students, and apply for a state facilities grant—all with direct UC Berkeley involvement—in order to open the school on time. UC Berkeley realized it did not have the capacity to do this in short order.
4. Recruiting from a broad, regionwide geographic area of wide diversity without drawing on a specific community or a particular school district, as other grantees had done.
5. Creating a Grade 6–12 secondary school, rather than just a high school encompassing Grades 9–12 as the ECI envisioned.
6. Postponing the determination of the actual site for the school, creation of an acceptable MOU with Aspire, choice of a charter approver (either a single school district or a county office of education), and the amount and locus of college course enrollments expected of students.

Campus leadership had also made clear that it would not allocate central funds or guarantee a facility and that UC Berkeley would not "own" the school and be subject to the accompanying financial and legal risk. Furthermore, UC Berkeley would not be liable for any funding shortfalls: "should the school ever encounter any financial challenge, the full strength and resources of Aspire Public Schools will be available to provide assistance in resolving the challenge" (Padilla & Pearson, 2003, pp. 18–19). Instead, UC Berkeley offered "numerous in-kind contributions" to the start-up process, including "developing and implementing a fund-raising strategy and the additional time of coordinators/liaisons, and other key staff, faculty and administrators" (Padilla & Pearson, 2003, p. 19).

These negotiated adjustments to the grant proposal, the spadework to build faculty commitment, and the CEP–GSE collaboration all added to the confidence of the UC Berkeley participants, up to and including the Chancellor and Executive Vice Chancellor. Particularly important also were that the ECI would allow sufficient flexibility to limit campus exposure while upholding UC Berkeley's standards, as evidenced by the extra year offered to plan and open the school, the availability and interest of a charter operator to administer the school in partnership, and the

---

[1] To meet the WWNFF grant deadline, all parties agreed to include Aspire Public Schools in the UC Berkeley grant submission due October 8, 2003, even though the ECI Faculty Committee was not to meet for the first time until October 15, 2003. On November 25, 2003, the ECI Faculty voted to fully endorse the partnership with Aspire Public Schools.

opportunity for Berkeley to exercise leadership in improving public education, as urged by UCOP and the state. As Berkeley and Aspire began to share language for an MOU, the words "collaboration" versus "providing feedback" emerged as major stumbling blocks. Was it UC Berkeley's school contracting with Aspire for services and advice, or Aspire's school seeking some UC Berkeley services and advice? Or, was there a model where both could claim ownership and responsibility? The workgroup and faculty advisory committee struggled with this primary conceptual question for the next two planning years (see Chapter 3) as drafts and redrafts circulated, but it is instructive that, once approved by both parties, the MOU has never been revisited to achieve consensus in the more than 10 years of this ongoing partnership.

## References

Padilla, G., & Pearson, P. D. (2003). *Grant proposal to the Woodrow Wilson National Fellowship Foundation for the Early College Initiative*. Berkeley, CA: Authors.

West-Faulcon, K. (2006, October). *From race preference to race discrimination: Does Proposition 209 permit remedial affirmative action?* Paper presented at the Equal Opportunity in Higher Education: The Past and Future of Proposition 209 Conference, Boalt Hall Earl Warren Institute, Boalt Hall School of Law, University of California, Berkeley, CA.

# 3 | Forging a Partnership with Aspire Public Schools

**RHONA S. WEINSTEIN**

*"Are we in a partnership with Aspire or are we simply consulted?"* (Early College Initiative committee notes, January 12, 2004)

T HIS CHAPTER DESCRIBES OUR EARLY years of boundary crossing—the building of a partnership with Aspire Public Schools and the co-design of our new early college secondary school. The chapter begins with the first official meeting, on October 15, 2003, of the Early College Initiative (ECI) committee, which was appointed by and reported to the Chancellor of the University of California (UC) Berkeley, to provide oversight for the development of the school. It spans the almost 2 years of planning with Aspire that culminated with the opening of California College Preparatory Academy (CAL Prep) on August 24, 2005. Minutes of the meetings, prepared by Robert Jorgensen and Gail Kaufman, as well as e-mail exchanges, provide a running commentary about the planning process, which informs the discussion here.

In this chapter, I describe the early expectations of UC Berkeley and Aspire as we tested the feasibility of our partnership. I then turn to the challenges we faced as well as the decisions we made in co-constructing a school that was reflective of our joint beliefs and expertise. This includes the work to develop partnership structures and governance guidelines, obtain a site and charter status, carve out a school vision, and recruit students and hire staff. Finally, I explore the inevitable tensions that arose and the progress made through our planning process. As we will see in forthcoming chapters, the issues raised during this planning time framed the research questions we addressed and foretold the struggles we would encounter in birthing this new school from blueprint to sustained reality.

Given the intent of the Bill & Melinda Gates Foundation's Early College High School Initiative—an effort co-supported by a number of other foundations—boundary crossing between institutions of secondary education and 4-year colleges was a core mediating principle. As described in Chapter 2, this pioneering initiative sought to seed new small secondary schools across the United States, which would offer both a rigorous college-preparatory education for *all* students and the opportunity to reduce the number of years to a college degree through *credited* college courses while in high school. The population of interest was students who faced disadvantages, most typically locked into an unequal education in large high schools and deprived of advanced course work. The Woodrow Wilson National Fellowship Foundation (WWNFF) was chosen as one of eight intermediary organizations to facilitate this effort, specifically for partnerships with 4-year colleges, by selecting grantees, distributing funds, and supporting the development of these partnered schools.

Boundary crossing was not going to be easy. The call for proposals from the WWNFF (March 28, 2002) forewarned about the enormous challenges inherent in merging high school and college experiences:

> High schools and colleges are entirely independent institutions . . . organized along different lines, they recruit faculty from different markets, they are funded differently, they are responsible to different oversight bodies, they have different pedagogical expertise, and they have developed missions and goals that have surprisingly few intersections. The early college initiative clearly requires a high level of coordination and cooperation between these two types of institution, and at the present nationally, there appears to be almost no coordination or cooperation. (p. 2)

In a *New York Times* article entitled, " 'Early College' Gains Ground in Education" (Arenson, 2003), Robert J. Baird, the director of school–university partnerships at the Woodrow Wilson Foundation at Princeton, described the necessary kinds of agreements between the high schools and colleges that are crucial to making the early college concept work. "They really have to blend the institutions, figure out how the courses mesh, and what happens when students don't perform at a certain level," Dr. Baird said. He continued,

It is very complicated, and it involves not just curriculum and content people, but admissions people and the registrar. That is why it is essential that the president or provost be involved and appoint a key point person. It puts the university on the line if they provide the credit.

We were already on the line for far more than university course credit, admittedly a steep hurdle, but also for the creation of a new high school.

The previous chapter detailed a first year of complex negotiations from invitation to commitment to develop an early college high school affiliated with the campus. The project, a collaboration between UC Berkeley's Division of Student Affairs (UGA) and the university's Graduate School of Education (GSE; see Chapter 2), involved multiple meetings with an increasingly stable group of people around the table, who became pivotal players in this initiative and ultimately chapter authors in this book. Critical decisions were reached during this initial year that would frame the effort. They included the decision (1) to create a new school rather than reform an existing school; (2) to adopt the model of a public charter school; (3) to partner with a charter management organization (CMO) rather than administer the school ourselves; (4) to begin the school at sixth grade; (5) to create a regional school not exclusively tied to a single district; and (6) to seek funding beyond the state average daily attendance funds (ADA) for planning, school start-up, and importantly research. Although we had yet to fully commit to our eventual charter district partner, Aspire Public Schools, we had proceeded with a grant submission to WWNFF to support planning and start-up costs for the new school.

These decisions, especially the charter model, the CMO partnership, and regional reach, were and continued to be controversial to some in the university. After much debate, they were viewed as essential to providing genuine freedom for UC Berkeley to innovate and engage in what it did best, such as curriculum development and research, unencumbered by the full responsibility of daily management of the school and without undercutting relationships with multiple districts in preexisting outreach programs. The CMO partnership proved critical as there was much to learn about the creation of new schools that went far beyond the expertise and available time of the university community. As we were to see, the university had other powerful ways to contribute beyond curriculum development. However, there remained many urgent decisions still on the table, among them, finalizing the UC Berkeley–Aspire commitment.

## Expectations at the Start: A Decision Made

The binder for the first meeting of the ECI committee on October 15, 2003, was almost too heavy to carry, let alone digest. It contained information about the committee (its charge, members, the agendas from preliminary meetings, the UC Berkeley background, and the grant proposal), the ECI, charter schools, Aspire Public Schools, and reports of interest. The timeline we created for these two planning years was even more daunting. It included for the first year alone—negotiation of a memorandum of understanding (MOU) with the charter partner, search for a school site, application for charter status and a State Charter Implementation Grant, development of vision, and creation of a fund-raising strategy. Tasks for the second year focused on hiring of the principal and teachers; an educational plan with curricula, instructional strategies, and college coursework; design of admission policy and recruitment of students; and planning for professional development and research.

At this first ECI committee meeting, we invited Professor Bruce Fuller, co-director of Policy Analysis for California Education, who summarized charter school research and pointed out the substantial challenges, including selection effects in admissions, sustainability, staff turnover, which schools lose students to charter schools, and pressure to do well on tests. We were thus armed with a significant prehistory, forewarned about charter challenges, and emboldened, perhaps naively, to address the laundry list of tasks, which in reality were entirely interactive.

From UC Berkeley's perspective, we had committed to create a "free-standing public charter school constantly innovating to develop college readiness, academic success, and early-college experiences for a wide diverse student body drawn from cities along the East Bay BART (Bay Area Rapid Transit) corridor, with emphasis on low-income, first-generation students" (memo to ECI members from Vice Chancellor Padilla and Dean Pearson, October 15, 2003). We wanted to make sure that we did not exclude special education students, and we envisioned a school that would ultimately span pre-K to Grade 12. In defining the kind of achievement we wanted to nurture, we were clear about wanting to increase the UC eligibility of these students. Among the districts close to UC Berkeley, only 23% of underrepresented minority students graduating in 2000 were defined as "college ready" by UC, as compared to 44% of Whites and Asians in the same year (Padilla & Pearson, 2003).

We also embraced the developmental framework for undergraduate achievement articulated by the UC Berkeley Commission on Undergraduate Education (Padilla & Porter, 2000). This included three phases: a cornerstone phase (development of skills and desire for lifelong learning through discovery-based learning environments), the engagement phase (deeper learning in a specific discipline or area of study, involving research methods, critical thinking, and evidence), and the capstone phase (involvement of students in independent and integrative scholarly pursuits such as research or design or service projects). UC Berkeley's hopes were to change the underlying culture of schools—in order to promote student engagement in rigorous problem-solving, foster a learning community for teachers, and put effective programs synergistically *together in one place* at the school level. We were clear that UC Berkeley needed to be an intrinsic part of this school and could not be removed. But we were equally insistent that we keep our promise to the school, because unmet promises are never forgotten. At the start, we saw our role more in design than operation—clearly a misleading dichotomy as we moved toward implementation.

On the other side, the expectations of Aspire were expressed in the PowerPoint presentation by the Aspire Leadership—Don Shalvey, Chief Executive Officer (CEO), and Elise Darwish, Chief Academic Officer—to the ECI committee meeting on November 17, 2003 (1 month later). Aspire saw the partnership as one where both would be better because of the collaboration. The presenters asked,

> Will we be able to work collectively on *the ways* scientists can inform science teachers, mathematicians enhance math teachers, historians and economists inform social science teachers, and assessment researchers enhance assessment? Can we figure out how coherent pathways, academies, education/employment blends and youth development experiences can seamlessly blend with "A–G" requirements? Would students be given special considerations in admissions, access to the expertise of Berkeley in summer sessions, pre-collegiate, and concurrent enrollment? (ECI committee notes, November 17, 2003)

After clarifying that there could not be any special advantage in admissions at UC Berkeley, the discussion focused on what each organization could and could not support. Aspire expressed openness to the university's sway over curriculum, pedagogy, and professional development as long as the Aspire network meetings were honored. But what

Aspire could not sacrifice was the calendar determined by staff and families; budget discipline around state and/or federal funding; graduation requirements; habits of mind; teacher teams; adherence to the state assessment system; and clarity on process, scope, and decision-making to ensure partnership success. UC Berkeley was concerned about promoting intellectual curiosity and deep knowledge in such a fashion that students would do well on standardized tests *and* meet university entrance requirements but would also perform well on measures of enhanced habits of mind. There was also a debate about the location of the school. Aspire placed schools where the students were—that is, locally. In contrast, UC Berkeley's intent was to locate the school close to university resources and close to the BART system but not to draw down from any particular district—that is, to recruit students regionally. Aspire agreed to work on the financial model for a school with these characteristics.

Although Aspire was judged very favorably by all, doubts still lingered about "going" charter and partnering with a charter management company rather than with a traditional district. Commonly raised concerns about charters included the potential for increased racial segregation or fewer special education students, given more limited access to needed services, as well as higher building-related and administrative costs. Furthermore, there was no evidence yet that charters actually change other parts of the public education system. An urgent memo from Robert Jorgensen on November 25, 2003 forced a decision:

> In awarding Berkeley the $400,000 grant, WW has included a condition that we designate a K–12 partner now—even if we were to change partners later. We're writing to seek your agreement to list Aspire as our current K–12 partner . . . Note that when we negotiate an MOU with Aspire or another charter operator, we will include an annual opt-out provision.

The ECI committee was asked to vote on this issue, agree or disagree, so that the grant acceptance process could be concluded. On shorter notice than was typical for scholars, UC Berkeley warmly embraced the partnership with Aspire Public Schools, and the grant was awarded. A *San Francisco Chronicle* article heralded the news that "UC Berkeley has won the latest grant from the Microsoft fortune to create an 'early college' school where disadvantaged students could finish high school while earning substantial college credit" (Burress, 2004).

# The Co-Construction of an Early College Secondary School

With funding assured for planning, a grant-required school opening no later than the fall of 2005, and a charter partner, we put a subcommittee structure in place in January, 2004, to address the key priorities of partnership and governance, facilities and charter application, educational vision (admissions, school design, early college requirements, and assessment), and fund-raising. CEO Shalvey appointed an Aspire staff member to work with each subcommittee. This strategy facilitated planning on multiple fronts, with committees reporting back at the monthly ECI committee meeting. By the next planning year, the list of tasks to complete was even longer. We prepared a timeline of tasks, noting the ones that had already been accomplished and the ones that needed to be addressed for the next year. Our subcommittee structures would change as we moved forward to address curriculum in specific disciplines over the summer break and to engage in recruitment, hiring, and curricular decisions in the second planning year. Our work on these issues spanned 2 years, but in the interest of clarity, the challenges discussed and decisions made are presented within the four key domains of partnership and governance, school site and charter, vision, and recruitment of students and staff.

## Key Partnership Structures and Governance

**Regularized Points of Collaboration**. For multiple organizations to collaborate in the creation of a setting—in this case, a new school—regularized points of contact between key parties need to be designed and institutionalized. Locally, we developed what we called four partnership structures, each critical to the task of co-construction. These four regularized and interdependent points of contact—an infrastructure of *layered collaborative efforts*—guided the work and enabled continual feedback loops. Together, they created an intellectually stimulating enterprise that fueled and sustained our long-term commitment to this project. At the state and national levels, we also became part of two networked improvement communities, which provided a broader set of resources and enlarged our perspectives. The process of setting goals, taking action, assessing results, and revising objectives, carefully guided and documented by Kaufman and Jorgensen, kept us on track. We were far from alone on this journey.

***Early College Initiative Committee.*** The first partnership structure we created was the ECI committee, the interdisciplinary oversight committee that met monthly and reported directly to the Chancellor, with the mission to establish and maintain policies for UC Berkeley regarding the development of the charter school. Among the ECI committee's strengths were that membership was strategically drawn from multiple disciplines across the campus and not solely from the GSE, that it included both faculty and staff, that it incorporated expertise from the Center for Educational Partnerships (CEP), that it had administrative clout with campus leaders as members, and that it was co-chaired by faculty from different departments (see Chapter 2). Campus leaders on the ECI committee included the Vice Chancellor for Undergraduate Affairs, the Dean of the Graduate School of Education, the Associate Vice Provost for the Faculty, the Academic Senate Chair, and the Vice Chancellor for Equity and Inclusion (a new post created in 2007). Key to its sustainability, the ECI committee's meetings were regularized to take place on the second Monday of each month from 3:30–5:00 p.m., making it possible to hold this time as "sacred."

Although the term of membership was set at 4 years, service continued well beyond 4 years for many of us. Of the initial committee of 14 members, two left the university, the incoming Vice Chancellor for UGA and GSE Dean replaced their predecessors as they stepped down, and five of the original members remained on board 10 years later. Thus, of the 12 individuals still at UCB, seven of the original members or positions (58%) are still at the ECI table. And three others have continued in other roles such as teaching seminars for CAL Prep students. New appointees also joined the ECI as expertise was added in areas relevant to families and social services, college offerings for high school students, community teachers or principals, and so on. This regularized context for collaboration enabled a predictable and sustained setting in which visitors could be invited, materials reviewed, and decisions made. Moreover, testament to the deepening collaboration, the ECI meeting came to include Aspire district administrators and the charter school's principal as regular members.

***Liaisons and the Liaison Planning Meeting.*** Although the ECI committee and its subcommittees proved sufficient, just barely, for planning, once the school became a reality with an opening date, we needed deeper university involvement. As we discussed joint responsibility, it was becoming very clear that implementation would depend upon released time for faculty and staff to become a regular presence in the school as liaisons and new partnership structures—for example, on-site partnership meetings (described below)—to foster this level of engagement. We created the position of university liaisons to the charter school to serve on the ground and attend a weekly meeting, again at a regularized time. Four individuals shared that role at the start, including two faculty members (Worrell, GSE, and Weinstein, Psychology), who for 2 years served as co-directors for development and research, and two staff members (Kaufman, UGA, and Jorgensen, GSE), who provided administrative leadership. As of this writing, both Worrell and Kaufman continue in these roles. Fund-raising efforts and the generous actions of the university offered teaching relief, research assistance, and redirected responsibilities that enabled this deeper commitment of faculty and staff. When the school opened, planning for certain topics shifted: university–school relations was a concern of the Liaison Planning Meeting, guidance and oversight was a concern of the the ECI committee, and co-construction of the school was primarily a concern of the School-Site Partnership Meeting.

*School-Site Partnership Meeting.* This meeting, held weekly at the school and at a regularized time, consisted of the principal, the UC Berkeley liaisons, and the regional superintendent from Aspire Public Schools. This meeting was the place where co-design, implementation, and evaluation took place. With its regularity and all partners at the table, plans could be put into action and problems could be resolved in a timely manner and with accountability.

*Other Structures.* As a place to assess how the partnership was proceeding and to address any trouble spots in our collaboration, a Partner Leadership Meeting between the UC Berkeley co-investigators (Vice Chancellor Padilla and Dean Pearson) and the Aspire CEO was instituted twice a year and later on a yearly basis. Additionally, by design, the Gates Foundation developed both a state by state and a national policy agenda for how to influence a blending of high school and college on a variety of issues, including concurrent enrollment and dual credit, funding streams, and teacher qualifications. Early college schools were grouped under intermediary organizations, in our case, the WWNFF. UC Berkeley and CAL Prep became the fifth WWNFF university-partnered school, joining schools at Hunter College, Brooklyn College, California State University (CSU) Los Angeles, and Dillard University.

WWNFF facilitated meetings twice a year among a growing network of early college secondary schools. These meetings, and the efforts of Jobs for the Future, a policy organization with responsibility for the entire

ECI, allowed for a sharing of challenges and strategies and coordinated data-gathering to evaluate how early college schools were faring. At the California state level, we began to network within the UC system with UC San Diego and the Preuss School, as well as with UC Davis and UC Los Angeles, which were also beginning partnerships and new schools, creating opportunities for meetings and school visits.

**Governance and the Memorandum of Understanding.** We agreed to the partnership, but the kind of governance and legal contract that would spell out our joint responsibilities had yet to be developed. How would we create a partnership of shared decision-making on significant issues such as determining the school's leadership, curriculum, assessments, and school climate? Among the structural options we explored were Aspire holding the charter subject to an MOU with UC Berkeley, UC Berkeley holding the charter subject to an MOU with Aspire, a vendor relationship, or a new nonprofit (501c3) organization of Aspire and UC Berkeley together. We discussed with legal counsel how these different governance options might affect liability issues, sustainability of structure, teachers and students, school integrity, and fund-raising. We were also aware that the mechanisms for start-up might need to be adjusted over time so that school could grow and flourish. On February 9, 2004, the legal advice from UC Berkeley and the UC President's Office recommended an affiliation agreement with the charter operator as the best course, with UC Berkeley negotiating for distinctive roles for each element in the design and development of the school. In holding the charter, Aspire ultimately would be responsible for the school (e.g., teachers would be Aspire employees), yet UC Berkeley's name would also be on the charter.

Multiple drafts of the MOU reflected the negotiations over relative roles and fallback mechanisms. As one example, what does it mean that UC Berkeley takes the first crack on an issue, such as curriculum, and what are the implications for both parties? Where UC Berkeley takes the lead, is it in effect only making a recommendation to Aspire? It was underscored by Aspire that UC Berkeley recommendations must be adjudicated within the context of available resources to the school. If UC Berkeley was not satisfied with the response by Aspire to the recommendation, it could take action to withdraw the use of its name. On the other hand, the default built into the MOU was that Aspire would act if UCB did not take the lead or follow-through. An example of the ongoing MOU tweaking noted that "The curriculum shall be consistent with UC eligibility requirements and all courses shall be approved by the Aspire Board of Directors as the

State Education Code requires" (Regents of the University of California & Aspire Public Schools, 2005, p. 8).

The UC Berkeley Business Contracts Office and Risk Management drafted the MOU's legal contract language, a suggested process for amending the MOU, and a dispute resolution process. Either party could terminate the contract. As charter holder, Aspire would ultimately be responsible for making school-related decisions. For some domains, UC Berkeley would have an equal role, whereas for others, one party would take the lead. There would be consensus of both parties on hiring a principal, work environment, support of teacher professional development, assessments, student enrollment in college classes, fund-raising, grants, media relations, site selection, and facility design. UC Berkeley would take the lead but consult Aspire on principles of school culture, enrollment policy and outreach, curriculum and instructional design, research on site, research on charter schools, placement of GSE student teachers, and professional development for the external educational community. Aspire would take the lead but consult UC Berkeley on the school calendar, school culture implementation and maintenance, scholastic program evaluation and reporting, parent relations, volunteer planning, human resources, financial systems, facilities systems, and legal compliance. In these ways, we described our roles and responsibilities, aiming for a collaboration that was transparent, effective, timely, efficient, cost effective, and ultimately good for students. The agreement was ultimately signed by both parties on October 26, 2005.

## Facilities and Charter Authorization

**Hunting for a School Site.** The time-consuming search for a school site led us to seven potential sites that might offer sufficient space for a secondary school. We had stiff criteria to meet—being on or close to the Berkeley campus and on a BART or bus line. Although it would have been ideal to garner a campus spot, such as with the early childhood education programs, the university was greatly overcrowded, with many programs relegated to off-campus locations and vying for a campus return. We encountered some pushback regarding the need for a campus slot, asking why we might prioritize a secondary school over programs for undergraduates. Furthermore, the city of Berkeley proved to be a dense and expensive urban space in which to buy or rent space. The ECI committee worked with the Aspire real estate team, met with campus administrators and space allocation committees, and toured multiple buildings, funding inspections and feasibility studies. We also stepped up fund-raising to identify a potential donor to fund a new facility. Despite intensive efforts, we had little success during the first year of facility hunting.

Obviously tied to the building decision and its locale was the charter application. We learned about chartering in California and had meetings with East Bay superintendents and with the Alameda County Office of Education, which had gained new legislative authority to charter schools directly, rather than after charter denial by a school district board. At the county level, the charter application would need to be signed by either parents (of 50% of students to be enrolled) or teachers (50% of the teachers we plan to hire). Preparation of a charter application would also need to specify an admission strategy. A draft charter petition that Aspire prepared gave Aspire students preference in admission, raising concerns at UC Berkeley about the conflicting goals of a regional student body versus a magnet school for Aspire students. We needed to work through these locale and admission strategies with our partner prior to submitting a mutually satisfactory charter application. And we desperately needed a school site.

**An Oakland District Site and Hybrid Model.** Pressure was building, because it was now less than 12 months before the school was slated to open in August 2005—a deliverable in our grant award from WWNFF. Discussed in our October 11, 2004, ECI committee meeting was a site in the Oakland School District at the soon-to-be-closed Golden Gate elementary school. An urgent decision was necessary because Oakland needed to inform families about the school closure by January, 2005. Although there were clear advantages, there were also a host of perceived problems. As a permanent site, this location was not on a BART route, was judged to be too far from the campus for easy access, and was not in a safe neighborhood. Furthermore, it represented a hybrid model of school design, with both community and regional admissions. We were concerned about working within one particular community (becoming more racially segregated; this was an African American community), about the anger of the community regarding the school closure, about the degree of independence with an Oakland District charter, and about the constraints of sharing space with a K–5 school because Aspire would locate a new elementary school at that same site. CEO Shalvey suggested that this site could be a first-step solution because the charter was authorized for up to 5 years and we could continue to search for a site closer to the campus. As to the ease of renegotiating a charter, Shalvey shared that Aspire had thus far opened 11 schools in 8 districts and negotiated 15 charters—only one superintendent remained in office during that period.

Admissions issues became a balancing act in the face of an actual school site, as simultaneously, we would have to fit within state charter law, satisfy the charter authorizer, meet Proposition 209 restrictions on recruiting by race, and reach the multiple goals for composing our student body. Tensions revolved around the enrollment criteria, with concerns raised about not wanting to "cream" a single district and target a particular demographic, or wishing for randomized admissions so we could better study the population. Aspire could secure an annual grant of $200,000 per year if 70% of the student population fell into the poverty range. Aspire suggested a change in admissions strategy in which lottery 1 (70% total) captured low-income students now enrolled in low-performing schools, lottery 2 (20%) captured students from founding families and Aspire feeder schools, and lottery 3 (10%) captured students from across the East Bay. The Federal criterion for low-income status was measured by family eligibility for free and reduced lunch.

But the feedback from the GSE faculty noted that lottery buckets as described would not generate a representative population allowing research conducted at the school to be sufficiently replicable. The GSE faculty envisioned a more representative population similar to that of the state of California or Alameda County. There was an additional concern that 70% low-income families was too high, and that if the school was not successful, the GSE would be blamed. The November 8, 2004, meeting of the ECI committee brought new information about charter restrictions, underscoring that student enrollment from the neighborhood could not be capped. We weighed both opportunities and liabilities. We could open on time, with a primarily African American population from the neighborhood, and have a demonstration site that would attract funding, or we could keep looking for an appropriate site and risk not being able to open on time or at all.

Could we succeed with a hybrid model, both serving a neighborhood but having greater diversity with regional membership or will we risk having two disparate cultures? On December 6, 2004, just 8 months before school opening, the Golden Gate site was endorsed, with 10 of 14 ECI committee members agreeing or strongly agreeing that we should proceed with opening a school at Golden Gate. We also agreed to focus on no more than one additional geographical area for recruitment during the first year—Fruitvale Central in East Oakland, with the hopes of increasing

Hispanic representation. We knew that we would have to pay attention to creating a strong sense of community at the school as the school would be made up of families from different geographical areas. The charter petition was submitted to the Oakland School District in December and passed on February 24, 2005.

## School Vision

Our visioning process for the school began with the big ideas. We continued to visit exemplar charter schools and shared our observations of what was working and what was not. Among the ideas on the table were redefining college readiness beyond the limits of the California A–G course requirements. Eligibility for the UC and CSU system (known as "A–G" requirements) rested in part on receiving a grade of "C" or higher in each of 15 yearlong college-preparatory courses depicted in Box 3.1. Although a cornerstone of our college-going curriculum, these requirements stood in the way of innovation, such as in multidisciplinary courses (e.g., English and social studies), project-based courses, and interdisciplinary courses (e.g., environmental science). We asked ourselves how could we capitalize on the more creative and self-directed learning experiences outside of traditional disciplines and outside of classrooms, so necessary for post–high school success. How could we diligently attend to teachers' relations with students and foster student leadership, initiative, and accountability? How could we create an environment of continual improvement and adoption of best practices? There were tensions between vision and practice as we struggled to reconcile the reality of a small school and flat organization with the possibility of teacher burnout, the goal of promoting student agency with a state-prescribed curriculum and self-contained classes, and the implementation of college courses with a compensatory curriculum for underprepared students.

CEO Shalvey, together with Darwish, identified a number of driving issues that concerned Aspire. How could we sustain the kinds of discussions that took place within the ECI committee meetings and continue to nurture a culture of innovation and learning—in the face of enormous accountability pressures? Shalvey pointed out that Aspire would have to take responsibility for raising test scores while creating the exciting, coherent curriculum being discussed at the ECI committee meetings. Furthermore, how could the financial stability of a small school be assured? Issues of financial stability had implications for how we grew the school, to what size, and how quickly. Shalvey suggested that the secondary school grow

**The Subject Requirement**

- **History/social science ("a")**—*Two years*, including one year of world history, cultures, and historical geography and one year of US history, or one-half year of US history and one-half year of American government or civics
- **English ("b")**—*Four years* of college-preparatory English that integrates reading of classic and modern literature, frequent and regular writing, and practice listening and speaking
- **Mathematics ("c")**—*Three years* of college-preparatory mathematics that include or integrate the topics covered in elementary and advanced algebra and two- and three-dimensional geometry
- **Laboratory science ("d")**—*Two years* of laboratory science providing fundamental knowledge in at least two of the three disciplines of biology, chemistry, and physics
- **Language other than English ("e")**—*Two years* of the same language other than English or equivalent to the second level of high school instruction
- **Visual and performing arts ("f")**—*One year* chosen from dance, music, theater, or the visual arts
- **College-preparatory elective ("g")**—*One year* chosen from the "a–f" courses beyond those used to satisfy the requirements above, or courses that have been approved solely in the elective area

Retrieved from http://www.ucop.edu/agguide/a-g-requirements/index.html

out, starting from sixth and seventh grades, and with ninth graders added in year 2 or 3. Aspire tracks their students' progress and has found that it takes extra resources if ninth graders are not well prepared through a feeder school or 6–12 model. The school would be judged early by test results on the Academic Performance Index (API) and Adequate Yearly Progress (AYP), under No Child Left Behind (NCLB); if we did not pass muster, the school's charter might not be renewed. We debated the implications of starting with sixth and ninth grade but reasoned that teachers would have to teach both sixth and ninth grade—a huge stretch—that would be difficult to support with sufficient preparation time. Ultimately, we decided to grow the school yearly, beginning at the middle school level.

The funder's rising expectations for their early college model raised the ante even further. The Gates Foundation urged WWNFF to expect 60 units of college credit during high school, up from the 30 units originally proposed. The May 3, 2004, Early College Subcommittee, with CEO Shalvey present, discussed tensions among Aspire secondary curriculum, UC Berkeley's school design and curricular ideas, and the Gates Foundation "early college" concept. Why accelerate students so greatly, we asked? What if students were not developmentally or academically ready for college-level courses? We recognized the problem not only with student preparedness but also with university readiness, because far too many first-year university courses require regurgitation, which turns off large numbers of students. A look at UC Berkeley courses identified the possibility of one-unit freshman seminars with just 10 students, as a more hospitable site for the high school students. Others spoke to the high cost of Berkeley units and the need to raise scholarship money for university courses.

Others raised the need to partner with a community college, which could offer a full year of high school credit for a one-semester class and where we could identify the courses that met the A–G requirements. Concerns, however, were expressed that a partnership with a community college and/ or individual differences in readiness might lead to tracking, with some students taking classes at UC Berkeley and some at a community college. Other questions arose. Should college classes be taken as a cohort or individually? Might we consider a 13th year to complete required college level classes, which state ADA funds could support? As a starting point, we began to work on issues of alignment. The school design subcommittee developed work circles in natural science, mathematics (math), humanities/arts, and social sciences to convene over the summer, each of which would choose a UC Berkeley course, review its curriculum, and present Aspire with options about how to coordinate high school and college levels so that students could be more successful in college.

Vigorous discussions continued on multiple fronts as our subcommittees reported back to the monthly ECI committee meetings. We worked hard to forge a joint mission statement with Aspire and to align our conceptual frameworks and data collection interests. We agreed that in the longer term, we would seek a widely diverse student body drawn from cities along the East Bay BART corridor with an emphasis on low-income students who would be the first generation in their families to enter college. We committed to preparing all students for college readiness leading to successful college experiences, with a positive school culture, challenging inquiry, and engagement at its heart, importantly, across a broadened array of domains, including social–emotional skills, arts, and sports. We pledged to build a research and design culture that encouraged experimentation in culture, curriculum, instruction, assessment, and professional development, and, capitalized on the expertise of the UC Berkeley campus and Aspire Public Schools. Debates continued about which habits of mind with what kind of rubrics to address, how to fit in formative assessment, what rich assessments to use, how to reconcile high-stakes testing with indicators of critical thinking, and ultimately how to align our proposed assessments so that they could be integrated into the assessment software for teachers.

## Student Recruitment and Staff Hiring

With a school site in hand and our charter under review, we adopted new ECI subcommittees by January 31, 2005: an Executive Committee (co–principal investigators, co-chairs of the ECI committee), Education Policy Committee, Curriculum Work Groups (math/science; English/social studies), Admissions, and Facilities. And we set new timelines—that the principal be appointed in April, with lead teachers in June and other teachers in July, and that student admissions be concluded by April 1. The school was scheduled to open on August 24, 2005, and end its first year on June 23, 2006. Working at record speed on student recruitment and hiring, we drafted a recruitment brochure, making clear the early college focus, the partnership between Aspire and UC Berkeley, and the research culture of the school. And we chose a name for our school: the California College Preparatory Academy, or CAL Prep. Recruiting began in earnest, with UC Berkeley undergraduates circulating flyers, a parade and barbecue at Golden Gate School, a community walk, and presentations at community centers and libraries. Similar efforts targeted the Fruitvale area in Oakland, the site of a large Hispanic population. We also recruited among UC Berkeley staff employed in housing, dining, and physical plant units, and we reached out to families with fifth and sixth graders who had used services from the Center for Educational Outreach.

In line with the MOU, the search for a principal and subsequently for teachers was a joint affair, by design. The principal search committee was co-chaired by a UC Berkeley member and an Aspire member, with its composition including two individuals from UC Berkeley, two from Aspire, one currently serving principal, and one local community member. The committee developed criteria to evaluate candidates, which included (1) a coherent vision that values teacher collegiality and distributed leadership, diversity and equity, and research; (2) instructional leadership; (3) management skills; and (4) the capacity to relate well to multiple communities, including receptiveness to the UC Berkeley–Aspire partnership.

From the candidates for principal, we asked for a vision statement, a professional development session to be given to a class in UC Berkeley's training program for principals, and a visit to an Aspire School to be interviewed by teachers. The ECI committee also conducted a final review of candidates. In keeping with Aspire staffing policies, hiring was at will with termination by either party, and a performance-based compensation plan was adopted where three factors had equal weight in merit pay decisions: (1) the results of an annual survey of parents, students, and staff; (2) the evaluation of the principal by his or her supervisor; and (3) school-wide performance on standardized tests. By April 26, 2005, Michael Prada, an experienced school administrator (6 years as assistant principal of a high school and 7 years as principal of a K–8 school, both Catholic) who was enrolled in the joint UC–CSU EdD program in Educational Leadership at UC Berkeley, emerged as the consensus candidate. He was offered and accepted the position as founding principal.

Principal Prada joined the ECI committee meetings in May, and we delved deeply into curricular discussions and teacher recruitment. As invited guest and math expert Professor Alan Schoenfeld reminded us, the good stuff is not in curriculum itself but in how it is implemented. He underscored the need for rigorous and robust intellectual standards (not the California math standards), curricula, assessments, and professional development aligned with those standards, as well as enough stability for professional development, defined within teachers' work week, to take hold. The perspective we were developing prioritized depth over breadth and an across-school curricular philosophy and pedagogy where all disciplines were approached as a form of sense-making. We reviewed California state standards as well as Aspire instructional guidelines and chose curriculum materials, such as a National Science Foundation–developed curricular reform called College Preparatory Mathematics (CPA Educational Program, n.d.) and a Full Option Science System (FOSS) science program developed by UC Berkeley's Lawrence Hall of Science (Delta Education, 2005). We also worked on how to create a culture of high expectations among the entire community and how to sustain them.

Teacher recruitment also began in earnest. We were hiring for Grades 6 and 7, with the capacity to grow upward. In middle school, one can teach with a multiple-subjects or single-subject credential, but high school teachers must have a single-subject, discipline-specific credential. By June 6, 2005, we had 37 applicants, with two teachers to be hired, and two more pending enrollment, covering English language arts, math, science, and humanities. We also applied for foundation grants to support an afterschool program and continued to look at school sites closer to the UC Berkeley campus for the future. The co-PIs sent a request for infrastructure funding to Executive Vice Chancellor Gray for $320,000 over 3 years, which would cover college enhancements, research and development, dissemination, fund-raising, as well as support staff and faculty roles.

## Inevitable Tensions and Undeniable Progress

These planning years were enormously fast-paced and intellectually exciting. There were the inevitable tensions both within and between the different cultures. On the UC Berkeley side, we drew lessons from the contentious start-up of UC San Diego's Preuss School and the early defeat of their proposal in the Academic Senate vote (Lytle, 2010; Rosen & Mehan, 2003). Its eventual adoption at UC San Diego rested upon a reframing of the Preuss School as a research endeavor rather than community service, to be placed under the oversight of a new research center called the Center for Research on Education Equity, Assessment, and Teaching Excellence (CREATE). Given differences between the UC San Diego and UC Berkeley charter school proposals—with the UC San Diego stakes higher because the Preuss School was to be fully run by the university and located on campus—we adopted another strategy for approvals. Our game plan included educating the campus community, engaging in vigorous discussion of alternatives, and seeking a buy-in rather than a formal vote.

Across these planning years, we began with broad faculty consultation; met with the administrative arm, including the Chancellor, Vice Chancellor, and representatives from the UC Office of the President; and worked with the Committee for the Protection of Human Subjects, Sponsored Projects, and the legal office. We made repeated presentations to groups across the campus, including the Chancellor's cabinet, Council of Deans, Faculty Academic Senate, CEP, and the GSE. Great questions were generated, the project became visible, and we strengthened the resources we could bring to this collaboration. In this way, the effort progressively became a campuswide project to which UC Berkeley ultimately lent its name.

Inevitably, however, there were the expected tensions around campus space, charter school choice, partnering outside a traditional school district and in a nonunion environment, and targeting first-generation college students, which resulted in a more segregated school (by race and income) rather than a heterogeneous one. Faculty from the GSE also criticized the lack of a formal vote on the vision plan prior to school opening. We continued to press for substantive input rather than a potentially divisive vote, seeing this effort as a joint and rapidly moving one, between UGA and GSE (with substantial representation from these two units assured on the ECI governing board) and, importantly, with Aspire.

Tensions on the other side, within the Aspire–UC Berkeley collaboration, included the pace of our joint work, as Aspire pushed to get the school up and running while UC Berkeley faculty called for more time to bring what had been learned from research to guide the development of the school. We also felt enormous strain between shorter term and longer term goals. In the press of the to-do list, we could not *yet* address a number of our prioritized goals, such as our research program, alternative assessments, professional development, and an envisioned organizational structure that would encourage positive two-way interactions with local districts. In addition, it proved difficult to balance externally mandated tests and local assessments to improve teaching. And although the MOU spelled out our joint and leadership responsibilities, it was far from clear in practice how the principal and ultimately the school should relate to two different partners. As Principal Prada so presciently asked in the ECI meeting on June 13, 2005, "Whom do I report to, and what is the difference between a collaborative relationship and a legal authority?"

During these years of collaborative and interdisciplinary work, there was also evidence of an important institutional change on UC campuses, with two members of the ECI committee as active players. We were buoyed by long sought and hard-won changes to the systemwide UC Academic Personnel Manual, which for the first time explicitly recognized diversity-related activities in faculty appointment and promotion. The revised criteria read, "The University of California is committed to excellence and equity in every facet of its mission. Research, teaching, professional and public service contributions that promote diversity and equal opportunity are to be encouraged and given recognition in the evaluation of the candidate's qualifications" (University of California, 2005, p. 4). What this meant on the ground was that efforts such as ours—intensive community engaged scholarship—would be valued and rewarded within the university incentive system with regard to initial appointments, merit increases, and promotions.

On June 14, 2005, we unveiled the progress made in a presentation given to the Chancellor's cabinet. In providing context, we underscored that UC Berkeley and Aspire, with their respective expertise and similar values, joined together to better serve students who face barriers to college-going by creating a highly effective secondary school that offers college preparation and college-level courses to underserved students. UC Berkeley was a natural candidate for this initiative given its historical commitment to a diverse student body to mirror California's diversity; its interdisciplinary research capacity; and its local districts facing low college-going rates, high dropout rates, and bimodal achievement. With academic expertise and reflective support, UC Berkeley could lead by creating a public school that embeds a culture of high expectations and achievement as well as provides a test site in which to realize a comprehensive research agenda. Among the objectives was a desire to develop a model of college readiness for the widely diverse population of California that advances knowledge about effective curriculum, pedagogy, culture, and leadership at a schoolwide level.

The new regional secondary school would be housed at the Golden Gate facility in Oakland, a 15-minute drive from campus. It was scheduled to open in the fall of 2005 with 120 sixth and seventh graders and grow to full capacity with 420 students in Grades 6–12 by 2010. We now had in place partnership structures and an MOU, on-site leadership (Principal Prada, teachers, UC Berkeley faculty and staff liaisons), an educational theme and principles, a funding model, and plans for student recruitment. State and federal per-pupil funding were secured for school operations. A UC Berkeley infrastructure request was under review, faculty leadership incentives were allocated (with Weinstein and Worrell as founding co-directors for research and development), and grant and fund-raising solicitations were underway. When we unveiled our theme—"A community learning by design, driven by a reliance on research and commitment to continuous improvement"—we envisioned interrelated layers of design for teachers and students. By using data to inform and establishing a supportive environment for reflection, teachers and administrative leaders would be able to improve their pedagogy and change instructional features. Students would hone skills of observation and understanding, make and test predictions, apply knowledge to social problems, create products that foster originality and ownership, and demonstrate competence through larger capstone-type projects that increase in challenge, complexity, and sophistication across grades.

With this presentation, the ECI committee initiative received the blessing of the campus administration as we raced toward the school opening. As our actual planning process revealed, we were clearly in partnership, not simply consultants.

# References

Arenson, K. W. (2003, July 14). 'Early College' gains ground in education. The *New York Times*. Retrieved from http://www.nytimes.com/2003/07/14/nyregion/ 14SCHO.html

Burress, C. (2004, January 13). UC wins grant for 'early college' school. *San Francisco Chronicle*. Retrieved from http://www.sfgate.com/education/article/BERKELEY-UC-wins-grant-for-early-college-2830477.php

CPA Educational Program. (n.d.). *College preparatory mathematics: A complete, balanced mathematics program for Grades 6–12*. Retrieved from http://www.cpm. org/

Delta Education. (2005). *FOSS middle school: Grades 6–8*. Retrieved from http:// delta-education.com/science/fossms/index.shtml

Lytle, C. (2010). *The burden of excellence*. La Jolla, CA: Plowshare Media.

Padilla, G., & Porter, C. (Eds.). (2000). *Commission on Undergraduate Education final report*. University of California, Berkeley.

Padilla, G., & Pearson, P. D. (2003). *Grant proposal to the Woodrow Wilson National Fellowship Foundation for the Early College Initiative*. Berkeley, CA: Authors.

Regents of the University of California & Aspire Public Schools. (2005, October 26). *Memorandum of understanding*, Berkeley, CA: Authors.

Rosen, L., & Mehan, H. (2003). Reconstructing equality on new political ground: The politics of representation in the charter school debate at the University of California, San Diego. *American Educational Research Journal, 40*, 655–682. doi:10.3102/00028312040003655

University of California. (2005). Diversity criteria. In *Academic policy manual, Section 210*. Retrieved from http://www.ucop.edu/academic-personnel-programs/ _files/apm/apm-210.pdf

Woodrow Wilson National Fellowship Foundation. (2002, March 28). *The Early College Initiative project description*. Princeton, NJ: Author.

# 4 | The California College Preparatory Academy Opens

**RHONA S. WEINSTEIN**

*"Other schools want you to go to the next grade," said Imani Keeling, an 11-year-old sixth grader, "This school wants you to go to college."* (Fred Dodsworth, *East Bay Daily News*, November 15, 2005)

*"There falls the shadow, as T. S. Elliot noted, between the conception and the creation. In the annals of innovation, new ideas are only part of the equation. Execution is just as important."* (Walter Isaacson, *Steve Jobs*, 2011, p. 98)

W E WERE OFF TO A GREAT START. On Saturday July 16, 2005, 65 parents and the Early College Initiative (ECI) committee, in celebration of one of its member's 60th birthday, cleaned the 1928 Golden Gate school campus in north Oakland and prepared it for painting. The California College Preparatory Academy (CAL Prep) would occupy the top floor, and the Berkley Maynard Academy, a new Aspire K–5 school, would occupy the bottom floor. Furniture, telephone lines, Internet, and curriculum materials were on order, but, not surprisingly, late. Surplus furniture was donated by the Graduate School of Education (GSE) and the National Writing Project. The Lawrence Hall of Science arranged for free science materials and teacher coaches, and University of California (UC) Berkeley undergraduates from the Center for Educational Partnership's Americorps Destination College program had committed to helping us build a college-going culture.

On August 24, 2005, CAL Prep opened its doors to 90 East Bay sixth and seventh graders, with plans to expand to a Grade 6–12 school with 420 students by 2010. The school was spotless and freshly painted, the principal warmly greeted the students, teachers came eager to collaborate with 2 weeks of prepared lesson plans, and classes began on time. A breakfast program and hot lunch were available, and parents were visible on the campus. The UC Berkeley partnership with Aspire was also noticeable; the principal's signature line read UC Berkeley/Aspire Early College High School, and there was a dedicated room for UC Berkeley partners. It was a shocking contrast to my earlier experiences in schools at risk for closure, where the halls and classrooms were dirty, classes were late in starting, and parents were not to be seen. The students who had attended the school in its prior incarnation appeared astounded at the transformation, as they sprinted from room to room squealing with delight.

Expectations for the school ran high. Fred Dodsworth (2005) in the *East Bay Daily News* announced, "Charter school instills college hopes in kids" in a school that last year had been among the lowest performing in the district. Dodsworth quoted Dionne Rowland, a sixth-grader, who reported that CAL Prep "prepares you for college . . . The teachers want us to excel. They graduated from great schools and they want us to go to those same schools." Carrie Sturrock (2005) proclaimed in the *San Francisco Chronicle*, "Stanford, Cal go to school: Universities run public campuses to prepare needy kids for college." She wrote of raised parental expectations, noting that CAL Prep parent Shawanda Ransom "hopes he [her stepson] gets what she never did: a college degree, which she now calls a necessary tool." But Sturrock also warned of the risk, noting that as university-run schools work with more challenging populations than their earlier laboratory schools for more privileged students—"there is no guarantee that universities will succeed any better than many traditional schools have."

This chapter charts the terrain between an idea and its execution, telling the story of the school's tumultuous first year, as it unfolded within a particular ecological context. The challenges we faced were normative, no different than that of other charter schools, described by journalist and teacher Jonathan Schorr in his 2002 book, *Hard Lessons: The Promise of an Inner City Charter School*. Charters carry our hopes because urban schools have "not met the challenge of crafting a single track, with academic achievement for all" writes Schorr (2002, p. 35). But this goal remains a high challenge indeed. In *Our School* (2005), the story of a charter school that beat the odds, journalist Joanne Jacobs quotes the principal's description of the first year as "collective insanity" (p. 33). What we had in our favor, however, was the partnership, with the weight of a charter district and a university behind us.

In this chapter, I describe our early program and the growing pains we experienced as a new-start school. Then, I turn to efforts we made to harness additional resources for this highly underresourced setting to address what we saw as urgent needs, and finally, I conclude with our planning for the second school year. Although these implementation struggles clearly humbled us, they were also pivotal in shaping the research questions we asked, our efforts to improve the school, and an emerging theory of how to meet the challenges of a single-track academic setting.

## Program at the Start

In this first year, the CAL Prep staff included principal Michael Prada, three teachers (mathematics [math], science, and English language arts), an office manager, and a custodian. All three teachers had multiple subject credentials, one with a California lifetime credential in Social Studies and another with National Board Certification. The principal held an administrative credential II and, as noted earlier, was enrolled in UC Berkeley's joint doctoral program in educational leadership. Given planning needs, on August 9, 2005, the decision was made to cap enrollment at 90 students: 60 for sixth grade and 30 for seventh grade, with a teacher–student ratio of 1:28.

As we had hoped, we had enrolled a population of the students who faced barriers to attending college. At school opening, student enrollment was largely low income (67% free and reduced lunch) and minority (82.14% African American, 11.90% Hispanic), and 13% were English language learners. Data showed that 82% of parents were without a college degree. Although we were not a regional school as originally envisioned in this first year, with 65.1% of CAL Prep's student body drawn largely from the city of Oakland, we did enroll students from 11 other cities. By our design, there were no academic or behavioral requirements for student enrollment and CAL Prep was advertised as a single-track, college-preparatory, and early college secondary school. The overarching vision embodied high expectations for all students, a rigorous curriculum, a developmentally appropriate thrust, and supports to enable students to meet these expectations.

In this first year, signaled by a *"College for Certain"* mandate, our *college-preparatory curriculum for all students* in math, English, and social studies/science was further enriched to include physical education, art, and music in the after-school program, as well as exhibitions, an independent capstone project of increasing challenge each year. The developmental thrust was reflected in a more *personalized environment* for these early adolescents through grade-level pods (where students moved as a group to classes) and small-group teacher–student advisories (held twice weekly). Supports included extended instructional time (longer day and year [183 days], and double periods of English and math for deeper coverage and catch-up), the building of an academic school community (2-week summer induction experience, dress code with school uniforms, honor roll, and "Perfect Punctiliousness" list), promoting parental collaboration (handbook, three Saturday Schools, biweekly newsletter, teacher welcome calls, and a scholastic homework site), and services in special education and mental health. Finally, professional development (PD) time for teachers was regularized by a minimum day on Wednesdays, with student dismissal at 12:30 p.m. but with after-school care available.

Regional Superintendent Elise Darwish served as the Aspire liaison in the weekly on-site partnership meetings with Principal Prada, and Weinstein and Worrell (co-directors for Research and Development) and Kaufman and Jorgensen (Early College Coordinators) represented UC Berkeley. The 1½-hour weekly meeting was scheduled for Monday afternoons, with Weinstein and Worrell also available each week for consultation and teacher PD. Principal Prada was quoted as saying that "he is relying on UC Berkeley professors to help the new school develop a sense of community and a culture that nurtures the students while making tough academic demands and sending the message that failure is not an option" (Maclay, 2005).

CAL Prep was formally dedicated on Monday, November 14, 2005 with both Aspire Chief Executive Officer Don Shalvey and Chancellor Robert Birgeneau in attendance to welcome the new students and their families. Shalvey began his impassioned remarks with this African proverb, "If you want to go fast, go alone. If you want to go far, go together." He told the students, "You have chosen to go far . . . You are pioneers . . . in shaping the personality of CAL Prep, you'll create opportunities for the students who will follow your lead . . . Each of you has greatness inside of you. Use it for the betterment of your families, community, and the place we call planet earth."

In his address, Chancellor Birgeneau spoke movingly about his tough childhood in Toronto, Canada. His luck came when a Catholic priest singled him out for a scholarship to a parochial high school in the suburbs. "Your luck and opportunity is ending up at CAL Prep," Birgeneau told the 85 CAL Prep sixth and seventh graders in the audience. "You are the vanguard group that we're depending on for the future of our state and we need you to achieve ... My dream is that I am going to come back here and one of you from the first graduating class is going to be standing up here as Chancellor of the University of California, Berkeley" (*GSE-bulletin*, January, 2006).

## Growing Pains in a New-Start School

My notes during that first year read, "We miscalculated how much time it would take [that is, to get the school up and running]!" Among the challenges we faced were resistance against the high academic demands, losses of students and teachers to attrition, constraints of a regional and very small school, and balancing of tensions within our collaboration. It was not surprising, perhaps, that life on the ground was far from the rosy educational vision that we had debated over years of planning. The twice-yearly early college conferences sponsored by the Woodrow Wilson National Fellowship Foundation (WWNFF) (November, 2005, in Princeton, New Jersey; February, 2006, in California) provided welcome support for these challenges as did our first meeting of our network of UC College-Going Schools, held in San Diego in the spring of 2006.

**Students.** We also underestimated how underprepared these students were for the level of challenge. As the three teachers tracked CAL Prep student benchmarks, we identified a bimodal distribution in reading level, with 38% to 40% at grade level and 50% below grade level on the Developmental Reading Assessment (Beaver & Carter, 2006). Of these underprepared students, 40% were reading two to three levels below grade expectations. The Lunch Time Justice program, a homework opportunity, drew 40 students, nearly half the school, on a day when the College-Preparatory Mathematics (CPA Educational Program, n.d.) problem of the week had stumped nearly everyone. There were enormous social-emotional needs, among them, a number of students who faced death in their families. There were serious issues of campus safety, with violent gang activity as well as incidents of school vandalism necessitating police intervention. In addition, students were reeling from the high expectations. A long talk I had with a student about his oral history project for exhibitions revealed that he had found the assignment too hard. Fighting to save face, he told me that he did not care: he wanted what he called a lazy job, rather than meeting these tough college-going expectations. Ultimately, this student left the school, despite our interventions to support his learning and encourage him to stay. It was examples such as these that fueled our concern about identity development in adolescents and the integration of academic and ethnocultural selves (see Chapter 15).

As we were to learn, the early emphasis on curricular rigor and strict standards (dress code, punctuality, and behavior), especially with a student population not accustomed to such high expectations, was met with pushback from students and families, resulting in a high rate of classroom management problems and disciplinary actions. Transitions between classes in narrow hallways meant for elementary school students also proved difficult and even during class time, the hallways were frequently lined with students sent out for disruptive behavior. Suspensions and attrition were high. During that first school year, 47% of the students received at least one suspension and 30% of the students left the school from August 24, 2005 through March 30, 2006. Students had come to CAL Prep with challenging needs and faced a school environment with high expectations yet few supports fully in place. In our ECI meetings, Regional Superintendent Darwish noted that it was harder to develop a culture here: "CAL Prep hasn't drawn from feeder schools, but instead from 11 different districts . . . We started late and attracted families who were dissatisfied with previous schools ['school hoppers'] and it took longer for kids to make connections when they come individually from so many communities."

**Parents.** The first Saturday School drew 70% of the parents, and the Open House brought out 66% of the families. Attendance at the School Council meetings was smaller, with the first meeting drawing only 10 parents. Given our hybrid model and the early compromise made to secure a school site, there were the expected tensions between neighborhood families, whose previous school had been closed (largely African American), and regional families, who made an active choice with greater travel time, to bring their students to CAL Prep (largely Hispanic).

It proved shocking to many parents just how hard the work was. The school was expecting things that had not been expected before. Is the homework valuable, parents asked? They noted far too many problems every night, and that they, themselves, could neither graph the results nor do the tables. The student exhibitions, which required a passing grade prior to promotion to the next grade, created great concern among the parents, especially the parents of students who did not pass the first time. In all, two thirds of the students passed on the first try, and multiple opportunities were given to ensure success. We wondered whether those students without family supports were among the failures: this was a problem we would address in subsequent years with additional supports. There were parental complaints about school decisions, such as a requirement for summer school for underperforming students in order to return to CAL Prep. Could we have known earlier and given a prewarning, we were asked? We were walking a tightrope—there was tension between keeping the school's door wide open and having sufficient resources to provide the differentiated support that was needed. Could CAL Prep be a school for everyone as we had expected?

**Teachers**. The three experienced teachers, working long hours, were tremendously overstretched and often did not have time for lunch or bathroom breaks. They faced huge classroom management issues in engaging students while upholding the expected rigor of the challenging curricula we had chosen. Behavioral infractions resulted in eviction from classrooms, and both teachers and students felt disrespected. Teachers could not find time to manage the tutoring program, where student volunteers were intermittent at best, yet they wanted to provide the oversight themselves. As they argued, given the depth of needs of the students, helpers such as tutors could not do a good job without the guidance of teachers. Two of the three teachers lasted the entire school year. In one subject area, we lost the first hire and the second replacement hire within the fall semester. On very short notice, we found a first-year teacher to join us for the spring semester, and Aspire provided a teacher coach.

**The Partnership**. As we coped with these growing pains, there were the inevitable challenges to the collaboration—disagreements, coordination problems, and accountability struggles. Over time, we worked through these issues. We argued about how to build the school culture—rigor or relationships first. We argued about the disciplinary system—strict management in the face of an unsafe campus or active engagement in keeping with an inquiry-oriented curriculum. And we argued about the relative weighting of academic versus whole-student development, such as in social-emotional skills, talents, and student initiative, so important to adolescents.

There were also tensions between the needs of both partners and the coordination of our work. Among the examples, teacher recruitment advertisements were created by the district rather than the school, often resulting in the omission of the UC Berkeley partnership at first pass. We needed to integrate UC Berkeley assessments (still in the planning stages) with those of Aspire (already developed and in use in other schools). There was a plethora of meetings to get scheduled and UC Berkeley–related meetings needed to be coordinated with those of the Aspire District. For UC Berkeley, this included our weekly on-site partnership meeting, monthly campus ECI meeting, twice-yearly WWNFF early college meetings, and PD sessions utilizing UC Berkeley faculty resources. For Aspire, their requirements included a 2-week summer PD for new teachers, two PD days for teachers, monthly lead teacher meetings, monthly principal meetings, and an annual town hall meeting for all staff.

Finally, there was strain between reflection and action, and questions about who was in charge. With the principal as leader, how is co-construction of school culture, as well as curriculum, pedagogy, and assessment, actually managed on a day-to-day basis? How do we weigh the consideration of alternatives with getting things done? It is a difficult balance between reflection now, which might save steps in the future and reconsideration later. Care must be taken not to undermine the leadership of the principal. Although it was ultimately Aspire's legal responsibility, it was clearly UC Berkeley's reputation at stake.

## Harnessing Additional Resources for an Underresourced Setting

This first year was exceedingly tough, so much so that it was difficult to welcome the constant stream of visitors (UC Berkeley faculty, funders, researchers, and school reformers) to the school—its development taking place under a looking glass. As we reflected on these growing pains in our meetings with the on-site partnership, the campus ECI committee, and with teachers, it was clear that we needed to prioritize goals and harness additional resources to address these implementation challenges—at least until the school grew in size to a fully funded model. One principle underlying our emerging theory of action was the need to create an adult-rich and opportunity-rich environment for these underserved students and for their teachers. Deep relationships and varied opportunities would support the growth of learning and teaching (Butterworth & Weinstein, 1996; Maton, 2000; Weinstein, 2002). Thus, we looked not only to raising funds but also to the innovative use of UC Berkeley and Aspire resources.

An overarching fund-raising priority—necessary for our survival—was to secure a permanent building for CAL Prep. The Golden Gate site, a compromise, was at near capacity and our planned expansion to a Grade 6–Grade 12 configuration by 2010 required additional space. Efforts to rent or buy a suitable building consumed a great deal of time, as the clock ticked away and rental of portable classrooms loomed on the horizon. Jointly, we identified three additional funding priorities for the first year—literacy intervention (given low reading levels), science instructional materials (for hands-on inquiry), and summer programs (to broaden student development). We attracted three major gifts during the fall of the school's first year, which we put to immediate use in winter and spring 2006. Happily, these three generous gifts became multiyear allocations.

One gift enabled us to purchase materials and equipment to support the use of experiments in our science program. Another gift allowed us to hire an additional teacher focused on literacy intervention and to implement a remedial reading program. After reviewing evidence-based programs, we chose Read 180 (Scholastic, n.d.), and Dean Pearson, along with education doctoral student Susie Goodin, designed an evaluation to inform subsequent improvements to the program. They also identified a need for a library to deepen literacy development for students, which Goodin followed up on for her dissertation research (see Chapter 8). The hiring of a literacy intervention instructor reflected our first use of the adult-rich principle; in addition to offering Read 180, this teacher was available to coteach, cover classes which freed teachers for collaboration, set up an after-school reading skills laboratory, and meet with groups as well as individual students.

A third gift provided funding for summer opportunities for students, a vital investment as research on extracurricular activities has shown strong effects on student achievement (Mahoney, Larson, & Eccles, 2005). Not only would summer programs help develop student talents, but they would also broaden exposure to new settings beyond these students' encapsulated neighborhoods. They would provide a first college experience. Nilofar Sami, a doctoral student in clinical/community psychology, identified and coordinated the summer program options with a place for every student free of charge. At UC Berkeley, we were able to offer slots in the Academic Talent Development Program, Alvin Ailey Camp [dance], Bay Area Writing Project, Cal Sci Program, Lawrence Hall of Science, Blue Camp, Grizzlies Sports, and Young Musicians Program. We also included programs from the Contra Costa College for Kids. Although many parents were hesitant to let their children go to a college campus, by March 20, 2005, 46 students were enrolled in programs at UC Berkeley or at other colleges. Working with undergraduates, Sami designed an evaluation of these summer experiences, the results of which were reported back to families and fueled the steady growth of participation over time. Sami held this role for 3 years until it was taken over by the director of the after-school program.

In addition to these funded efforts, which supported science instruction, catch-up in reading skills, and talent development, we worked to make school more joyful despite the hard work and to expand connections to UC Berkeley. Worrell started an after-school choir, similar to what he was doing at the GSE. The CAL Prep Chorus sang with the GSE chorus in a 2006 spring concert at UC Berkeley. We instituted a Spirit Week, where our newly named CAL Prep grizzlies were "Grrrr-owling for Knowledge," and we explored bringing sports teams into the after-school program. We offered a 9-week CAL Science Saturday program on campus, a visit to learn about the UC Berkeley Library, and participation in CAL Day, when UC Berkeley opens its campus to the community. UC Berkeley faculty gave presentations in classrooms and UC Berkeley Americorps volunteers organized a Career Fair for students and their families. And at the end of the school year, CAL Prep sponsored a Student Showcase, where students presented their academic work to parents and the community.

We also identified priorities for teacher PD. Our joint wish list included substantial coaching for beginning teachers, regularized times for teacher collaboration in site-based PD, and an annual summer retreat where UC Berkeley faculty and CAL Prep staff could work together. In staff meetings, to which we were invited monthly, we collaboratively set agendas for each meeting and reported back on what had been accomplished. Ultimately, teachers took on the writing of agendas. In this first year, drawing upon campus resources, we created PD opportunities on positive classroom/school climate, the Algebra I syllabus, and student exhibitions. As one example, we held a dinner (February, 2006) at the UC Berkeley Faculty Club for CAL Prep staff and the ECI committee to both welcome two new teachers and prepare for student exhibitions. The teachers presented the two exhibition topics: an oral history writing project for sixth graders and an applied math problem of scale (measuring carpet for an apartment) for seventh graders. Students were required to conduct research (interviews and scale drawings, respectively) and then prepare a written poster and oral presentation for an audience of their peers and community members, who graded their performance on specific standards. Working together, guided by research on the learning cycle of invitation, exploration, concept formulation, and application (Lawson, 1995; National Research Council, 2000), we generated questions to challenge students and direct the postpresentation inquiry by community members.

Other efforts were underway with regard to strengthening the college-preparatory curriculum and creating the early college curriculum.

Although we began with a Grade 6–7 school, WWNFF was pressing for an entire early college curriculum by year's end. The ECI set up three committees (Humanities, Math and Science, and Early College) composed of faculty, teachers, and Aspire partners to create a scope and sequence of courses that would be rigorous, aligned, and innovative in meeting the A–G requirements needed for UC admission. Their charge included identifying habits of mind and learning outcomes, assessments, student supports, numbers of teachers needed in which content areas, sequencing of content that matched state testing and provided opportunities for integrative synergies, and indicating college-credit courses that met A–G requirements.

In preparation for early college classes, we recruited a new partner, a local community college, where the earning of college credits was more affordable. On January 12, 2006, we had our first meeting with Vista Community College, renamed Berkeley City College (BCC), to develop a partnership for the college classes to be offered on-site at CAL Prep. Our initial offering was to be a two-semester conversational Spanish class for seventh and eighth graders planned for the next school year. Under concurrent enrollment, students could earn six BCC college credits for the year at no cost for tuition, simultaneously with earning middle/high school credit. BCC would pay for the instructor, CAL Prep would pay for books at approximately $100 per student, and both institutions would share the cost of an instructional assistant. We envisioned a sequence of Spanish courses from seventh to ninth grade that would meet the UC language requirement and accumulate 18 college credits.

## Positive Steps Forward

As the year progressed, we saw small improvements—more students were on the honor roll and fewer on probation. Students began to encourage each other to follow the school rules. Although the October benchmark results showed that only 1.4% of students tested proficient in math, by year end 22% of students met grade-level standards on state tests: The corresponding percentage in English language arts was 24%. This performance level earned us an Academic Performance Index (API) of 648 and a decile score of 2 on a scale of 1 to 10, virtually at the bottom as compared to all California schools. We clearly had work to do.

CAL Prep experienced a stream of visitors to the school and in classrooms even during this demanding first year. Faculty at UC Davis were considering an early college secondary school and on February 2, 2006, visited CAL Prep, interviewing students, staff, and ECI committee representatives. In the spring, 40 principals and teachers from the University of Chicago's Urban School Improvement Center visited. Our students proved to be enthusiastic guides in describing how the teachers challenged them here and helped them overcome obstacles in their learning. Becoming a student ambassador and leading school tours became a powerful motivator for students. The visitors reported being impressed with the early college vision, the collaboration, and the teachers' use of data to chart students' growth, a process spearheaded by Aspire. One visitor shared that she could feel the spirit of the hard-working school as students prepared to walk in the door—welcome evidence of an improvement in school climate.

The WWNFF also offered additional grant support to help a second Aspire School, Lionel Wilson College Preparatory Academy, evolve into an early college high school. We agreed to collaborate and share expertise, but not to participate at the same level of partnership or with UC Berkeley's stamp on it.

We held a mid-year review about the UC Berkeley–Aspire partnership in March, 2006, to talk about the feedback we obtained from all the partners, including the principal and teachers. It was agreed that we had achieved openness and transparency, a shared commitment to making the school work, and all partners fully at the table. We had jointly developed protocols for principal and teacher hiring that had worked smoothly. We at UC Berkeley underscored what an incredible opportunity it was to work simultaneously with a district and a school to address the problems of equity and excellence in new-start settings. We also identified a host of problems that remained to be resolved. These included securing a larger building nearer the campus, paying for college courses, leveraging UC Berkeley gifts to develop a multiyear funding plan, and initiating our research agenda. We wanted to implement an alternative discipline system that promoted a positive culture as well as learning and self-regulation rather than compliance to external rewards (National Research Council, 2001). We needed to fix program elements that were not working, such as counseling needs that could not be met with a single mental health intern, uneven tutoring opportunities (UC Berkeley volunteers were not always reliable in showing up or in integrating with teachers' goals), and advisories that had been difficult to mount. And we needed to establish decision rules on the ground, regarding which issues reach which levels of review and what UC Berkeley's role would be in teacher separation and principal evaluation.

## Plans for the Next Year

Recruitment was underway for the next year's sixth grade class and for openings to be filled at the seventh and eighth grades. We made the decision to add students at the upper levels, despite the fact that new students might start behind the others. Enrollment updates as of May 4, 2006, showed 62 new sixth graders, 62 seventh graders, and 41 eighth graders, with a waiting list. Thus, for the second year of CAL Prep (2006–2007), we were on target to meet the projection of 165 students, with two classes at each grade level and seven teachers to be hired. Three of the four teachers on board in spring 2006 intended to return the next year: we lost one of these teachers due to dual career constraints and a move out of state. Of the five new teachers hired, two (one a PhD student in Mathematics Education at UC Berkeley and one drafted from another Aspire School) were specifically targeted to strengthen CAL Prep's math program (see Chapter 11).

Among many initiatives for the school's second year was the expansion and integration of special education and mental health services available to students. Aspire planned to continue their contract with the Oakland District Special Education Local Planning Area. For this, Aspire paid an encroachment fee per enrolled student and obtained the support of a resource specialist for Individual Educational Plans and a school psychologist, who would work across 14 Aspire charter schools. We designed an expansion of these services to include two mental health interns—one from the clinical psychology program at UC Berkeley and one from the counseling program at Saint Mary's College—who would participate in an integrated services practicum to be supervised by Worrell. The goal was to build a collaborative team that could interface with the Oakland district services and teachers in developing both preventive schoolwide interventions and targeted treatment interventions for groups and individual students.

As part of a preventive thrust, we continued our work on building a positive school climate and fostering student engagement in learning. An important part was the creation of a whole school compact (as a student I will . . ., as a parent I will . . ., as a staff member I will . . .), which would make explicit the values and expected behaviors of the CAL Prep culture for students and their families as well as the staff. These were among our first steps, with more to come as we deepened our development of student supports (see Chapters 13 and 14).

This next year we planned to strengthen our capacity for school improvement by supporting teacher inquiry about practice. Aspire trained teachers to use the Edusoft Assessment Management System (Riverside Publishing Company, 2001–2006) in a process called the cycle of inquiry, in order to regularize data analysis of student learning outcomes to inform instructional revision (e.g., Copland, 2003). Two sets of discipline-based teams in math/science and English/humanities—linked to increase thematic integration—would meet every 3 to 4 weeks with UC Berkeley participation. To increase faculty engagement, we created the role of campus critical friends who joined these inquiry teams, to both learn from teachers and bring perspectives from research (see Chapters 11 and 12).

Our plans for the next year also included the development of a research program. During this opening year, we, the UC Berkeley partners, moved between multiple roles—design, consultation, direct service, and research. In this very small new school, deeply underresourced at the start, we felt the press to respond to service needs, evident in Worrell's school choir and planned integrated services practicum, Sami's summer programs and work with the Parent Advisory Council, Weinstein's sessions on climate, and the development of college opportunities by Kaufman and Jorgensen. In this first year, as we jointly built the research and development culture specified in both the UC Berkeley–Aspire memorandum of understanding and the school handbook, our research activities were largely informal. We used every occasion to collaboratively develop surveys, with input from staff, students, and parents. These were given anonymously and, when analyzed, informed us about unmet needs and needed next steps in program refinement. Although our involvement in direct services at the school consumed much time, often in conflict with time needed for research activities, this involvement in practice offered a priceless opportunity to better understand the challenges at hand and deepened our relationship with our school partners.

At both our partnership and ECI meetings, we debated the direction of our emerging research program and its fit within the data-gathering activities of our partners. Aspire was committed to first, analysis of student achievement (in frequent benchmark testing and year-end state testing) to inform instructional strategies, and second, yearly surveys assessing the satisfaction of students, parents, and staff. Here, we obtained useful data about the progress both at CAL Prep and in comparison to other Aspire schools. Jobs for the Future developed a Student Information System for the Early College High School Initiative, and WWNFF spearheaded studies in early college schools with 4-year college partners. These efforts required regular data uploads and provided useful reports on how these schools across the country were faring.

At the table, as we explored the problems we had faced with the implementation of advisories, such as frequent cancellations, inappropriate materials, and lack of student interest, our partners turned to us and said, "How about UC Berkeley taking over the design and implementation of advisories during the school's second year?" This was a challenge that we could not turn down nor undertake without an evaluation.

In a spring 2006 report to the ECI, we outlined the kinds of studies we at UC Berkeley might spearhead as a means of using data to shape the development of the school. We noted the need to pursue research grants to support these endeavors, and to obtain approvals from our institutional review board, the Committee for the Protection of Human Subjects, and from CAL Prep. We tasked the on-site partnership meeting as the place for research study approval, adopting the principle that any study conducted at CAL Prep must be judged to be of practical use to the school.

Developed through this collaborative process, we committed to design studies, descriptive studies, and model development. The Read 180 program evaluation was already underway. In the design of advisories (Chapter 5) and a library (Chapter 8), we would conduct two program implementation and evaluation studies. The ECI committee underscored the importance of identifying patterns of and factors that fueled student attrition and of tracking student achievement (Chapter 9). Sami shared her emerging dissertation ideas about the tough transition into middle school (in this case, a high-expectation setting) and the potential mismatch between student needs and the socialization practices they encountered at school and at home (Chapters 6 and 7). And early on, we also pressed for the development of a model of school-based support, drawing from research evidence and best practices (Chapter 14).

Although this first year was unbelievably challenging, we ended on a high note, optimistic that in time we would collaboratively resolve these challenges and strengthen what we could offer these students. Our greatly overstretched teachers reported feeling lucky to have this learning opportunity, a belief that was shared across the partnership.

## References

Beaver, J., & Carter, M. (2006). *Developmental Reading Assessment* (3rd ed.). Upper Saddle River, NJ: Pearson.

Butterworth, B., & Weinstein, R. S. (1996). Enhancing motivational opportunity in elementary schooling: A case study of the ecology of principal leadership. *Elementary School Journal, 97,* 57–80. doi:10.1086/461849

Chancellor inspires students at Cal Prep dedication. (2006, January). *GSE-bulletin*. Retrieved from http://vocserve.berkeley.edu/admin/publications/bulletin0601/0601calprep.html

Copland, M. A. (2003). Leadership of inquiry: Building and sustaining capacity for school improvement. *Educational Evaluation and Policy Analysis, 25*, 373–395. doi:10.3102/016237370250004375

CPA Educational Program. (n.d.). College preparatory mathematics: A complete, balanced mathematics program for Grades 6–12. Retrieved from http://www.cpm.org/

Dodsworth, F. (2005, November 15). Charter school instills college hopes in kids. *East Bay Daily News*. [No longer being published]

Isaacson, W. (2011) *Steve Jobs*. San Jose, CA: Simon & Schuster.

Jacobs, J. (2005). *Our school: The inspiring story of two teachers, one big idea, and the charter school that beat the odds*. New York, NY: Palgrave MacMillan.

Lawson, A. E. (1995). *Science teaching and the development of thinking*. Belmont, CA: Wadsworth Publishing Company.

Maclay, K. (2005, August 24). "CAL Prep" opens to East Bay 6th, 7th graders. UC Berkeley Press Release. Retrieved from http://www.berkeley.edu/news.media/releases/2005/08/24_capprep.shtml

Mahoney, J. L., Larson, R. W., & Eccles, J. S. (2005). *Organized activities as contexts of development: Extracurricular activities, after school, and community programs*. New York, NY: Psychology Press.

Maton, K. I. (2000). Making a difference: The social ecology of social transformation. *American Journal of Community Psychology, 28*, 25–57. doi:10.1023/A:1005190312887

National Research Council. (2000). *How people learn: Brain, mind, experience, and school*. Washington, DC: National Academy Press.

National Research Council. (2001). *Community programs to promote youth development*. Washington, DC: National Academy Press.

Riverside Publishing Company. (2001–2006). *Edusoft Assessment Management System*. Rolling Meadows, IL: Author.

Scholastic. (n.d.). *Read 180*. New York, NY: Author.

Schorr, J. (2002). *Hard lessons: The promise of an inner city charter school*. New York, NY: Ballantine Books.

Sturrock, C. (2005, October 30). Stanford, Cal go to school: Universities run public campuses to prepare needy kids for college. *San Francisco Chronicle*. Retrieved from http://www.sfgate.com/education/article/BAY-AREA-Stanford-Cal-go-to-school-2598428.php

Weinstein, R. S. (2002). *Reaching higher: The power of expectations in schooling*. Cambridge, MA: Harvard University Press.

# II | Collaborative Research Informs School Development

# 5 | Learning from Teacher–Student Advisories

**RHONA S. WEINSTEIN, NILOFAR SAMI, AND ZENA R. MELLO**

*"I learned mostly how to get over hardships in life and advisory taught me to move them aside."*

*"I learned just because you are different doesn't mean you can't get along."*

*"I learned to do words not do actions."*[1]

ADVISORIES ARE SMALL-GROUP SETTINGS FOR students led by teachers and staff. The voices of middle school youth, echoed above, illustrate the kind of learning that took place in advisories at California College Preparatory Academy (CAL Prep). Among many functions, advisories are used to personalize teacher–student relationships and strengthen student advocacy. Although a key feature in our charter application, advisories were never fully implemented during the tumultuous first year of the school. As we approached the school's second year, the University California (UC) Berkeley was pressed by Aspire to take the lead in developing an advisory program. Despite feeling stretched beyond our limits, we (faculty member, graduate student, and postdoctoral scholar) jumped at this challenge.

A common advisory curriculum offered a schoolwide training opportunity—rare in the subject-matter world of secondary schools—to foster student engagement in learning and build a positive school

---

[1] All quotations from students and teachers are taken verbatim from their completed questionnaires, with no changes made to syntax or spelling.

culture. As designers, we wanted to incorporate evidence-based practices in advisory activities and, importantly, evaluate our efforts. This opportunity provided us a unique window on three aspects of program development (design, implementation, and evaluation) of a frequently used practice about which empirical evidence is sparse. In keeping with the tenets of community-engaged scholarship, we also wanted to give voice to the perspectives of teachers and students, making clear that their ideas were reflected in the advisory program. By using mixed methods and an iterative plan—providing feedback and making adjustments—we modeled a reflective and responsive process. In these ways, we mirrored the instructional improvement goals of the cycle of inquiry underway for subject-matter teams.

In one dizzying academic year, we collaboratively developed, implemented, and evaluated 50 advisory lessons in twice-weekly sessions from October through June. Lacking a randomized or control group design, this single case study cannot speak to advisory group effectiveness, but, importantly, it can examine sources of variation in implementation and *perceived* program effects. As average results fail to tell the whole story, research about the factors that explain variation is critically important, both for the knowledge base and program improvement (Weiss, Bloom, & Brock, 2013). Using a within-intervention and contextualized design in this high-expectation secondary school, we explored student and leader factors that explained within-school variability in perceived advisory effectiveness.[2] In telling this story, we present highlights of advisory design, evaluation results, and lessons learned.

## Research on Advisories

The history of advisories has roots in the early-20th century Dalton House school (Semel & Sadovnik, 2008) as well as in many movements, including guidance, middle school, and the identification of adolescence as a distinct age group whose needs must be addressed in schooling (Carnegie Council on Adolescent Development, 1989; Galassi, Gulledge, & Cox, 1997). Mac Iver and Epstein (1991) described advisory groups as one of many responsive practices that serve to "provide each student with

[2] This study was conducted with a Research Enabling Grant from University of California, Berkeley and a Woodrow Wilson National Fellowship Foundation Grant, funded by the Bill & Melinda Gates Foundation, to the first author.

a teacher who knows, cares about them, or is available as a mentor or advisor" (p. 592).

This personalization is especially critical as the transition to secondary school poses risks for the adjustment of adolescents. Academic expectations rise, school structure changes from single to multiple teachers, and students become more anonymous (Alvidrez & Weinstein, 1993). Such shifts in structure coincide with a developmental period of enormous biological, psychological, and social changes—requiring new knowledge of self, new identities, new allegiances with adults and peers, and increased autonomy (Wigfield, Lutz, & Wagner, 2005). It is this mismatch between secondary school design and developmental needs that heightens adjustment problems (Eccles et al., 1993). A large body of research shows a decline in motivation, self-concept of ability, and achievement during this critical transition to both middle and high school, with the risk even greater for ethnic minority and low-income youth, who come underprepared and are more likely to be placed in lower academic tracks (Anderman & Mueller, 2010; Hanewald, 2013; Langenkamp, 2015). Advisories have been widely used as a *transition* mechanism to help ease this adjustment into secondary schooling.

Beyond transition needs, advisories have also become a permanent feature of school design. Reform efforts to improve academic preparedness for low-income and minority youth, both in the redesign of large comprehensive high schools and in the creation of small charter schools, have adopted advisories as an organizational feature to promote personalization of teacher–student relationships and to build a communal setting (Darling-Hammond, Ancess, & Ort, 2002; Phillippo, 2013). Finally, advisories offer a school-based context from which to implement empirically validated programs that promote positive development, such as social-emotional learning (SEL), character education, and programs addressing mental and physical health (Greenberg et al., 2003). For example, SEL is now mandated by the Illinois State Board of Education, with curricular standards developed across the grades (Illinois State Board of Education, 2010). A recent meta-analysis by Durlak and colleagues (2011) provides evidence of SEL program effectiveness not only for social-emotional skills but also for academic performance. At the secondary level, advisories may provide a dedicated niche for such instruction.

It is not surprising, then, that there are many different uses for advisory. Galassi and colleagues (1997) propose a typology of six different advisory orientations, which include (1) advocacy (adult–student relationship), (2) community (group identity), (3) skills (developmental guidance),

(4) invigoration (relaxation), (5) academic strategies (educational performance), and (6) administrative tasks (housekeeping). Yet despite the widespread use of advisories, there exists remarkably little research on the practice (Anfara, 2006). Much of the evidence for advisory effectiveness is "indirect, inferred, or based on methodologically-weak studies" (Galassi et al., 1997, p. 319). Studies lack control groups, pre- and post-measures, objective indices of program effects, and separate tests of program elements.

But in reality, advisories pose a tremendous challenge for evaluation, given differences in goals, components, duration, grade levels, settings, and institutional support. Most critically, advisories are "rarely a school's *sole* strategy for supporting students and fostering personalization" (Makkonen, 2004, p. 11). Furthermore, although meta-analyses have shown the effectiveness of specific prevention curricula, for example, with regard to social-emotional skills, especially when implemented with fidelity by trained personnel, freestanding demonstrations do not necessarily translate into successful implementation in the school-based advisory context (Durlak & DuPre, 2008; Galassi et al., 1997). Conclusions about the effectiveness of advisories are yet to be drawn.

To advance understanding, as Galassi and colleagues (1997) suggest, research must move toward greater specificity of the advisory intervention—asking how effective is this kind of advisory, for this group of students, in this setting, and for which outcomes. Makkonen (2004) presses for more localized evaluations that are tailored to the objectives of specific programs and for assessments that can inform improvement. Others also underscore that the creation of effective programs for youth development rests upon identifying factors that contribute to successful implementation and exploring how particular school ecologies interact with program elements (e.g., Durlak & DuPre, 2008; Gregory, Henry, & Schoeny, 2007). One recent example of research that takes on this contextual challenge is Kate Phillippo's (2013) ethnographic study of advisory practices in three high schools, where she finds enormous variability within and between schools as teachers enact these expanded roles.

To address the need for a more contextualized study of advisory implementation, we identified four specific aims. First, given many possible purposes, we explored whether the goals for advisories were aligned between teachers and students—a needs assessment that shaped the advisory program. Second, we investigated whether student satisfaction varied by advisory goal. Third, we asked what characteristics of students or advisory leader predicted differences in student-perceived advisory effectiveness and learning. Finally, we explored what advisory leaders identified as helpful or unhelpful in advisory implementation and training.

## Advisory Design

### California College Preparatory Academy in Year 2

In 2006–2007, there were 150 students enrolled at CAL Prep in a Grade 6–8 middle school. Of these, 53% of seventh graders and 35% of eighth graders were returning students. As designed, CAL Prep continued to enroll a low-income (64% free or reduced lunch), ethnic minority (65% African American, 28% Latino, 7% mixed/other), and first-generation college population (85%), with 46% male students, 7% English language learners, and 4% with individual learning plans. Based on statewide tests from the previous year, these students were low achievers, with 76% below proficiency in English language arts and 78% below proficiency in mathematics (math). Class size was 30 students for sixth and seventh grades and 15 students for eighth grade. At each grade level, students were divided into two cohort groups who took all their classes together. There were seven teachers (two returning from the previous year) and three instructional assistants. Each subject area (English/social studies, math, and science) had two teachers and one assistant, with an additional teacher for reading intervention. Each subject-matter teacher taught three double-period classes, with four preparation periods per week. Two of the teachers were male, five were Caucasian, one was Latina; and one was African American. The principal was Latino.

### Vision of Teachers and Students

Defining goals for advisories emerged as a crucial first step in light of the heterogeneity of purposes described in the research literature. Beginning with a needs assessment, we collected anonymous information from staff and students about their advisory goals, information that was shared and used for planning.

**Teachers.** In our interviews with the CAL Prep staff about the reasons underlying failed advisories here or at other schools, we uncovered themes familiar in the advisory literature. Barriers to success loom large, arising in all stages including conceptualization, implementation, and maintenance (Brown & Anfara, 2001; Galassi et. al., 1997). We learned about insufficient back-up coverage in the event of leader absences and routine cancellation of advisories, which greatly disappointed students. Teachers reported that the provided materials did not relate well to their students' experiences or to the school's needs. A handbook of discrete advisory activities proved too unstructured, whereas a set of lesson plans about character education was deemed too prescriptive. Teachers called for ongoing training beyond one summer session to support this program. These experiences suggested to us that we needed to recruit a teacher–collaborator, appoint substitute leaders with a clear absence plan, and provide ongoing staff development. These data were also our introduction to the tension between curricular-driven versus teacher-driven approaches.

We used the typology of Galassi and colleagues (1997) to create a goal measure, adding a seventh orientation, which we labeled community applications. We asked teachers and staff ($N = 7$, 70% response rate) to anonymously rank order the purpose for advisories among these seven different goals from 1 (*most important*) to 5 (*least important*). The highest ranked goal was *advocacy* (adult–student relationship) in keeping with the school's charter description (four of the seven gave it the highest score). *Skill* or *social-emotional development* was ranked next (four of the seven gave it the second highest score) and *academic strategies* was ranked a close third (four of the seven gave it a 2 or 3 rating). Particularly striking was the variability among teachers in the relative importance of different advisory goals, with some teachers ranking community-building, administration, and community applications very highly. Thus, teachers were not on the same page at the outset.

**Students.** Given that students are rarely asked for their input, we chose to more broadly assess their hopes for advisories, with a series of open-ended questions implemented as the initial activity of their first advisory session. We asked students to write about (1) topics they would be interested in learning about, (2) conditions that would make the advisory group the best group they had ever been part of, (3) activities in the school that would build on their strengths and interests, and (4) what they would want their advisory leader to know about them. In all, 79% ($N = 118$) of students completed this survey. Thematic analysis of the topics for advisories revealed four primary goal domains: community-building (with peers), social-emotional development (especially friendships), academic development, and community/world issues.

First, students wanted to be known and to know others in deeper ways. They wished to be asked, "How was your day and how are you feeling and why?" or "How is life going so far?" They wanted to get to know the students so that they could "learn about everyone's goals and what they [students] want to be when they grow up" and "share experiences, talents, and embarrassing moments." Second, students were eager to develop social skills, such as how to improve friendships ("what to look for in other people so I can become close to my classmates" and "how to get along and work with others no matter how different they are"). They wanted help in handling complex situations such as "how to deal with people who tease you or whom you don't like" and "being supportive when people make mistakes so they don't feel bad." Students were also curious about adolescent development ("stages of growth we go through"), about personal development ("how to be a better me," "how to be a leader," "how to keep a positive attitude," and "how to face my fears") and how to get help with family problems. Third, in the academic domain, they wanted to learn about college, how to be organized, and how to make school better. Finally, they pressed for discussions on a wide range of topics (about other people's cultures, race/color, why there is racism, Black on Black crime, why there is war, African American history, pollution, life, how to get a job, and how to get used to death and loss), as well as opportunities to contribute beyond school to the community, such as in "helping others, feeding the needy."

The advisory vision of students differed from that of their teachers in several ways, including the primary focus on peer relationships and breadth of their needs, which included a desire for authentic and relevant discussion. In identifying important features of advisories, students asked for an experience that would "link our hearts and minds" and involve "lots of laughing, talking, telling stories." They wanted real relationships ("to know each other from deep inside"), time for deep talk ("give us time to talk . . . about what is going on" and "to talk about things that people don't usually talk about"), and to build a caring community. They described this community as "everyone becoming a family," "everyone has each other's back," "everyone on the same page," and "all the hating to stop." In order to create such an advisory, advisory leaders would need to "make us relaxed and comfortable." And students also recognized that they would need to behave well, that is, listen to the advisory leader, be kind to one another, and allow everyone to talk and participate.

Students had a long wish list for schoolwide activities, which included music, theater, dance, all kinds of sports, cooking, gardening, clubs (spelling bee or math club), homework help, field trips, and community projects. They also noted "social activities for girls to help them stay out of fights and conflicts with each other." In a school with such a strong academic focus, they were eager to grow as a whole person and in nonacademic ways, vitally important to the task of adolescent identity development.

The majority of students, but not all, wanted to be known and understood by their advisory leader. They wanted their advisory leader to learn "what my culture is," "my interests," "my hidden strengths," "my birthday," and "about my family." Some wished to share personal family information such as having "not seen my father for past 3–4 years" or "not getting along with sibling." They hoped that their advisory teacher would "try to communicate with me," "see what I learn," and know the different parts of me. These parts included "the nice, sweet, and good side of me," "that I am not mean," "I am not a bad student," "I don't like to read," and "how loveable I am." A small minority of students desired more privacy, expressing their feelings in these ways: "I can be shy, quiet, angry, talk a lot, want to be left alone and not known"; "I do not want [the] leader to know a lot about me"; and "I like to be alone and not disturbed . . . it may look like I don't care but I'm trying to concentrate." This honest and richly detailed vision etched by the students, shared in a faculty meeting at CAL Prep, proved enormously moving to teachers as well as helpful for advisory development and training.

## Designing Advisories and the Evaluation

In meetings with staff and guided by data, we jointly made decisions about the organizational features of advisories, goals and curriculum, institutional supports, and evaluation. The pace was fast as we balanced the roles of developer, trainer, and evaluator in the face of an urgent deadline to get advisories running. As noted, the advisories were implemented from October, 2006, through June, 2007, in twice-weekly 30-minute sessions at the end of the school day. The development of curriculum, training, and evaluation continued throughout the year.

**Advisory Features.** A schoolwide curriculum was chosen to facilitate staff training because a differentiated grade-level curriculum was beyond our resources in this small setting. Mixed-gender and mixed-grade (6–8) groupings were used to create nine advisory groups of 15 or so students. Advisory leaders included 10 individuals—seven teachers; a counselor intern; and two office staff, who served as co-leaders. Additional staff members were trained to provide substitute capacity in the event of advisory leader absences. Due to staff attrition, 2 of the 10 advisory leaders (20%) were replaced mid-year.

**Goals and Curriculum.** Our data suggested that an advisory goal of advocacy alone, although written into the charter and highest rated by teachers, would ignore both variation in teacher goal rankings and the expressed needs of students, for whom the development of peer relationships was critical. After much discussion, we chose four goals for advisories: teacher–student relationships (advocacy), peer relationships and belonging (community-building), and skill-building in both academic and social-emotional domains. We named our emerging curriculum "A Caring Community of Learners and Leaders."

For lesson development, we culled from empirically validated programs to teach psychosocial and academic skills as well as available advisory curricula. We looked for activities that would promote active and engaged learning, and were aligned to adolescent needs for increased voice and responsibility as well as to college-readiness objectives of developing skills in reflection, analysis, problem-solving, and self-regulation (Conley, 2010; National Research Council, 2004). In all, 50 lessons were created or adapted to focus on the development of community, learners, and leaders (see Table 5.1). Most but not all lessons, such as the UC Berkeley ropes course or the film *Akeelah and the Bee* (Fishburne & Atchison, 2006), were implemented during advisory period. Some were single lessons, such as advisory norms, and others comprised a unit, such as five lessons on the prevention of social aggression and bullying (Cappella & Weinstein, 2006). In order to meet site needs and allow students to apply these skills, we timed advisory activities with schoolwide milestone events. This meant recurring visits to the themes of learner (e.g., malleable ability), leader (e.g., prevention of social aggression), and community (e.g., trust-building) in order to prepare for report card conferences, returns from school breaks, and state testing. Advisories were graded for degree of student participation.

**Institutional Supports.** The role of advisory leader was a broadened one, not only meeting typical academic needs, but also the social-emotional needs of students, all in the context of learning a new curriculum. We provided resources to support this role expansion. A binder of lessons and supplementary materials for each advisory period was distributed to the leaders and placed in the staff room, with additions made each month as the curriculum was developed. To better meet teacher and student needs, we provided lesson plans but also encouraged advisory leaders to adapt materials, bring their unique contributions to the curriculum, respond to

TABLE 5.1 Themes and Topics of Fifty-Lesson Advisory Curriculum

| A CARING COMMUNITY OF LEARNERS AND LEADERS | | |
|---|---|---|
| **CREATING A** *CARING* **COMMUNITY** | **DEVELOPING** *LEARNERS* | **DEVELOPING** *LEADERS* |
| Dreams for advisory[a] | Learner strengths[e] | College student visits[i] |
| Respect/disrespect[b] | Getting smart[f] | Leaders/conflict resolution[j] |
| Advisory norms/listening[c] | Goals/report card[g] | Prevention/social aggression[k] |
| Trust-building (ropes course)[d] | Test preparation strategies[h] | Prevention/stereotyping[l] |

[a]Data collection. [b]Weinstein (2002). [c]Chappelle & Bigman (1998). [d]UC Berkeley experience. [e]Live Wire Media (1997). [f]Dweck (2000); *Akeelah and the Bee* (Fishburne & Atchison, 2006). [g]Leadership Public Schools (2006). [h]Aspire Public Schools (2006). [i]UC Berkeley experience. [j]Live Wire Media (1997). [k]Cappella & Weinstein (2006). [l]Simulation Training Systems; Alpha-Beta Game (adaptation of Bafa' Bafa' intercultural simulation).

student issues, and share expertise with each other. In biweekly Friday staff meetings, new advisory lessons were presented, role-played, and discussed, with debriefing about previous lessons.

**Evaluation.** Competing demands, such as the press for immediate action in practice (e.g., getting advisories running) versus reflective research design in the university, forced compromises. Among these compromises was the proposed use of largely non-identifiable data that enabled a fast-track application to the UC Berkeley's Committee for the Protection of Human Subjects. Although this decision resulted in an expedited project approval, it limited our capacity to link data across students, teachers, and time periods, ruling out pre- and post-measures. Thus, in addition to our initial needs assessment, our formative mixed-methods evaluation focused on student and teacher evaluations of advisories *post-advisory* in June, using both quantitative and qualitative methods. Measures and analyses are described in our presentation of results.

## Students Evaluate Advisories

In all, 73% of the students completed questionnaires post-advisories. Students were asked to provide demographic and performance information (gender, grade, ethnicity, honor roll), and indicate their advisory section. They rated their advisory class on three new six-item scales, which measured overall satisfaction and domain-specific satisfaction with teachers and peers. The *General Rating of Advisory* ($N = 110$, $\alpha = .91$) assessed the overall degree of learning, enjoyment, and improvement in relationships with teachers and peers. *Climate with Peers* ($N = 109$, $\alpha = .92$) focused on the peer climate of respect, support, and appreciation. Using the same items, *Climate with Teacher* ($N = 109$, $\alpha = .94$) examined the teacher climate of respect, support, and appreciation. Students responded to each item using a five-point scale from 1 (*disagree a lot*) to 5 (*agree a lot*). Open-ended questions tapped student assessments of advisory leaders, including their effectiveness, strengths, and suggestions for improvement. Students were also asked to indicate what they learned from their favorite advisory lesson and from each of six selected advisory activities.

Students were largely positive on average about the quality of their advisories. They rated their advisories favorably on all three scales: *Overall Advisory* ($M = 3.53$, SD $= 1.07$), *Climate with Peers* ($M = 3.58$, SD $= 1.04$), and *Climate with Teacher* ($M = 3.76$, SD $= 1.14$). Looking at the data in another way, positive ratings of advisory were endorsed by 42% to 67% of the students (see Table 5.2). Importantly, providing evidence for domain differences, students reported significantly more satisfaction with the quality of teacher relationships achieved in advisories than that of peers, $F(2,98) = 4.99$, $p < .01$.

## Variation in Advisory Effectiveness

Given that students were nested within advisory classes, multilevel modeling analyses were conducted to explore variation in perceptions of advisory effectiveness. A two-level model was generated where Level 1 included student qualities (e.g., grade, gender, ethnic group, honor role status) and Level 2 included advisory classes and advisory leader efficacy to predict student ratings of overall advisory effectiveness (Table 5.3). We created a simple dichotomous variable that captured observed advisory leader efficacy. Two of the authors independently rated advisory leaders (more/less) on how comfortable and knowledgeable they appeared in talking about advisory teaching in staff meetings. Raters achieved 89% interrater agreement, with the single disagreement reconciled in discussion. In the two cases with multiple leaders (co-leaders, teacher change), the lower score was used in analysis. Five of nine advisories were rated as having more efficacious leaders. This two-level analysis allowed us to examine how advisory-level characteristics such as leader efficacy were related to students' reports of overall advisory effectiveness, beyond student-level variation.

TABLE 5.2 Advisory Rating Items, Means, and Percentage Agreement

| ADVISORY ITEMS | M | "AGREE A LOT" OR "AGREE A LITTLE" | |
|---|---|---|---|
| **Overall Advisory** | | N | % |
| 1   Overall, my advisory class provided an orderly and safe place in which to learn. | 3.86 | 73 | 67 |
| 2   Overall, I enjoyed the activities that we engaged in, in my advisory class. | 3.55 | 61 | 56 |
| 3   Overall, I learned a great deal from the activities in my advisory class. | 3.58 | 64 | 60 |
| 4   Overall, my academic skills improved as a result of activities in my advisory classes. | 3.21 | 45 | 42 |
| 5   Overall, my relationship with my *peers* improved as a result of the advisory classes. | 3.50 | 58 | 54 |
| 6   Overall, my relationship with my *teachers* improved as a result of the advisory classes. | 3.50 | 56 | 54 |
| **Advisory Peers** | | | |
| 1   Overall, I feel supported by my *peers* in my advisory class. | 3.47 | 57 | 53 |
| 2   Overall, I feel respected by my *peers* in my advisory class. | 3.50 | 59 | 55 |
| 3   Overall, I feel accepted by my *peers* in my advisory class. | 3.80 | 72 | 67 |
| 4   Overall, I feel appreciated by my *peers* in my advisory class. | 3.57 | 57 | 54 |
| 5   Overall, I felt understood by my *peers* in my advisory class. | 3.49 | 56 | 53 |
| 6   Overall, my opinions were taken into consideration by my *peers* in my advisory class. | 3.65 | 65 | 60 |
| **Advisory Teachers** | | | |
| 1   Overall, I feel supported by my *teachers* in my advisory class. | 3.68 | 64 | 59 |
| 2   Overall, I feel respected by my *teachers* in my advisory class. | 3.73 | 66 | 62 |
| 3   Overall, I feel accepted by my *teachers* in my advisory class. | 3.84 | 70 | 66 |
| 4   Overall, I feel appreciated by my *teachers* in my advisory class. | 3.76 | 70 | 65 |
| 5   Overall, I felt understood by my *teachers* in my advisory class. | 3.77 | 71 | 66 |
| 6   Overall, my opinions were taken into consideration by my *teachers* in my advisory class. | 3.81 | 69 | 64 |

TABLE 5.3 Multilevel Modeling Estimates of Observer-Rated Teacher Efficacy: Predicting Overall Advisory Experience Controlling for Student-Level Characteristics

|  | COEFFICIENT | STANDARD ERROR |
|---|---|---|
| Intercept | 3.87** | 0.67 |
| **Class-level** | | |
| Perceived confidence | 0.69* | 0.24 |
| **Student-level** | | |
| Grade | −0.22 | 0.15 |
| Gender | 0.12 | 0.20 |
| Ethnic | 0.09 | 0.09 |
| Honor roll | −0.37 | 0.21 |

$*p < 0.05.$ $**p < 0.001.$

Student perceptions of advisory effectiveness did not vary by type of student. Indeed, advisories were rated as equally effective no matter the gender, grade, ethnicity, or achievement level of the student. Instead, the advisory leader proved to be the significant factor in predicting student satisfaction. Students in advisories with more efficacious leaders, as rated by observers, reported higher ratings of advisory satisfaction (a 0.69 unit increase, $p < .05$) compared to their counterparts in advisories with less efficacious leaders. These findings hold after taking into account student-level characteristics and the nested nature of the data, providing evidence of linkage between the ratings of observers (in staff meetings) and students (in advisory sessions).

## Qualities of Highly Rated Advisory Leaders

Next, we compared the three highest-rated and three lowest-rated advisories, offering insight into student perceptions of effective advisory practice. Students reported that more effective advisory leaders led with strength ("a great leader" and "strong powerful woman") and kept the class focused ("very good controls" and "keeping the class together and organized"). These leaders were characterized as "respectful, fair, and understanding" as well as knowledgeable and skilled. The effective advisory leader "knows what she/he is talking about," "explains things well," and "listens to the shy people." Leaders were also admired for special qualities and described as "awesome," "kind hearted," "passionate," and "loyal and cool to hang out with." One student wrote he/she was "woken up, never bored or sleepy" in advisory. Remarkably few ideas for improvement were offered, with one student sharing, "I like the way she/he is because she/he is special to me." There was one request that "yelling needs to stop" with advice to the advisory leader to "try not to get overwhelmed and frustrated." Students did suggest that advisories should have "a little more fun" and do "different activities, to let people get the stress out."

In contrast, less highly rated advisory leaders garnered more muted and variable praise. Some students described their leaders as "an okay advisory leader," "boring sometimes," and "sometimes all right," whereas others noted that "she/he was really good" and "smart caring loving understanding." But students did identify many positive assets, such as effort ("great, she/he tries her/his hardest," "tried to calm us down when we were loud," and "try's no matter what") and listening skills ("is willing to lissen and help"). They also underscored their leaders' considerable accomplishments, which included "had good thoughts on what he/she was teaching us," "got us to become all friends," and was "able to teach the class new activities." One critical differentiating quality about which students offered advice concerned the need for stronger classroom management skills ("have a lil' more class management . . . be a lil' bit more evil . . . could wait until the class is listening to give instructions"). They also called for an improvement in attitude ("talk more calmly," "have to work on their attitude," and "needs to be more patient") and in explanatory skill ("explain better the activities").

## Student Learning

In student descriptions of their learning in six advisory units, we see that students could articulate benefits from the different curricular threads. Students reported changed attitudes and behaviors. For example, in lessons about learner strengths, a student wrote that it "helped me believe in myself and stop catching attitudes." The lessons on respect taught another student that "respect is the key to everything in life." Lessons on conflict resolution and social aggression gave students alternative actions (e.g., "Now instead of going off on something I can talk calmly to them" and "To use the strategy not to respond back but tell a teacher"). The unit on test preparation strategies enabled one student to learn to "do what you know first." And in playing the intercultural game, another student wrote that "it helped me by making me understand how it feels to be a different race." These comments also illustrate that not all students learned equally.

For some, these were lessons that they already knew ("I'm created with so many different cultures so I already appreciate different cultures") or found difficult ("I was confused half the time") or boring ("I know most of the stuff"). For other, the lessons were never fully implemented ("We never got through it nobody knew how to shut up").

We examined student reports about what they learned in their favorite advisory activity as a function of advisory group membership. In higher-rated advisories, there was greater evidence of learning. For example, 87% of students (vs. 60%) could identify something they learned rather than leaving the item blank or reporting that "I didn't learn anything from those activities." Furthermore, in many but not all cases, their responses appeared more differentiated and thoughtful. As examples, their answers described learning about "how to deal with anger and don't take it out on someone else" and "how to show empathy ... connect and help people out." In lower-rated advisories, student responses were largely less developed and more general, such as learning "more info about things I don't know" and about how to "support other cultures."

## Teachers Evaluate Advisories

We also created a questionnaire for advisory leaders, to be completed after the advisories and that included ratings of advisory effectiveness, curriculum usage, and open-ended questions. The *General Rating of Advisory* scale ($\alpha$ = .81) used five of the six items from the student scale, with the "safety of the advisory climate" item omitted. Leaders rated the degree of student learning, enjoyment, and improvement on items such as "overall, my students enjoyed the activities that we engaged in my advisory class." They also rated how often they used the advisory curriculum materials on a four-point scale from *always* to *rarely*. Open-ended questions solicited suggestions about training, resources, advisory features, and content. In the press of year-end activities, only 5 of 10 advisory leaders completed these questionnaires, limiting the representativeness of the sample. However, additional feedback from advisory leaders was provided at the year-end staff meeting and is incorporated here.

Similar to the views of students, leader ratings were largely positive ($M$ = 3.48, SD = 0.50 on a five-point scale) and four of five leaders reporting curriculum usage as *always* or *often* on a four-point scale. These advisory leaders were largely positive about the helpfulness of the materials, as the following comments indicate:

Material ... beneficial to create class discussions that were fresh and eye opening.

It was wonderful to have a ready-made plan to deliver.

Materials were user-friendly, detailed, and could be easily used/adapted.

I liked the structure and common themes.

In contrast, one advisory leader found the material "incredibly overwhelming ... there was an abundant amount expected, little time given ... and little depth."

Views about advisory training were more variable. Some leaders found the Friday staff meetings "very helpful to prepare us for that week's advisory," and for those not able to be present, "information was always accessible and/or I was able to get support from a staff colleague." Other leaders expressed the need for more or less support. On the ground, in the face of multiple demands, advisories were sometimes given short shrift on the Friday meeting agenda; the training was sometimes cancelled and handled via e-mail. As one staff member described it, "They [the trainings] were too sporadic and too far from the activities to remember." One teacher suggested having "someone observing to see if we are all actually doing something related to the topic." Greater support was especially crucial for those leaders who were not teachers:

As someone who doesn't typically act in a teaching capacity, I would have benefited from some support. However, in being open to the experience, I learned through trial and error how to improve efficacy.

Many leaders lauded the Alpha-Beta Game (an intercultural experience that required a high level of training) precisely because of the consistent help provided by our teacher–collaborator who visited advisories to monitor and support. In contrast, report card reflections were undermined by administrative constraints that delayed the availability of reports and limited preparation time.

Throughout, however, there was unresolved tension between a curricular approach and a teacher-directed approach, judged more responsive to the needs of students. One leader urged, "keep providing a framework which students can dialogue on a variety of topics." However, another leader suggested less support ("I am comfortable with advisory") as well as less direction ("I am comfortable finding applicable lessons and activities"). Similarly, another leader wrote that "from discussions with students, there would be more buy-in if students had a voice in how time was used. Many wanted to do homework, socialize, and use the time for fun, community-building activities that were not 'academic' oriented."

Advisory leaders were unified in their suggestions for improvement, which included (1) a longer advisory period of 45 minutes given class transitions; (2) same-grade groupings; (3) more trust-building activities earlier in the year; (4) less breadth, more depth, and more active curriculum; and (5) more training about how to engage students and build relationships. In their words, a longer period would allow "enough time for a proper discussion to occur and one that is not rushed," more attention to trust building would create "a safe place for the kids to express themselves," and greater depth would overcome the problem that "students cannot just jump into stuff they have never experienced before."

## Lessons Learned

In one fast-moving year, we collaborated in the design, implementation, and evaluation of a schoolwide advisory program with multiage groups of students from Grades 6 to 8. Our 50-lesson curriculum targeted multiple goals, including relationship-building with both teachers and peers, and skill development in both academic and social-emotional domains. It drew from empirically validated activities where possible, but it also matched the needs of the setting. A variety of institutional supports provided scaffolding for advisory leaders. In an iterative way, this case study mapped processes of advisory construction and outcomes in order to understand sources of variation in program desires, effects, and supports. Its strengths included collaborative and data-driven advisory development, the viewpoints of both teachers and students, domain-specific indices of perceived effectiveness, and a controlled test of the factors that predicted advisory differences. What do these findings teach us about strengthening advisories at CAL Prep, and with what implications for research and policy?

First, advisory goals mattered a great deal. In this high-expectation middle school setting, the goals of teachers and students for advisories diverged. Teachers ranked student advocacy (personalized relationships with students) as most important, whereas students held far broader hopes—to include peer relationships and greater understanding of self and the world. For CAL Prep, this evaluation underscored the unmet developmental needs of students in Grades 6 to 8. It identified the importance of blending academic rigor with social-emotional development (especially in the domain of peers) and of student interests beyond academics (i.e., adopting a whole-student approach). But it also underscored the challenges of meeting these multiple goals within advisories. Advisories as constructed were perceived by students to be more successful in strengthening relationships with teachers than with peers. This domain-specific result finds support in the sparse literature (e.g., Espe, 1993). It calls for more emphasis, more time, and/or different approaches, such as building a stronger school culture, to strengthen adolescent peer relationships. Skill-building programs have been found to be most effective when practice is sequenced, active, focused, and explicit, as well as when implementation problems are absent (Durlak et al., 2011). These findings mirror feedback from our advisory leaders that a narrower curriculum, approached with greater depth as well as more scaffolding for both teachers and students, would improve the strength of program reach.

Second, there was documented variation among advisories in student ratings of effectiveness, linked to projected leader efficacy, specific leader qualities, and differential learning outcomes. The important role of efficacy beliefs in the teaching of advisories is also identified by Phillippo (2013). In the eyes of students, successful advisories got the work done (they were focused and well-managed) but in ways that were respectful, sensitive, and worthy of admiration. More effective leaders appeared able to adapt the lesson, meeting the needs of both curriculum and student (perhaps with the deep, authentic talk that students envisioned), and ultimately, becoming important role models (Pianta & Hamre, 2009). These findings highlight the importance of improving program implementation as unevenness in practice undermines outcomes, such as what students learned (Durlak & DuPre, 2008). Finding out about student-identified advisory differences proved to be uncomfortable for advisory leaders. All had worked so hard and experienced many successes, a fact sensitively recognized by students. But indeed there were tremendous constraints (e.g., not all leaders were teachers, there were replacements, and training was uneven) as well as clear challenges of a multiple-goal curriculum.

Finally, the feedback from teachers underscored the need for coherence between advisory goal (structure and curriculum), school mission, administrative capacity, and available staff training. As the implementation study of Gregory and colleagues (2007) suggests, time for training and professional development, an advisory coordinator, and principal leadership are all needed to improve implementation. The researchers shared the leaders' perspective that there was insufficient time for staff training. In the face of multiple priorities at this new school, meeting times were often derailed for other purposes, jeopardizing advisory training and the advocacy role, which relied on regularized access to student information. Importantly, success in meeting multiple advisory goals required the melding of different kinds of supports, further taxing institutional capacity. The work of advisories, in schools such as CAL Prep, must interface smoothly with and advance the preparation of students to be ready for college and successful there—inevitably linking academic and social-emotional objectives. Schools must avoid the layering of independent programs, competition among objectives, and additional teacher preparation that is, ultimately, not sustainable. Not surprisingly, in her ethnographic study of three high schools, Phillippo (2013) found the most consistency of practice within those schools that provided an "aligned advisor role structure" (p. 80).

In conclusion, mounting a multiple-goal, engaging, relevant, and school milestone-based curriculum for advisories proved to be a tall order. Although advisories offer a promising site for the use of empirically validated prevention and SEL programs (Foreman, Olin, Hoagwood, Crowe, & Saka, 2009), there is substantial work to be done to adapt such curricula to school needs, milestone events, multiyear programs, and staff and school capacity—factors likely at play in their underutilization in educational settings. And although leaders were favorable about the advisory curriculum, there were disparate views about a curricular versus a teacher-directed approach to advisory.

These contextualized findings bring us back full circle to the single goal of deepening the teacher–student relationship (so that teachers can advocate for their students) and to the student-expressed need for authentic conversations that touch both hearts and minds (which may rest on less programmed time). Recent research captures the importance of experienced personalization. For example, Ryzin (2010) documented that those students who identified their advisory leader as a secondary attachment figure (40% of the sample) reported greater engagement in school and showed greater achievement gains as well as adjustment. Furthermore, in a study of 14 redesigned small schools, McClure and colleagues (2010) found that student-perceived personalization in school was more predictive of grade point average and standardized achievement scores than student-perceived learning in advisories. Future research on advisories, using a randomized control design to test different advisory models, might tease out the relative contribution of strengthened teacher–student relationships versus learned skills or attitudes to gains in student attainment.

This collaborative project stimulated an investment by students and teachers alike in the advisory program as well as deep conversations among the staff about future directions for advisories. And we learned that middle school students can be vivid and good reporters about advisory leader practices, consistent with observer perceptions. They are a largely untapped resource that can be used in program improvement, as is done in college classes.

## Postscript

The feedback that students provided about advisories was used by the school in subsequent years, both inside and outside of the advisory context. Although student clubs did not get off the ground during this first advisory year, in subsequent years, a student council and student clubs were implemented, and the after-school program was expanded to include sports teams, arts, drama, cooking, gardening, and debate. Advisories were also continually refined under the direction of the dean of students, and later under the wraparound services coordinator (a teacher) in collaboration with the principal. To build a stronger school culture, a schoolwide theme (CARRIES) was chosen to clarify the mission and more clearly articulate the expected qualities (integrating academic and social-emotional attributes) that students needed to carry them to and through college. The CARRIES attributes reflect a cooperative citizen, assertive activist, rigorous problem solver, responsible role model, inquisitive scholar, empathetic contributor, and self-controlled success (see Chapter 13).

Advisories are differently organized now. Teacher advocacy for students (i.e., the creation of an academic family) is defined as the primary advisory goal. Single-gender and single-grade groups currently meet twice a week (once for social-emotional development and once for academics) and remain together across school years, nurturing longer term connections. All staff members serve as advisors and meet within grade-level groups to determine their own activities, guided by the CARRIES attributes and with help from resource books. Advisories continue to serve an important function in the school. As one student described it, "Advisory class is the one class I like the most. I can be myself in that class. I can share my feelings." Every year at the high school graduation ceremony, each advisory teacher publically describes the growth of his or her advisees (sharing their own growth as well) over the course of their CAL Prep years. This part of the ceremony culminates in a group hug that poignantly reflects the sense of being known, valued, and belonging that the advisory program has nurtured.

# References

Alvidrez, J., & Weinstein, R. S. (1993). The nature of "schooling" in school transitions: A critical re-examination. *Prevention in Human Services, 10*, 7–26. doi:10.1300/J293v10n02_02

Anderman, E. M., & Mueller, C. E. (2010). Middle school transitions and adolescent development. In J. L. Meece & J. S. Eccles (Eds.), *Handbook of research on schools, schooling, and human development* (pp. 198–215). New York, NY: Taylor & Francis.

Anfara, V. A. (2006). *Research summary: Advisory programs.* Westerville, OH: Association for Middle Level Education. Retrieved from http://www.nmsa.org/Research/ResearchSummaries/AdvisoryPrograms.tabid/812/Default.aspx

Aspire Public Schools. (2006). *Advisory binder.* Oakland, CA: Author.

Brown, K. M., & Anfara, V. A. (2001). Competing perspectives on advisory programs: Mingling or meddling in middle schools? *Research in Middle Level Education Annual, 24*, 1–30.

Cappella, E., & Weinstein, R. S. (2006). The prevention of social aggression in girls. *Social Development, 15*, 434–462. doi:10.1111/j.1467-9507.2006.00350.x

Carnegie Council on Adolescent Development. (1989). *Turning points: Preparing American youth for the 21st century.* New York, NY: Carnegie Corporation.

Chappelle, S. & Bigman, L. (1998). *Diversity in action.* Hamilton, MA: Project Adventure.

Conley, D. (2010). *College and career ready: helping all students succeed beyond high school.* San Francisco, CA: Jossey-Bass.

Darling-Hammond, L., Ancess, J., & Ort, S. W. (2002). Reinventing high school: Outcomes of the Coalition Campus Schools Project. *American Educational Research Journal, 39*, 639–673. doi:10.3102/00028312039003639

Durlak, J. A., & DuPre, E. P. (2008). Implementation matters: A review of research on the influence of implementation on program outcomes and the factors affecting implementation. *American Journal of Community Psychology, 41*, 327–350. doi:10.1007/s10464-008-9165-0.

Durlak, J. A., Weissberg, R. P., Dymnicki, A. B., Taylor, R. D., & Schellinger, K. B. (2011). The impact of enhancing students' social and emotional learning: A meta-analysis of school-based university outcomes. *Child Development, 82*, 405–432. doi:10.1111/j.1467-8624.2010.01564.x

Dweck, C. S. (2000). *Self-theories: Their role in motivation, personality and development.* Philadelphia, PA: Taylor & Francis.

Eccles, J. S., & Midgley, C., Buchanan, C., Wigfield, A., Reuman, D., & Mac Iver, D. (1993). Development during adolescence: The impact of stage/environment fit on young adolescents' experiences in schools and families. *American Psychologist, 48*, 90–101. doi:10.1037/10254-034

Espe, L. (1993). The effectiveness of teacher advisors in a junior high. *The Canadian School Executive, 12*(7), 15–19.

Fishburne, L. (Producer), & Atchison, D. (Writer/Director). (2006). *Akeelah and the bee* [Motion picture]. United States: Lionsgate.

Forman, S. G., Olin, S. S., Hoagwood, K. E., Crowe, M., & Saka, N. (2009). Evidence-based interventions in schools: Developers' views of implementation barriers and facilitators. *School Mental Health, 1,* 26–36. doi:10.1007/s12310-008-9002-5

Galassi, J. P., Gulledge, S. A., & Cox, N. D. (1997). Middle school advisories: Retrospect and prospect. *Review of Educational Research, 67,* 301–338. doi:10.3102/00346543067003301

Greenberg, M. T., Weissberg, R. P., O' Brien, M. U., Zins, J. E., Fredericks, L., Resnik, H., & Elias, M. J. (2003). Enhancing school-based prevention and youth development through coordinated social, emotional, and academic learning. *American Psychologist, 58,* 466–474. doi:10.1037/0003-066X.58.6-7.466

Gregory, A., Henry, D. B., & Schoeny, M. E. (2007). School climate and implementation of a preventive intervention. *American Journal of Community Psychology, 40,* 250–260. doi:10.1007/s10464-007-9142-z

Hanewald, R. (2013). Transition between primary and secondary school: Why is it important and how can it be supported. *Australian Journal of Teacher Education, 36,* 62–74. doi:10.14221/ajte2013v38n1.7

Langenkamp, A. G. (2015). Academic vulnerability and resilience during the transition to high school: The role of social relationships and district context. *Sociology of Education, 83,* 1–19. doi:10.1177/0038040709356563

Leadership Public Schools. (2006). *Advisory binder.* San Francisco, CA: Author.

Illinois State Board of Education. (2010). *Illinois learning standards: Social-emotional learning.* Retrieved from http://www.isbe.state.il.us/social_emotional/standards.htm

Mac Iver, D. J., & Epstein, E. J. (1991). Responsive practices in the middle grades: Teacher teams, advisory groups, remedial instruction, and school transition programs. *American Journal of Education, 99,* 587–622. doi:10.1086/443999

McClure, L., Yonezawa, S., & Jones, M. (2010). Can school structures improve teacher-student relationships? The relationship between advisory programs, personalization and students' academic achievement. *Education Policy Analysis Archives, 18.* 1–21. Retrieved from http://epaa.asu.edu/ojs/article/view/719.

Makkonen, R. (2004). Advisory program research and evaluation. *Horace: The Journal of the Coalition of Essential Schools, 20,* 11–13.

National Research Council. (2004). *Engaging schools: Fostering high school students' motivation to learn.* Washington, DC: National Academy Press.

Phillippo, K. (2013). *Advisory in urban high schools: A study of expanded teacher roles.* New York, NY: Palgrave Macmillan.

Pianta, R. C., & Hamre, B. K. (2009). Conceptualization, measurement, and improvement of classroom processes: Standardized observation can leverage capacity. *Educational Researcher, 38,* 109–119. doi:10.3102/0013189X09332374

Ryzin, M. V. (2010). Secondary school advisors as mentors and secondary attachment figures. *Journal of Community Psychology, 38,* 131–154. doi:10.1002/jcop.20356

Semel, S. F., & Sadovnik, A. (2008). The contemporary small-school movement: Lessons from the history of progressive education. *Teachers College Record, 110,* 1744–1771.

Simulation Training Systems. (2009). *BaFa' Bafa' educational edition.* Retrieved from www.simulationtrainingsystems.com

Weinstein, R. S. (2002). *Reaching higher: The power of expectations in schooling.* Boston, MA: Harvard University Press.

Weiss, M. J., Bloom, H. S., & Brock, T. (2013). *A conceptual framework for studying the sources of variation in program effects.* New York, NY: MDRC. Retrieved from http://www.mdrc.org/publication/conceptual-framework-studying-sources-variation-program-effects

Wigfield, A., Lutz, S. L., & Wagner, A. L. (2005). Early adolescents' development across the middle school years: Implications for school counselors. *Professional School Counseling, 9,* 112–119. doi:10.5330/prsc.9.2.2484n0j255vpm302

Live Wire Media. (1997). *Wise Lives Curriculum: Grades 6–8.* Santa Cruz, CA: Author. Retrieved from https://www.livewiremedia.com/WiseLivesCurriculumBinder

# 6 | The Student Transition into an Early College Secondary School

**NILOFAR SAMI AND RHONA S. WEINSTEIN**

*"I need encouragement from teachers and family. I need freedom, respect, and kindness at the school."*[1]

*"I don't want them to expect so much from all of us as kids."*

*"It is up to me if I want to learn or not."*

N LIGHT OF RESEARCH FINDINGS about the decline in both engagement and achievement as students transition from elementary to middle school and from middle to high school, California College Preparatory Academy (CAL Prep) was designed to better meet adolescent needs while offering a college-preparatory education for first-generation college students. Thus, by design, CAL Prep provided a small and untracked school setting with transition support resources that included (1) advisories (see Chapter 5), (2) a pod structure where students moved as a class to different teachers, and (3) an eighth-period homework session. These features were introduced to strengthen relationships with teachers and peers and to bridge the home–school gap in academic support.

Despite these supports, however, observations during the school's first 2 years as a middle school suggested that students were struggling mightily to adjust to the high level of challenge. To learn more about the nature of this struggle and its possible link to the school transition, we designed a

---

[1] All quotations from students are taken verbatim from their completed questionnaires, with no changes made to syntax or spelling.

multimethod study—in partnership with school staff—to be implemented in the spring of the school's third year (Sami, 2011). In this chapter, we draw on selected findings that guided changes we made in the ongoing development of CAL Prep.

## Research on Student Adjustment to Secondary School

### Developmental Stage–Environment Fit

There is a large body of research evidence about student adjustment difficulties in the transition to secondary school, with the decline in engagement and achievement even steeper for low-income and ethnic minority students (Anderman & Mueller, 2010; Benner, 2011; Hanewald, 2013). As Eccles and colleagues (1993) have suggested, the mechanism underlying diminished student functioning is the mismatch between the developmental stage of adolescents and features of secondary school environments that fail to support student needs. Also, as the study by Barber and Olsen (2004) has shown, it is structural changes in the school—not the developmental stage of students or grade level—that have a negative impact on student adjustment.

At transition, most typically, students move from a smaller setting to a larger one, where they are exposed to multiple teachers across disciplines. They experience enhanced curriculum rigor alongside ability-based tracking, less teacher support and greater teacher control, and fewer decision-making opportunities (Alvidrez & Weinstein, 1993; Eccles et al., 1993). These structural changes increase anonymity while decreasing student autonomy and disrupting the support of peers and teachers. These changes also occur at an important time of identity development when adolescents, who are undergoing enormous biological, psychological, and social changes, need to be known, to exercise their will, and be supported by deep relationships with both teachers and peers (Wigfield, Lutz, & Wagner, 2005).

The adjustment risk is even greater for ethnic minority and low-income youth, who are more likely to arrive in secondary school underprepared and, hence, relegated to lower academic tracks with greater risk of dropout. They are more likely to have come from schools with fewer resources and from families without college experience, who may not know how to support their students (Langenkamp, 2015; Seidman, Lambert, Allen, & Aber, 2003). These youth also face societal messages filled with negative racial-ethnic stereotypes about achievement and social pressure from peers to disengage from academics (Altschul, Oyserman, & Bybee, 2006).

Although studies have charted variation in transition processes by different population groups, less attention has been paid to the social context—understanding how the qualities of school environments, into which the transition takes place, might magnify or minimize maladjustment. For example, secondary schools that are organized with family pods have students with more favorable perceptions of the school environment and better adjustment (Barber & Olsen, 2004). We know little about the transition of underprepared minority and low-income students into more favorable educational environments—that is, with greater challenge as well as increased support, rather than the more normative lower-track classrooms to which these students are commonly exposed.

## Assessing Mismatch of Needs and Environment

Student perceptions of their environments have been the primary means through which the mismatch hypothesis has been tested as a factor in student adjustment to the transition. Studies differ in the features of perceived environments studied, environments surveyed, and methods of assessment used. Most studies of transition have identified developmental socialization practices (creating connection and providing autonomy) as key features of what constitutes a supportive environment for adolescents. Both longitudinal and cross-sectional studies consistently report a decrease in student-perceived connection, at school and home, during the transition to secondary school. Also, student perceptions of greater connection with teachers (during the transition) and greater connection with family (prior to the middle school transition) have been found to predict higher achievement across core subjects (DuBois, Eitel, & Felner, 1994; Seidman et al., 2003). The findings with regard to student-perceived autonomy have been less consistent.

For low-income and ethnic minority youth, both academic and ethnocultural socialization practices are also important domains to be studied, especially in the transition to a high-expectation school setting. High expectations and academic involvement from both teacher and parent have been found to be related to higher student engagement and achievement (Grolnick, Kurowski, Dunlap, & Hevey, 2000; Jeynes, 2003; Régner, Loose, & Dumas, 2009). Yet teachers often communicate lower expectations to poor and ethnic minority youth, even in the face of equal achievement (Weinstein, 2002). And despite high academic expectations for their children, parents with less education and family income are less likely to be involved in their children's schooling (Jeynes, 2005; Lopez,

Sanchez, & Hamilton, 2000). Students experience considerable decline in parent and teacher academic involvement in the transition from elementary to secondary school (Eccles et al., 1993; Kuperminc, Darnell, & Alverz-Jimenez, 2008).

For ethnic minority students, racial-ethnic socialization may be a critical domain of support during the transition to secondary school, especially with regard to the developmental task of forging an integrated ethnic and academic identity. Ethnic minority parents engage in racial-ethnic socialization practices to provide their children with tools to successfully deal with social inequalities, discrimination, and negative stereotypes that they may face (Hughes et al., 2006). A study by Oyserman, Harrison, and Bybee (2001) provides evidence that an intervention to encourage ethnic minority students to view achievement as an important part of their in-group identity resulted in higher grades and fewer absences for intervention as compared to non-intervention students.

Two different methodological approaches to studying mismatch have been used. The first method *explicitly* assesses the degree of mismatch between student ratings of real and ideal environments (e.g., Trickett & Moos, 2002). The second measure assesses mismatch *implicitly* by examining student perceptions of real environments, making the assumption that positive ratings of environments reflect needs being met (e.g., Gutman & Midgley, 2000). To our knowledge, no study has compared these two methods of assessing mismatch in predicting student adjustment. Furthermore, although transition studies such as those described above have focused on ratings of school and home environments, it is a rare study that assesses both contexts (see Barber & Olsen, 1997). Our interest here was also to capture student perceptions of the mismatch between home and school, which to our knowledge, has not been directly assessed.

## Framing the Study

Our inquiry provides a unique window on issues of transition in a number of ways. First, taking a contextual, mixed-method, and largely cross-sectional (except for achievement) approach, we situated our study within a challenging and supportive early college middle school. Here, we contrasted the experiences of students new to CAL Prep (transitioning students) with old hands at CAL Prep (returning students), looking for factors that might distinguish student attitude about school (school belonging) and academic performance (mathematics [math]). Our interest in math achievement was driven by the link between student success in math during middle and high school and success in postsecondary schooling (National Mathematics Advisory Panel, 2008). Second, we broadened our assessment of contexts (school, home, and home–school), socialization practices (developmental, academic, and ethnic-cultural practices), and types of mismatch (ratings of real–ideal differences versus real environments, and student-identified mismatches). By also including open-ended questions, we were able to explore barriers at school and at home that students, themselves, identified as standing in the way of their success in a setting like CAL Prep.

Our goal in this study was to systematically test the role of transition status and student perceptions of mismatch (between needs and qualities of environment) in predicting both a sense of school belonging and math achievement. Based on findings from the research literature, we expected to find that (1) perceived mismatch of need and environment would be greater for transition students than for returning ones; (2) greater mismatch at school and at home, and between home and school would predict less school belonging and lower math achievement for transition students; and (3) beyond the effects of mismatch, higher levels of teacher socialization practices (real environment) would predict greater school belonging and higher math achievement.

## Method

### Sample

Given our focus on middle school, all students in the sixth to eighth grades (but not the ninth grade) were invited to participate. Of the 174 eligible students, 89% ($N = 154$) participated, with 45 sixth, 56 seventh, and 53 eighth graders in the sample. The sample was balanced by gender (51% female, $n = 78$) and transition year (49%, $n = 75$). Transition-year students included students from different grade levels (56% [$n = 42$] in sixth grade and 44% [$n = 33$] in seventh or eighth grade). The majority of the students self-identified as African American (38%, $n = 58$,) and Latino (32%, $n = 49$), followed by biracial or multiracial, part African American or Latino (27%, $n = 42$), and other (3%, $n = 5$). A majority of the students were eligible for free or reduced lunch price (58%, $n = 89$). These students were predominantly English-only speakers (81%, $n = 125$) and had parents or caregivers who had not completed college (83%, $n = 128$).

## Measures

**Demographics.** Student information collected from school records included gender, race/ethnicity, English language learner, lunch status, grade level, grade level pod, year at school, and transition status.

**School Belonging.** School belonging was measured by the 18-item Psychological Sense of School Membership scale (Goodenow & Grady, 1993; $\alpha = .85$). Students were asked to rate their agreement on items such as "It is hard for people like me to be accepted here."

**Mathematics Achievement.** Achievement measures included first-quarter math grades and California STAR Test (CST) math achievement scores (using continuous rather than proficiency scores) from prior and current school years.

**Socialization Scales.** Table 6.1 lists the scales and the psychometric properties of the scores in this sample. Developmental socialization included student perceptions of connection ("I can count on my parents [teachers] to help me out") and autonomy ("my parents ... tell me that I should not question them," and "how often are students' ideas used in the classroom?"). Academic socialization reflected educational aspirations ("How far in school do you think your parents [teachers] expect you to go?") and academic support ("How often do your parents [teachers] discuss your academic progress with you?"). Racial-ethnic socialization measured group connectedness ("My parents [teachers] have taught me that it is important to feel that I am part of my racial-ethnic community"), group achievement ("My parents [teachers] have taught me that it is important for my family and my racial-ethnic community that I succeed in school"), and awareness of racism ("My parents [teachers] have taught me that some people will treat me differently because I am [racial-ethnic group]").

Parallel measures of these three domains of socialization practices were created, with wording altered to apply to the teacher in general (given multiple teachers) or primary caregiver. Each set of items was yoked: students first answered all the questions within a domain based on their *real* experience and then completed a similar set of questions about their *ideal* experience. Scales were repeated four times: the home environment (real and ideal) and the school environment (real and ideal). Mismatch was calculated by subtracting the ideal score from the real score, using absolute

TABLE 6.1 Socialization Practices

| DOMAIN | MEASURE AUTHOR AND YEAR | # OF ITEMS (RESPONSE RANGE) | TEACHER α REAL/IDEAL | PARENT α REAL/IDEAL |
|---|---|---|---|---|
| **Developmental** | | | | |
| Connection | My parents–my teachers (Steinberg et al., 1994) | 9 (1–4) | .81/.80 | .71/.76 |
| Autonomy | My parents–parent (Steinberg et al., 1994) | 9 (1–5) | — | .67/.82 |
| | Decision making opportunity–student (Eccles & Midgley, 1989) | 7 (1–5) | .66/.69 | — |
| **Academic** | | | | |
| Expectations | Academic aspirations (Goldenberg et al., 2001) | 1 (1–7) | — | — |
| Involvement | Parental involvement (Reynolds, 1992) | 9 (1–3) | .67/.79 | .57/.84 |
| **Racial-Ethnic** | | | | |
| In-group connectedness | Racial-ethnic identity (Altschul et al., 2006) | 4 (1–5) | .92/.95 | .79/.89 |
| Embedded achievement | | 4 (1–5) | .87/.91 | .68/.86 |
| Awareness of racism | | 4 (1–5) | .89/.91 | .76/.79 |

differences. A score of a 0 indicates a match and the higher the score, the greater the perceived mismatch.

Students were also asked two open-ended questions about the barriers they experienced at school and at home: "What do you need in order to become a successful learner in this school" and "Are there things that make it difficult for your parents/guardians to be able to support you at school and with class work?" A thematic reading of student responses identified 12 types of barriers that impede learning, which were subsumed under the three conceptual domains (within person, school, and family) articulated by Adelman and Taylor (2010). Multiple responses from students were coded to indicate the frequency of endorsement for each category. Table 6.2 illustrates the categories, interrater agreement between two trained raters, and student rankings.

## Data Analysis

Data analysis included (1) an examination of nonparametric correlations among mismatch scores, transition status, and student demographic variables; (2) a series of paired $t$-tests to explore differences in student

TABLE 6.2 Student Perceptions of Barriers in Learning at School

| BARRIERS | INTERRATER AGREEMENT (%) | STUDENT ENDORSEMENT (%) | RANKED FREQUENCY |
|---|---|---|---|
| **Person Factors** | | | |
| Work habits | 95.5 | 46.4 | 3 |
| Attitude/behavior | 100.0 | 35.3 | 6 |
| **School Factors** | | | |
| School facility | 87.2 | 35.3 | 6 |
| Activities | 96.7 | 51.1 | 2 |
| Climate | 83.0 | 54.2 | 1 |
| Teachers | 90.8 | 42.5 | 4 |
| Peers | 85.0 | 13.7 | 10 |
| **Family Factors** | | | |
| Distance | 85.7 | 5.2 | 12 |
| Jobs | 98.0 | 31.4 | 8 |
| Demands | 54.9 | 23.5 | 9 |
| Understanding | 91.0 | 38.6 | 5 |
| Communication with school | 81.5 | 9.2 | 11 |

perceptions of real versus ideal environments in three contexts (school, home, and home–school), and (3) a series of hierarchical regressions to predict school belonging and math achievement. Because there was no significant relationship between grade-level pod (in which students were nested) and school belonging or math achievement scores, hierarchal linear modeling was not required.

In a series of hierarchical regressions to predict student school belonging ($N = 154$) and math achievement ($N = 115$) in the spring of the school year, we tested first the effects of first-quarter grades (for belonging) or prior-year math achievement (for year-end math achievement); second, transition status (new or returning student); third, the contribution of perceived mismatch (total score for school, home, and home–school mismatch); and fourth, the interaction between transition status and perceived mismatch in these three domains. A second series of hierarchical regressions tested the additive effect of real socialization practices in the classroom in predicting both school belonging and math achievement. As the results for the additive effect of real socialization practices were not significant for math achievement, we limit our discussion to the school belonging analysis. In this analysis, eight predictor variables were entered in three blocks to explain school belonging: first-quarter math grades in Block 1; total mismatch at school, home, and home–school in Block 2; and teachers' developmental socialization, academic expectations, academic involvement, and racial-ethnic socialization in Block 3. Because transition status and its interaction term were not significant in the previous regression analysis, they were dropped from this analysis.

## Student Perceptions of Mismatch and the Transition into the California College Preparatory Academy

### Mismatch Between Needs and Environment

In contrast to many studies, we found that student perceptions of mismatch in this setting—on any domain or any context—were not significantly greater for transition students than for continuing students. Instead, all students reported measurable gaps between their real and ideal environments at both home and school. Also, regardless of gender, ethnicity, income, or grade level, all students experienced similar degrees of mismatch between their needs and their reality in both school and home contexts. These results show us that, in the context of CAL Prep, perceived mismatch was not unique to the transition year and that perceptions of mismatch did not disadvantage one subgroup of students over another. One could say that there was equity of experience within this school environment.

Furthermore, the experience of mismatch was greater at school than at home. At school, significant differences between real and ideal ratings were found for five of seven socialization scales, with mismatch scores ranging from 1.76 (Cohen's $d$ = 0.40) for awareness of racism to 9.27 points ($d$ = 2.01) for autonomy. At home, mismatch scores had a narrower range (from 0.03 to 3.74), and only the autonomy scale showed a significant and meaningful difference ($d$ = 0.69). In the classroom, students reported less developmental socialization (connection and autonomy) and less racial-ethnic socialization than they would have ideally preferred—for example, "I need support . . . no strictness" at school. They also hoped that teachers would "help us and remind us who we [are] and where we come from [so we] are proud." However, with regard to academic socialization practices (expectations and help) at school, students did not experience a mismatch between what they received and what they wanted.

At home, students reported greater satisfaction of their needs. Here, the only significant mismatch was in autonomy, where, similar to their ratings of teachers, students wanted more autonomy from their primary caregivers than they received. At home, one student wanted parents "not to baby me so much," whereas in school, another student wished to be "doing what *we want* in class." Also given more mismatch at school than at home, five of the seven home–school comparisons were significant ($p_{corrected}$ < .002), with effect sizes ranging from 0.68 to 0.86. Importantly for this high-expectation setting, students rated their teachers and parents similarly with regard to academic expectations, with no significant differences in ratings between home and school.

## Predicting School Belonging

What did we learn about the role of transition status and perceptions of mismatch in how connected students felt to school? Tested with the full sample of 154 students, our regression model predicted only 14% of the variance in school belonging (see Table 6.3). Not surprisingly, students with higher first-quarter grades in math reported significantly more connection with school in the spring (explaining 3% of variance in school belonging). In this setting, however, beyond the effects of early achievement, transition status did not predict school connection, either alone or as

TABLE 6.3 Regression Predicting School Belonging and Current Year Math Achievement

| PREDICTORS | STUDENT OUTCOMES | | | | | | | |
|---|---|---|---|---|---|---|---|---|
| | SENSE OF SCHOOL BELONGING | | | | MATH STANDARDIZED ACHIEVEMENT TEST | | | |
| | ADJ. $R^2$ | $\Delta R^2$ | $B$ | $\beta$ | ADJ. $R^2$ | $\Delta R^2$ | $B$ | $\beta$ |
| Step 1: First-quarter math grade /Prior year math achievement[a] | .03* | .03 | 0.18 | .19* | .57*** | .57 | 0.69 | .76*** |
| Step 2: Years at school | .03 | .00 | -1.71 | -.07 | .59* | .02 | 18.54 | .13* |
| Step 3: Total school mismatch | .04 | .01 | -0.62 | -.17 | .59 | .00 | -0.42 | -.02 |
| Step 4: Total home mismatch | .11** | .07 | -1.14 | -.27* | .59 | .00 | -2.10 | -.10 |
| Step 5: Total home–school mismatch | .12 | .01 | -0.89 | -.18 | .60* | .01 | -3.81 | -.15* |
| Step 6: Total school mismatch × years at school | .14 | .02 | 1.44 | .36 | .61 | .01 | -5.99 | -.31 |
| Step 7: Total home mismatch × years at school | .14 | .00 | -0.79 | -.14 | .61 | .00 | -3.30 | -.13 |
| Step 8: Total home–school mismatch × years at school | .14 | .00 | 0.24 | .04 | .62* | .01 | -9.02 | -.32* |

NOTE: Adj. = Adjusted.
[a]First-quarter math grade was used to predict school belonging and prior year math achievement was used to predict current math achievement.
*$p < .05$. **$p < .01$. ***$p < .001$.

a moderator of the relationship between mismatch and belonging. Thus, transition students were as connected to school as were returning students, and the relationship between mismatch and school belonging was not stronger for transition students.

However, despite the finding that students reported greater mismatch at school, it was perceived mismatch at home that significantly predicted school belonging (accounting for 7% of the variance). Students who felt a greater gap between their needs and their environment at home reported less connection to school. We get a sense of what these less connected students felt they were missing at home from students' open-ended responses about their families:

> They never know all the details. Quick to judge me for things that aren't my fault.
> Doesn't gather all of the facts. Not involved. Not supportive.
> Sometimes they think things are easy when they're hard and then [they] pressure a lot.
> Study with me. Help me when I'm going through a problem.
> The help [from my parents] that would benefit my education ... to be a little more supportive.

Given that it was home mismatch, rather than school mismatch, that proved most predictive of student connection to school, we asked whether actual teacher practices in the domain of developmental, academic, and ethnic-cultural support made a difference to students— beyond the effects of unmet needs outside of school and early or prior achievement. In this analysis, 27% of school belonging was significantly predicted by our overall model. Beyond the effects of achievement and home mismatch, teachers' socialization practices (i.e., the real environment as reported by students) uniquely predicted an additional 14% of the variance in school belonging (see Table 6.4). In particular, higher connection to teachers and autonomy inside the classroom predicted higher school belonging, whereas in contrast, higher academic involvement by teachers predicted less connection to school (see Table 6.4). Neither academic expectations nor racial-ethnic socialization practices of teachers predicted school belonging.

Students who felt more connected to CAL Prep described the developmental support they received from teachers in these ways. Teachers tried to connect with them on a personal level ("check us and ask how our day was"), were caring ("treat me like they care about me"), offered advice

TABLE 6.4 Real Socialization versus Mismatch in Predicting School Belonging

| PREDICTORS | ADJ. $R^2$ | $\Delta R^2$ | $B$ | $\beta$ |
|---|---|---|---|---|
| Step 1: First-quarter math grade /prior year math achievement | .03* | .03 | 0.18 | .19* |
| Step 2: Total school mismatch | .13** | .10 | −0.01 | −.00 |
| Total home mismatch | | | −1.20 | −.29* |
| Total home–school mismatch | | | −0.90 | −.18 |
| Step 3: Teacher connection/autonomy | .27** | .14 | 3.53 | .52** |
| Teacher school expectations | | | 0.49 | .05 |
| Teacher academic involvement | | | −0.74 | −.19* |
| Teacher racial-ethnic socialization | | | 0.05 | .05 |

NOTE: Adj. = Adjusted.
*$p < .05$. **$p < .001$.

on personal life issues ("Ms. [J] give[s me] advice on everyday life struggles"), and helped students to feel less stressed ("relax and breath[e]"). Students also indicated that the teachers did not put them down ("do never put me down"), but provided encouragement ("keeps [up] my motivation"; "help us with our confidence"; "they don't give up on me"; and "you can do it, never give up on what you want").

These results highlight the important role of perceived mismatch at home (not the transition itself or mismatch at school) as a part of feeling less connected to CAL Prep. But importantly, beyond the mismatch effect, teachers' provision of support and autonomy in the class made a positive contribution to school connectedness. That we explained only 27% of the variability in school belonging suggests other explanatory factors not measured here. In a subsequent section, the open-ended responses of students provide additional clues.

## Predicting Math Achievement

We tested the same questions in a smaller sample of 115 students, for whom we had both prior-year and year-end math achievement scores. Overall, 62% of the variance in math achievement was accounted by our model (Table 6.3). As expected, higher prior-year math achievement predicted higher year-end math scores, explaining more than half of the variance. The other predictors added another 5% of unique variance in year-end math achievement, with the interaction between years at school and home–school mismatch having the highest beta.

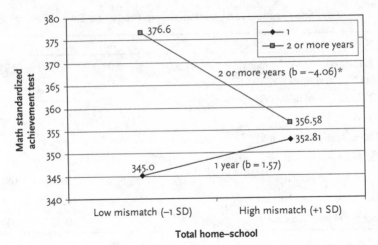

FIGURE 6.1. Total home–school mismatch, years at school, and math achievement.

These results mean that both transition status and perceptions of mismatch interacted in predicting math achievement, but not in the direction anticipated. Instead, beyond the effects of student achievement differences at entry, the mismatch between home and school predicted lower math achievement for returning, not transition, students (see Figure 6.1). For transition students, there were no significant differences in math performance under high versus low mismatch conditions. Again, these results fail to support the uniquely risky nature of the transition year. But they do underscore that the undermining of math achievement—in the face of a home–school mismatch—appears for continuing students alone, albeit with small effects.

Students' open-ended responses illuminate features of this home–school divide. Students report high parental expectations that match the high academic expectations of the school, but they also paint a sensitive picture of their parents' challenging lives, which leave them less able to academically support their students. Students report that their parents were unable to help because they did not have time or because they did not understand the subject matter, given their own educational level or differences in how subjects are currently taught. Here are some student comments:

Mom works 10 hours. Is very busy, has to help sisters [H.] and [G.]. Dad doesn't live with me, so can't help me. Mom sometimes doesn't know the material I need help on.

My parents have problems doing to[o] much work at their job. My parents can support [me] but only for a minimum time.

She don't now [know] how to read ingles. She has to go to work. Don't know how to do difficult math.

Well my mom went to second grade so can't really help me in homework and my dad is always working.

My mom didn't learn the same stuff we are learning now because we are learning new things.

This identified mismatch between home and school, between what the school expected and what parents could provide in terms of help, proved problematic for students in their subsequent years at CAL Prep, in response perhaps to even more challenging work.

## Students Identifying Barriers to their Success

Whereas the previous analyses used predetermined scales to assess student perceptions of mismatch between their needs and environments, this analysis draws from students' own words in describing what they experienced as barriers at CAL Prep. Fully 98% of the students reported barriers to their success in school and 75% described barriers at home that affected their work at school. As illustrated in Table 6.2, the most frequently cited barrier was school climate and the least cited barrier was the distance of families from this regional school. We also explored whether the reported barriers differed by the grade level of students. Using chi-square analyses of grade-level trends among the 12 types of barriers, we found only one significant grade-level difference. With each higher grade level, a greater proportion of students cited the limited range of activities in the school as a barrier, 34.0%, 39.3%, and 77.4%, for sixth, seventh, and eighth graders, respectively, $\chi^2 = 22.84$, $p < .001$.

We look here in more detail at the top five student barriers to success. The most frequently cited barriers reflected *school* (climate [1], activities [2], teachers [4]), *person* (student work habits [3]), and *family* (understanding [5]) domains. In their concerns about school climate, students pushed back against the structure and demands of the school. They preferred a school setting that was less strict and provided easier work: "I don't want them to expect so much from all of us as kids." They had a long list of wants: a more flexible dress code (with no uniforms and free dress), no summer or Saturday School, no exhibitions, longer recess and less homework, and no Friday or late detentions. They also desired a "high school feeling ... more freedom and privileges," "lockers so we don't have to carry around all those bags," and "CAL Prep on a larger campus instead of with little kids." And they wrote about autonomy: "if we had more freedom to choose classes" or "off-campus lunch because we are in high school," they would feel better about school. Some students missed their old school and friends, writing, "me being at my old school ... me not being here." Students also wanted a broader selection of "fun" activities that included dances, a football team, more clubs and sports, a school band, metal class, and more field trips—an opportunity to balance the hard academic work with development in other domains. As one student described it, "having time to express ourselves creatively would be awesome."

With regard to their teachers, although many students lauded the support of teachers, others asked for better, more helpful, and slower teaching, more teachers of color, more respect and understanding from teachers, and deeper relationships. Here are some comments:

> Teachers to explain more and not expect me to learn this in one day.
> I want the teachers to be nicer ... or to change some teachers.
> Talk to you more respectful instead of telling me to always sit down.
> Do more fun things with the teachers, have time to do, well, just talking about all of us, lastly to see what connections we have with the [teachers].

Students also recognized the challenges of classroom management, asking for better control of classrooms ("make the teachers who cannot control the students be able to control the students") and more severe consequences for disruptive and failing students ("to make the students who are rude and who do not try to get an education ... leave the school;" "To be more harder [meaner] to the bad students, suspend all the bad kids"). As one student commented, "I would like that only smart students stay at CAL Prep ... at the end of the year students with a D or F be kicked out." There was awareness that not all students were ready for or responding well to the high academic demands of CAL Prep. One student who did not perceive teachers as a barrier wrote, "nothing really 'caus the teachers are very helpful to us but sum student are not aprishitive."

Students also understood that their own work habits and attitudes needed to be changed in order to meet the high expectations of the school. As one student said, "you need to be prepared and ready to learn, supplies, and good learning skills, you need to focus, you need to study, you need to do all the work." Another student wrote that "in this school you need perseverance, a want to learn, and a positive attitude." For some students that meant "not to talk or think about boys and friends that much," "not to be lazy," and to "stay dedicated."

Among the parental barriers, more than one third of the students pointed to parental lack of understanding, either about the class material or about what is going on with the student in school or at home, as a critical impediment in their success. They did, however, recognize the tremendous strain on their parents. Among their examples are, "[my parent] does not know how to do the work," "they can't help me with my homework," "speaks and reads a different language," and "sometimes they think things are easy when they are not." Of interest, barriers that parents mentioned (see Chapter 7), such as physical distance from the school and parental communication with the school, were noted by very few students.

In summary, gleaned from students' own words, the biggest barriers for half of these early adolescent students lay in the rigorous academic and behavioral press of the school climate and in the dearth of fun and developmentally salient extracurricular activities. Importantly, this latter concern about limited activities increased with age. Although not tested here, these aspects of their school environment might have also interfered with their connection to CAL Prep.

## Lessons Learned

### A Note of Caution

As this was largely cross-sectional look at school transition, except for the achievement results, we cannot speak to adjustment to the transition nor determine the directionality of relationships, both of which are best tested with a longitudinal design. Although guided by theory about the temporal order of effects, it is also possible, for example, that students who feel less connected to school are prone to see more unmet needs at home, rather than vice versa. We were also limited by spring assessments (which may already reflect some form of adjustment for transition students) and transition into multiple rather than single grades (which makes it difficult to disentangle grade-level and transition effects).

However, this comparison of two cohorts of students—those new to CAL Prep (transition students) and those continuing for a second and third year (returning students)—has several strengths. We examined transition issues of minority and low-income youth in a high-expectation and early college middle school setting, one with a rigorous and nontracked curriculum for all students and with transition supports. We broadened the socialization practices studied (beyond developmental support to include academic and racial-ethnic practices) the contexts explored (including school, home, and home–school), and the types of measurement utilized (including real–ideal mismatch, real practices, and student-identified barriers). Finally, we systematically tested for domain-specific effects in two arenas of student functioning (school belonging and math achievement), most importantly, controlling for the effects of prior or early academic performance differences on these variables.

## Key Findings

For this group of largely low-income and ethnic minority sixth to eighth graders, the transition year at CAL Prep, as compared to the second or third year, did *not* carry with it greater unmet needs, less connection with school, and lower achievement. Indeed, for math alone, perceptions of greater mismatch between home–school environments predicted lower achievement for continuing but not transition students—in response, perhaps, to the progressively challenging work across the grades. Perhaps our design elements (cohort classes, advisories, and a homework period) did reduce the experienced disjunction for students between elementary and middle school. Or perhaps the transition into more complex school settings is a developmental process unfolding across multiple years, with cumulative disadvantage over time for students who are struggling (Benner & Graham, 2009). This finding underscores the importance of setting-comparative and longer-period studies in drawing conclusions about transition processes.

Thus, similar to the findings of Barber and Olsen (2004, 1997), perceptions of unmet needs were not a phenomenon of the transition year alone. And students viewed their home environment as closer to their ideal than the CAL Prep school environment—especially with regard to feelings of connection and ethnic-racial teaching. Yet there were two domains where student perceptions about home and school were more aligned. Students wanted more autonomy than they got, both at home and at school, and they reported similarly high academic expectations from both parents and teachers. And happily for a school concerned with equity of experience, perceived mismatch was not greater for any demographic group.

Even though students wished for more from their teachers, it was perceived mismatch outside of the school context—at home and between home and school—that proved to be predictive of their school belonging and math achievement, respectively. Different domains of perceived mismatch explained different domains of student functioning, which, themselves, were unrelated. For school connection, it was greater unmet needs at home that predicted less belonging. For achievement, it was greater home–school gaps that predicted lower performance in math. Also, the students who reported higher school connection were not necessarily the students with higher math achievement.

But inside school practices also mattered mightily. Most importantly, student reports of teachers' actual practices in the classroom (the real environment) emerged as an additive factor in predicting school belonging. Actual practices, as reported by students, had unique explanatory power, beyond the effects of student early grades and unmet needs at home. Specifically, higher developmental socialization from teachers at school (connection and autonomy but not racial-ethnic teaching or academic support) spelled greater belonging to school. Indeed, academic support had a negative relationship to school connection: more support was linked to less belonging. This finding could be explained by items on this measure that reflect support after (rather than before) academic failure, at which point it may be too late to nurture school engagement. In the domain of math achievement, however, there was no evidence of a similar additive factor.

Finally, although the data obtained across multiple measures of mismatch provide a consistent picture of student experience, the student-identified barriers also uncover another domain of mismatch, likely operative in a high-expectation school. These different instruments confirmed first, the students' need for a deep connection with teachers, and second, unmet needs at home (lack of understanding) and between home and school (lack of parental knowledge and help). However, a school climate of *too high* academic and behavioral demands—in the absence of *too few* fun and talent-expanding activities—also stood as a very large barrier in the eyes of students, a critical mismatch between their needs and the school environment. The enormous amount of work that students must do in order to be successful in a college-preparatory program comes as a great shock—given that these students arrive greatly underprepared and from schools with far lower academic expectations and given their dreams of a fuller and more "typical" middle and high school experience. A study by Julie Edmunds and colleagues (2010) of students who leave early college high schools points to these same barriers as the primary reasons given for school attrition, a pattern we saw as well in the early years of the school (see Chapter 9).

## Applying these Findings to California College Preparatory Academy

These findings shed new light on transition theory—underscoring the importance of studying transition processes in the context of school characteristics, over longer developmental periods, and through domain-specific links between types of mismatch and different student outcomes. For us, findings such as these shifted our thinking away from the transition year itself toward the availability of supports across all years needed to nurture the growth of academically underprepared students. Despite our initial interest in the role of academic support and ethnic and cultural practices, it proved to be connection with and autonomy from teachers that was related to student connection to school, importantly beyond the effects of unmet needs at home. Thus, we directed our efforts toward strengthening the capacity of teachers to connect with students and provide developmentally appropriate supportive teaching (e.g., Pianta & Hamre, 2009). We also sought additional opportunities to nurture student autonomy, for example, by having students take the lead in family–school conferences and serve as mentors to younger students. We did not compromise, however, on our high academic and behavioral expectations but interlaced these expectations with support. We worked hard to be what Lisa Delpit (2012) has called warm demanders—holding students accountable to high expectations but expressing care and concern in its communication.

By now, both the advisory and transition studies revealed student longing for a fuller development, so critical for adolescents. We expanded our program of enrichment opportunities and extracurricular activities, deemed as essential as our goals for academic and social-emotional learning. These findings also focused our attention on narrowing the home–school gap that students identified (in understanding and in academic help) and was found to be critical to math achievement. Mehan (2012) described similar conflicts between home and school among low-income minority students in the college-preparatory Preuss School at UC San Diego, where students reported that "they [parents] just don't understand what I am going through" (p. 96). Our students provided lots of suggestions about home–school communication. Some placed the onus on parents, suggesting that their parents needed to "meet with teachers," "find out what to do," and "review things on each subject I take." Others thought that the school needed to teach parents how to be helpful. Students indicated that there is a "lack of teacher[s] telling my parents what goes on at school." Students with Spanish-speaking parents reported that "there is not a lot of Spanish things" at school and their parents need "translators" at school. Students suggested that the school "teach them some of the curriculum I am learning."

The needs that students so eloquently raised in this chapter were met in subsequent years, evident to us in their own analyses of their educational trajectory at CAL Prep, which they presented as their senior exhibition projects. Culling from different student presentations, we learned about bumpy journeys with numerous challenges, including families that did not understand the demands of school and tremendous financial and personal struggles. But among the turning points that ultimately shifted a trajectory of failure toward success (acceptance at a 4-year college and a definite career plan) were membership on a team such as sports or debate, which offered skill development and mentorship opportunities; participation in a field or college trip, which deepened relationships with teachers; and love for just one subject-matter class, which prompted the comment "I love geometry". After rigorous questioning by peers and community judges, and a successful passing grade, these students reached for their cell phones to notify family, friends, and teachers alike, all awaiting news in the wings. Success was hard-earned and they owned it, as one student acknowledged in the quote that opens this chapter: "It is up to me if I want to learn or not."

## References

Adelman, H. S., & Taylor, L. (2010). *Mental health in schools: Engaging learners, preventing problems, and improving schools*. Thousand Oaks, CA: Corwin.

Altschul, I., Oyserman, D., & Bybee, D. (2006). Racial-ethnic identity in mid-adolescence: Content and change as predictors of academic achievement. *Child Development, 77*, 1155–1169. doi:10.1111/j.1467-8624.2006.00926.x

Alvidrez, J., & Weinstein, R. S. (1993). The nature of "schooling" in school transitions: A critical re-examination. *Prevention in Human Services, 10*, 7–26.

Anderman, E. M., & Mueller, C. E. (2010). Middle school transitions and adolescent development. In J. L. Meece & J. S. Eccles (Eds.). *Handbook of research on schools, schooling, and human development* (pp. 198–215). New York, NY: Taylor & Francis.

Barber, B. K., & Olsen, J. A. (1997). Socialization in context: Connection, regulation, and autonomy in the family, school, and neighborhood, and with peers. *Journal of Adolescent Research, 12*, 287–315. doi:10.1177/0743554897122008

Barber, B. K., & Olsen, J. A. (2004). Assessing the transitions to middle and high school. *Journal of Adolescent Research, 19*, 3–30. doi:10.1177/0743558403258113

Benner, A. D. (2011). The transition to high school: Current knowledge, future directions. *Educational Psychology Review, 23*, 299–321. doi:10.1007/s10648-011-9152-0

Benner, A. D., & Graham, S. (2009). The transition to high school as a developmental process among multiethnic urban youth. *Child Development, 80*, 356–376.

Delpit, L. (2012). *Multiplication is for White people: Raising expectations for other people's children.* New York, NY: The New Press.

DuBois, D. L., Eitel, S. K., & Felner, R. D. (1994). Effects of family environment and parent-child relationships on school adjustment during the transition to early adolescence. *Journal of Marriage and Family, 56*, 404–414. doi:10.2307/353108

Eccles, J. S., & Midgley, C. (1989). Stage/environment fit: Developmentally appropriate classrooms for early adolescence. In R. E. Ames & C. Ames (Eds.). *Research on motivation in education* (Vol. 3, pp. 139–186.). New York, NY: Academic Press.

Eccles, J. S., Midgley, C., Wigfield, A., Buchmanan, C. M., Reuman, D., Flanagan, C., & Mac Iver, D. (1993). Development during adolescence: The impact of stage-environment fit on young adolescents' experiences in schools and in families. *American Psychologist, 48*, 90–101. doi:10.1037/10254-034

Edmunds, J. A., Arshavsky, N., Unlu, F., Luck, R., & Bozzi, L. (2010, September). *"They try their best here to keep you": Lessons learned from a study of early high school leavers.* Greensboro, NC: SERVE Center at the University of North Carolina at Greensboro.

Goldenberg, D., Gallimore, R., Reese, L., & Garnier, H. (2001). Cause or effect? A longitudinal study of immigrant Latino parents' aspirations and expectations, and their children's school performance. *American Educational Research Journal, 38*, 547–582. doi:10.3102/00028312038003547

Goodenow, C., & Grady, K. E., (1993). The relationship of school belonging and friends' values to academic motivation among urban adolescent students. *Journal of Experimental Education, 62*, 60–71. doi:10.1080/00220973.1993.9943831

Grolnick, W. S., Kurowski, C. O, Dunlap, K. G., & Hevey, C. (2000). Parental resources and the transition to junior high. *Journal of Research on Adolescence, 10*, 465–488. doi:10.1207/SJRA1004_05

Gutman, L. M., & Midgley, C. (2000). The role of protective factors in supporting the academic achievement of poor African American students during the middle school transition. *Journal of Youth and Adolescence, 29*, 223–248. doi:10.1023/A:1005108700243

Hanewald, R. (2013). Transition between primary and secondary school: Why is it important and how can it be supported. *Australian Journal of Teacher Education, 36*, 62–74. doi.org/10.14221/ajte2013v38n1.7

Hughes, D., Rodriguez, J., Smith E. P., Johnson, D. J., Stevenson, H. C., & Spicer, P. (2006). Parents' ethnic-racial socialization practices: A review of research and directions for future study. *Developmental Psychology, 42*, 747–770. doi:10.1037/0012-1649.42.5.747

Jeynes, W. H. (2003). A meta-analysis: The effects of parental involvement on minority children's academic achievement. *Education and Urban Society, 35*, 202–218. doi:10.1177/0013124502239392

Jeynes, W. H. (2005). A meta-analysis of the relation of parental involvement to urban elementary school student academic achievement. *Urban Education, 40,* 237–269. doi:10.1177/0042085905274540

Kuperminc, G. P., Darnell, J. D., & Alverz-Jimenez, A. (2008). Parent involvement in the academic adjustment of Latino middle and high school youth: Teacher expectations and school belonging as mediators. *Journal of Adolescence, 31,* 469–483. doi:10.1016/j.adolescence.2007.09.003

Langenkamp, A. G. (2015). Academic vulnerability and resilience during the transition to high school: The role of social relationships and district context. *Sociology of Education, 83,* 1–19. doi:10.1177/0038040709356563

Lopez, L. C., Sanchez, V. V., & Hamilton, M. (2000). Immigrant and native-born Mexican-American parents' involvement in a public school: A preliminary study. *Psychological Reports, 86,* 521–525. doi:10.2466/PR0.86.2.521-525

Mehan. H. (2012). *In the front door: Creating a college-going culture of learning.* Boulder, CO: Paradigm.

National Mathematics Advisory Panel. (2008). *Foundations for success: The final report of the National Mathematics Advisory Panel.* Washington, DC: U.S. Department of Education. Retrieved from http://www2.ed.gov/about/bdscomm/list/mathpanel/report/final-report.pdf

Oyserman, D., Harrison, K., & Bybee, D. (2001). Can racial identity be promotive of academic efficacy? *International Journal of Behavioral Development, 25,* 379–385. doi:10.1080/01650250042000401

Pianta, R. C., & Hamre, B. K. (2009). Conceptualization, measurement, and improvement of classroom processes: Standardized observation can leverage capacity. *Educational Researcher, 38,* 109–119. doi:10.3102/0013189X09332374

Régner, I., Loose, F., & Dumas, F. (2009). Students' perception of parental and teacher academic involvement: Consequences of achievement goals. *European Journal of Psychology of Education, 24,* 263–277. doi:10.1007/BF03173016

Reynolds, A. J. (1992). Comparing measures of parental involvement and their effects on academic achievement. *Early Childhood Research Quarterly, 7,* 441–462. doi:10.1016/0885-2006(92)90031-S

Sami, N. (2011). *Student perceptions of school and family socialization: Predictors of adjustment in the transition to an early-college secondary school* (Doctoral dissertation). Available from ProQuest Dissertations and Theses database. (UMI No. 3449067)

Seidman, E., Lambert, L. E., Allen, L., & Aber, J. L. (2003). Urban adolescents' transition to junior high school and protective family transactions. *Journal of Early Adolescence, 23,* 166–193. doi:10.1177/0272431603023002003

Steinberg, L., Lamborn, S.D., Darling, N., Mounts, N.S., & Dornbusch, S. (1994). Over-time changes in adjustment and competence among adolescents from authoritative, authoritarian, indulgent, and neglectful families. *Child Development, 64,* 754–770. doi:10.2307/1131416

Trickett, E. J., & Moos, R. H. (2002). *A social climate scale: Classroom Environment Scale manual: Developmental, applications, research* (3rd. ed.). Palo Alto, CA: Mind Garden.

Weinstein, R. S. (2002). *Reaching higher: The power of expectations in schooling.* Cambridge, MA: Harvard University Press.

Wigfield, A., Lutz, S. L., & Wagner, A. L. (2005). Early adolescents' development across the middle school years: Implications for school counselors. *Professional School Counseling, 9,* 112–119.

# 7 | Parent Involvement and the Home–School Divide

NILOFAR SAMI, FRANK C. WORRELL, AND RHONA S. WEINSTEIN

*"I need more feedback from teachers when he needs to do better . . . I don't need to find out from a report card."* (Parent)

*"Check in with teachers periodically . . . attend Sat. School and info nights."* (Teacher)

As a REGIONAL SECONDARY SCHOOL, California College Preparatory Academy (CAL Prep) faced special challenges in building family–school connections, given the distance parents needed to travel to the school. Yet CAL Prep worked hard to create a partnership with families, with involvement practices that spanned all six types of the typology identified by Epstein and colleagues (2009). Epstein (2001) argued that parental involvement has been too narrowly defined by (1) participation (volunteering, attending school functions, and membership in parent–teacher associations), (2) creating home environments and rules that support academic learning, and (3) helping children with homework. Often, parents from low-income and ethnically and linguistically diverse communities find these school-driven expectations of parental involvement challenging and difficult to meet (Jackson & Remillard, 2005; Ramirez, 2001).

Moreover, recent research has demonstrated that there are a variety of ways that parents—particularly those from diverse groups—are involved in their children's learning, with positive links to achievement (Jeynes, 2010; Pomerantz, Moorman, & Litwack, 2007). These more home-centered supports include parents holding high academic expectations and sharing the value of education (Gill & Reynolds, 1999); parent–child communication that is open, supportive, and loving (Rimm-Kaufman & Pianta, 2005); and a parenting style that is high on both support and structure (Steinberg, Lamborn, Darling, Mounts, & Dornbusch, 1994).

The parent involvement typology developed by Epstein and colleagues (2009) characterizes a fuller range of both home-centered and school-centered practices that parents might engage in and that schools might strengthen in building positive family–school partnerships. The six types of involvement include (1) parenting skills at home that support the intellectual, social-emotional, and behavioral development of their children; (2) learning activities at home that include homework help and academic monitoring; (3) bilateral communication between home and school about school programs and student progress; (4) volunteering in and attending school events; (5) involvement in decision-making at school through a parent or parent–teacher organization; and (6) collaboration with community resources that provide services to families, students, and the school.

In Year 3, more emphasis was placed on promoting bilateral communication between home and school around the development of shared expectations. These practices included (1) transparent recruitment (advertising for a first-generation college population and encouraging school visits prior to enrollment); (2) a signed contract (committing both parents and students to school participation); (3) a newsletter sent to students, teachers, and parents; (4) an open invitation to make appointments with teachers; (5) quarterly family–school conferences that were student-led; (6) scheduled coffee hours (the "second cup of coffee") with parents and administrative staff as a forum for suggestions and concerns; and (7) a parent satisfaction survey at the end of each academic year.

In addition, opportunities for skill-building (parenting strategies, academic help at home) took place most often in four Saturday Schools spread across the school year, which parents and their students were urged to attend. Parental volunteers were sought to help with school events. A Parent Advisory Council operated to provide feedback to the school and to develop programs to increase parent participation. The annual parent satisfaction survey could also be seen as a governance opportunity, because the merit increases of both teachers and principal were based in part on the ratings received from parents. Community collaborations included events on the University of California (UC) Berkeley Campus to which parents and students were invited.

Yet despite the parent involvement practices in place at CAL Prep at this time, all of us witnessed the struggles of parents to adjust to the high academic expectations of the school. And, as we saw in Chapter 6, some students experienced a home–school mismatch, with implications for their achievement in mathematics (math). We asked ourselves how we could learn more about this divide between home and school that could improve our practices. In Year 3, we examined the involvement practices of parents as well as the barriers experienced by both parents and teachers, so that we could determine the nature of the work ahead of us in building a stronger collaboration between home and school. In framing our approach to this investigation, we first looked to the research literature.

## Research on Parent Involvement

Both home and school environments play a critical and interactive role in supporting student engagement in learning and student achievement (Bronfenbrenner, 1979; Pomerantz & Moorman, 2010). The research literature shows that students of more involved parents have stronger academic performance at both the elementary (Jeynes, 2005b) and secondary (Jeynes, 2005a, 2007) school levels. Moreover, recent meta-analytic work (Jeynes, 2012) yielded effect sizes of 0.29 and 0.35 for pre-elementary/elementary and secondary students, respectively, suggesting that the positive effects of more involved parents on achievement are similar across the grade levels. Yet at a time when parental support is still needed, students experience a decrease in parent involvement in the transition from elementary to secondary school (Eccles, et al., 1993; Kuperminc, Darnell, & Alvarez-Jimenez, 2008).

There is also evidence of a parent involvement gap that may disadvantage some students over others. Families from higher socioeconomic levels and with higher educational attainment report greater involvement (Jeynes, 2005a, 2005b). Furthermore, the type of involvement varies by the socioeconomic status and ethnic-cultural background of families (Lareau & Calarco, 2012). These findings point to the importance of examining the ecologies of parent involvement in context. Families living in poor, urban environments may experience additional stressors (e.g., fewer social and community service supports) that can have a negative impact on their adjustment to the demands of school environment (Seidman, Lambert, Allen, & Aber, 2003). In addition, adolescents in urban schools, more likely to be African American and Latino, often experience greater incongruence between attitudes and values at home and at school (Lee & Bowen, 2006). This disconnect may loom larger in the context of the high expectations of a college-preparatory secondary school for a first-generation college population.

A disconnect between home and school may arise when parents from diverse backgrounds need assistance in how they can be involved but appropriate help is not provided (Chavkin & Williams, 1989; Williams & Sanchez, 2013), or when the school view of parental involvement may differ from that of parents (Lloyd-Smith & Baron, 2010). For example, Ramirez (1999) reported that some teachers wanted parental involvement to be limited to communication (what Barge and Loges [2010] have described as information transmission), whereas some parents envisioned a deeper partnership. Conflict is possible when home-centered parenting strategies—particularly those from low-income and diverse groups—are not acknowledged or appreciated by the school (Jeynes, 2010; Pomerantz et al., 2007). Conflict can also occur when the academic demands of school are not understood or are so great that they cannot be met by struggling families or by students with extensive family responsibilities and culturally different obligations (Mehan, 2012).

Although parent involvement implies action on the part of parents, the onus is on the school to foster a collaborative family–school partnership that supports student learning (Epstein, 2001). Indeed, the provisions of No Child Left Behind (2002), which hold schools accountable for students meeting academic proficiency standards, also mandate that schools actively involve parents in their children's education.

In this chapter, we turn our attention to parent involvement practices and the relationship between parents and teachers as they nurture students on their academic journey. Learning from this literature, we examine the challenges that both parents and teachers face and the types of help they need—parents from the school and teachers from parents—to better support student attainment. Finally, we share how CAL Prep used what was learned from this study to inform changes in school practices.

## Method

### Participants

The study was carried out from mid-March 2008 to mid-June 2008. We focused on the middle school population, inviting parents of all sixth to eighth grade students to participate. The final parent sample ($N = 64$) represented a little more than a third (37%) of the primary caregivers of the 174 eligible students. Caregivers were predominantly mothers ($n = 51$, 80.0%) from low-income backgrounds ($n = 42$, 65.6%) and spread across educational levels [did not complete high school ($n = 5$, 7.8%), graduated from high school ($n = 14$, 21.9%), completed some college ($n = 20$, 31.3%), and had a 4-year degree or more ($n = 15$, 23.5%); missing data ($n = 10$, 15.6%)]. Student characteristics reflected diversity in ethnicity [African American ($n = 22$, 34.4%), Latino ($n = 21$, 32.8%), and biracial/multiracial ($n = 19$, 29.7%)] and gender ($n = 35$, 54.7%).

Students in all three grade levels were represented in this sample: sixth ($n = 21$, 32.8%), seventh ($n = 25$, 39.1%), and eighth ($n = 18$, 28.1%). Although the students of participating caregivers did not differ significantly from the students of nonparticipants on demographic characteristics, achievement, and attendance, they did have significantly fewer detentions. The teacher sample included 11 of the 12 teachers (92%) and all were early-career teachers with fewer than 10 years of experience. Eighty-two percent of these teachers were female and 58% were European American.

## Interview/Survey Questions

Primary caregivers were asked three open-ended questions in an hour-long interview:

What kinds of things do you do and say to support your child in school?

Are there things that make it difficult for you to be able to support your child at school and with schoolwork?

What kind of help do you need to support your child at school and with class work?

Interviews were conducted in the primary caregiver's preferred language, with 72% ($n = 46$) conducted in English and 28% ($n = 18$) conducted in Spanish. Teachers completed a survey where they were asked a question similar to the third question for parents: "What kind of help do you need from parents to be able to support your students at school and with classwork?"

Responses for each question were coded for the *presence* (1) or *absence* (0) of each of the six types of involvement (parenting, learning at home, home–school communication, volunteering, school decision-making, and community collaborations) identified by Epstein and colleagues (2009).

Interrater agreement for each of the six categories and for parents and teachers was high, with interclass coefficients of 0.78 to 1.0 in a two-way mixed effects model. Frequency counts were tabulated by question and by parent involvement type. Open-ended responses were examined to capture the themes raised by parents and teachers.

## Results

### Parent Involvement Practices

Table 7.1 shows the range of parental involvement practices reported by this sample of caregivers, with most noting their use of parenting and academic learning strategies at home (98.4% and 67.2%, respectively). Parents emphasized that they provided social-emotional support, shared their valuing of education, and created home environments conducive to learning. As one parent said, "I hug him or simply speak to him, telling him not to get discouraged, to relax, take breaks, and then continue doing his homework."[1] Another parent talked about setting limits—"I set boundaries upon electronics, schedules. No games on Monday through Thursday." And a third parent reported emphasizing the longer term utility of being in school, telling her daughter that "she will have a better life, better things, better economic situation, and not have to work as hard as her family."

Parental academic support ranged from providing academic resources to assisting with homework. For example, one parent noted that if her son did not understand something, "he can ask his [older] sister or I will take him to the library or search on the internet." This theme of providing assistance in completing schoolwork or finding someone who could do so was present in many of the responses, as illustrated in the following comment: "Have you done your homework? Is there anything you need help with? I'm here for anything you need. If I can't help you, I will find someone who can." Interestingly, although more than half of all parents provided academic resources, far fewer parents assisted their child by directly helping with homework.

In contrast, and despite the structures designed to facilitate these activities (e.g., Saturday School, second cup of coffee), only a small minority of parents report engaging in communication activities between home

---

[1] All quotations from parents and teachers were taken verbatim from their completed interviews or surveys, with no changes made to syntax or spelling.

TABLE 7.1 Parent Involvement Practices and Help Needed

| | PARENT (N = 64) | | | TEACHER (N = 11) |
|---|---|---|---|---|
| | PRACTICES (%) | DIFFICULTIES (%) | HELP NEEDED (%) | HELP NEEDED (%) |
| **Home-Centered** | | | | |
| Parenting at home | 98.4 | 10.9 | 9.4 | 41.7 |
| Learning at home | 67.2 | 17.2 | 17.2 | 66.7 |
| **Home–School** | | | | |
| Home–school communication | 9.4 | 18.8 | 42.2 | 58.3 |
| **School-Centered** | | | | |
| Volunteering/ participation | 12.5 | 48.4 | 0.0 | 0.0 |
| School decision-making | 3.1 | 0.0 | 21.9 | 0.0 |
| Community collaboration | 1.6 | 0.0 | 0.0 | 0.0 |

and school and in school-based activities such as volunteering, school decision-making, and community collaboration (see Table 7.1):

> When the teachers call, I show up, I'm there . . . part of second cup of coffee parenting group.
> [I] come to school and go to her class.
> I always try to go to the meeting because she [my child] gets happy when I go.

## Difficulties: A Divide Between Home and School

It is important to underscore that a small minority (18%) of these parents did not face any difficulties supporting their child, because their child was doing well or they had access to resources or the school was doing its part. For example, parents made the following comments:

> He doesn't really ask me for help with school work since he already knows.
> She pretty much does it herself. I like when she stays after school to do homework, that's been a great help . . . I can help her but not a whole lot. After-school help, I encourage it.

I am very resourceful. If I can't help him, I will find someone to help him. We are able to handle everything.

Teachers do a good job alerting me when there are issues to do with focus and achievement, we stay on top of support issues ... Once we learn there are problems, we manage them.

The teachers already make themselves available—I will ask them if I do need their help.

However, the majority of the parents in this sample reported difficulties. Furthermore, an examination of the patterns in Table 7.1 also shows a gap between teachers and parents in the domains where they express the need for help from each other. Although most parents felt comfortable with their home-centered strategies (with less than 20% expressing the need for help from the school on parenting and learning concerns), a substantial percentage of teachers identified these home-centered strategies as domains where more parental help was required. On the other hand, with regard to home–school communication, more than 40% of the parents and almost 60% of the teachers underscored the need for more help from each other. Almost 50% of the parents reported that they had difficulty with volunteering and participating in school events and 20% of the parents wanted a role in school decision-making, but these were not domains noted by teachers. The comments from parents and teachers suggest that both groups perceived a lack of support from the other side, with specific expectations about the ways each side could provide more support to students. These differences in perceptions about where help is needed (and what kind of help) are illustrated in these next sections.

## Home-Centered Practices

Some parents reported difficulties in assisting their children with homework and providing social-emotional support. Parents wanted to be academically involved, but they faced challenges that were related to limited academic skills, the language barrier, or time constraints. Therefore, students who asked for academic help at home were not always able to get it:

Her school work and assignments—I don't understand them and so can't help her. I try to do the tutoring if the assignments are something I know.

Considering I've been out of school ... things are very different, not like how things were when parents were in school.

I can help him but math is hard for me . . . I don't understand some of his homework, I only went to high school and my level is low compared to (his) homework . . .

Being a single parent makes it difficult because you have to work and do the overall general house maintenance. I'm running in so many directions all the time. When she ask me for help on homework, she has to wait and there's a long delay before I can actually help her.

Parents looked to the school and teachers to provide more support for them so that they could better support their sons and daughters. These parents shared that "Saturday School had become less useful when it stopped showing parents how to help students" and suggested that "if examples [of math] were sent home, they would be able to assist with homework." Other parents asked for help in explaining the relevance of the work to the students, as they themselves did not understand the point of the assignment. Some parents called for improvements in the tutoring services to support students outside of the classroom. One parent said that

The school needs more centralized tutoring sessions . . . When she [her daughter] went to the after school tutoring program, it was a free for all. She was there for nothing, just socializing and I took her out of it. She would get home with no homework done. It was a complete waste of time. Even if there were no structures, there should be quiet time so at least she could get some work done. However, it would be more useful if it was more structured, and if there was quality tutor time where they could help with the things she's having difficulty with.

Teachers also experienced difficulty in supporting students academically. They felt drained and could not provide extra help to compensate for the perceived lack of direct academic support from home. Teachers reported not having enough time and resources or noted that the large number of students requiring help made it difficult to provide assistance to everyone who needed it. One teacher put it this way:

Time. Too many other commitments within the school so we don't have time to meet. If we meet with staff, we can't support kids. If we meet with kids, we don't have time to meet with staff. Large work load—teaching too many different classes. 120 students with three different preps . . . Always rushed.

Another teacher described feeling overwhelmed: "The sheer number of students who need support makes it nearly impossible to help them all . . . Sometimes I don't have the tools/materials I need to be able to help students (broken copiers, clear directions, supplies, etc.)."

From the teachers' perspective, most believed that the parents could provide more direct and indirect academic support for their children. One teacher suggested that parents create a more "structured and monitored homework time with expectation of one to two hours per night," engage in the "development of discussion skills and time to read/review together," and "check binders, backpacks, and supplies regularly." The sentiment about checking up on completed homework every night was repeated by several teachers, and one teacher added that parents who were familiar with classroom content should help "students with homework and study." Teachers also perceived that there were things that parents were not doing or could do more of, such as talking "to their student about the importance of an education," providing "space/time for schoolwork (no television, no siblings to watch)," and establishing "consequences at home for poor grades or poor attitude."

In contrast to the above differences, parents and teachers expressed similar challenges in providing social-emotional support to students due to their poor attitudes and motivation. One parent reported:

> I have nothing to motivate (him). He loves sports and engineering stuff, both of which CAL Prep does not provide, so I am at a loss on how to best motivate him. I need help . . . I'm not winning the race with them. I say to them but my words just go in one ear and come out the other.

Another mother stated (regarding her daughter), "I ask her questions about homework, etc. She always says she gets it but sometimes I [find] out she doesn't get it. For some reason she doesn't take up my offer to help." Another parent described her need for help with her daughter's attitude ("hormones—going through her right now"), as all she gets is "attitude and sarcasm." Most importantly, teachers expressed concerns similar to those of parents regarding how to foster students' positive attitudes and social-emotional functioning. As one teacher noted, "[if] students don't meet me half way, it's difficult to [get] their best out of them." Another teacher underscored that it is "difficult for myself to always find the method in which to motivate students."

## Home–School Communication

Both parents and teachers also reported difficulty around home–school communication to support student learning. Both sides expected that it was the responsibility of the other side to improve the communication across the divide. The general theme for many of the parents was the need for more complete, understandable, reliable, and timely communication from the school. One parent was concerned about English fluency: "I speak broken English, so I can't really translate what I want to say to the teachers and school. It's a big barrier for me. " Another found the school's outreach unclear: the "binder [is] so confusing and stakes [are] high with it. Not having a good place to go to at school to know what expectations and things [are] need." A third parent expressed tremendous frustration in communicating with the school around her child's disability:

> I gave CAL Prep a lot of information on him and his IEP but they didn't do anything . . . At first I was getting feedback and then that stopped. Only teacher [Ms. A.] gave feedback. [The teacher's] responses were reactionary and I wanted her to let me know early so that I can help fix the behavioral problems at home and not tell me 3 to 4 weeks later. I expect for him to obtain a good education for later in life. The fact that I wasn't getting the feedback I asked for . . . and it felt like a slap in the face.

Other parents felt that CAL Prep was so complicated that they needed much more information than would be necessary at other school sites. One parent said, "I need a week-long course at CAL Prep and how it works. I need to be overly briefed. I need connections with other people." Several parents also wanted an easier way to reach teachers, especially around student work. For example, one parent wanted an "easier way to get in contact with teachers. I know there's a website but it's not user friendly. If I e-mail a teacher, I would like a response back." Another parent wanted more timely notifications of poor academic performance:

> I need more feedback from the teachers when he needs to do better . . . . I don't need to find out from the report card. I need to know when his grades start dropping so there's time to bring it back up. They don't have to call me since I'm at the school, they can tell me when they walk by . . . a couple of words.

Similar sentiments were expressed about information on homework and projects "so that I know what she needs to do for school and homework— and what to expect from the teachers."

One parent lamented about the need for more timely communication and suggested that the school should not depend on students to convey information home:

> Have more notice of when things are going to happen. For example, if they have a field trip, I will get a note 2 days in advance and that's just not enough time to plan. Communicate better—usually parents know of school field trips or activities through word of mouth through the kids. And kids are just not reliable and not good with details . . . The solution should be e-mails directly from school to parents regarding notification of school trips or field trips or general announcements etc., and should *not* depend on the kids to tell these information to the parents.

Teachers also reported difficulties with home–school communication, but they expected parents to take more responsibility. Therefore, teachers perceived parents as not being responsive to the school's communication when school reached out. One teacher noted that "parents are not checking in with students on academic progress" and another underscored the problem of "families that are difficult to reach." Teachers wanted parents to take more initiative to attend school meetings, check the school website, and call them. Teachers wanted parents to "check in with teacher periodically [and] attend Sat School and info nights," as well as "check Power School regularly to know if work isn't being turned in." In addition, a teacher wanted parents to take the initiative to "talk to me to check in on their students' progress. They can tell me about their child and needs I may not know about." Teachers shared that it was difficult for them to communicate with all families and wanted "families to understand that I need to support 90 students and they need to step up and support their students by contacting me rather than expecting me to make every call. I cannot feasibly contact every student who misses an assignment. It isn't possible."

## School-Centered Practices

Parental participation in volunteering, school events, and the parent advisory organization proved difficult and was limited largely due to lack of time:

My commute. Traveling distance from work to home. I leave at
5 p.m.—even though it's a reverse commute, it's still far. Thus, I often
miss parent meetings after school, or meetings held during afternoons,
I have to miss all those. If I attend, I would have to take time from
work or half day from work.

Time—just not enough hours in the day. I would love to be more
involved in school, would love to be more active in school or in her
classes if I had more time.

I have work and school and my husband works so we're not actually
able to be at the school all the time and help with classroom activities,
but we make sure we go to all the other needed stuff.

Hard for me to come in . . . because of my classes.

Saturday School is a great idea, it is not always available for me to
attend.

However, one parent who had the time indicated that there were other
concerns as well: "When I go to his classes, I'm not being utilized. I'd like
to be utilized, not just sit. I don't see a real draw, from teacher to parent."
Still another parent noted tension between ethnic groups within the school,
having an impact on Latino families in particular, who were joining the
school in growing numbers: "(This is) the African American area . . . since
they tell us that we don't belong there and to go back to our schools . . .
I feel that this is not such a problem for our (son), it is a problem I experience with other parents."

Although few parents were or wished to be involved in school decision-
making, some parents did feel the need for greater input into the practices
of the school. Their comments reflected changes that they wanted to see in
the school rather than ways in which parents could participate in decision-
making. For example, parents suggested that the school needed (1) "different ways to monitor the children" with regard to discipline, (2) a more
centralized and organized tutoring system, (3) better classroom organization, and (4) larger classrooms. And although teachers expected volunteer
help and parental attendance at school events, they, too, did not envision a
role for parents in school policy-making.

## Discussion

As we interpret these results, a note of caution is in order, regarding the
small and potentially nonrepresentative sample of parents who participated.

Although 92% of the teachers participated, only 37% of the parents did—a little more than a third of the caregiver sample. Moreover, as previously indicated, the parents who participated in the interviews had students with fewer disciplinary infractions, suggesting that these interview comments might be a conservative estimate of parental concerns. However, it is also possible that this sample reflects the subset of parents who harbored the most concerns. Nonetheless any concerns, even from a minority of parents, need to be addressed.

This study also reflects a number of strengths, seen in the inclusion of both parent and teacher perspectives, a differentiated examination of parent involvement (home, school, and between home and school), and the use of mixed methods. The qualitative data paint a vivid picture of the concerns of parents and teachers, and the quantitative analysis of reported difficulties within domains allows us to contrast their views, a rare comparison. It is such a comparison that enables us to see both parents and teachers as struggling with different as well as similar problems that need better support.

Among the findings, most parents reported active home-based involvement—first, in providing social-emotional and motivational support to their children, and second, in offering academic support at home. But parents did struggle with volunteering and participation at school (in activities or governance), the most traditional of parental involvement strategies. They also identified problems in helping their students academically and in home–school communication. Similar to findings in the literature, CAL Prep parents reported experiencing barriers to providing direct academic support because of language barriers, not recalling material learned during their own schooling, not understanding the high-level course work, or not completing high school (Jackson & Remillard, 2005; Ramirez, 2001, 2002; Williams & Sanchez, 2013). However, parents were resourceful in finding alternative supports when they were not able to directly help their students with homework. The commitment of parents to "resource-providing" home-based involvement reflects an important, but often overlooked, support for students (Pomerantz & Moorman, 2010, p. 402).

The most important lesson here is that parents and teachers saw things differently, with a gap in perceptions about how much support was provided by each side as well as a gap in expectations about who was responsible for providing support to the students. Parents and teachers were engaged in a delicate dance of learning about contextual constraints on both sides, earning trust of the other and opening the door for communication. As one teacher noted, "I need parents to trust that I have their child's best interest in mind." And as a parent underscored, "I need to feel that there is space here at the school for parents to be in." Perhaps one of the most surprising aspects of these findings, and difficult for us to hear, was the similarity of these findings with concerns raised in the extant literature on parental involvement despite a set of structures put in place to make CAL Prep different.

## Home–School Mismatch

This home–school mismatch was seen in all three domains of home-centered, home–school communication, and school-centered practices. Although almost every parent reported home-based efforts to support their children's academic aspirations and indeed asked for additional help around academics, teachers believed that parents could do more in the academic domain, especially around homework. What parents did not understand was that teachers themselves were feeling overwhelmed with the underpreparedness of so many of their students and turned to parents for additional support. What teachers did not fully appreciate was that parents were not up to the academic challenge of homework help, without more information about *how* to support their children's learning activities. Also, teachers were unaware of the other forms of parental support at home and its importance to student attainment (Jackson & Remillard, 2005; Pomerantz & Moorman, 2007; Ramirez, 2002).

Although both parents and teachers identified home–school communication as a problem, both sides expected the other side to take the initiative. Teachers wanted parents to "check in" with the school more frequently, to attend the Saturday schools and information nights regularly, and to use the online system to check up on their children's performance. They interpreted the communication difficulties as a lack of concern on the part of parents and an unwillingness to reach out to the school. On the other hand, parents felt that there was not enough communication from the school: they viewed the communication received as often unclear, not timely, and they wanted the school do to more. Both sides also experienced difficulty in reaching each other.

Despite the fact that parents supported their students at home, there was a strong expectation for school-based involvement—an expectation especially difficult for low-income, minority parents to meet (Jackson & Remillard, 2005; Ramirez, 2001). Parental obstacles were predominantly related to time constraints and not being able to take time off from work. Teachers expressed frustration when parents could not come to the school, attributing their absence as a reflection of disinterest in their children's learning. These erroneous perceptions of parents find support in the research literature (Carreón, Drake, & Barton, 2005; Jackson & Remillard, 2005; Pomerantz & Moorman, 2010). This is not surprising for two reasons: (1) most teacher education programs do not specifically prepare teachers to collaboratively engage with diverse families (Epstein et al., 2009) and (2) schools often do not set a clear and effective structure for communication to flow in both directions (Ramirez, 2001). Although teachers and schools heavily emphasize school-centered supports, they fail to realize the critical role that they play in encouraging home-centered supports, which are more important (Pomerantz & Moorman, 2010).

## Bridging Home and School Through Use of Parent Feedback

The views of these CAL Prep parents, alongside those of teachers—obtained early in the evolution of the school in Year 3—provided the school with important information to guide our program development. Although we believed we had created a welcoming school environment that facilitated frequent and trusting communication with families, it was clear that the practices in place were not working as effectively for parents, teachers, and students as they could. In response, the school made a number of changes that included more on-site academic support for students, more timely and individualized outreach to parents, more support for teachers in professional development, and educational programs for parents. In Year 3, when these interviews and surveys were obtained, the school had redirected its resources to hire a dean of students. The dean's role was designed to focus on improving the school climate and developing early interventions around student academic and behavioral difficulties that would reengage these students in classroom learning. This dean became the school's third principal at the beginning of the fourth year, and served four years in that role, which allowed her to institutionalize many of the strategies that she had begun developing (see Chapter 13).

One of the parents' greatest concerns was their inability to assist student with homework. This concern was also shared by students, with implications for their math achievement (see Chapter 6), and teachers, who argued that they could not realistically provide individual support to so many students in need. The school day was extended to include an eighth period, which could be used as a study hall, with tutors under teacher supervision available to assist with homework, or as a time to work with a teacher individually or in a small group for teaching interventions. Peer tutoring was also incorporated into the eighth period. The principal also created "office hour" slots during the school day for teachers to do individual work with students and make calls to parents. Saturday School and the after-school program were redesigned to allow students to receive academic assistance. Finally, the school adopted a common set of core values for CAL Prep that clarified the mission of the school for students, teachers, and families.

With regard to the concerns about home–school communication, the principal expanded the information flow beyond a weekly newsletter, through a monthly calendar of activities, and regular e-mails with home-work assignments due and updates, thus providing the type of informa-tive and timely communication that parents desired. Having a Dean of Students and longer-term advisory leaders enabled more individualized calls to parents. There was also an increased focus on supportive teaching in professional development provided for teachers. The school counselor offered monthly informational sessions on topics related to college and adolescence to parents.

## Conclusion

CAL Prep continues to evolve each year. As a response to these data, the school took both the initiative—a proactive first step—and the onus of responsibility in making sure that parents were heard and collabora-tively engaged. By better supporting teachers (in professional develop-ment opportunities and school structures that improve their outreach to students and parents) to better support parents and students, we were able to shift what was at the start an uncomfortable distance to a more trusting partnership with families. Among the important lessons learned here is that academic rigor cannot be sustained without a variety of academic and social-emotional supports, and that these supports must be provided not only to students, but also to families and teachers.

## References

Barge, J. K., & Loges, W. E. (2010). Parent, student, and teacher perceptions of paren-tal involvement. *Journal of Applied Communication*, *31*, 140–163. doi:10.1080/0090988032000064597

Bronfenbrenner, U. (1979). *The ecology of human development: Experiments by nature and design*. Cambridge, MA: Harvard University Press.

Carreón, G. P., Drake, C., & Barton, A. C. (2005). The importance of presence: Immigrant parents' school engagement experiences. *American Educational Research Journal, 42*, 465–498. doi:10.3102/00028312042003465

Chavkin, N. F., & Williams, D. L. (1989). Low-income parents' attitudes toward parent involvement in education. *Journal of Sociology and Social Welfare, 16*(3), 17–28. Retrieved from http://search.proquest.com/docview/617721063/abstract/142D8A78E6CFD84A4B9/1?accountid=14496

Eccles, J. S., Midgley, C., Wigfield, A., Buchmanan, C. M., Reuman, D., Flanagan, C., & Mac Iver, D. (1993). Development during adolescence: The impact of stage-environment fit on young adolescents' experiences in schools and in families. *American Psychologist, 48*, 90–101. doi:10.1037/10254-034

Epstein, J. L. (2001). *School, family, and community partnerships: Preparing educators and improving schools.* Boulder, CO: Westview Press.

Epstein, J. L., Sanders, M. G., Sheldon, S. B., Simon, B. S., Salinas, K. C., Jansorn, N. R.,...Williams, K. J. (2009). *School, family, and community partnerships: Your handbook for action.* Thousand Oaks, CA: Corwin Press.

Gill, S., & Reynolds, A. J. (1999). Educational expectations and school achievement of urban African American children. *Journal of School Psychology, 37*, 403–424. doi:10.1016/S0022-4405(99)00027-8

Jackson, K., & Remillard, J. T. (2005). Rethinking parent involvement: African American mothers construct their roles in the mathematics education of their children. *The School Community Journal, 15*, 51–73.

Jeynes, W. H. (2005a). The effects of parental involvement on the academic achievement of African American youth. *The Journal of Negro Education, 74*, 260–274.

Jeynes, W. H. (2005b). A meta-analysis of the relation of parental involvement to urban elementary school student academic achievement. *Urban Education, 40*, 237–269. doi:10.1177/0042085905274540

Jeynes, W. H. (2007). The relationship between parental involvement and urban secondary school student academic achievement: A meta-analysis. *Urban Education, 42*, 82–110. doi:10.1177/0042085906293818

Jeynes, W. H. (2010). The salience of the subtle aspects of parental involvement and encouraging that involvement: Implications for school-based programs. *Teachers College Record, 112*, 747–774.

Jeynes, W. H. (2012). A meta-analysis of the efficacy of different types of parental involvement programs for urban students. *Urban Education, 47*, 706–742. doi:10.1177/0042085912445643

Kuperminc, G. P., Darnell, J. D., & Alvarez-Jimenez, A. (2008). Parent involvement in the academic adjustment of Latino middle and high school youth: Teacher expectations and school belonging as mediators. *Journal of Adolescence, 31*, 469–483. doi:10.1016/j.adolescence.2007.09.003

Lareau, A., & Calarco, J. M. (2012). Class, cultural capital, and institutions: The case of families and schools. In S. T. Fiske & H R. Markus (Eds.), *The secret handshake: Social class divides in face-to-face encounters* (pp. 61–86). New York, NY: Russell Sage Foundation.

Lee, J., & Bowen, N. K. (2006). Parent involvement, cultural capital, and the achievement gap among elementary school children. *American Educational Research Journal, 43*, 193–218. doi:10.3102/00028312043002193

Lloyd-Smith, L., & Baron, M. (2010). Beyond conferences: Attitudes of high school administrators toward parental involvement in one small Midwestern state. *The School Community Journal, 20*(2), 23–44. Retrieved from http://search.proquest.com/docview/921295274/abstract/142D8A78E6CFD84A4B9/7?accountid=14496

Mehan, H. (2012). *In the front door: Creating a college-going culture of learning.* Boulder, CO: Paradigm.

No Child Left Behind (NCLB) Act of 2001, Pub. L. No. 107-110, § 115, Stat. 1425 (2002).

Pomerantz, E. M., Moorman, E. A., & Litwack, S. D. (2007). The how, whom, and why of parents' involvement in children's academic lives: More is not always better. *Review of Educational Research, 77*, 373–410. doi:10.3102/003465430305567

Pomerantz, E. M., & Moorman, E. A. (2010). Parents' involvement in children's schooling. In J. L. Meece and J. S. Eccles (Eds.), *Handbook of research on schools, schooling, and human development* (pp. 398–416). New York, NY: Taylor & Francis.

Ramirez, A. Y. (1999). Survey on teachers' attitude regarding parents and parental involvement. *The School Community Journal, 9*, 21–39. Retrieved from http://search.proquest.com/docview/62405550/abstract/142D8A78E6CFD84A4B9/4?accountid=14496

Ramirez, A. Y. (2001). "Parental involvement is like apple pie": A look at parental involvement in two states. *The High School Journal, 85*, 1–9. doi:10.1353/hsj.2001.0019

Ramirez, A.Y. (2002). A secondary school: Teachers' and their view on parents. *American Secondary Education*, 27–42. Retrieved from http://search.proquest.com/docview/62336796/abstract/142D89A70BFCC8B4E48/6?accountid=14496

Rimm-Kaufman, S. E., & Pianta, R. C. (2005). Family-school communication in preschool and kindergarten in the content of a relationship-enhancing intervention. *Early Education Development, 16*, 287–316. doi:10.1207/s15566935eed1603_1

Steinberg, L., Lamborn, S. D., Darling, N., Mounts, N. S., & Dornbusch, S. M. (1994). Over-time changes in adjustment and competence among adolescents from authoritative, authoritarian, indulgent, and neglectful families. *Child Development, 65*, 754–770. doi:10.2307/1131416

Seidman, E., Lambert, L. E., Allen, L., & Aber, J. L. (2003). Urban adolescents' transition to junior high school and protective family transactions. *Journal of Early Adolescence, 23*, 166–193. doi:10.1177/0272431603023002003

Williams, T. T., & Sanchez, B. (2013). Identifying and decreasing barriers to parent involvement for inner-city parents. *Youth and Society, 45*, 45–74. doi:10.1177/0044118X11409066

# 8 | Making Room to Read: The Evolution of a Secondary School Library

**MARJORIE (SUSIE) GOODIN AND P. DAVID PEARSON**

*"There's definitely kids carrying around a lot more books,
which is nice. And it sounds like such a simplistic measure of
it, but I don't think it is. Because before I just never saw kids
carrying around books, **ever**... You know—that's, I think,
been the biggest difference—that because of the library,
kids have books and kids are reading and kids are learning
how to find books that they're interested in."* (Ms. Stuart,
September 28, 2010)[1]

W HEN I (GOODIN) FIRST VISITED CALIFORNIA College Preparatory
Academy (CAL Prep) in the winter of the 2006–2007 school
year, it was to evaluate a reading intervention program that
was being implemented for underachieving readers. In its second year,
the school was striving on many fronts to provide resources and programs for its 150 low-income, minority students. These efforts included
a grant-funded commercial reading intervention program as well as an
initial effort to provide access to books in small classroom libraries and
a collection of donated and yard-sale books, many of them ragged and
out-of-date. From questionnaires administered to and interviews conducted with staff and students during the reading intervention evaluation
study in the 2007–2008 year, we discovered a common interest in building a school library—to more deeply engage students in reading. Given

---

[1] All quotations are taken verbatim from surveys and interviews, and pseudonyms are used
throughout to disguise data from individuals. This example is a comment from a teacher.

the University of California, Berkeley's partnership with the school, the expressed need for a library seemed a good opportunity both for research and for program development.

What happens when a school without a library decides to create one? To answer this question, we embarked on a library-building enterprise at CAL Prep over the span of Years 4 to 6 of the school's history (i.e., 2008–2011). This is the story of the evolution of this library—its birth, growth, fits and starts, successes, and setbacks. By tracking the development of school library resources and programs at a secondary school where no library existed, we were able to explore the processes and elements of library formation as it impacts the literacy and learning environment. The research questions included probing the nature of the students' responses to increased access to library resources, gauging the impact of library services on the collaborative engagement of content area teachers, and defining the essential elements contributing to success or failure of the library evolution in this particular school environment (Goodin, 2011).

Our hunch was that by improving available resources, enhancing opportunities for access and choice, and developing the library dispositions of the students (American Library Association, 2009), there might be observable changes in students' reading attitudes, engagement, and achievement at the school. These library dispositions include habits of mind and attitudes that guide student thinking and intellectual behaviors. We thought that these elusive dispositions might be measured through actions taken to access library resources and to read independently.

Many teachers, such as Ms. Stuart, recognized the importance of reading in students' lives. Knowing that the difficulty of underachievement in reading has an impact on many students' performance in school and prospects for college and career, teachers and researchers strive to discover the best ways to "hook kids on books." At the secondary level, it is imperative to engage students in a broad range of texts with diverse perspectives to prepare them for lifelong reading. We wondered if part of the solution to reducing secondary reading achievement gaps is living quietly, in plain sight, in the often unrealized resources of a school library and school librarian,[2] both existing in a familiar instructional site where multiple literacy practices are accommodated with diverse materials every day (Goodin, 2007, 2009).

---

[2] School librarians have been called library media specialists, library media teachers, and now in many places, teacher–librarians. In this chapter, we use the term *librarian*.

## Design Research Approach

Concerns about library efficacy have been studied in established school libraries over the past decades by many researchers (Achterman, 2008; Baughman, 2000; Lance, 2002; Robertson, 2003; Smith, 2001), but none have studied library effectiveness in a school where formerly no library existed. In studying a school library in this unique, iterative fashion, we hoped to illuminate the essential nature of its impact on the school's literacy environment. Our study followed the tenets of Design Research by seeing the work as "engineering" or constant redesign based on site response (Cobb, Confrey, diSessa, Lehrer, & Schauble, 2003; Reinking, & Bradley, 2008). The data we gathered from fall 2008 through spring 2011 included student reading surveys and questionnaires ($n = 85$), formal and informal interviews of 12 staff members and 9 students, and public records and notices. These sources were supplemented by 10 to 15 hours of field observation a week, photographs, and data from library automation software that automatically collected circulation and collection figures.

We knew from the outset that this library would have to be unique because of the physical constraints imposed by the limited space available at the school, so we worked to build library dispositions and a distributed library by developing better classroom libraries, constructing a small, focused central collection, and providing access to public library services. We viewed the school library project as an intervention—one that sought to develop a culture of reading and information use with adolescents—by (1) attending to access, choice, motivation, and engagement in reading and by (2) collaborating with amenable content-area teachers on instructional supports.

Research in three important areas—reading comprehension instruction, independent reading, and engagement/motivation in reading—have pointed the way to effective, positive, and interesting reading experiences and, by implication, to library facilities and affordances as a foundational resource. At the same time that there is a consensus for the cognitive benefits of wide reading of diverse texts (Biancarosa & Snow, 2006; Brozo, Shiel, & Topping, 2007; Moje, Overby, Tysvaer, & Morris, 2008), the issue of providing access to diverse texts is rarely pursued in concert with the call to encourage wide reading. In fact, very few education researchers have recognized the growing body of research documenting the relationship between effective school library programs and reading achievement gains measured in standardized test scores (Krashen, 2004; Lance, 2002).

It seemed to us that research on reading development and school library efficacy might be combined in a design study to build a school library. The design research approach adopted required that the library intervention be negotiated over time with the school community, including students, staff, and teachers, as they responded to the library and thereby influenced its evolution. The resulting ethnographic study, to observe one small school's effort to construct and respond to a library, tracks the evolution of a secondary school library program over the course of three school years from fall 2008 to spring 2011.

## A School Library Situates in a Third Space

The story of this library starts with the idea of *third space* (Gutiérrez, Baquedano-López, & Turner, 1997; Leander & Sheehy, 2004). Third space is a construct that is descriptive of accommodation and potential change among entities—for instance, among languages, literary traditions, cultural traditions, or sets of beliefs. The school library can be a third space for both individual learning and collaborative instructional practices, a third space for teaching and learning, or a third space for students navigating between in-school content area requirements and out-of-school literacy practices and discourses.

In addition, the library encompassed three dimensions of space—physical space, curricular space, and ideological space. The requirements and complexities of building the physical facility emerged first as the effort to provide library resources competed with other compelling needs for facility space at the school. The issue of curricular space for a library program intersected with the mission and goals of the school as a whole as teachers struggled to integrate the possibility of library service in an already crowded curriculum and schedule. Descriptions of ideological space, a space that encompassed the deep beliefs and understandings held by students and staff about school library functioning, emerged both in interviews and in statements expressed as the learning community accessed library resources over the course of the study. In each dimension, the library has an essential "in-between-ness" about it—it occupies a third space between traditional school literacy practices and the authentic literacy practices of students out of school. Thus, the school library juggles the diverse goals of schooling and out-of-school priorities by maintaining a stance in the middle, serving both.

# Physical Space and Access: Matter Matters

## Library Desire and Design

The first turning point for development of a school library came in of the fall of 2008, when the school received a curriculum grant to provide print resources supporting writing and project work in the content areas. Staff made the decision to support the building of a small library facility to house the new curriculum materials. Building a library program where none previously existed first entailed developing the physical space for library service, including the essential elements—collection, furniture, and technology. Over the course of several months, we negotiated the space for a small collection, created a design for the space allocated, developed bids for the requisite equipment and books, and established the necessary vendor accounts. By the late spring of 2009, the emerging library became a visible presence in the corner of the all-purpose room at CAL Prep, generating interest in staff and students, even though it was not yet operational. A small school library began to evolve in colorful cabinets, as did the beginnings of a library program. By January, 2010, we moved the fledgling library with many more cabinets to the stage in the all-purpose room (see Figure 8.1). The collection grew from a start-up of 598 books to more than 3,000 books by the end of more than two and one half years of development.

FIGURE 8.1. The California College Preparatory Academy Library, January, 2010. (Photo taken by Susie Goodin.)

When we started the library-building process, it was with the notion of "build it and they will come." Because we knew from our earlier research at the school and from encouragements from the principal that the school community wanted a library, we assumed that the library would be a welcomed addition. Even so, we found that the desire for a library was complicated and sometimes compromised by other priorities for space allocation. For instance, in the first full year (2009–2010), the limited times for library use at the end of the day in eighth period were frequently trumped by assemblies, academic rewards and award parties, and school spirit events. In spite of these conflicts, the principal, staff, and students expressed genuine receptivity to the concept of a school library.

## Student Access to Texts: "Can I Have Another One Just Like It?"

The key factors we found connected to increasing student library use were the number of diverse texts available, the number of days the library was accessible, the gender and age of the students, and the collaborative engagement of the teachers. Over the course of the 2009–2010 school year, every expansion in library service was matched by an increase in student use. For instance, after only 11 days of access, 77 out of 194 students had checked out one or more books. This number represented 40% of the students, who borrowed 110 books over the course of the first four and a half weeks after opening. As the collection expanded to nearly 2,000 books at the end of the library's first year (2009–2010), 82.6% of the students had visited at least once, and all but 13 of those students checked out a book of interest on their first visit (see Figure 8.2).

Given our findings that 8.2% of the students surveyed at CAL Prep owned *no* books of their own and 17.6% had read *no* books for pleasure in the preceding 12 months, we believe that expanding access to interesting books was a factor in increased circulation. Once students understood that books that they *wanted* to read were available, they returned to the library requesting similar titles, and became, at the same time, more open to consulting with the librarian.

**Access and Equity.** Access to library resources encompasses both physical and intellectual access. On repeated occasions during the study, the library could not operate during its limited, regularly scheduled hours because library time was superseded by other scheduled gatherings in the all-purpose room, rendering physical access impossible. Beyond

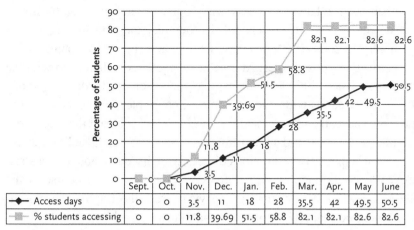

| | Sept. | Oct. | Nov. | Dec. | Jan. | Feb. | Mar. | Apr. | May | June |
|---|---|---|---|---|---|---|---|---|---|---|
| ◆ Access days | 0 | 0 | 3.5 | 11 | 18 | 28 | 35.5 | 42 | 49.5 | 50.5 |
| ▦ % students accessing | 0 | 0 | 11.8 | 39.69 | 51.5 | 58.8 | 82.1 | 82.1 | 82.6 | 82.6 |

**Days of library access 2009–2010**

FIGURE 8.2. Cumulative access days and circulation data from September, 2009–June, 2010.

providing physical access to a wide range of texts for student use, those wishing to promote library use also found that they must introduce students to diverse texts as a way of making the library resources familiar and approachable. Goodin used revolving displays organized by genre and topic as well as book talks in the library and classrooms to connect students to interesting books. Together, these efforts could offset the lack of equity in access that is well documented for low-income learners (Darling-Hammond, 2000; Neuman & Celano, 2001). Circulation figures at the end of the first 7 months of limited operation in 2009–2010—1,154 book circulations for approximately 190 students—demonstrated that students responded to increased access, although not uniformly by grade or gender (see Table 8.1).

TABLE 8.1. Number of Students Accessing the Library, Grades 8–11, November 10 to December 17, 2009

| GRADE LEVEL | NUMBER OF STUDENTS | NUMBER OF STUDENTS ACCESSING THE LIBRARY | PERCENTAGE ACCESSING |
|---|---|---|---|
| 8th grade | 56 | 35 | 62.5 |
| 9th grade | 60 | 32 | 53.3 |
| 10th grade | 56 | 5 | 8.9 |
| 11th grade | 20 | 4 | 20.0 |

NOTE: The 11th-grade class consisted of only one section with 20 students, reduced to 19 students in the school year.

Another issue related to access was sound—more specifically, noise! During the two regularly scheduled times that the students could visit the library in 2009–2010, that is, lunchtime and study hall, sound played diametrically opposed roles. At lunchtime, the large hall echoed with the boisterous voices of 200 students, and the sheer din made one-on-one book conversations with students almost impossible. During study hall in the same space, the requirement for absolute silence meant that book conversations between student and librarian had to be conducted in uncomfortable whispers. Both situations discouraged discourse about books and proved to be an ongoing barrier to access throughout the course of the study, relieved only by small group visits from the English classrooms when more normal productive conversation was possible.

**Early Adopters and Late Entries.** There were gender and age differences in students' response to the addition of school library services. We were able to index access rates for gender and grade by using the Student Use Agreement signed by each student upon initial use of the school library, even recording the first book selected by each student on that occasion. Consistent with earlier research findings that younger students spend more time reading independently (Cullinan, 2004), the 8th and 9th grade students were the early adopters of the library (see Table 8.1). Within the first 5 weeks, 58% of the 8th and 9th graders had visited the library, whereas only 12% of the 10th and 11th graders had done so.

Gender also factored into library usage. In the first 5 weeks of operation, girls at all grade levels accessed the library to a much greater degree than boys; for example, 88% of 8th-grade girls versus 62% of 8th-grade boys and 38% of 11th-grade girls versus 8% of 11th grade boys visited the library in that time period. It may have been more difficult to attract boys to the growing collection, in part because books that might appeal to them (Moje et al., 2008; Smith & Wilhelm, 2002) were in short supply. Goodin's prior experience as a librarian suggests that nonfiction titles that are both appropriately challenging and relevant to many boys' out-of-school interests are simply more difficult to find. Indeed, one boy remarked that he wanted books that "tell him about stuff," and many male students responded positively as the collection of biographies and other nonfiction materials grew. Ms. Tallub, the experienced English teacher, offered the same reflection about specific genres appealing to boys:

> And I think there is a gender difference often time between the type
> of reading that girls like to do and that boys like to do, and I think

that nonfiction is a part of getting some of those more hesitant boys interested in reading (June 17, 2010).

However, as the library collection grew and was increasingly informed by students' requests and responses to the available selections, so did the circulation of books, especially in the eighth and ninth grades.

## The Red Cart Benefit and the Blue Notebook Effect

The early limits in physical space and the ongoing scheduling obstacles to student access did have some benefits. We discovered that by working on collection development during the lunch hour, the evolving library was both visible and transparent. The students saw the number of books in the collection grow day by day as Goodin processed them for library circulation with labels, stamps, and barcodes. Early in the building process, a red library cart served as a workstation, and we found that many students were interested in the process and asked questions as they waited in the lunch line nearby. Thus, the red cart resulted in an unplanned promotion of the library in an authentic manner.

Another serendipitous outcome of the crowded corner start-up library in 2009 was Goodin's notebook. As students noticed the work on books, they also commented on them and made suggestions about books they would like to see acquired for the library. Soon, Goodin was writing their suggestions and names in a small blue notebook to record the expressed preferences. This procedure introduced an element of transparency to the construction of the library, as students realized that we were buying and stocking the books they wanted. It became clear from students' eagerness to make recommendations about books they liked and those they hoped to read that the highly visible and transparent nature of the initial efforts had the unanticipated consequence of drawing students into the process.

An important part of the value of making connections to students' interests in developing the library collection was the overt respect it displayed for adolescent literacy practices. By attending to student interest, the librarian validated students' ability to make meaningful choices about the texts they read voluntarily, nourishing the motivation to read in the process (Gibson, 2010; Hughes-Hassell & Rodge, 2007; Worthy, 1996). Furthermore, giving students some power in selecting texts, especially in choosing a broader range of texts than the typical library fare—by providing student-suggested graphic novel titles, for example—allowed students to "write themselves into the world" of literacy engagement (Wade & Moje, 2000, p. 622).

## Students' Reading Habits: "Choose Better Books"

Over the course of this study, students actively reported their preferences in books: during informal conversations and reader's advisory moments as well as in formal surveys and interviews. Individual enthusiasms for particular titles were commonplace as students requested and recognized book titles: "You have *Rocket Boys*?" When a book was a good match for a student, by topic and reading level, that student's positive reaction to reading was evident in their motivation to check out the book, to find more titles by the same author, and even to submit their names to waiting lists for very popular books.

**An Issue of Motivation.** Although motivation to read independently is a complex matter, this study confirmed observations from other researchers (e.g., Guthrie & Davis, 2003). First, if we want students to want to read, we have to show them it is worth it by modeling and revealing our own enthusiasm, finding ways to attract attention to reading as a satisfying experience, and consulting with students about what they want to read and learn. The most compelling evidence of this claim was the regular discourse students had with the lead author about books they loved. Student response to book talks was another time to have an observed effect on students' motivation to read; after every book talk session, which introduced titles of interest, students were eager to check out the titles.

A second related claim confirmed in this study is that engagement is closely aligned with motivation to read (Brozo et al., 2007). If we define engagement as simply the amount of time that students are actually reading and measure it with evidence from circulation records and observed attention to books at the school site, then engagement with books was evident at the school. Increasing circulation figures, observations of students reading, and teachers' observations of students "flashing their book covers in the hallways" support the conclusion that access to the school library improved reading engagement for many students. Another sign of the impact of engagement and its effect on motivation to read was demonstrated in the phenomenon of books "going viral" in the student population. We observed that as specific titles gained popularity and produced an increased demand for those books, many students were motivated to request the same titles for independent reading. These books became "contagious."

**"Stage Fright."** However, the highly visible nature of the library on stage was not conducive to increased library use for all students. Data indicated that there was a social consequence to moving the library onto the stage in where it was in plain (and elevated) sight of the student body during lunch and study hall. It appeared that many students did not want to be seen as library users when the whole school could observe them, although there were differences observed in the free access of lunchtime and the library pass system utilized during study hall. During lunch, a library visit was a sign of nerdiness, but during study hall, it served as a badge of resistance, with some students using the library as a "get-out-of-study hall" pass. Most students' use of the library was strongly influenced by peer relationships. For a great many students, that meant that they needed some privacy to risk library engagement. We found that it helped to partially screen the stage with a whiteboard and to organize scheduled visits by small groups of students during regular class periods in order to offset the perceived nerdiness associated with independent library use.

## Summary: Access and the Physical Dimension

By the end of the 2009–2010 school year, we reached a ceiling of 82.6% of students making initial contact. Although some mostly younger students had become regular users of the library, others had not made any contact. The resistance to library use was both social and physical. For some students, the very visible position of the library was a deterrent, as they did not want to be seen using the library by peers. Other students chose to visit publically and sign out self-selected texts, especially those who had engaged in the process of selecting books for the library as they made acquisition recommendations. School expectations for sound levels also played a role in library usage when either too much noise or demands for silence had an impact on library discourse. However, as library usage increased and the school community recognized its value to literacy development, the library moved from a space on the periphery in the all-purpose room to the stage, a more central place in the school, perhaps signaling a change in status.

## Curricular Space: A Library Program's Uncertain Welcome

Building students' individual dispositions to use the school library represented just the first layer of library construction; the second level included making connections with the teachers' curricular goals. The nature of school librarianship encompasses curriculum support along with support for independent learning, and at CAL Prep, the former was slow to be established. Collaborative efforts among teachers require time, conversant objectives, and trust (Monteil-Overall, 2005; Small, 2001). The first two concrete efforts to collaborate with teachers occurred at the beginning and end of the 2009–2010 school year; collaboration on classroom libraries for independent reading emerged at the start of the school year, and joint work on the culminating research project for eighth graders developed at the end of the year. Both were cautious initial efforts to collaborate, and neither was completely successful.

### Independent Reading Program

When the 2010–2011 school year began, two of the three English teachers expressed interest in enhancing their small classroom libraries in support of an independent reading program. By the second semester, however, the teachers requested the removal of most of the books from their classrooms, saying that the time required to manage even a small library was overwhelming. The obstacle they reported was a lack of time—time to provide books, time to allow students to read, and time required to teach the standards necessary to prepare students for standardized tests in the spring. We continued to work together as we scheduled book talks and students rotated in small groups into the library for 15-minute visits to select books. However, the difficulty in finding time for reading revealed an ongoing tension in priorities for developing literacy. Although both English Language Arts and school library standards support independent reading and inquiry, and reading a broad range of diverse texts can indirectly enhance content learning, library standards played second fiddle to the urgency of covering other content standards (DeVoogd, 2009; Garan & DeVoogd, 2008; Guthrie & Wigfield, 2000).

So why was independent reading time in school so underutilized by teachers? Certainly one reason was the primacy of testing in the current culture of school accountability. The valuing of test scores and grades on assigned texts introduced a conflict with students' preference to read self-selected books. Another reason was the lack of teacher knowledge about contemporary young-adult literature. Lacking a familiarity with popular young-adult literature interfered with teachers' ability to promote accessible and interesting free-reading selections. Perhaps more important, the contestation of which texts are worthy influenced many teachers' attitudes about independent reading. As a teacher Mrs. Scott reported, she did not approve of graphic novels and did not consider them a literary genre. Restriction of some texts was common (Gibson, 2010; Jago, 2004; Samuels, 1983), but this could be counterproductive when encouraging adolescents to develop individual book preferences and literacy abilities. At CAL Prep, the tension between assigned and independent work was evident in the lack of strong support for implementing the independent reading program as a linchpin in the school's literacy curriculum.

## Collaborations Around Student Research

At the heart of school library effectiveness studies is the issue of collaboration between librarians and teachers (Loertscher, 1988; Monteil-Overall, 2005; Small, 2001). When school library professionals work together with teachers in planning and implementing projects and programs, student achievement levels increase (Achterman, 2008; Baughman, 2000; Lance, 2002; Smith, 2001). At CAL Prep, our initial focus on building the collection evolved into a focus on integrating resources and schedules to maximize student access and information literacy instruction. At the end of the first school year and the beginning of the second school year of operation (2010–2011), a collaborative initiative manifested in several research projects with 8th, 9th, and 11th graders.

Through a combination of class visits and small group research visits, students were given a taste of research strategies and bibliographic instruction, but it was evident from their responses that more research experience would be beneficial. For instance, students had very limited understanding of how to search a subscription database or a library catalog, and most did not know how to locate materials in the library once a title record was produced in search results. In piecemeal fashion, Goodin was also able to engage English teachers and the Spanish teacher in collaborative partnerships for literature circle work, book club initiatives, and independent reading assignments for out-of-school completion. These were initial, if somewhat limited moves in the direction of an integrated library program. Because collaborative efforts take time, as does the development of trust between collaborating partners, we expect that the library program at CAL Prep may grow over time if the library is valued in content areas.

## Ideological Space: Unearthing Student and Staff Beliefs

At the foundation of a library's efficacy is the history of school library use held in the memories, experiences, and expectations of school community members. As teachers, administrators, and students related their own personal regard for libraries in their particular past experiences, a set of beliefs about libraries—what we call the ideological space—was manifested at CAL Prep. Over time, in conversations, decisions, and challenges that accompanied the construction of the library, beliefs about libraries surfaced. For example, although the staff expressed a strong belief in the value of independent reading and inquiry, their ability to provide opportunities for those activities was compromised by the tightly controlled instructional standards and heightened attention to standardized testing.

Every teacher interviewed referred to the constrictions of standards and standardized testing when describing the limitations they experienced in teaching *past the test*. As Ms. Tallub imagined a different educational scenario, she said (June 17, 2010),

> I would reduce the emphasis on CSTs [California Standards Tests], most especially for the higher grades because I think there's a danger with standards in that they are what you need to graduate high school. And that can become constraining when what they really need to be prepared for is college, if that makes sense.

As we uncovered elements for successful library operation and met obstacles to building a library resource and program at this site, we became increasingly aware of the intricate web of overlapping beliefs and expectations influencing the way that literacy was taught in this school's setting and the ways in which the library was utilized—or not.

### Believing in the Power of Libraries (Or Not)

Three main categories of beliefs had a strong impact on the integration of a school library at CAL Prep: (1) beliefs held by teachers about the value of libraries in curriculum areas, (2) an institutional regard for the value of school libraries, and (3) students' beliefs about reading competence and library use. In the case of the teachers and staff, youthful experiences with libraries were more positive, but they had limited experience in using school libraries in preservice or in-service education. All 12 staff members had positive experiences with libraries before training or becoming teachers, whereas only 3 of the 10 credentialed teachers had pedagogical connections with libraries before teaching. As a result, although CAL Prep teachers believed that school libraries might have a beneficial influence on learning, they had limited experience and understanding of the possibilities for collaborative partnerships with the librarian in their curricular area.

In an age of accountability, a school library's mission to promote independent learning plays second fiddle to test preparation when scheduling is considered. Thus, incidental learning suffers, although we know that independent reading is a vitally important source of increased vocabulary and general knowledge (Cullinan, 2004; Nagy, 1988). Even CAL Prep's principal, who increasingly demonstrated appreciation for library resources as the library grew and wanted to "regularize library work," was hard pressed to help the staff include information literacy in the curriculum. In an era when the benefit of independent and informal learning is undervalued, school library programs are often relegated to the nonessential in the curriculum.

Student beliefs about the value of library use and their individual reader identity—beliefs about personal competence in reading (Hall, 2007, 2010)—are the last major category in a web of beliefs we uncovered. A majority of the students at CAL Prep believed themselves to be good or very good readers, regardless of test scores, the actual amount of time they spent reading, or the regularity of their library use. Moreover, we learned from student and staff interviews that being seen as library users was socially risky for many students. Furthermore, underperforming readers had two barriers to overcome when approaching the library to obtain independent reading materials: (1) they risked the badge of nerdiness by using the library in full public view and (2) they risked the label of struggling reader during attempts to find appropriately challenging books.

## A Content Literacy Conundrum

One ongoing conundrum in the literacy field involves the incorporation of literacy instruction within the content areas. Just as O'Brien, Stewart, and Moje (1995) described, content area teachers at CAL Prep recognized the discrepancy between their sense of responsibility for literacy instruction and their actual practice of literacy instruction within their content areas.

When faced with the question, who is responsible for literacy instruction, most of the staff reluctantly admitted that it fell mainly on the English teachers. Research suggests that content area teachers reject research-based strategies for content literacy either because (1) the strategies do not fit well into the norms of their subject disciplines or (2) after adapting the strategies to the subject area, they become (paradoxically) uninteresting (O'Brien et al., 1995). In addition, the infusion of independent reading texts as part of an expanded literacy curriculum occasionally generated a negative response as mathematics (math) and science teachers found students engaged in clandestine reading during class. The negative responses to students' reading on the part of these teachers highlighted the tension between general literacy instruction and content area curriculum expectations.

This is not to say that teachers were opposed to the library. As one math teacher, Ms. Stuart, explained in regard to her support of independent reading, "Math is most important to me, but most of them are not going to be mathematicians. At the end of the day, I want them to experience the passion of learning" (September 28, 2010). But given the press of standards and testing, teachers often opted out of allowing students to make choices that advanced general literacy proficiency over content area knowledge. Whether based on time constraints, a focus on testing objectives, a focus on teacher autonomy, or a tightly constricted schedule, CAL Prep teachers were caught between the need to be relentlessly standards-based and their concern about student growth.

## Conclusions

Our design study sought to situate a new school library within the learning community of a small secondary school in hopes of understanding the ways in which it might contribute to the learning environment and reading lives of its students. The impetus for building one small secondary school library "from scratch" began with an idea for conceptualizing the place of a school library within a school's culture, was reinforced by a clearly expressed desire for library resources, and expanded to become the topic of this research (Goodin, 2011). Our study revealed the extent to which tensions between a school library's mission and other school objectives shape a library's efficacy and acceptance. We concluded that the school library exists in a third space defined by constant tensions in three categories: an *ideological space* balanced between in-school and out-of-school learning priorities; a *curricular space* caught between curriculum requirements and individual learning desires; and a *physical space* competing for accessible learning spaces.

This study, spanning 3 years of involvement in library building, is limited by virtue of being about one small school and including one researcher. Although Goodin (2011) identified as a participant observer in the most active sense—by building the program, and teaching, and observing—she started with a clear bias as a teacher–librarian. In addition, the nature of being a researcher positions one on the periphery of an institution—attempting to maintain a semi-objective distance—rather than at the center of the learning community being studied. At this site, Goodin's part-time, volunteer status as consulting school librarian and researcher may have complicated teachers' potential responses to collaborative overtures.

## Significance for Research and Policy

In recent years, qualitative research has once again taken a backseat to quantitative work on literacy. It certainly is true that the messy navigation of complex systems, such as those operating in education settings, offers little in the way of simple solutions. On the other hand, it may be that naming the messiness of ecological systems is exactly the research that needs to be done. It is only by taking on the complexity of educational sites rich with possibility from cross-currents of dictate and desire that research can illuminate "emergent systems" (Brooks, 2011, p. 108). In the case of school libraries, the nonlinear approach to a complex of factors can rejuvenate our understanding of their value. Although studying multiple elements interacting in a developing pattern runs counter to the prevailing quantitative and linear research paradigms in vogue today in education, in human interactions, the component parts of a school or culture do not sort easily into disaggregated factors, but evolve organically in dynamic complexity (Fullan, 2002). The resultant change cannot be attributed to one specific variable, but in the end, must be grappled with as the consequence of an ecosystem that is not explained by simple reductionist forces. School libraries must be researched in this contextual fashion to uncover the true worth of their contribution to literacy.

Opportunities for literacy growth expand if we understand the school library as a site for students to express individual agency through choice of texts and literacy practices, as a "space for elaborating strategies of selfhood ... that initiate new signs of identity, and innovative sites of collaboration, and contestation, in the act of defining the idea of society itself" (Bhabha, 1994, p. 1–2). Our hope is that by describing the elements of library function in relation to literacy development as we built one small school library, we might clarify the interwoven nature of libraries and literacy curriculum, alerting all to the opportunities inherent in a school library—including the simple opportunity for students to read a lot more books.

It is also our hope that by describing the elements of school library functioning in relation to literacy development, clarity of purpose might be achieved for both libraries and literacy curriculum. In this era of increasing digital access to information, there are doubts about the benefits of school libraries. If the value of the school library is invisible, it can be dismissed as peripheral to learning environment—initiating a cycle of misunderstanding, underuse, undervaluation, and subsequent underfunding. Yet, creating balanced literacy programs, valuing the power of differentiated literacy practices, and honoring the diverse learning interests of students are all explicit priorities of school librarianship. In this study, we hope to alert policy makers to missed educational opportunities if school libraries practices are not topics of preservice and in-service education. If teachers and administrators become familiar with library literacy standards, become aware of the breadth of young people's literature and their combined potential for literacy growth, one can imagine a renewed drive for funding of school libraries to provide equitable access to all students. In a time of accelerating technical change, school libraries may be the "slow food of education," but we hoped to expose their significance as potential rich sites of lifelong learning by accommodating student agency in learning.

## Lessons Learned

When summing up the findings in this case, the good news is that the CAL Prep school library continues (at this writing, more than 2 years after the data for this study were collected) to serve students in some historical and traditional ways. Access to library resources at school, both print and nonprint, *does* matter. At CAL Prep, the school community responded to the construction of a library in primarily positive ways: increasing patronage and circulation, expanding collaborative partnerships between disciplines, and exploring avenues for physical expansion. We saw, as Robertson (2003, p. 196) did, a "cascade of changes," from changing the facility, to changing attitudes, to changing practices, and to changing use policies. Although our findings do not speak directly to student reading achievement measured in standardized test scores, the logic of the Matthew effect of reading (Stanovich, 1986) encourages us to assume some positive consequences from the increased volume of reading seen at the site.

A second realization arising out of this study pertains to the powerful impact of time pressures and curricular control exerted on teachers in the age of accountability. At CAL Prep, the majority of teachers reported the sense of being in a curriculum bind, a tug-of-war between the requirements of core curriculum standards and their desire to pursue other educational objectives with their students. Even though ensuring equity of access to books and the time to read, supporting student motivation to read, and implementing criteria for schoolwide sustained silent reading were valued concerns, independent reading programs did not thrive in the English department. Dedication to the standardized curriculum in pursuit of higher test scores made independent reading a lower priority. Unfortunately, one consequence of privileging one source of knowledge construction over another is the disenfranchisement of some students for whom self-selected texts in multiple formats are crucial to engagement in reading. A school library can offset such disengagement with the provision of texts that students want to read.

Third, our conclusions in regard to the success of a distributed library at the site—in classrooms, online, and in the community—reflect the complexity of student and staff beliefs about the value of a school library and independent reading. These beliefs, in turn, were related to personal histories of library training and experiences that influenced whether or not the library was utilized. Students' sense of identity as readers was connected to their willingness to perform as readers and library users on the stage. Teachers in the content areas differed in their use of the library resources depending on whether or not they believed that library use in supported their curriculum goals.

Finally, there was an ongoing tension in terms of resources for the school programs more generally and resources for the library. CAL Prep is a small school with a small budget and substantial needs. Thus, there were other resource shortfalls beyond the lack of physical resources. Many of the books were purchased through dedicated grants, and Goodin donated her time to the project as she pursued her dissertation. How do small schools with many needs choose among the many competing priorities? Should a librarian be hired at the expense of a subject-matter teacher? And how might some of the tensions have played out if the school had both the physical and financial resources to have full-time librarian in a well-stocked library?

# References

Achterman, D. L. (2008). *Haves, halves, and have-nots: School libraries and student achievement in California.* (Unpublished doctoral dissertation). University of North Texas, Denton, Texas.

American Library Association. (2009). *Standards for the 21st century learner.* Chicago, IL: American Association of School Librarians.

Bhabha, H. K. (1994). *The location of culture.* New York, NY: Routledge.

Baughman, J. C. (2000). *School libraries and MCAS scores.* Paper presented at a Symposium sponsored by the Graduate School of Library and Information Science, Boston, MA.

Biancarosa, G., & Snow, C. E. (2006). *Reading next—A vision for action and research in middle and high school literacy: A report to Carnegie Corporation of New York.* Washington, DC: Alliance for Excellent Education. Retrieved from http://www.all4ed.org/publications/ReadingNext/ReadingNext.pdf

Brooks, D. (2011). *The social animal: The hidden sources of love, character, and achievement.* New York, NY: Random House.

Brozo, W., Shiel, G., & Topping, K. (2007). Engagement in reading: Lessons learned from three PISA countries. *Journal of Adolescent and Adult Literacy, 51,* 304–315.

Cobb, P., Confrey, J., diSessa, A., Lehrer, R., & Schauble, L. (2003). Design experiments in educational research. *Educational Researcher, 32*(1), 9–13.

Cullinan, B. E. (2004). Independent reading and school achievement. *School Library Media Research.* Retrieved from http://www.ala.org/aasl/SLMR/vol3/independent/independent.html

Darling-Hammond, L. (2000). New standards and old inequalities: School reform and the education of African American students. *The Journal of Negro Education, 69,* 263–287.

DeVoogd, G. (2009). Rechecking the research and the professional role of teachers: A response to Timothy Shanahan. *The California Reader, 42*(2), 4–15.

Fullan, M. (2002). The complexity of the change process. In *Change forces: Probing the depths of educational reform* (pp. 19–41), New York, NY: The Falmer Press.

Garan, E. M., & DeVoogd, G. (2008). The benefits of sustained silent reading: Scientific research and common sense converge. *The Reading Teacher 62,* 336–344.

Gibson, S. (2010). Critical readings: African American girls and urban fiction. *Journal of Adolescent & Adult Literacy 53,* 565–574.

Goodin, S. M. (2007). *School libraries: An unrecognized third space for the practice of multiliteracies* (Unpublished master's thesis). University of California, Berkeley.

Goodin, S. M. (2009). *Embrace complexity: Responding to interwoven motivation resources of adolescent readers* (Unpublished manuscript). University of California, Berkeley.

Goodin, S. M. (2011). *Room to read: Tracking the evolution of a new secondary school library.* (Doctoral dissertation). Available from ProQuest Dissertations and Theses database. (UMI No. 3498970)

Guthrie, J. T., & Davis, M. H. (2003). Motivating struggling readers in middle school through an engagement model of classroom practice. *Reading & Writing Quarterly, 19,* 59–85.

Guthrie, J., & Wigfield, A. (2000). Engagement and motivation in reading. In M. L. Kamil, P. B. Mosenthal, P. D. Pearson, & R. Barr (Eds.), *Handbook of reading research, III* (pp. 403–422). Mahwah, NJ: Lawrence Erlbaum Associates.

Gutiérrez, K., Baquedano-López, P., & Turner, M. G. (1997). Putting language back into Language Arts: When the radical middle meets the third space. *Language Arts, 74,* 368–378.

Hall, L. A. (2007). Understanding the silence: Struggling readers discuss decisions about reading expository text. *The Journal of Educational Research, 100,* 132–141.

Hall, L. A. (2010). The negative consequences of becoming a good reader: Identity theory as a lens for understanding struggling readers, teachers, and reading instruction. *Teachers College Record, 112,* 1792–1829.

Hughes-Hassell, S., & Rodge, P. (2007). The leisure reading habits of urban adolescents. *Journal of Adolescent and Adult Literacy, 51,* 22–33.

Jago, C. (2004). *Classics in the classroom: Designing accessible literature lessons.* Portsmouth, NH: Heinemann.

Krashen, S. D. (2004). *The power of reading: Insights from the research.* Westport, CT: Libraries Unlimited.

Lance, K. C. (2002). Impact of school library media programs on academic achievement. *Teacher Librarian, 29*(3), 29–34.

Leander, K. M., & Sheehy, M. (Eds). (2004). *Spatializing literacy research and practice.* New York, NY: Peter Lang.

Loertscher, D. V. (1988). *Taxonomies of the school library media program.* Englewood, CO: Libraries Unlimited.

Moje, E. B., Overby, M., Tysvaer, N., & Morris, K. (2008). The complex world of adolescent literacy: Myths, motivations and mysteries. *Harvard Educational Review, 78,* 107–154.

Monteil-Overall, P. (2005). Toward a theory of collaboration for teachers and librarians. *School Library Media Research, 8,* 1–31. Retrieved from http://www.ala. org/aasl/sites/ala.org.aasl/files/content/aaslpubsandjournals/slr/vol8/SLMR_ TheoryofCollaboration_V8.pdf

Nagy, W. E. (1988). *Teaching vocabulary to improve reading comprehension.* Washington, DC: Office of Educational Research and Improvement. Retrieved from http://files.eric.ed.gov/fulltext/ED298471.pdf

Neuman, S. B., & Celano, D. (2001). Access to print in low-income and middle-income communities: An ecological study of four neighborhoods. *Reading Research Quarterly, 36,* 8–26.

O'Brien, D. G., Stewart, R. A., & Moje, E. B. (1995). Why content literacy is difficult to infuse into the secondary school: Complexities of curriculum, pedagogy, and school culture. *Reading Research Quarterly 30,* 442–463.

Reinking, D., & Bradley, B. A. (2008). *Formative and design experiments: Approaches to language and literacy research* [An NCRLL Volume]. New York, NY: Teachers College Press.

Robertson, M. N. (2003). *Participants' perceptions of the impact of the Wonder of Reading program* (Unpublished doctoral dissertation). Rossier School of Education, University of Southern California, Los Angeles, CA.

Samuels, B. G. (1983). Young adult literature: Young adult novels in the classroom? *The English Journal, 72*(4), 86–88.

Small, R. V. (2001). Developing a collaborative culture. *School Library Media Quarterly, 4*, 1–4. Retrieved from http://www.ala.org/aasl/sites/ala.org.aasl/files/content/aaslpubsandjournals/slr/vol4/SLMR_CollaborativeCulture_V4.pdf

Smith, E. G. (2001). *Texas school libraries: Standards, resources, services, and students' performance*. Austin, TX: Texas State Library and Archives Commission.

Smith, M. W., & Wilhelm, J. D. (2002). *Reading don't fix no Chevys*. Portsmouth, NH: Heinemann.

Stanovich, K. E. (1986). Matthew effects in reading: Some consequences of individual differences in the acquisition of literacy. *Reading Research Quarterly, 21*, 360–407.

Wade, S. E., & Moje, E. B. (2000). The role of text in classroom learning. In M. L. Kamil, P. B. Mosenthal, P. D. Pearson, & R. Barr (Eds.), *Handbook of reading research, III* (pp. 609–627). Mahwah, NJ: Lawrence Erlbaum Associates.

Worthy, J. (1996). Removing barriers to voluntary reading for reluctant readers: The role of school and classroom libraries. *Language Arts, 73*, 483–492.

# 9 | Tracking Student Indicators Across Time

**RHONA S. WEINSTEIN, JUSTIN F. MARTIN,**
**LIONEL H. BIALIS-WHITE, AND NILOFAR SAMI**

*"An ominous feeling of confusion, complacency, and hostility lingered in the halls. The playground and neighboring parks were riddled with fights. It was survival of the fittest. For the first 2 years of its life, CAL Prep knew this as its dark reality. This would be known as CAL Prep's phase of Mayhem. However, illumination & stability were right around the corner. . . . Class of 2012, we have come a long way . . . No matter what, we are a family . . . Always remember that our future is as bright as we make it. Never let the darkness around you, consume you. Use the light and tools you have been equipped with to make a positive future."* (Xavier Taylor, Graduation Speaker, California College Preparatory Academy, June, 2012)

*"Is there an award to give CAL Prep? Maybe a Nobel peace prize? Because they transformed an Oakland girl with no hopes to a cooperative citizen, who helps her peers when they need it and is a 4.0 student."* (Senior Alana Banks, California College Preparatory Academy, in Ness, 2012)

DID WE INDEED MOVE FROM the "mayhem" of California College Preparatory Academy (CAL Prep)'s early years to the transformation of lives—earning a Nobel peace prize in the eyes of one student? The previous chapters captured these earlier times, in CAL Prep's opening year and in studies of programmatic features implemented along the course of the school's development. This chapter describes the academic outcomes achieved by our students—from school inception to the high school graduation of two classes—with a lens focused on ups and downs as well as on advances across the 7 years. It provides a case example of how under more optimal conditions, the trajectory of first-generation college students can change—those who were once underprepared are now bound for 4-year colleges. Following this status report, the chapters to come describe pivotal qualities of the school, progressively shaped, that may have made such achievement possible.

Scholars have paid scant attention to the evolution of school start-ups into more mature schools with programmatic and instructional coherence and consistent outcomes (Betts & Hill, 2010). Also, not surprisingly, many caution that evaluations of school design outcomes should begin at points of greater maturity and not judge outcomes *too* early. Yet it is this flux—the challenges, the bumpy but steadfast journey, and the revisions in design and practice– that interests us in this book and provides important lessons for growing stronger schools.

Although an examination of a single case cannot speak to school effectiveness, it can depict patterns in achievement and attainment, paying close attention to changes in school context and student population. A systematic examination of student indicators provided feedback critical to the improvement process, illustrating whom we were serving, how far we had come in reaching our goals for student attainment, and what remained to be done. It also allowed us to explore the array of alternative explanations for achievement results, addressing methodological concerns that Henig (2008) raises in claims made about program effects. These include threats to internal validity (who enrolls and who leaves) and external validity (individual vs. population growth). As one example, Henig (2008) underscores how few studies report fully on student attrition.

In recent years, a series of lottery-based studies of model secondary schools, both charter and non-charter, provides more rigorous evidence of substantial school impacts, such as improved academic preparedness, graduation rates, and college-going for student populations who have not been well-served by the educational system. A lottery-based design is a natural randomized experiment that compares a treatment group of those admitted to the school with a control group who failed to gain admission, controlling for the role of selection factors in the outcomes achieved. These studies include evaluations of KIPP middle schools (Tuttle et al., 2013) and New York City Small Schools of Choice (SSCs; Bloom & Unterman, 2013; Unterman, 2014). These also include an evaluation of early college high schools (Berger et al., 2013, 2014) and the Preuss 6–12 School (Bohren & McClure, 2011). What these school designs share is the provision of a college-preparatory curriculum for all students. Despite decidedly different ecological contexts (in selection criteria, student demographics, and school configuration) and substantial variation in method (in time of assessment of school and student), these lottery-based studies provide a comparative context for the case analysis presented here.

We begin with a brief look at some of the challenges CAL Prep faced as it matured—challenges that greatly extended the timeline to becoming a fully functioning high school. Shifts in school context immediately stimulated questions about our student population (who entered and who left) and about which factors (student selection, school maturation, or student growth) might explain student outcomes. Did our population change and did we continue to serve the student population we had targeted? Did rates of student attrition diminish as the school matured and what factors predicted who left and who stayed? Regarding academic progress, was subject-matter mastery on statewide standardized tests on the rise, could we point to individual growth rather than population shift for these gains, and were we indeed reducing the achievement gap for African American and Latino students as compared to county and state results? Finally, in comparative terms, how did we fare in helping all students graduate as college-eligible and college-enrolled, with college credits already under their belt?

To answer these questions, we drew data from a variety of sources. These included the narrative records of Early College Initiative (ECI) committee meetings and analyses conducted by research teams at University of California (UC) Berkeley, Aspire Public Schools, and the Woodrow Wilson National Fellowship Foundation (WWNFF). We also used data from CAL Prep's self-study report (Reed & Cortez, 2010) for the Western Association of Schools and Colleges (WASC), student self-report data from the 2012 National College Advisory Corps Report, and college-going data from the National Student Clearinghouse, supplemented by information from Aspire and CAL Prep. We drew on county, state, and national comparisons, where possible.

The data presented here highlight the special challenges of bringing underprepared, low-income, and first-generation college youth into new secondary schools that offer an accelerated college-preparatory program with the highest of expectations for all. The collaborative process and analyses such as these informed the building of a coherent and aligned college-preparatory school culture, the nature of which will be described in forthcoming chapters.

## The Rubber Hits the Road: From Flux to Stability

Like all new schools, especially those that grow a grade level each year, CAL Prep was a dynamic setting, buffeted by forces both within and outside the school. In the journey from a new-start to a mature school, we faced three critical challenges along the way. These included (1) a site change from Oakland to Berkeley shifting charter authorization from the Oakland district to Alameda County; (2) a configuration change from the planned Grade 6–12 to a Grade 9–12 school; and (3) changes in staffing and leadership.

### Site and Configuration

The difficulty of securing a suitable and affordable site on or close to campus for the planned Grade 6–12 model had enormous implications for the ultimate design of the school and its financial viability. The population density and high real estate prices in communities within transportation reach of the UC Berkeley campus as well as the absence of a major donor conspired to limit school site options. Our first location at Golden Gate in Oakland, where we shared space with another Aspire elementary school a floor below us, proved untenable after 3 years—even with added portables—due to space restrictions and the difficulties of combining younger and older students on such a small campus. This led to a move in Year 4 to a somewhat larger site in Berkeley (St. Joseph the Worker School). As with every challenge, there were both negative and positive consequences. The move ended CAL Prep's status as a neighborhood school (a potential factor in lowering the enrollment of African American students) and reduced the degree to which the Aspire elementary school served as a feeder school to CAL Prep. Furthermore, given continuing size limitations even in the new location, this move derailed plans for a Grade 6–12 secondary school and limited school size to 225 instead of the envisioned 450 students.

Thus, during Years 1 to 2, CAL Prep operated as a middle school. The ninth grade was introduced in Year 3, and CAL Prep functioned as a full high school by Year 6, without any middle school grades (see Table 1.1 in Chapter 1). This pattern of growth—adding a new grade each year and dropping middle school grades—posed challenges for programming, teacher hires, course preparations across the middle school–high school divide, and program evaluation. Teachers spoke of the need to adjust for differences in preparedness between Aspire feeder school students and students coming from other schools and of the foreshortened time period for catch-up and acceleration, once high school status was reached. A student body of 225 students also constrained the variety of classes that could be offered and the school's financial strength. However, on the positive side, this change in site brought CAL Prep to a safer location, closer to a regional school model as originally designed, and within walking distance to the Berkeley campus, facilitating a deeper contact between the school and the university.

## Turnover

As described in Chapter 4 and made vivid in the quotations that open this chapter, the early years were tough. We struggled to implement a rigorous academic program in the face of the enormous underpreparedness of students—that is, to interweave acceleration with remediation. Also, we struggled to grow the school to size and achieve stability in leadership and teaching staff. During the period studied here, there was administrative turnover, with three principals in 7 years. Greater stability was achieved in Years 4 to 7, when the Dean of Students from the prior year became principal, thus providing 5 years of administrative leadership (see Chapter 13). Our partnership underwent changes as well, with the three regional superintendents from Aspire participating in our weekly school-site meeting (Elise Darwish for Years 1 and 2; Gloria Lee, for Years 3 to 5; and Tatiana Epanchin-Troyan for Years 6 and 7) and two of our four UC Berkeley liaisons continuing in these positions (Weinstein for Years 1 to 2; Jorgenson for Years 1 to 5; Worrell and Kaufman for Years 1 to 7). Darwish became Chief Academic Officer and Principal Prada became Director of Student Support Services for Aspire, and Weinstein continued her research role as well as ECI committee membership. These transitions went very smoothly, in part because of the very strong collaborative processes and regularized communication that was built into the Aspire and UC Berkeley partnership.

Attrition occurred for teachers as well, especially in the early years. In the first 2 years, student ambassadors, who led tours, would point out the pictures of their teachers in the entrance of the school and tell visitors, "This one is gone, that one is gone."[1] Among the reasons for the initially high teacher turnover were classroom management problems with a largely underprepared population. Similar to what has been documented in

---

[1] All quotations from students are taken verbatim from their completed questionnaires and narrative records, with no changes made to syntax or spelling.

the research literature especially with African American students (Gregory & Weinstein, 2008), a delicate dance ensued where teachers pressed hard for respectful behavior but students demanded signs of teachers' respect first. Other reasons included spousal geographic moves and a mismatch, mutually felt, between the needs of teacher and school.

In the first year, the small school staff included three experienced teachers (mathematics [math], science, and English Language Arts [ELA]). One teacher left during the year and was replaced, and only one of these four teachers returned the following year (turnover rate of 75%). In its second year with seven teachers on board, two left mid-year. But of these nine teachers (including two "leavers" and two replacements), seven teachers returned for Year 3 (turnover rate of 22%). Among these recruits were two teachers of color who contributed to diversifying the school staff. Importantly, four of these teachers remained at least 5 years (with three still on the faculty), and other long-serving teachers in the third year and beyond arrived. Together, these individuals emerged as the stable and core leadership for the school. Although several teachers continued to leave each year (e.g., 28% turnover from Year 6 to Year 7), some of these changes were in response to the Aspire policy to use teacher reassignment to strengthen other schools—a policy that had also benefitted CAL Prep.

## Student Population

### Who Enrolls

In this set of analyses, we examined student population demographics across the first 4 years of the school, given the site change from Oakland to Berkeley. Enrollment policy focused on the regional recruitment of students who faced barriers to going to college, including being English Language Learners, and coming from low-income families (as determined by eligibility for the Free and Reduced lunch program) as well as families whose members had not graduated from college. Also, there were no academic or behavioral requirements for enrollment. In the first few years, having opened as a largely neighborhood school within an African American community, we gave preference to siblings of enrolled students, neighborhood students, and students from other Aspire schools, with a smaller regional emphasis. With the site move, enrollment preferences included first, siblings of enrolled students; second, students from Aspire schools; and third, other students who faced barriers to attending college.

When the number of applicants exceeded capacity, lotteries were used in order of these preferences to determine which students gained admission.

**The School's First Year.** In its first year at the Oakland site, the school attracted a population of students that was slightly more male and predominantly African American (see Table 9.1). A majority of the students were eligible for free/reduced lunch, and most parents did not have college degrees. Almost 15% of the students were English language learners and 11% had special education classifications. CAL Prep's location in a recently closed under-performing neighborhood school drew students largely from one city, although the other students came from 11 other communities. Also, academic performance at the start was markedly low. On the October benchmark tests, few students tested proficient in math (1.4%) or writing (0%), with the majority of students scoring far below or below basic in these subjects. Looking at first-quarter grades, the majority of students received a grade of C or below in math and English. These descriptors point to a greatly underprepared student body, representative of the first-generation college population we had hoped to attract.

**From Years 1 to 4.** With October 1 as the enrollment cutoff date, we conducted a series of chi-square analyses to test differences in student demographics in the school's first year (a Grade 6–7 middle school in Oakland) and fourth year (a Grade 7–10 school in Berkeley). Although the student body was 2.3 times larger, a comparison of Year 1 to Year 4 showed significant change on only two of the seven demographic characteristics studied (see Table 9.1): ethnic makeup and city from which students were drawn. The school population was becoming *less* African American, *more* Latino, and *more* regional, but there were no significant differences in gender, free/reduced lunch status, parent education, and students with special needs. Changes in the enrollment of English language learners and special education students also reflected non-significant fluctuations. With regard to the early October performance levels of students, however, there were significant differences between Years 1 and 4. Although proficiency levels were still low in math (1.0%) and writing (10.7%), a lower proportion of students were performing at far below basic in math and in writing. Furthermore, students receiving first-semester grades of C and lower dropped substantially in math and English.

Thus, by Year 4, the school still enrolled a population that was mostly ethnic minority, low-income, from families who did not complete college, and largely low-performing. But the ethnic and regional mix of its students had shifted as had early-year academic benchmarks. One consequence of

TABLE 9.1 Student Demographics and Early Benchmarks/Grades for Year 1 and Year 4

|  | YEAR 1 | YEAR 4 |
|---|---|---|
| Number of students | 84 | 203 |
| % Male | 53.6 | 47.3 |
| % African American* | 83.3 | 57.1 |
| % Latino* | 10.7 | 38.9 |
| % Free/reduced lunch | 59.5 | 58.1 |
| % English language learners | 14.3 | 9.4 |
| % Special education classification | 10.7 | 15.8 |
| % Parents without a college degree | 82.0 | 75.4 |
| % Host city students* | 65.1 | 26.1 |
| % Far below basic in math* | 67.6 | 40.8 |
| % Far below basic in writing* | 58.5 | 8.6 |
| % With C grade or lower in math* | 84.2 | 43.8 |
| % With C grade or lower in English* | 70.2 | 50.7 |

NOTES: Ethnic makeup $\chi^2 = 22.33$, $p < .001$; host city $\chi^2 = 38.90$, $p < .001$; change in math proficiency $\chi^2 = 18.39$, $p < .001$; change in writing proficiency $\chi^2 = 85.64$, $p < .001$; grades in math $\chi^2 = 29.09$, $p < .001$; grades in English $\chi^2 = 6.79$, $p < .01$.

the move from Oakland to Berkeley was that the school became more regional in nature with an accompanying increase in the Latino population. Still low-performing, the school also enrolled a smaller population of the lowest performers on benchmarks as well as on first quarter grades.

## Who Leaves

**Rates of Student Attrition.** Attrition during the course of this first year was high, with 34% of the students leaving CAL Prep. As the school matured across 4 years, the *within-year* attrition rate dropped from 34% to 21%, 11%, and 9%, respectively. Joiners during each school year remained a relatively small percentage (11%, 3%, 7%, and 3%, respectively). A second report on student mobility (Vogt & Jaeger, 2009), which examined entering cohorts of students, confirmed a similar decline in *cross-year* attrition from spring to fall reenrollment across 4 years (27%, 25%, 16%, and 0%, respectively). Thus, over time, there was increased stability in the student population.

**Predictors of Attrition.** Drawing from three data sets, we explored the role of grade level, student demographics and school maturity, and student-perceived barriers or needs in predicting return status. Cross-year attrition was found to be greater among students in the higher grades. The 2010 WASC Report examined student mobility from spring to fall re-enrollment. After CAL Prep's first year, 65% of seventh graders did not return versus 47% of sixth graders. And after the second year, 65% of seventh graders and 63% of eighth graders did not return as compared to 40% of sixth graders. Data collected in Sami's transition study (Chapter 6) confirmed this same pattern after CAL Prep's third year. The greatest proportion of non-returning students was at the eighth to ninth grade transition to high school and 57.1% of all non-returners were from the eighth grade class ($\chi^2 = 6.87, p < .05$).

We also created a database of all students who had been enrolled at CAL Prep during its first 4 years ($N = 391$) and identified 115 (29%) who were "leavers" at any time. Using a series of logistic regressions to predict attrition status, we first tested gender, ethnicity, lunch status, suspensions, entering year, parent education, and entering achievement in independent analyses, and then we tested the significant predictors within a single equation to examine unique effects. Four of the eight—ethnicity, free/reduced lunch, suspension status, and year of school—were significant predictors of attrition. African American students were 1.82 times more likely to leave the school than students who were not African American ($p < .01$, CI $= 1.11–2.99$), as were students who were suspended ($p < .01$, odds ratio $= 1.92$, CI $= 1.14–3.24$). Students who entered CAL Prep in the earlier years were more likely to leave than students who entered CAL Prep in the later years ($p < .001$), with the estimated odds of a student leaving CAL Prep decreasing by 0.67 for every unit increase in the year of the school (CI $= 0.53–0.85$). However, students receiving free/reduced lunch were 0.53 times *less* likely to leave CAL Prep than students who paid for lunch ($p < .01$, CI $= 0.34–0.82$). Entering achievement level, parent education, and gender did not predict student attrition.

When these four variables were entered into one equation, neither lunch status nor suspensions remained significant. Importantly, this analysis underscores two *independent* predictors of attrition—ethnicity (Blacks at greater risk) and school immaturity (early years at greater risk). In this final model, the estimated odds of a student leaving CAL Prep was 1.90 times ($p < .001$, CI $= 1.03–3.49$) as great for African American students than for non–African American students, and 0.77 times lower (CI $= 0.59–1.00$) for every unit increase in year of the school.

Using this same database to identify the subset of students who had also participated in Sami's transition study (see Chapter 6), we explored whether the students who left and the students who persisted differed in reported barriers and socialization needs, as reflected on ratings of their ideal teacher. Non-returners compared to returners were more likely to implicate qualities of teachers ($\chi^2[1,153] = 5.83$, $p < .01$) and peers ($\chi^2[1,153] = 4.53$, $p < .05$) as barriers to their success. Those students who left the school described their feelings in the following ways, suggesting that they might have stayed if "The teachers respected us, and was nicer to us"; "Teachers be more easier, give less detentions, [and] more free dress"; and "The students were less rude." This comment, from a sixth grader, an African American girl, reflects these concerns:

> The teachers won't have to gives us so much work, the teachers won't have to be so rude and disrespectful . . . I say this because . . . we are just kids and I don't think some of them know that . . . we talk to them so rude because it is like strangers trying to gang up on us just because we are kids.

A series of analysis of variance tests also revealed significant differences between returners and non-returners on three of the seven socialization scales for ideal teacher. Non-returners desired more connection, $F(1, 147) = 2.29$, $p < .05$, more academic involvement, $F(1, 147) = 4.30$, $p < .05$, and more awareness of racism, $F(1, 147) = 2.58$, $p < .05$, from their teachers that did returners. But no differences were found between groups on their ideal for autonomy, academic expectations, and other aspects of ethnic-relevant teaching. In sum, non-returning students felt that the expectations of the school (academic and behavioral) were too high, school life was too structured, and teachers and peers did not respect them for being themselves. They also craved a closer relationship with teachers, one more understanding of race and racism (see Chapter 10). Thus, although diminishing in size as the school matured, there remained a group of students who felt less served by the school.

## Indicators of Student Academic Success

Here, we looked primarily at student performance on state standardized tests and at the educational attainment of our first two graduating classes. Given annually in Grades 2 to 11 until 2013, the California Standards

Tests (CSTs) assessed student performance relative to state standards, with scores assigned at one of five levels: *far below basic, below basic, basic, proficient,* and *advanced.* Not vertically aligned between school years, the CSTs do not allow direct comparisons of scaled scores from one year to the next. However, student proficiency level scores can be analyzed between grades. The Academic Performance Index (API) is California's weighted average of performance in academic subjects that ranges from 200 to 1000, with the target as 800 or above. When reached, schools are no longer given specific growth targets for subgroups to meet, as reflected in Adequate Yearly Progress (AYP) which is an accountability provision required by the No Child Left Behind Act (2002) for schools and districts receiving Title I monies. As California has adopted the Common Core Standards, the CSTs were suspended in 2012 and new tests were developed.

### Early Results: Years 1–2

As described earlier, students began CAL Prep with proficiency levels on fall benchmark tests at the very bottom (e.g., 1.4% proficient in math). But by the end of the school's first year, the percentage of students who achieved proficiency or above on the CSTs was 24% in ELA and 22% in math. This level of performance earned an API of 648 and a decile score of 2 on a scale of 1 to 10. A year later, these proficiency levels inched up to 35% in ELA and 44% in Math. The second API of 725 garnered a mid-range decile score of 5 statewide but a score of 10 compared to schools with similar income levels and ethnic makeup.

**Matched Student Growth.** Given that the API tracks the performance of school populations rather than individuals, did this upward change in achievement simply reflect a different student body or, importantly, was there evidence of individual student growth across these first 2 years? Individual growth analyses conducted by Aspire revealed that CAL Prep had accelerated the learning of two thirds of its lowest performing students (far below basic) by one to two levels. Furthermore, 36% of the student body went up at least one to two proficiency levels in ELA, and 49% of students did so in math. In a study conducted by ECI member David Stern (2009), these CAL Prep matched growth scores were compared to matched growth scores in four Bay Area school districts with comparable populations, and the results favored CAL Prep in all cases. As one example, 36% of CAL Prep students increased their performance in ELA by one or more levels, whereas only 22.7% of students did so in Oakland. Similarly for math, the corresponding percentages were 49% (CAL Prep) and 21.2% (Oakland). Thus, there was evidence for individual growth in proficiency at CAL Prep, independent of any population shift, and these gains surpassed the gains documented by school districts with comparable populations. Also accompanying these academic gains were improvements in behavior. An examination of the records of the 48 students enrolled for both school years showed a significant decrease in suspension rates from 33.3% in Year 1 to 10.4% in Year 2 ($\chi^2 = 6.97$, $p < .01$). Thus, even in the school's earliest years, we had evidence that individual students were showing both academic and self-regulatory growth.

A More Stable School: Years 4–7

**Recognition in Year 4**. In 2008–2009, CAL Prep was one of only 30 middle and high schools designated a California Title 1 Academic Achievement Award School. This award was granted because all students were making significant progress toward proficiency on California's academic content standards and socioeconomically disadvantaged students doubled their achievement targets for two consecutive years. Also in 2009, 100% of the 10th graders at CAL Prep passed the California High School Exit Examination in math and 91% passed in English, as compared to 48% of African American and 53% for Hispanic/Latino students on statewide comparisons who passed both parts of the test (Becker, Wise, & Watters, 2009).

**Algebra I in Eighth Grade**. Successful completion of Algebra I early in secondary school is an important marker for access to advanced math classes in high school, college-going, and success in science, technology, engineering, and mathematics (STEM fields), although opinions continue to shift about when this subject should be taken. All eighth graders at CAL Prep completed Algebra I in 2009–2010. As a whole, 71% scored proficient or advanced, exceeding the performance of White students where corresponding pass rates were 56% in the state and 52% in Alameda County. Within Alameda County, the pass rates were 19% for African American students and 24% for Hispanic/Latino students.

**Academic Performance Index Growth Over 7 Years**. The school also saw steady growth in the API index from 2006 to 2012 (see Figure 9.1). By Year 4 of the school, the API had surpassed the target score of 800, the

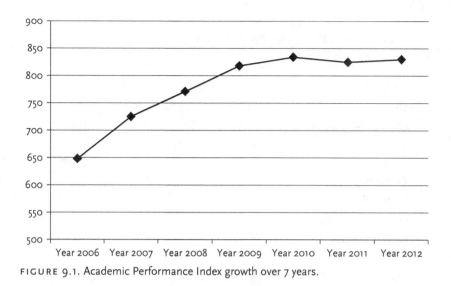

FIGURE 9.1. Academic Performance Index growth over 7 years.

state's measure of a high-performing school. Also, since 2009, the school earned decile scores in the 9 to 10 range as compared to all schools as well as to similar demographic schools. This rise was especially noteworthy because CAL Prep added upper grades and more challenging classes yearly until 2011–2012.

**Closing the Achievement Gap.** An Aspire report of the 2010–2012 CSTs for CAL Prep provided comparative data on rates of proficient or advanced for each academic subject by underrepresented ethnic group and economically disadvantaged students—and as compared to county and state rates. These proficiency rates for CAL Prep ranged from 40% to 93% at a school level, with CAL Prep's performance in 7 of the 13 subject areas demonstrating grade-level proficiency for 60% or more of its students. Importantly, in all subject-matter areas, the performance of African American, Latino, and economically disadvantaged students at CAL Prep exceeded by a wide margin the performance of these groups in Alameda County as well as in the state. Table 9.2 shows these results for two subject areas where we clearly see both success, especially with regard to closing the achievement gap, and work still to be done to bring all students up to proficiency. The 2011 CST results also demonstrated that CAL Prep did not have any achievement gaps based on ethnicity or socioeconomic status in ELA or math and the school met the English proficiency and growth metrics for English language learners. On the California English Language Development Test, 75% (*n* = 32) of the

TABLE 9.2 Comparative Proficiency Data on the California State Standards Tests by Subject (2010–2012)

| | CAL PREP | ALAMEDA | CALIFORNIA |
|---|---|---|---|
| **Subject X** | | | |
| All | 90% | 59% | 53% |
| African American | 100% | 31% | 37% |
| Latino | 85% | 41% | 40% |
| Economically disadvantaged | 87% | 40% | 41% |
| **Subject Y** | | | |
| All | 54% | 44% | 43% |
| African American | 55% | 14% | 23% |
| Latino | 53% | 22% | 27% |
| Economically disadvantaged | 50% | 47% | 29% |

NOTE: Academic subjects are nonidentified given the small size of the school and number of teachers. Data taken from Aspire Public Schools (2012).

students tested proficient and advanced, and those with matched results met the state target for growth.

**College-Ready Metrics.** Aiming for a level of preparedness that would help students avoid remedial courses in college, CAL Prep increasingly focused on assessing college readiness, in part as defined by the Early Assessment Program, a joint effort in California of the State Board of Education, the California Department of Education, and the California State University system (CSUs). These are *augmented* standards tests taken in 11th grade, which then allow for 12th grade interventions. Early results showed greater college readiness, as judged by both conditional and college-ready measures, in math (80% and 75% for classes of 2011 and 2012, respectively) than in ELA (24% and 45%, respectively), where efforts need to be directed.

## Two Graduating Classes

**High School Graduation Rates**. Table 9.3 shows the academic attainment of our students. The cohort analysis drew from state data, where the tracking of students had been uneven. The *estimated* adjusted cohort graduation rate—the percentage of entering ninth grade students at CAL Prep who graduate from *any* California high school with a regular diploma

TABLE 9.3 High School Graduation Rates and Postsecondary Enrollment

| OUTCOME | CAL PREP | | CALIFORNIA | | |
| --- | --- | --- | --- | --- | --- |
| | 2011 (n = 17) | 2012 (n = 44) | ALL | AFRICAN-AMERICAN | LATINO |
| Adjusted cohort HS grad | 83% | 75% | 79% | 66% | 74% |
| HS grad | 94% | 91% | | | |
| College courses | 4 | 6 | | | |
| College enrolled | 100% | 100% | 41% | 36% | 39% |
| 4-year college | 75% | 83% | 17% | 14% | 14% |
| UCs | 31% | 20% | 7% | 4% | 4% |
| CSUs | 44% | 55% | 11% | 10% | 10% |
| Private college | 0 | 8% | NA | NA | NA |
| 2-year college | 25% | 17% | 23% | 22% | 25% |

NOTE: HS = high school; grad = graduation rate; UCs = University of California; CSUs = California State University. All percentages are rounded. The adjusted 4-year cohort high school graduation rate reflects the percent of students in the 9th grade cohort at CAL Prep who graduated from *any* California high school with a regular diploma in 4 years: These are estimates as state tracking of students who received degrees elsewhere is incomplete. State graduation rates were obtained from ed-data (http://www.ed-data.k12.ca.us/). High school graduation rate reflects the number of students enrolled in 12th grade who graduated at the end of the school year. An analysis of student transcripts yielded the number of college courses passed while in high school. College enrollment figures for CAL Prep reflect the numbers of on-time high school graduates who are enrolled in college in the fall of the next year. These data were drawn from Beyond 12 and the National Student Clearinghouse and augmented by data from Aspire and CAL Prep. State comparisons of college enrollment were obtained from California Postsecondary Education Commission reports for 2009 for college-going in California.

in 4 years—was 83% (Class of 2011) and 75% (Class of 2012). This cohort rate places CAL Prep around the state average but higher than the cohort rate for African American and Latino students (see Table 9.3). However, this is an unfair comparison because these graduation rates, for the subgroup of students who persisted at CAL Prep, were achieved with more challenging requirements—a C or better in all A–G course requirements, exhibitions passed yearly, successful completion of three to five college classes, and an acceptance into a 4-year college. Also, these first two ninth grade cohorts began their journey in less than ideal circumstances (a Grade 6–9 school in Oakland and a Grade 7–10 school in Berkeley), *before* CAL Prep matured into a full high school.

When we look at the high school graduation rate of enrolled seniors, this rate rose to 94% (class of 2011) and 91% (class of 2012). In order to meet the stiff graduation requirements, the 8% of students across these

2 years who did not graduate on time enrolled for a fifth year as "super seniors." Within these graduating classes, 59% of the Class of 2011 and 77% of the Class of 2012 had attended CAL Prep for 4 or more years. We expect these persistence rates at CAL Prep will continue to increase.

**College Courses and College Preparation.** An analysis of student transcripts revealed an average of four (Class of 2011) and six (Class of 2012) completed college courses—with 12 to 18 college credits earned while enrolled in high school. Student reports matched these transcript results. The National College Advisory Corps, which sends recent college graduates into high-need high schools to help students overcome college-going barriers, surveyed the 2012 CAL Prep seniors ($N = 35$, 80% participation) about their college preparation, providing comparative state and national data from 168 high schools across nine states (Evaluation and Assessment Solutions, 2012). Overall, 70% of CAL Prep students reported taking three or more college classes for credit while in high school, more than twice the national rate of 28%. Self-reports also revealed that 71% of students received a grade point average (GPA) of 3.0 or above (as compared to 54% nationally) and that 38% were accepted at four or more colleges, more than twice the national rate of 16%. It is of interest that 63% of these CAL Prep seniors (compared to 38% nationally) listed parent expectations among the top two most important reasons for going to college.

**College Enrollments and Persistence**. All graduating seniors were enrolled in college the next academic year, as tracked by Beyond 12 and the National Student Clearinghouse, and augmented by Aspire and CAL Prep (see Table 9.3). Most striking was the number of CAL Prep graduates who enrolled in 4-year colleges and universities, which at 75% and 83%, respectively, for the first two graduating classes, is more than five times the rate for African American and Latino students in California. It is also twice the national rate of 37.5% for all recent high school "completers" (National Center for Educational Statistics, 2014). Furthermore, a high percentage of students enrolled in the UCs, the most selective tier of the California postsecondary system. The rates of 31% (2011) and 20% (2012) greatly exceed both the college-going rates as documented in Table 9.3 and the eligibility rate of California public high school graduates (13.4%), African Americans (6.3%), and Latinos (6.9%) for UC admission (Griffin, 2009). Across these first two classes, six students were admitted to UC Berkeley, a particularly rewarding outcome for the partnership. Although a thorough examination of college persistence data is beyond the timeline studied in this book, preliminary data provided by CAL Prep are promising. Overall, 81% of the Class of 2011 was still enrolled in postsecondary education (at either a 4-year or 2-year college) in the third year beyond their high school graduation. For the Class of 2012, this persistence rate was 88%, as of their second year out of high school.

## Student Indicators in Context

### Overview

The pattern depicted here reflects a steady upward path of academic accomplishment, despite a series of challenges to CAL Prep's stability as a new-start school. Schools that add a grade a year have a longer lasting newness problem, and CAL Prep did not achieve *full* high school status until Year 6 of the seven years examined. Regional schools also encounter additional challenges in building community across a larger geographical terrain. Also, the change in school site as well as in grade configuration meant a shift from a neighborhood to a *fully* regional school and from a planned Grade 6–12 to a Grade 9–12 high school. By CAL Prep's fourth year, however, greater stability of school staff and administrative leadership had been reached, and with increased institutional stability, student attrition was also reduced. A close look at who entered and who left CAL Prep underscored some change in the characteristics of enrolled students. Over time, the student population became more regionally drawn and more Latino, with a decrease in the enrollment of the very lowest achievers. Yet CAL Prep continued to serve the students it intended to reach—underrepresented ethnic minority, low-income, first-generation college, and greatly underprepared students.

In this school with a more challenging curriculum (college-preparatory blending high school and college courses), the performance of its students, assessed at a population-level on standardized tests, improved each year. The rates of subject-matter proficiency outpaced county and state statistics for Whites as well as underrepresented minorities, thereby closing the achievement gap. Although the adjusted ninth grade cohort graduation rate was about average for the state—notably in the face of tougher graduation requirements and with four to six college courses under students' belts—100% of the seniors enrolled in college upon graduation. A high percentage of these graduates chose 4-year colleges, especially those at the top tier of competitiveness such as the UCs, and at rates that exceeded state results for this population. These rates of admission to highly selective universities stand in contrast to findings from Domina and Ruzek's (2012) study of K–16 partnerships in California, which documented boosts to California State university admissions but not to the UCs. But even with this high level of attainment, there was considerable work still to be done—subjects where proficiency levels lagged, gaps between proficiency on tests and actual college readiness, students needing a fifth year to complete requirements, and school "leavers" who at CAL Prep were disproportionately African American.

## Evidence of School Effects

Could these results be attributed to *school* effects or might they instead reflect *student* differences? Were there biases in the sample that stemmed from selection (parental choice and more motivated families) and/or from attrition (dropout of low achievers), thereby creating a pool of students more likely to succeed regardless of school qualities? Although a case study of a single school cannot answer this question, there are clues that speak to both sides of this issue. On the side of potential student differences is evidence in the regional nature of the school (requiring a greater parent commitment to transportation), student-reported parental expectations as a reason for college-going (63% as compared to 38% in a national sample), and the drop at entry across school years in the very lowest achievers. Alternatively, on the side of school effects is evidence of individual student growth across the school's first 2 years that surpasses the growth of comparable school districts, school maturity effects on reductions in attrition, and increases in 4-year persistence rates at CAL Prep from the 2011 to 2012 cohorts.

Importantly, our findings largely match the results of recent lottery studies, which provide more rigorous evidence of substantial positive school impacts as well as a point of comparison for this case study. While ruling out selection effects, the lottery studies' findings also underscore some attrition effects at play. As an example, the Preuss School study for class of 2010 showed higher standardized test performance (except for sixth grade math), completion of A–G course requirements, and GPA for Preuss students as compared to lottery-control students, as well as a 74% rate of intent to register in 4-year colleges for Preuss students, with no comparison group noted (Bohren & McClure, 2011). Although targeting a first-generation college population, Preuss School, in contrast to CAL Prep, screens for academic potential through letters of support from teachers and personal statements. Bohren and McClure (2011) also point to greater attrition of lower-performing students from Preuss as compared to the comparison group, which could account for some part of the achievement differences. The New York City SSCs, with a sample of 14,608 students and a 4-year cohort analysis, garnered higher 4-year graduation rates (71.6% vs. 62.2%) and college enrollment (49.0% vs. 40.7%), with 29.7% versus 23.2% headed to 4-year colleges as compared to lottery-control students (Unterman, 2014). This report also notes an attrition rate of approximately 30% of students who do not graduate from high school on time or enroll in college.

Closest to our model is the Early College lottery-based evaluation of 10 schools in five states that demonstrated significantly higher performance for early college students as compared to control students on ELA state assessments (but not math or GPAs), high school graduation rates, and college enrollment while in high school (Berger et al., 2013). Of interest, there was a similar attrition rate from high school of 17% for early college students and 19% for comparison students. Their results also show higher enrollment in a 4-year college, both one year earlier (23.6% vs. 8.5%) and normatively (48.9% vs. 43.3%). Also, based on student survey data, 49.1% of early college students reported having earned at least one full year of college credit or 60 units upon high school graduation versus 5.5% of comparison students.

Given that early college courses were a mandated feature, it is of interest to compare results across CAL Prep and the Early College lottery study. At CAL Prep, as determined from course transcripts, all graduating students successfully completed approximately one semester of college courses (four to six courses) in the context of a 10% rate nationally. In contrast, Berger and colleagues (2013) noted that more than a third of the early college students did *not* enroll in any college classes but based on self-report, more than half of the students completed a full year of college classes, as the Gates Foundation Early College Initiative had intended. Thus, CAL Prep more consistently met the goal of enrollment in college courses but not at the level of earned credit expected. Among the constraints that CAL Prep experienced were scheduling conflicts, balancing remedial interventions with college courses, the uneven quality of courses, and the cost, which earlier had been free at community colleges but with the economic recession now incurred a charge. The UC Berkeley partnership offered additional but non-credited opportunities for students to take summer session classes, freshman seminars, and a week of college seminars on campus. As compared to CAL Prep, 8 of the 10 early college high schools were located on college campuses, and 7 of 10 reflected partnerships with community colleges rather than research universities, making college course accrual easier.

## For All Students

Although this growing literature strongly supports school effects, attrition—albeit unevenly studied—may remain a problem for such high-expectation and accelerated secondary schools. In their study of 10 early college high schools, Edmunds and colleagues (2010, p. 48) raised the question of whether an accelerated model is for everyone: "The Early College High School model faces a challenge. Its very strengths—a challenging, focused academic program with high expectations—attract many students while simultaneously driving a few youth back to traditional high schools."

For students at CAL Prep, the greatest barrier lay in the high academic and behavioral demands of the school, as students pressed for more freedom and more fun—a finding also reported by Edmunds and colleagues (2010). The rigor was enough of a barrier for some not to return, especially at the point of transition from eighth to ninth grade. And looking across the first 4 years, beyond the effects of student achievement, parent education, income, and gender, both school immaturity and student ethnicity predicted student attrition. Even as the school matured, African American students were almost twice as likely as Latino students to leave CAL Prep.

As measured in Year 3, at the heart of our students' reasons for leaving the school was not only the concern about the "hard" work but also the quality of the teacher and student relationships, where they felt a lack of respect, connection, and academic support as well as the need for more awareness of racism. Their perceptions reflect the divide between African American students and their teachers, documented in high school settings where such students are overrepresented in disciplinary infractions for defiance (Gregory, Skiba, & Noguera, 2010). But as Gregory and Weinstein (2008) have shown, although African American students behaved more defiantly with teachers they perceived as untrustworthy, the perceived expression of teacher caring and high expectations was associated with more cooperative behavior and a diminished discipline gap.

In contrast, Edmunds and colleagues (2010) reported that Hispanic/Latino students were more likely, on average, to be the school "leavers" in the 10 early college high schools they studied. It is difficult to tease out the reasons behind the ethnic differences in student attrition across these two studies, except to note contextual differences such a change in school location in our study and enormous variability in student composition among the 10 early college high schools, limiting the usefulness of an average attrition rate. As documented in national samples, although African American and Latino students leave high school at similar rates (Heckman & LaFontaine, 2010), studies of student dropout and school transfers during high school paint a complex picture of influential factors, stemming from qualities of students, family and neighborhood, and schools (Rumberger, 2011). Future research about student attrition rates and about the success of acceleration for all must look beneath the averages, exploring contextual variation in school model, location, and configuration, ethnic and income makeup, and school maturity that may help explain the conditions that magnify and minimize patterns of student attrition.

## Acting on the Data, Again and Again

Specific targeted interventions, based on analyses of data, contributed in our view to the improvements seen each year. Among many efforts, Aspire provided teachers and school with analyses of how subgroups of students performed on standardized tests in each subject domain. UC Berkeley offered data on school "leavers" and school "stayers." Action on these data, as noted in the CAL Prep WASC Report (2009), promoted "social-emotional belonging and well being which seem to play a large part in increasingly stable enrollment numbers" (p. 16). Given normative student concern about limited school activities, we broadened the extracurricular program—creating opportunities for talent development, student choice, and schoolwide fun activities more typical of high school settings. Teachers worked hard to develop the trust of students as the first step of engaging them in instruction (Chapter 11) and to create an ethnically relevant curriculum that addressed cultural achievements as well as an understanding of the history of racism (Chapters 10 and 15). We also built a robust system of student supports (Chapters 13 and 14). Also, in order to develop a stable core of teachers, we reached out for exceptional talent in the ranks of UC Berkeley graduate students and teachers from other Aspire schools and provided strong coaching and professional development (Chapters 12 and 16). In essence, we worked actively to grow our own—both teachers and students.

The hard work continues at CAL Prep—increasing the level of challenge in instruction and introducing more rigorous assessments with a deeper focus on college readiness and writing. Preparation for the Common Core Standards and different achievement tests is underway. We continue to explore the conditions needed for successful college credit accrual and the advantages of Advanced Placement classes versus early college classes. In addition, we have begun to investigate the barriers that students experience in college and the supports they need to be successful.

This bumpy but upward trajectory of increasingly positive outcomes, in the context of challenges faced and actions taken, is the most important lesson here. It provides an existence proof of how much low-income and first-generation college students can achieve, given a change in educational conditions. Not attained in a day or a year, such improvements required thoughtful focus, revision, and time. Attrition rates and the incorporation of newcomers cannot likely explain all of these positive outcomes. These results, evident early (the first two graduating classes) and in a school without admission criteria, are especially promising, given our hopes to repair the educational pipeline for those student populations facing dramatic disparities in access to and success in a college-preparatory education. The chapters that follow reflect the voices of administrators, teachers, and researchers in illuminating critical elements in school design and subject matter instruction that may have played a mediating role in the development of students' academic preparedness for college and their identity as college-bound youth.

## References

Aspire Public Schools. (2012). *CAL Prep comparative data state and county level.* Oakland, CA: Author.

Becker, D. E., Wise, L. L., & Watters, C. (Eds.). (2009). *Independent evaluation of the California High School Exit Examination (CAHSEE): 2009 evaluation report.* Alexandra, VA: HumRRO.

Berger, A., Turk-Bicakci, L., Garet, M., Song, M., Knudson, J., Haxton, C., ... Stephan, J. (2013). *Early college, early success: Early College High School Initiative impact study.* Washington, DC: American Institutes for Research.

Berger, A., Turk-Bicakci, L., Garet, M., Knudson, J., & Hoshen, G. (2014). *Early college, continued success: Early college initiative impact study.* Washington, DC. American Institutes for Research.

Betts, J. R., & Hill, P. T. (2010). *Taking measure of charter schools: Better assessments, better policymaking, better schools.* Lanham, MD: Rowman & Littlefield.

Bloom, H. S., & Unterman, R. (2013). *Sustained progress: New findings about the effectiveness and operation of small public high schools of choice in New York City.* Oakland, CA: MDRC.

Bohren, A., & McClure, L. (2011). *The Preuss School at UCSD: Academic performance of the class of 2010.* La Jolla, CA: The Center for Research on Educational Equity, Assessment, and Teaching Excellence. University of California, San Diego.

Domina, T., & Ruzek, E. (2012). Paving the way: K-16 partnerships for higher education diversity and high school reform. *Educational Policy, 26,* 243–267. doi:10.1177/0895904810386586.

Edmunds, J. A., Arshavsky, N., Unlu, F., Luck, R., & Bozzi, L. (2010). *"They try their best to keep you:" Lessons learned from a study of Early College High School leavers.* Greensboro, NC: SERVE Center, University of North Carolina at Greensboro.

Evaluation and Assessment Solutions for Education. (2012). *2011-2012 student survey report: Cal Prep High School.* Chapel Hill, NC: National College Advising Corps.

Gregory, A., Skiba, R. J., & Noguera, P. A. (2010). The achievement gap and the discipline gap: Two sides of the same coin? *Educational Researcher, 38,* 59–68. doi:10.3102/0013189X09357621.

Gregory, A., & Weinstein, R. S. (2008). The discipline gap and African Americans: Defiance or cooperation in the high school classroom. *Journal of School Psychology, 46,* 455–475. doi:10161/j.jsp.2007.09.001.

Griffin, A. (2009). *College-going and university eligibility: Differences between racial/ethnic groups* (CPEC Report 09-11). Retrieved from http://www.cpec.ca.gov/completereports/2009reports/09-11.pdf

Heckman, J. J., & LaFontaine, P. A. (2010). The American high school graduation rate: Trends and levels. *The Review of Economics and Statistics, 92,* 244–262. doi:10.1162/rest.2010.12366.

Henig, J. R. (2008). *What do we know about the outcomes of KIPP schools?* East Lansing, MI: The Great Lakes Center for Education Research & Practice. Retrieved from http://greatlakescenter.org/docs/Policy_Briefs/Henig_Kipp.pdf

National Center for Educational Statistics. (2014, April). *Public high school four-year on-time graduation rates and even dropout rates: School years 2010-11 and 2011-2012.* Washington, DC: U.S. Department of Education. Retrieved from http://nces.ed.gov/pubs2014/2014391/tables.asp

Ness, C. (2012, May). *Against formidable odds, four from CAL Prep are entering Berkeley this fall.* Retrieved from http://newscenter.berkeley.edu/2012/06/04/31377/

No Child Left Behind (NCLB) Act of 2001, Pub. L. No. 107-110, § 115, Stat. 1425 (2002).

Reed, M., & Cortez, M. (2010). *CAL Prep WASC self-study: An Aspire public school in partnership with UC Berkeley.* Unpublished document, California College Preparatory Academy, Berkeley, CA.

Rumberger, R. W. (2011). *Dropping out: Why students drop out of high school and what can be done about it.* Boston, MA: Harvard University Press.

Stern, D. (2009). *Analysis of individual student changes on California Standards Tests during 2006-2007 school year.* Unpublished paper, Graduate School of Education, University of California, Berkeley.

Tuttle, C. C., Gill, B., Gleason, P., Knechtel, V., Nichols-Barrer, I., & Resch, A. (2013). *KIPP Middle Schools: Impacts on achievement and other outcomes.* Oakland, CA: Mathematica Policy Research. Retrieved from http://www.kipp.org/results/ mathematica-study/mathematica-2013-report

Unterman, R. (2014). *Headed to college: The effects of New York City's small high schools of choice on postsecondary enrollment.* New York, NY: MDRC. Retrieved from http://www.mdrc.org/sites/default/files/Headed_to_College_PB.pdf

Vogt, K., & Jaeger, L. (2009). *Student persistence and incoming performance: School D.* Unpublished report. Princeton, NJ: The Woodrow Wilson Early College Network.

# III | Equity and Excellence in a High School Setting

# 10 | Equity in the Teaching of History

**RYAN GROW**

*"I hope to learn about **my** history."* (Student at California
College Preparatory Academy)

E QUITY IN A CLASSROOM IS an ever-present challenge for a conscientious teacher. Different cultures, languages, ethnicities, skill levels, values, and socioeconomic statuses form a web of obstacles that is formidable for a teacher to contemplate, and even more formidable to navigate. History class is a particularly apt setting for highlighting equity in a school. The themes of history are often concerned with equity, with the struggles for it, with the fair application of it, with the denial of it to minorities or the powerless. The themes of religious freedom, abolition of slavery, women's suffrage, imperialism, suppression of minorities, public education, genocide, and so on are all touched on in the course of a typical survey history course, as is found in most public high schools in California, and the issue of equity runs strong through them all. As a history teacher, the concept of pedagogical equity is essential to teaching about the struggles for political, economic, and social equity.

As I write these words, I am concluding my eighth year as a California College Preparatory Academy (CAL Prep) teacher, the last six as the sole history teacher on campus. The development of equity in the history curriculum of CAL Prep aligns very closely with my own development as a teacher, and I have not always been successful. It is important, I think, for teachers to be able to recognize, even if they do not always reflect, the social and cultural starting points for their students. This recognition facilitates empathy. When I was first hired at CAL Prep, I had little sense of this. I grew up in a household where everyone older than me had gone to college and expected the same from me. I attended the University of California, Davis and did as well as I wanted to at the time. My friends had all gone to college. We all spoke standard English and spoke it well, and we were encouraged, often. This was what I called and referred to as "life." When I started at CAL Prep, I discovered that this perspective, my social and cultural starting point, was often widely divergent from those of my students. Consequently, for my first few years, I was often an inequitable teacher with the best of intentions.

## Toward Pedagogical Equity

There are many ways human beings have used to divide themselves over the centuries, and the first duty of a classroom culture must be to knock away as many of these divisive barriers as possible. Pedagogical equity is based on several different aspects of equity. These include equity of theme, equity of access, and equity of experience; the lack or misappropriation of any of these can create an unbalanced or unfair classroom environment.

### Equity of Theme

Equity of theme concerns the particular lessons of history that are taught in the class. Because history is a rich and complex subject, not everything can be squeezed into the school year; some things must be left out. The choice of what gets taught and what gets ignored is one criterion by which equity of theme is judged. It is possible, as we shall see, to create a narrative of American history that essentially is true but that also leaves entire populations of people out of the story. Such inequities of theme create a biased and dishonest view of our past that fails to celebrate the important contributions of some peoples to our American present.

**Going Beyond the Standards.** For many years, US history classes have been based on standards set by state departments of education. These standards were the result of a nationwide movement in the 1990s to mandate minimum levels of education in American schools. Using results of standardized tests as a benchmark, one can argue that this movement has been successful, but tests and standards do not reflect everything that is desirable in a classroom environment. Indeed, the History–Social Science Content Standards for California Public Schools, originally adopted in 1998, have a certain narrowness of focus that leads to a very compartmentalized view of the development of this nation, and they can lead to inequities in the classroom if rigidly adhered to. The portrayal of African Americans in the standards provides one example of such narrowness. If one were to use only the California Content Standards for US history as a guide, one would conclude that African Americans played a vitally important role in the development of this country, solely by agitating for an expansion of their civil rights.

The African American experience, as laid out by the California Content Standards for US history, can essentially be summarized as follows:

> African Americans were brought here as slaves, their enslavement caused a conflict which led to compromises to the original framing of the Constitution, then later a Civil War. After the Civil War, they were technically free, but not actually free, so they fought for their civil rights and they eventually, after many reverses and dangers, won.

This summary certainly touches on some of the more important parts of African American history, but it is also a narrow and overly simple conceptualization of African Americans' historical legacy. Based on this summary, one could conclude that all African Americans were either slaves or freedom fighters. Were there not, an African American student might well ask, any inventors, any teachers, any entrepreneurs, any (nonsharecropping) farmers in the wide stream of Black history? These are excellent questions, and it is the responsibility of an equity-minded teacher to help students find answers to these and similar questions.

The conceptualization of Native Americans' role in American history is even narrower—and possibly irresponsible. Of the approximately 81 separate, US history standards in the California Content Standards, only one mentions Native Americans. Curiously, the standard asks the history teacher to explain how the African American Civil Rights Movement of the 1950s and 1960s influenced the "agendas, strategies, and effectiveness" of other groups fighting for their own civil rights such as Native Americans, Hispanic Americans, and Asian Americans. This standard reflects a profound gap in the history of this country, and the conscientious teacher needs to go beyond the standards and find space in his or her pacing guide to point out that there were Native Americans living where we live now *before* the arrival of other racial or ethnic groups, and that this was their land, but was taken from them over the course of the nation's growth.

Fortunately, things are in flux in the world of education. Many states, including California, are adopting a new approach to curriculum expectations in the form of the Common Core standards. These standards are advertised as concentrating more on development of academic skills in students rather than particular pieces of content knowledge. This approach, theoretically, should allow teachers to feel less constrained in what they teach, opening the door to a broader viewpoint of what constitutes content mastery. As of this writing, Common Core has yet to address history and the social sciences, and so it remains to be seen whether or not students from marginalized backgrounds will be enabled to see their own stories reflected in the history of the United States.

**Allowing Students to See Themselves in History.** Students are curious! Every year I get questions that begin with "When are we going to learn about ...?" I still remember a question that I was asked in my first year as a teacher at CAL Prep. I was hired mid-year to replace a departing teacher, teaching humanities with a world history component, and I was new to the community and leaning heavily on the textbook to get through the first few months. Jared[1] asked me, "When are we going to learn about Africa?" I didn't know. So I looked through the textbook, and there was only one chapter that addressed sub-Saharan Africa, and a few paragraphs on Mediterranean Africa and the expansion of Islam, but that was not what Jared was talking about.

I had expected an entire unit of study on the second largest continent, but there was just the one chapter. I found myself temporizing: "I'm not sure just yet, Jared." And Jared, an African American kid, went away with his question unanswered. Jared stands out in my mind as my first failure as an equitable teacher. I had failed in reassuring him about the equity of theme in my classroom. Perhaps it was an understandable failure. I was a new teacher taking up a new job in the middle of the academic year in a new city. There were bound to be mistakes. But this one rankled, and I resolved that the next time a curious student asked me a question that began "When are we going to learn about ...," I would have an answer. It might not always be the answer the student might want—history is a vast subject, after all—and some things must be left out, but the answer would be thoughtful and purposeful. If I am serious about equity of theme in my classroom, then that much, at least, I owe to students such as Jared.

---

[1] All names used are pseudonyms.

## Equity of Access

The second aspect of equity is equity of access. In a high school classroom, the teacher facilitates a student's access to educational materials in a much higher proportion than in a university setting, where students are often expected to act as autonomous, independent agents in the process of gaining an education. High school teachers, therefore, have a great deal of influence over the quality and substance of their students' education, simply because they provide so much of the content and context. One of the main responsibilities, then, of a high school teacher is to ensure that students' access to education is as open as possible.

Equity of access can take many forms, and cultivating it in the classroom poses one of the greatest challenges for high school teachers. In fact, equity of access can distinguish master teachers from novices. Because of the great range of learning histories and students' perceptions of themselves, their abilities, and their school experiences, creating an equitable, accessible classroom environment is exceptionally difficult. What works well for one student may not work well for another, and what works for that other student may not work at all for the 3rd or the 4th or the 27th student in the room. Sitting down with a blank sheet of paper or a newly opened Microsoft Word file and designing a learning experience to accommodate the needs, personalities, and histories of 30 high school students is one of the most humbling and intimidating experiences a new teacher faces. Also, when one realizes that a teacher usually sees five or more groups of students a day, the enormity of the challenge readily becomes apparent.

**Supporting Individual Differences.** Fortunately for the struggling teacher, some general ideas enable him or her to forge an equitably accessible classroom environment for a great majority of the students encountered. Much like one's diet, a classroom environment should have variety. A tool kit of varied pedagogical strategies allows a diverse group of students to access the content of the class successfully. When people consider exactly how they access information, they quickly arrive at the five senses: sight, sound, smell, touch, and taste. A close consideration of the five senses gives a teacher insight into techniques for creating an equitable classroom environment, from the point of view of access.

Not all of the five senses can be used in similar proportions. Smell and taste, in particular, are rarely available as pedagogical tools, although occasionally, when bringing a time period to life in a visceral way for the students, they can be invaluable, as when studying the Romantic response to the machine-driven inhumanity of the Industrial Revolution, we bring in sprigs of daffodils for the students to smell while analyzing William Wordsworth's poem of the same name. But such occasions are rare. This leaves us with sight, sound, and touch. Touch is the next most rare, but it can be very powerful.

History, properly understood, is an investigation into varying interpretations of data. The historian sifts information, weighs facts, creates hypotheses, constructs arguments, evaluates sources of information, and supports conclusions. It is the scientific method applied to the past. The professional historian spends a great deal of time and effort in the "field": picking through library stacks; digging up old midden heaps; skulking around in churches, castles, and temples; and talking to people who have the information or memory they want. It is old-fashioned sleuth work, with "truth" the ultimate prize. The high school history teacher has a difficult time replicating these conditions. A class of students generally sits for about 50 minutes, with no travel budget beyond the cost of a ticket for the local bus. Creating a lesson of historical investigation, with the consequent development of critical thinking skills, is a challenge. The use of realia can, to some extent, aid in this.

Students love realia, the artifacts or facsimiles of the past, which they can pass around, handle, turn over, question, interrogate, and create inferences from. Every time they are used in class, the lesson is a success. Unfortunately, there is something abstract about history, which I suspect is one of the reasons it is so underappreciated, but realia give shape and substance to the abstraction. For students who have difficulty casting images in their minds, for those with disabilities, these objects become lessons in themselves, illuminating ideas that before were merely vague shadows or guessed-at mirages. Even those students who had been following the lesson with attention, who had conceived themselves well versed in the subject, are fascinated with artifacts. Everyone can touch, and almost everyone likes to touch.

In a history classroom, the options for realia are almost limitless. Woven baskets and chipped arrowheads when studying Paleolithic cultures, ammunition cans and helmets from Army surplus when studying World War II, gas masks and radiation tags when studying the Cold War—any of these can become a lesson that can be accessed equally by all students in the classroom. It is really restricted only by the teacher's imagination. A long-term dream of mine, for example, is to teach a unit on the French Revolution with a fully operational guillotine at the front of the room, open for examination. Currently, however, there are certain prejudices (and perhaps laws) against bringing heavy, sharp, dangerous objects into the classroom, which must be overcome before such a dream can become reality. But no progress was ever made by accepting the status quo, so I remain hopeful.

For all its benefits, however, teaching through the sense of touch has severe limitations. It is inefficient in conveying information, it is subject to wildly inaccurate hypothesis–conclusion relationships (as when a student concluded that a flying shuttle, used in textiles, was "probably a canoe for Barbies"), and it does not capture the narrative of history well, providing more of a snapshot of an idea than a sense of cause and effect. Touch can be used like punctuation, adding a question mark or putting an exclamation to an idea, but, by itself, touch is inadequate to provide students with equitable access to a history curriculum. This brings us to sight and sound, the most common senses used by a history teacher, or any teacher.

In my experience, sight is the most important sense for teaching. Humans are, as a whole, a visual species. We have excellent, binocular, color vision, and we access much of the world with it, so it must be a major part of an equitable classroom curriculum. Vision offers many opportunities in a history classroom. The use of maps, for example, can give a sense of proportion to world events, elicit an understanding of geopolitics, allow learners to place historical protagonists in their memory palaces, or give those with an organizational bent opportunities to impose order on the content (by the use of color coding, movement arrows, and so on). Also, once the curriculum has moved into the 20th century, film and video can be used as primary sources, to give students firsthand accounts of the time period under study. World War I is always more vivid and affecting after showing the students film clips of the soldiers suffering from shell shock following the Battle of Verdun and the psychological treatments they were forced to endure. Such visuals provide "punch" to any lesson, allowing students access to ideas and emotions formerly blocked or obscured for them.

Visual demonstrations are also useful, perhaps essential, for students to build their understanding of the manipulation of ideas. There is very often a sense among students that the visual world is the real world, that reality and vision are one and the same. The entire art and science of advertising is based on taking advantage of this very common misunderstanding, and it is the responsibility of a teacher, especially a history teacher, to give students the mental tools to properly analyze the evidence of our eyes. Certainly, propaganda plays an important role in any well-conceived history curriculum. Students can be taught the critical thinking skills to resist blind acceptance and to view information with appropriate skepticism. An hour or two of sieving the conspiracy websites devoted to the assassination of John F. Kennedy, for example, plus access to YouTube, can give a history teacher all the material he or she needs to conduct a lesson on the nature of trustworthy evidence. (Who knows, perhaps a student will finally prove conclusively the identity of the president's assassin.)

Hearing is the basis for most pedagogy and is particularly apt in a history curriculum. History is, after all, the greatest story ever told, rich in conflict, with fascinating characters, life lessons, and exultation and tragedy in equal doses. Sometimes, despite the many tools and technologies available to a modern teacher, the best way to convey a story is to tell it. A story artfully told—with passion, with precision, with awareness of one's audience—is still one of the most engaging forms of entertainment. Show a movie in class and some kids fall asleep; have them read a document and they will whisper to each other or pull out a phone. But tell them a story, and tell it well, and every student listens. It is as ancient a mode as exists for transmitting information, a throwback to the origins of the family fire, and it works exceedingly well.

In addition to being engaging, effective lecturing or story telling is very efficient. A lot of information can be transmitted in a relatively short amount of time, although one must be careful to not overwhelm students with a flood of new facts, figures, and connections. When I begin to hear deep sighs, see pencils drop to desks, or notice eyes staring fixedly straight ahead or at the ceiling, I know I have reached the saturation point and that it is time to change my approach. I have found that 30 minutes of solid information flow is the capacity of the average high school class. Moreover, it is difficult to express complex ideas using only the spoken word. As an exercise, try explaining American constitutional theory without any visual tools.

The best pedagogy for history should involve the use of multiple modalities. Teachers who are concerned with giving their students the best chance to access the information in the classroom will ensure that their lessons are filled with variety. Although finding a "tried and true" lesson formula that can be used day after day would immediately eliminate much time and effort from a teacher's life and lighten considerably a teacher's load, it is a dangerous temptation. A teacher who decides that he or she will teach a certain lesson in only one way is probably reaching some proportion of his or her students and shutting out others, and this practice is no longer equitable.

Could the students adapt to this template and learn anyway? Perhaps. Certainly, students have some responsibility for making the most of their own education, and it is right to expect great things from them. But it edges into the arena of self-righteousness to expect all students to learn from a single way of teaching, and conformity is not the same as achievement. Besides, high school students exist along a wide spectrum of emotional, mental, and physical maturity. Some of them may not understand why they are not learning in a certain class, and some may recognize that they need something different but may not believe that the problem is not of their doing; others may have been conditioned by difficult experiences outside the classroom to surrender in the face of adversity. A teacher concerned with equity should consider these possibilities when crafting lessons. The job is to teach, after all, not to expound. An effort should be made to reach students from all backgrounds, and the best way to do that seems to be to include as much variety in lesson plans as possible, drawing from the full range of learning modalities.

**Supporting Students with Disabilities.** There are some students, unfortunately, who will find it difficult to rise to high expectations, no matter how varied the pedagogical techniques used in the classroom are. Very frequently, there are students with disabilities in the classroom, and creating an environment where they can access the curriculum is a challenge that is unique for each student, because disabilities rarely manifest in exactly the same way. For these students, school can be a grinding, disheartening experience. Day after day, in class after class, they are aware that they "don't get it" and think that they are "slow," and they believe that the forest of upraised hands will never include their own. Moreover, as their ability to access a lesson is impeded by their disability, their confidence and will to achieve are diminished. These students are often the first to give up. Finding creative ways to include them in the classroom conversation, give them opportunities for success, and help them build a positive academic identity is an enormous challenge for equity in a classroom.

Disabilities are unique to individuals, but they do have some common symptoms that can be broadly addressed. One of the commonalities I have observed is a feeling of helplessness. There is so much to learn, and learning even one thing can be a challenge for these students. One student of my experience (Jennifer) spent 2 to 3 hours a night on her homework for just my class. Then she did her English, math, and science homework, too. Her disability made it difficult for her to retain content information. Often, by the time she finished the last sentence of a paragraph, she had forgotten what the first sentence was about. So, she would read the paragraph again, and again, until she got it. She was staying up to one in the morning every night, determined to be a good student, but she was quickly running out of reserves to continue. Willpower such as this should be fostered and rewarded, not pushed to its uttermost limit of endurance.

Jennifer needed some modification of expectations in order to find success. The solution the teachers found for her was to not do all of her homework. Thirty minutes a night, per class, they decided, constituted a valiant effort on her part, and she would get full credit for the work she did in that allotted time. She was to put her effort into creating quality, not quantity. Interestingly, her test grades in my class went up after we instituted this modification for her. She was doing less homework, but what she was doing was of better quality, and she was retaining it.

Modifying the expectations of a lesson or assignment is a technique that can be very useful for creating equitable access for students with disabilities. Just having fewer items to attempt, or fewer paragraphs to read, can mitigate the helpless feeling so many students with disabilities experience in their daily routine, leading to increased effort, increased self-confidence, and greater participation in the classroom. Other modification possibilities include using an audio book in place of a paperbound book, reading a summary of a primary source document rather than the document itself, or working in a study group instead of individually. The modifications are fluid and adjusted as necessary to find the right level for the particular student. Teachers want their students to be challenged, not overwhelmed. Equity of access is not dependent solely on the actions of the teacher; students must be given opportunities to express their own ideas, construct their own arguments. Access implies action on the part of the learner.

## Equity of Experience

The third variety of equity for which a history teacher (or any teacher) is responsible is what I call equity of experience. Whereas equity of access focuses on the mechanics of a lesson, how information is delivered to and received by the students, equity of experience is more subjective. It is concerned with less tangible but equally important aspects of the students' interaction with the classroom and its pedagogy. Equity of experience is framed by several important questions. Do the students see themselves as a part of the classroom culture? Are they expected to learn? Can they explain the relevance of the curriculum to their own lives? Do they have a "stake" in the class? Teachers who strive for equity of experience in their classrooms hope that every student can answer these questions in the affirmative. I will now look at each of these questions.

**Establishing a Positive Classroom Climate.** Nearly every problem an educator has with managing students can be solved by creating the right classroom culture. Indeed, management problems rarely occur in a class with a strong culture, and the lack of a strong classroom culture is one of the main reasons why new teachers have such a rough time of it. All teachers create a culture in their classroom, whether they intend to or not, and all teachers are role models, whether they intend to be or not. As the fount of power in the classroom, students instinctively look to the teacher to understand how to react to even the smallest incident. It is important to always be cognizant of the fact that high school students are still in the process of forming their social identities, and they will take their cues from different sources, experimenting until they find what is successful.

A teacher who is consistent, cheerful, responsible, calm, firm, and fair, will find students in the classroom reflecting many of these same qualities. In contrast, a teacher who is arbitrary, snappish, preferential, moody, blaming, and indecisive will find similar qualities in the students in that classroom. Often, the cheerful, well-behaved students in the first class will be the unmanageable, impolite students in the second class, adapting their behavior from one class to the next in response to the culture in each classroom. Creating the correct classroom culture requires an ongoing awareness of decisions made, tone of voice, facial expression, word choice, and a host of other small details, and it is incredibly difficult to master. But a classroom will never be successful unless it has the right culture. Nothing is more important.

There are many ways in which human beings have divided themselves over the centuries, and the first goal of a positive classroom culture is the removal of as many of these barriers as possible. It is an old political technique to get a people proud of "who we are," to rally a nation, to create a sameness among individuals. Properly harnessed, the forces unleashed by this process are immensely powerful, sending people off to war, encouraging new levels of economic production, spurring scientific advancement. A successful classroom culture (or, even better, schoolwide culture) operates in the same way. Students should know, when they walk into a classroom, that it is their classroom, that they are welcome, and that they belong. It is up to the teacher to create this feeling, this "classroom nationalism." With it comes the opportunity for education for all; without it, it is difficult for a teacher to accomplish much.

Creating classroom nationalism revolves around the expectations a teacher has for his students. Most students want to do well. They rely on the teacher to explain what doing well in this class means, and then holding them accountable for doing well. Thus, the essence of a successful classroom culture involves both a clear vision for success and consistent expectations of success. If the vision and level of expectations are set before the students at the beginning of the year, explained, reiterated, and firmly held to, a successful culture will develop. Students will strive to meet the expectations; they will learn to rely on the word of the teacher; and, as part of the expectations of success will include students working together, they will learn to trust each other.

Respect and trust are the foundations of any successful relationship, including the web of relationships that form a classroom culture, but nobody can be told to respect and trust other people. Respect and trust are grown through daily interactions. If a teacher's actions are worthy of trust, they will receive trust from the students, eventually. Students who trust their teacher are willing to be managed by the teacher and follow the teacher's directions, and once this is established, an equitable classroom culture is formed.

**Avoiding a Negative Classroom Climate.** In terms of equity of experience, a positive classroom culture is essential. Nobody can learn in a room with a malignant culture, and few will learn in a room where the culture is half-formed, apathetic, or inconsistent. If the teacher has a clear vision of success for the students, and enforces that vision, a positive classroom culture will develop. The only way the teacher can derail it is by making students feel that success is unattainable. Students want to do well, but if they feel they cannot do well, they will never truly join the class. There are many ways by which the teacher can make students feel that success is unattainable. Some are conscious actions on the part of the teacher, and some are unconscious.

Students may feel that success in a classroom is unattainable if the expectations for success are not clearly explained. This is particularly so in classes where grades are often based on the judgment of the teacher. Math and science classes often involve assignments where the criteria for success are objective and clear. When asked to solve for $X$, there is usually only one right answer. History classes and English classes, however, are often asking students to defend arguments, draw conclusions, and write evaluations of events or passages. Such assignments are much more open to interpretation and misunderstanding. It is easier for a student to feel slighted on a grade for an essay than for a mathematics equation. If the teacher in these circumstances is not careful and conscientious about his or her grading policy, students can become frustrated, angry, and mistrustful. If this occurs, trust is broken. Students cannot feel they are receiving an equitable education if they cannot trust the evaluations of their teachers.

Similarly, equity in the classroom can be compromised by decisions the teacher makes on the spur of the moment in front of the entire class. Students must feel that their voices are important in guiding classroom discussion and moving the education process forward. It is very common for newer teachers to damage their classroom culture in this respect by the manner in which they choose classroom participants. "Why was William Lloyd Garrison significant to the evolution of the abolition movement in the United States?" I might ask. Immediately, several hands (I hope) would shoot up from individuals wanting to provide an answer. Choosing one person to answer the question is fine. But I should notice if the next time I ask a question, the same few hands rise again. And the next time, as well. Every class has a few "frequent fliers" when it comes to answering questions. To preserve equity of experience in my classroom, I have to be aware of these students and purposefully not call on them when I ask a question. These students are usually fast-processing, high-skilled, high-willed students who love to participate and are probably the first hands raised in most of their classes. To call on them from time to time is a good thing, but teachers have a tendency to always call on the first few hands they see, the result of which is that they deny an essential part of the classroom experience—participation with and feedback from the teacher—to many other students in the class.

There are several ways to combat this tendency, which is very strong, and to make sure teacher attention is distributed equitably among the students. The first is to allow a certain amount of time between asking the question and looking for an answer. Some students would love to participate but have a lower skill level or a slower processing time, and reaching the correct answer or a thoughtful response takes a little longer for them. A slow, mental count to three after asking a question often results in more hands and a higher quality of answers. Some teachers at our school also use "equity sticks," popsicle sticks or tongue depressors labeled with each student's name that they can pluck from a jar, to ensure that every student has an equal opportunity of being a participant in class. At other times, I have used a clipboard with a seating chart of the class on it, and checked off students whose voice I have heard during the period. It is not always possible to get to every student in one period, but I can make sure that over the course of the week every student will participate.

This aspect of equity of experience, participation, is especially important because there are certain students who would take an absolutely passive role in class if they were allowed to, missing out on the active part of their education. There are other students who would not mind being more active but are intimidated by their classmates and remain silent. There is a sophomore class I had that happened to feature an unusual large number of extroverted, highly intelligent boys. As a consequence, many of the introverted students found it difficult to contribute in class from day to day and week to week. In extreme situations such as these, it is necessary sometimes to institute a special rule to ensure equity of experience is achieved. In the past, I have instituted rules such as (1) girl, then boy, then girl, and so on; (2) students call on other students; or (3) Kalvin does not talk any more. Special rules such as these are useful, insofar as their intention is made clear to the class and, like all other rules, they are enforced consistently.

Another way to promote equity of experience in the classroom is to promote and celebrate the process of thinking rather than getting the correct answer. No matter a student's background, no matter his or her skill level, everyone can think and reason, and a classroom culture that defines success by the quality of reasoning, even if it is only for the first step of a 10-step problem, will allow every student to experience a measure of success. Thus, the advanced students in a history class, for example, can take on the Communist Manifesto in all its revolutionary glory, analyze it, defend it, attack it, and draw conclusions, whereas the students with greater learning challenges can do something a bit simpler, such as creating their own definition of what communism is, or categorizing the differences between communism and capitalism. These are very different tasks, but they celebrate the same kind of success: encountering a new concept and making sense of it using reason and evidence. Some experimentation is required to find the right levels for a particular class, but critical thinking can be made available to all students and can create the equitable educational experience that makes for an effective classroom.

One of my favorite techniques is to create gradated assignments, where students can select their own level of challenge. One example of this comes from a lesson in which my class analyzed primary documents from the Holocaust. I identified nine different Holocaust documents of varying levels of difficulty and posted them around the room, in what I considered to be an ascending order of difficulty. Students were told to analyze at least three of the documents over the course of the class. I explained the assignment to the students, and I was very transparent about the levels of difficulty. One girl, Stacy, had a question, "Do we have to do a hard one?" She was not a strong reader, and I knew that assignments like these caused her anxiety. "No," I said. "Evaluate your own skill level, and choose what you think is best for you, but try to challenge yourself." The students then distributed themselves according to their self-perceived abilities. After 10 minutes, I had them switch from their first choice to a second document. Stacy had originally chosen the easiest document, but now she skipped to the middle of the room, where the intermediate-difficulty documents were. "It's not as hard as I thought it would be," she told me subsequently.

Stacy's experience was typical in that lesson. Many other students also chose to advance to more challenging texts after their first self-assessment indicated that their skills were higher than they expected. They could attempt this additional challenge without anxiety because the analysis— the thought process—was the same whether they worked with an easier or harder document. Students who feel their efforts and thoughts are valid no matter what will often opt for greater challenges when anxiety about performance is removed.

## Conclusion

As a history teacher, the opportunities for inculcating critical thinking in the classroom are many and varied. The domain of history is itself one giant exercise in critical thinking, a continuing argument over the interpretation of known evidence, and a thorough searching for new evidence to strengthen known arguments. Opening that experience to students is a fantastic lesson on the nature of historical "truth," but it also conveys to them a sense that they could contribute something to the monumental conversation. Their reasoning is important! It also sends a message to the student, perhaps to a student who had had previously little faith in her own academic abilities: "this is a way you can learn." Learning is not just about answers, it is about thinking, and student can be given evidence that they can think, and think well.

This approach gives confidence to the student, maybe in a way it had never before been given, and it sets an equitable expectation of learning in the classroom. Students do not always have to arrive at a predetermined answer, but they do have to show evidence of thought. Not only is this approach equitable, but it also fuels hope. Students who can only make it to Step 10 with the greatest mental exertion often become fatigued from the constant effort. If they often find they have arrived at the wrong answer after tremendous effort, in time they will often give up and refuse to try even Step 1. But if they know they can learn from the process of the steps, and if they know the teacher will credit them for their best attempts that show thinking, they will be inclined to give it a shot. Students want to do well, but they also do not want to be perceived as failures. Teachers can engineer their lessons and assignments so that they promote genuine thought and deep analysis and minimize the possibility of failure for a student who is willing to try. These assignments validate the student's thought process, and such validation leads to a sense of competence in the student, in the best sense.

At the end of the day, the goal of any teacher is to get the students to think, to learn, and to learn to think. If we do not consider equity in the design and implementation of our curriculum, then we will forever be failing a portion of our students. We must measure equity on the basis of results; we cannot rely on intentions. I *meant* to include all of the kids, so I am equitable, right? No. If only such reasoning were true, I would be able to talk about all the marathons I meant to run. Just like the would-be marathon runner, we have to hold ourselves accountable. If we sign up, we have to run it, or our intentions will not be true. Engaging in pedagogical equity requires a lot of work, but it is good, necessary, and important work. An equitable classroom, an equitable curriculum, and equitable delivery will allow all students the opportunity to discover their highest intellectual potential, and to define the limits of their own ignorance which, to a curious mind, are the boundaries from which to explore.

# 11 | Math and *Not Just About Math*!

**SARAH SALAZAR AND STACY THOMAS, WITH RHONA
S. WEINSTEIN**

*"Just over half of San Francisco's class of 2014 is on track to
graduate, which means more than 1,900 high school juniors
have just three more semesters to catch up on the credits for
newly required college-prep coursework they need to get a
diploma."* (Jill Tucker, *San Francisco Chronicle,* November
19, 2012)

*"Students failing algebra rarely recover."* (Jill Tucker, *San
Francisco Chronicle,* November 30, 2012)

*"Bleak future for males of color unless state acts, report
warns."* (Jill Tucker, *San Francisco Chronicle,* December
4, 2012)

N THE QUOTATIONS ABOVE, JOURNALIST Jill Tucker speaks to the pervasive roadblocks ahead for many students, especially male students of
color, in an era of higher academic requirements. For example, schools
are under increased pressure to prepare all students to reach a higher level
of mathematics (math) proficiency that will enable successful entry into
competitive state colleges and universities. Higher-level math skills are
also essential for study in the fields of science, technology, engineering,
and math (STEM)—occupations that are critical to economic competitiveness, where proficient students are in short supply, and where ethnic
minorities and females are largely underrepresented (Carnevale, Smith, &
Melton, 2011). In California, these higher expectations for mathematics
proficiency require that all students take Algebra I, viewed as a gateway

course for college readiness, earlier in their school career in eighth grade, and successfully complete both geometry and Algebra II (advanced algebraic reasoning) in high school.

Yet as a recent study of 24 school districts in California has shown, more than one third of students needed to repeat Algebra I in 9th or 10th grade, and of those repeaters, only 9% reached proficiency the second time around (Finkelstein, Fong, Tiffany-Morales, Shields, & Huang, 2012). New ways of teaching advanced mathematics are clearly needed, especially for students who are underprepared for math proficiency in the earlier grades and who while in high school fail to understand the subject matter when presented the first time around.

How can we think differently about the teaching of mathematics? What kind of teaching enables minority and low-income students to be successful in advanced math, readies them for entry into and successful completion of college, and engages them in math-related fields—especially when they arrive underprepared from underresourced schools? Most importantly what kind of teaching instills an interest in, indeed a love of mathematics, or at least not a fear of it?

This chapter presents the reflections of two math teachers at California College Preparatory Academy (CAL Prep)—reflections obtained in a 3-hour interview conducted by Weinstein (December 13, 2012). Both teachers joined the faculty in the second year of the school in August of 2006 and were plucked from other settings. They were brought in to both strengthen and diversify the teaching staff at CAL Prep. Stacy Thomas arrived with 7 years of teaching experience, and Sarah Salazar was a first-year teacher. Thomas taught at CAL Prep for 5 years, serving as the lead math teacher until June of 2011, when he moved to serve as Dean of Academics at another Aspire school. Salazar, currently serving as both Dean of Students and a math teacher, has just completed her 7th year at CAL Prep.

With the goal of eliciting critical qualities of their teaching practices, Weinstein (RW) asked questions about (1) their history that brought them to this school, (2) their conceptualization of how to teach math, (3) their evolution as math teachers, (4) factors that fueled their growth, (5) examples of students who succeeded and students who failed, and finally (6) their experience of the partnership between University of California (UC) Berkeley and Aspire. This conversation yielded 83 typed transcript pages, which Weinstein thematically organized in response to each question and edited for readability.

Three goals important to the success of STEM programs were highlighted in the recent National Research Council Report entitled *Successful K–12 STEM Education* (2011). These include the learning of STEM content, development of positive attitudes toward STEM subjects, and creation of lifelong learners. Just the title of this chapter, in their own words, "Math and *Not Just About Math*," reveals such a teaching approach where the focus on content knowledge is simply not enough.

The journey these teachers take with their students begins with the teacher–student relationship and evolves as they work to develop student agency and confidence in the face of increasingly more difficult challenges. Their reflections speak to what they call the "unspoken part of the curriculum" and to the climate they created in the classroom, where it was cool to engage deeply in math. Among the themes that characterized their lively and interactive exchange was the continuing struggle to balance mathematical rigor, basic skill remediation, and importantly, life lessons in reaching the students. Also, it was essential to weigh the scaffolding they provided—not too much, not too little. Especially important for adolescents, there was time to puzzle it out, have fun, laugh, and celebrate small steps of success. Both Salazar (SS) and Thomas (ST) brought with them a love of math as well as a deep commitment to students of color—including taking responsibility when students failed. Importantly, they also were open to their own continuing growth as teachers and as a result, the math program at CAL Prep, as other programs, was built with patience and support, over time, brick by brick.

## History: Path to California College Preparatory Academy

### Plucked from Other Settings

ST: Before I was at CAL Prep, I had been at another Aspire school for 4 years, and before that, I was at another independent school for 3 years. I did some summer teaching of math. Although in college, I did start in engineering, I ended up majoring in social science, more because I wasn't prepared for the rigor that was being asked from me. But I was always definitely attracted to math and, possibly, you know, sharing my experiences with young people. When I came to CAL Prep, I actually wasn't really even considering leaving where I was before. I thought I have a good thing here. Why would I leave that? I remember the CEO of Aspire (Don Shalvey) calling me in his office and asking if I would.

My initial reaction was just like, "No way. I don't think I want to do that." I think one of the things that opened the door for me to actually do it was that I was considering being a principal, and I figured I needed to have some experience in another setting. And the other thing that sealed the deal for me is when I actually visited the school. I was reminded why I got into teaching in the first place—I definitely wanted to teach young people, particularly students of color in Oakland. I saw a school culture that can use some assistance and I felt like I can contribute to that. Where I was before was doing fairly well and wouldn't necessarily miss me terribly. So I decided to make a move and try something different, so I could learn more and possibly help out.

ss: Well, as you know, I was in graduate school in a PhD program in Math Education. I loved math when I was younger. I was a really tiny, little thing when I was in high school. I probably weighed 100 pounds. My hair weighed more than I did. And math was always the great equalizer for me, especially proofs. I always loved proofs. Because if I could prove it and I knew it worked, nobody could say I was wrong. That, in and of itself, just made me fall in love with math. So I majored in math. I worked in classrooms when I was an undergrad and did an undergraduate teaching fellowship, where I got to work in local high schools. Some of the high schools were so wealthy, and just had everything. You know, you walk into their math classrooms and it's like everything you can imagine. And then you go into a math classroom in poorer areas, and they have nothing. And it really, really bothered me. And I thought, OK, I definitely like math; I definitely like teaching. I'm going to go to grad school; I'm going to do it. But when I got to grad school, I was just miserable. It was so far removed from actually working with kids. There was a lot of working in a classroom, observing kids but there wasn't a lot of actually being with kids and doing math with kids. And I just really missed it. So when you suggested, Rhona, that I look at CAL Prep, I said "OK, this might be the thing that keeps me going."

So I started as an instructional assistant just to help the math department—to sit in classrooms and redirect kids, stay after school and give them some fun math to do, challenging and helping kids that needed it. Be the positive face of math. That's what Michael Prada, the principal, asked me to do. He said, "Just be you and get them to like math a little bit more." When the science teacher left, they needed to do some shuffling (moving a math teacher into science). He asked me if I wanted to teach. I'd never taught before, ever, on my own. So I did it. I'm not going to abandon these kids in the middle of the year if they've already been abandoned. The worst case scenario is that I know that this isn't for me, and I go back to finish grad school. Best case scenario, I love it. And the best case scenario happened. I just fell in love with it.

## Teachers Who Look Like Me

ss: I remember that when I was in high school, I never had a teacher that looked like me. I never had a teacher who understood what it was like to have parents like mine. I had to fight to get into the Honors and the AP classes. And a lot of my teachers took for granted that I was there: "Oh, well, you're here, so obviously your parents are well-off, and obviously it's going to be easy for you to graduate from high school." And in some respects it really was. But in a lot of respects it wasn't. My parents always wanted me to go to college but they didn't really know the ins and outs of it. And when I saw those kids at CAL Prep, I totally identified with them, especially the ones that wanted to go to Cal, to go to college. Already in sixth grade, they had bought it. You know, some of those were our weakest students. And I just remember thinking that this is what I need to do. I think that it's been a big asset—understanding where the kids are coming from. I think it's also been a big liability. I take their success personally, which is a good thing but it's hard. It can be really challenging sometimes to look at them and know that for some of them, the alternative is walking the streets of Oakland.

RW: You were nodding your head, Stacy, in terms of Sarah's background. Did you have a similar experience?

ST: Yeah, 100%. As an African American, I also did not have any teachers of color or very few, and definitely not in mathematics. You know, I think it just presents a different perspective. I'm not saying that students are able to learn necessarily more from instructors of color, but I think there is something to be said about somebody that definitely looks like you, that you think you can identify with. There's that intangible quality of possibility.

ss: I agree. I don't think that I'm a better teacher because I'm Hispanic or Latina. I believe that it gives me an opportunity to have a conversation with students about the fact that I did it and I have the same background as you. You can do this.

# Theory about the Teaching of Mathematics

## Letting the Students Do the Thinking: Developing Agency

RW: Your master's thesis . . . You might want to say a word about it, because you observed some important things that must have influenced your teaching.

SS: It's interesting because I teach a remedial algebra class now. It's definitely influenced my work over the last 2 years. So for my master's thesis, I observed an honors algebra class, a standard algebra class, and an Algebra IA class. The IA class was a full-year course spread out over 2 years (the first year for linear equations, solving equations, graphing lines, systems of equations, and the second year for parabolas, quadratics, and factoring). And a lot of kids were still getting tracked into IA and kids were still failing IA semester by semester. So I wanted to look at that and I started just sitting in classes and observing. I think the teachers were very well intentioned, in wanting to support and scaffold kids, and make sure that they had access to the mathematics. But I noticed they were doing all the thinking for the students. They would draw the picture of what the kids were supposed to do, draw the proportion, label every piece of the proportion, and then have the kids use the calculators to punch in the numbers. It was almost *over-scaffolded*. And I remember thinking that if the IA class has the whole year to do a semester of work, let the kids grapple for a day, help them the next day.

So it's been one of the things that I keep coming back to in teaching this remedial algebra class now. I have to deal with a lot of basic skills work. They need it but I'm not going to use that as the basis for my curriculum. So we do a lot of what I call happy fun math Zen time, where we just kind of puzzle around. I say, "I don't know. What do you guys think we should do?" "What do you mean, Miss Salazar, you don't know the answer?" And I say, "Yeah, I just made up some numbers. Let's see what happens." There are days when I have to scaffold things really heavily. But there are days when I just let them play, and I let them see what's going on.

ST: And I actually want to give you some credit because [laughs] you say it's remedial algebra, but with the students you had last year, they scored the highest throughout the whole organization. Students that hadn't been so successful in math before, you just totally transformed them and showed them that they could do it.

ss: They did it. They did the work. [As another example of puzzling it out], C. A. is doing an independent study. She said, "I just want to teach myself something." And I said, "Oh, you can teach Stats. You can take my lesson plans and my teacher's manual, and I'll grade all the work. You can take it at your own pace." She's doing it. She is working really slowly, but I'm not helping her. And she's doing maybe a section a week, whereas I taught a section every other day. She's only made it through two chapters, but she's killing it. And she loves it.

I love watching them [the students] give math instruction. I had a really trippy experience. I went into Mr. R.'s classroom—he's our Calculus teacher. And I'm sitting down, observing him, taking notes. All of a sudden I look up—N. R. is at the board and she's presenting a Calculus problem. She's finding the limit of a function. OMG [oh my god], I taught her how to add fractions. And this is why the years of not sleeping was totally worth it. Yes! It felt really good. That was the highlight of my month. [Laughs]

## Developing Trust: Building Student Confidence

rw: So what is it about math, Stacy, that's especially difficult for students, all students but especially students of color? What's gone wrong in the teaching of math that explains their fears, their disinterest, and failure?

st: I think that most people who go into education, at least at the elementary level, are liberal arts or English majors. So their understanding of the material is limited. Or even how they teach it is limited. And more time will be spent on language arts, whether it's reading or writing. Then the students miss out on somebody who really knows math. On the flip side, you get educators, especially in the secondary level, that know the material well—just brilliant minds—but they are really bad educators. When I talk to students, I pretty much can see, "Yeah, you probably didn't have good teaching." And it took me a while to understand that one of the goals I had in the class is just building their confidence in math. It is more than "I need you to understand this particular content" or "I need you to do this proof." "I really just need to show you that you *can* do this."

ss: You have to be a cheerleader.

st: Yeah. I'm going to scaffold enough so you can get that and I will build you up to success for the more challenging things.

ss: But at some point I'm going to pull all of those scaffolds away. You'll be just fine. You'll be scaring [laughs] people [with how much you know].

st: Exactly. I've had to really think about teaching math itself. Early on in my teaching career I used to think that math was the be-all, end-all. They had to do this and do it this way. Then I started to understand that I'm really teaching them how to be a better Stacy. [Laughing] I started to realize that for you to understand what I'm doing, I need to get you to trust me. You're not going to listen to me because I'm the teacher, the authority [and that's one of the mistakes I used to make, even starting at CAL Prep]. They weren't going for that. [Laughter] I realized that I need to build a relationship with you, earn your trust, and maybe then you'll think that what I have to say is worthwhile. And what I'm telling you is that there's a world outside of your immediate area, a greater world, and it holds a lot of wonder. It holds a lot of options for you—outside of how you solve this equation. These are some intangibles that, you know, I don't see that much with secondary math teachers who can be really tied to their content. They're [the students] not going to get anything if we keep doing that. *It's just finding that balance—support, scaffolding, withdrawing scaffolding—and you don't have to do all the work for them. The art is at what pace and how to do it.*

rw: At the start of CAL Prep, and there is a lot of research on it, particularly for African American students, there was this dance (Gregory & Weinstein, 2008). The students would say, "I'll trust him and I'll respect him or her if they respect me." And the teachers would say, "You respect me first [laughter], and then I'll respect you." How do you see this issue of respect and the building of trust? Who should make the first move? It's one of the dynamics that turn students of color away from school.

ss: I can handle giving the respect first. I'm the grown-up, the mature one.

st: There are a lot of teachers that are scared of the students. They don't want to say that outright but you can kind of tell. They feel that if I give in a little bit, I've lost power. And then I'm not going to have the control that I perceive I need to have.

ss: I don't think it's about giving in.

st: I don't either [laughs].

ss: I was a first-year teacher too. And I was nervous all the time. I don't think it's about giving in but about taking the time. So you do this every day. Shake their hand as they come in the door. Look at them in the eye and say, "Good morning, so great to see you. How was your night? How's your mom doing?" You know, these are all the things that we do with our colleagues. The more you show respect to them, you're just modeling the behavior you want back.

ST: Exactly.

SS I think it's hard for new teachers, for the same reason that you said. They're scared about losing all control. If I give an inch, what if they take [laughs] a mile? And they will, unless you do something about it. But that doesn't mean you have to be hard and strict; you can be warm and strict. You have really high expectations. But you'll crack a joke and giggle. You'll know things about them and you'll mention it. You show genuine caring for them and that's what makes them trust you. That's what makes them respect you, because you respect them. From Day 1 you respect them. Call them by their last names. "Miss S. how are you doing today? I missed you the last two days. Where were you?" They notice that. "Oh, she/he noticed I wasn't here?" Whoa! No teacher's called me out on that before." They notice these things. That's respect.

## How Math Practices Changed in the Evolution of California College Preparatory Academy

### Emphasizing Math Discourse

SS: We started Algebra I in eighth grade, which is standard now in California. Our kids did pretty well in algebra from the beginning. At that point we had had them in sixth grade and seventh grade, so they trusted us. Algebra I became the thing that the kids did. You know, you're cool if you get into Algebra I. And we still had the kids who failed. And we still have kids who struggle. I think the biggest change overall has been our philosophy. Our first few years we were really stuck in [this approach]: "I'm going to teach you how to graph a line because you're going to know how to graph a line." Now "You're doing this for the thinking, for habits of mind. And you're doing this to learn how to be a student, how to overcome really hard obstacles." I think our conversations now, at least in the last 2 to 3 years, have been more about "What is it that you're trying to get out of this, the bigger purpose?"

sᴛ: Yeah, I think Sarah and I working with each other for so long and the conversations that we had moved us toward a discourse-rich environment. Having the students actually discuss the problems and their thinking. We started understanding that we need to do that more. It's [also] working on school culture. For the senior class (that just graduated in '12), there were just so many of them for whom it was cool to be intellectual. This is cool—this is what I'm about.

sꜱ: Then other students would buy in because the cool kids are doing it.

sᴛ: Young people are influenced by their peers a lot, especially at that age. So if the cool kids are actually doing, I'm going to do that too.

sꜱ: I think we have done a very good job of getting kids to speak about math and speak the language of math. They're not perfect. But you can go into any classroom at CAL Prep, and within the first 15 minutes you're going to see four to five kids up at the board presenting problems. And they're going to turn to the class and say, "This was my problem. I did this because of this. I tried this. It didn't work. Anybody have any ideas?" They'll ask each other questions: Not only "Why did you get 4?" but also "Could you have solved this in another way?" And it's one of my favorite things when somebody comes in my room and asks, "Oh, where is Miss Salazar?" "Oh, she's sitting over there in the middle of the room. She's not even standing. She's just sitting, we're running this," you know? But it's cool. Our kids speak math. Our kids can stand in front of each other and say, "This is what I did." I don't think they could have done that our first couple years [laughs].

sᴛ: No. Professionally I wasn't ready for that.

## Holding onto High Expectations

sᴛ: It becomes acceptable for people to say, "I'm just not good at math." But you don't say, "I'm not a good reader." We have to change that low expectation.

sꜱ: I don't think I was ready, gutsy enough, to hold them to that high expectation. What if they fail publicly? Whereas now I think that it's OK if they fail publicly, because they're going to face it. They're going to be successful [at some point]. If they don't know how to do it, they'll ask for help and somebody will help them get to the finish line. What you don't want to do is, "Oh, yeah, I'm moving you ahead because you're super smart." You want it to be, "*I think you can handle the work.*"

ST: Like Sarah said, we're going to be tough on them. We had credibility with them and their families. And we knew we weren't trying to steer them wrong. I'm going to be tough but I'm going to support you in that. I'm going to do the best I can so that you can be successful in this.

SS: Yeah. I'm going to absolutely love you, full force *love* you. But I'm not going budge on this expectation. Some of these kids have crazy life stories and they're just 15, 16. But I'm not going to budge. I'm not going to bend the rules so that you like me. I respect you enough to hold you to the same expectation as everyone else.

## Celebrating Successes along the Way

SS: I love math. And I want all of my kids to go to Calculus and be math majors, and solve crazy problems that have never been solved before. I do. But I know [laughs] that not all of them are going to. And I do think it's more about teaching them ways to think, about changing their minds, and about letting them know that they can overcome things that are really, really scary to them. It is about working so hard at something, and then when you get it right or when you grow by five percentage points, that's a big deal. I have a freshman right now who, at the beginning of the year, could only do 4 multiplication problems in 3 minutes. And she's in ninth grade. Four! And now she's up to 17 in 3 minutes. Every time she gets one higher, it's like, "Yeah! High five! That's awesome. I can't believe you did it 2 days in row!" I will cheer for her and at this point, now, other kids are saying, "Yes! You did it? You broke 20! Are you going to do it tomorrow?"

RW: [Laughs]

SS: "But can you believe!" They're cheering her on, even though they know she's much lower skilled than they are. Algebra I probably isn't the best placement for her. She probably needs Pre-algebra. But she's in Algebra I. I'm going to celebrate it. I let her use a calculator for the algebra but I make her practice multiplication. I'm going to celebrate every small, little success. A student who always gets Cs on a test, finally gets a B—I am going to snap a picture and text that to them. You got a B! You find out Saturday morning; you don't even have to wait 'til Monday morning. Those little things make such a difference for kids who hate math!

## Including the Parents

sт: I think that a lot of students that we work with bring preconceived ideas about school. School hasn't necessarily always been a positive experience for them or their families. But the great thing I think about working with Aspire, working at CAL Prep, is that the parents care enough to get them into the school, the school of choice. I see students doing things above what their parents ever did. And their parents feel intimidated by that. They don't know how to support them, even hold their students accountable. The student will try to get out of it some way. This can lead to discussions at home about school in general, but in particular math, that are not always positive.

ss: I do think one of the things we do a good job with is empowering families to help their kids with math. Once we started offering Algebra I, the kids started surpassing their parents, and the parents couldn't help with the homework. So we taught parents how to look at what was written down as homework and then just say like, "OK, what were the problem numbers? Did you do those problem numbers? Let me check that." Or teaching them that OK, you don't have to be able to help them, but drop them off 20 minutes early to get the help they need.

sт: Or allow them to stay later.

ss: Yeah, for a long time, Stacy would stay after school until 5:00 o'clock, every day, basically teaching the class again for any student willing to stay. You know, he always had a packed room, always. But it worked.

## What Deepened Our Math Teaching and Program

### A Collegial Partner in Math

rw: So you say in the beginning you weren't ready or you weren't quite there. What helped you get ready?

ss: I think we started pushing each other.

sт: That's exactly what I was going to say. [Both laugh] Unfortunately, I came to CAL Prep a little bit arrogant, thinking I knew quite a bit. Then I got taken down a few pegs, having to rethink my approaches. Collaborating with Sarah just pushed me immensely as an educator— got me to look at what she was doing. She was asking what I was doing and there were a lot of conversations about how we can get better. I don't think I was always willing in the beginning, but then I developed the notion that I need to get better at this. I was very fortunate to have a colleague who can do that with me.

RW: So you had time or made time.

ST: Any time we could. It could be math meetings, it could be after school. We would just go in each other's room and we'd chop it up.

SS: "Check out this cool technique I just saw." "OMG, you have to see it."

## By Design: Extended Block for Math

SS: I think a lot of it [pushing each other] was due to time, you did mention time. We had time to play because we did have the extended block—100 minutes of instruction every day. And I remember they took it away—so I only have 100 minutes every other day. I want 100 minutes every day with every kid because it takes off the pressure and they can learn at their own pace. Because we had that extra time, we could experiment. If we spent 30 minutes on something and it failed, it was OK. When we got to the point where we were comfortable experimenting, we had enough credit with the kids where we could say, "We're just gonna try this out. Bear with me; let's see what happens." We were transparent with the kids about instructional decisions. "Hey! You guys have been really struggling with this. We're going to go back to basics for a day. We're working on integers. I know you guys are working on graphing problems right now. But we're going to spend the day adding and subtracting integers because you need it." Just being totally and completely transparent about what we're deciding to do, why we're deciding to do it. And since we had the credibility, they weren't going to question our decisions because they believed in us. They trusted us. Their families trusted us. We trusted us [laughs]. We trusted ourselves enough to make professional decisions.

## By Design: Locked Schedule

RW: The schedule is allowing them to get what they need but not be off track for the advanced work.

SS: I do the master schedule for the school. I lock all the math classes, so Algebra I is locked with Geometry. There's a Geometry section that's locked with Algebra II. There's an Algebra II section that's

locked with Geometry and Precalculus. It's hard for other departments because they see our class sizes as being smaller. But in order
to give kids the math classes they need, we have to have these classes
locked because we're such a small school. For example, if we didn't
have the classes locked, if a student failed Geometry, we don't have
any way to offer them Geometry the next year unless they stay in
ninth grade and repeat *all* the ninth grade classes. But what we've
done is locked Geometry next to an Algebra II class, allowing students to repeat *one* class.

RW: What does that mean, you've locked it?

SS: They're at the exact same time every single day. We have to make a
Monday–Wednesday, Tuesday–Thursday, and Friday schedule. It's
really complex and a big math problem. But it's what needs to be
done for our students because we're not as big as we need to be to
have the course offerings that we need. I would love to have three
course offerings for seniors, so that they can take Precalculus if they
need it, Calculus if they need it, Stats if they want it, and have all
those courses offered. But with such a small staff and California's
ADA (average daily allowance) funds, we're never going to get the
funding to have a larger staff.

ST: Those things are huge challenges. And not all the classes are small.
Some are big. J. [a teacher] had 36 students. But we make those sac-
rifices . . . to give the students the opportunity to take that class. And
it's really hard, again, in a small school to offer all that and find math
educators that are solid, it's very difficult. And when you find good
ones, you take care of them [laughs] and make sure that they know,
"Hey, you're doing a great job. We really . . ."

SS: [Overlaps] You're valued here.


## Growing Your Own Math Teachers

SS: That's something I did, growing your own. [Laughs] We found the
newest math teacher at CAL Prep through the Cal Teach program at
Cal. Aspire was starting its [teacher] residency program. I reached
out to her and begged her to apply for it. And I was like, "Please.
Come here. I'll work with you." I had her all last year. I trained her.
She has been Aspirized. And so now when I changed roles this year,
she took over my position. So we literally grew our own. She's still
a first-year teacher, totally green. But, man, her first year is stronger
than any I've seen. So we have people coming in with 3 years of

experience who are nowhere near where she's at in her first year. I think the residency program is really promising. I really do. You have a master teacher with somebody who is brand new to the teaching profession 4 days a week, full time. You get to let them like fail early, fail often. "Yes, you're going be all by yourself. You'll be just fine. And you'll fail and it'll be fine. You'll fix it. I'm not going fix it for you." And that's why this year she's not struggling with the things that other first-year teachers struggle with.

RW: What pays for the residency program?

SS: A grant. And individual school sites pay in a little bit because they end up getting an extra body out of it. The residents don't get paid much. They only get paid a small stipend, maybe $7,500 a semester. I'm a big fan. I think it's an interesting model of teacher education and it has a lot of promise.

## Students Who Made Advances and Students Who Could Not be Reached

### The Students Who Knock Your Socks Off

SS: I've got one that's going to knock your socks off.

ST: I'm interested [laughs].

SS: A. W. is taking AP Calculus.

ST: Wow! Really! Awesome!

SS: She got a B+. A. W. always had the skill—real good with numbers, real good with basic skills. She didn't believe though. No belief whatsoever that math was at all important, that math was her thing. She thought she was horrible in math forever. But at the start of this year, she said, "Calculus is kinda cool. Like these problems are a page and a half long. It's really cool." And she just completely turned around over the year. I've never seen her so successful. And for her to be carrying around a Calculus book with pride. That book is 15 pounds [laughs].

ST: C. T. wants to become a math teacher. She said, "Yeah, Mr. Thomas, I want to be a math teacher. I want to teach math." I'm like, "Well, great!" Wow!

SS: In seventh grade math, I thought she was this little, tiny girl. I thought she was going to kill me, she hated it so much. But she wants to be a math teacher, just fell in love with it. Math, it's a great equalizer. Nobody can tell you you're wrong if you're right.

RW: I'm surprised you use the term that it's a great equalizer, because I always felt, there was only one answer, and if I didn't get it, I . . .

SS: Well, there are solutions that are more elegant. I talk to my kids about elegance a lot. Once you've solved it, great. But try to find something a little more elegant, with fewer steps, a neater line of argument.

ST: Well, what you're saying is there's more than one way to get to San Francisco. [Laughs]

SS: Yes! I spend an entire lesson on this every year. There *is* more than one way to get to San Francisco. I have them list every possible way they can get to San Francisco. And we have a conversation about how many ways. You can drive. You can take the F line. You can take BART. You can take the ferry. You can go over Richmond Bridge and the Golden Gate Bridge. You can take a helicopter. That's like the [ultimate] status. If they've got a really good solution, you just take the helicopter.

ST: You can go south and you go San Mateo or Dumbarton Bridge.

RW: You can go by sailboat.

SS: You could, you could! You can swim. People do it. And the kids are always saying, "OMG, you're so cheesy, Miss Salazar. I can't believe it." But once they get to multistep equations, or when they get to word problems, or when they get to these things that are really big and bulky, I say: "Oh yeah, let's [take] the helicopter." And they're like, "OMG! That's why! That's why!" It's just this funny little story. It started as a joke, but it's turned into [a metaphor]: So many ways to get to San Francisco.

## The Students We Failed

ST: When I'm thinking of the successes, I sometimes focus on [laughs] the ones that I didn't do such a great job with. Early on at CAL Prep, I don't think I was totally equipped to deal with students who did have the huge gaps [in their preparation]. For example, I remember, the second year I was there, students coming in to Algebra I in eighth grade had a really difficult time. I didn't really know what to do. Now talking to Sarah, I would definitely rethink how I scaffold, but at the time it was really tough. And a lot of those students aren't still at CAL Prep anymore. I really need to hone in on how I can reach more students. I think we've gotten better at that. I know Sarah has, obviously, from her results on algebra scores.

ss: One of the problems with Algebra I is that it is a revolving door of teachers. You put brand new teachers with the hardest course and with the most challenging population of students. It's not the kids that are challenging. It's the content, the rigor of the content, and the fact that everybody is placed in this one course at the same time, regardless of preparation.

st: Exactly, regardless of preparation.

ss: You can't expect those teachers to last more than a few years because you burn them out. And you can't expect those kids to learn very much because they don't have an expert in front of them. There are two ways in which we lost kids or not lost them but haven't done a good job of serving. We have some kids who've made it as seniors but still don't have the mathematical proficiency they need [I think we never got them to change their minds about what they're capable of]. So I think of S. B. She hasn't overcome that hump yet of believing that she can be somebody who does mathematics. Now she's taking that problem-solving course with Ms. Y. and I'm starting to see glimmers of it. She knows now that when the calculations get hard, that doesn't mean that she's dumb. She can use a calculator and she can focus on the richness. But then there are the kids who we have just lost, like D. B. Actually he's like my child. I love this kid. I'd do anything for him—go take him to get his GED [graduate equivalency diploma], anything that involves his schooling. But we just lost him. I think we are competing with all these outside pressures. Some of our kids, they come to school and it's the only place where they get to be a kid.

st: Mm hmm.

ss: So they act out because they don't get to act out anywhere else in their life. They don't get to yell at anybody at home because there's nobody at home. They don't get to sleep at home because they're taking care of all the little ones, so they sleep during class. They don't get to be a big shot at home because they've got an older brother, who is running the streets, and he's the big shot at home. So they're going to be the big shot on campus. So I think for D. B., he didn't get to be a kid anywhere else, and, unfortunately, because he acted like a kid, he made very immature decisions. I think that drove him out. And, you know, I ran into him today. He's been in and out of jail—no money, no education. He didn't finish school. I'm still trying to push him to go get his GED. But there are no jobs.

st: Right.

SS: And it's so easy to tell him, "Oh, go get your GED. You'll, you'll be fine then." But when you can't afford to go take the test! And I teach his younger sibling right now, who said, "I know who you are. D. told me who you are. He says that I just need to do what you say." And I'm like, "Yeah, pretty much."

ST: [Laughs]

SS: I'm so protective of those kids that I know don't have anything outside, because if we lose them, they're lost. At least their families have known enough to get them into our schools. But if those kids are at a large high school, there's no safety net for them there. There's nobody to catch them. That's another reason why advisory is great.

## Has the Partnership Between Aspire and the University of California, Berkeley Made a Difference?

### A Focus on Getting Better

ST: For me, coming from another Aspire school that didn't have the partnership, I really appreciated what the partnership brought in terms of the discourse to the table, just the idea of how we could get better. This discussion seemed to be ingrained at the school. I don't think that would exist necessarily without the partnership. The school I'm at now, it doesn't exist like that in the same way, and the school I was at before, didn't . . . . I really notice the partnership has brought that.

### Increased Resources: Opportunity-Rich and Adult-Rich

ST: Cal Teach and other things have pointed us in a direction that we might not have been looking before.

SS: Auditing college classes is huge.

ST: Helping with ATDP [Academic Talent Development Program] summer program at UC Berkeley—it's invaluable.

SS: In terms of math, I think Ms. R. from Lawrence Hall of Science was really instrumental in pushing us. I don't want to say off the precipice, because it sounds so negative, but she pushed us out of our comfort zone. It was "Try this cool math problem that I found." "Just do it [an assessment] to look at the data, just see what you find." I don't think we need her in the same way now, but the timing [at the beginning] was very, very good. Now, because of the continued relationship with UC Berkeley and Cal Teach—we have so many undergrads on our campus. On any given day, we have three or four kids in math and science classrooms just hanging out. Sometimes they're doing instruction (guest lessons of really cool, interesting problems) and sometimes they're just sitting in the back next to a group of kids, saying, "Hey, isn't this problem cool?" It's a wealth of people. You know? Schools don't have a lot of people [laughs].

RW: Adult-rich is a term that I used in terms of what schools need—adult-rich environments.

SS: We're actually very adult-rich compared to most schools. I think our ratios are really good. You know, Ms. W. and I split a teaching position. And we split a dean position, dividing the dean responsibilities in terms of our strengths. She is very good at organizing large school systems, like testing and after-school programs. I work best with kids, one on one, and coaching teachers. Over the last 3 years we've been able to get really creative with the way we fund positions. And [now] we've been able to build school culture in a different way. Before, we were trying to change the school culture from, quite honestly, a mess, toward getting the academics in place. Now it's how do we enrich their experience so it's a high school experience? How do we leverage our relationship with other Aspire high schools to have a prom, homecoming, to have a big rivalry with GSP [Golden State College Preparatory Academy] during basketball season? If we had started with that, we never would have gotten the academics down.

ST: More on the adult-rich notion. It has meant exposing them to an outside world. They actually have to interact with people from the outside world. Constantly having a lot of visitors—how do I interact with those visitors, what's appropriate, what's not appropriate? It's actually a pretty big thing. The two schools I worked at before, there are visitors now and then, but they can be protective: "who are you? I don't know how much I should really be interacting. I don't know how much I trust you." But the partnership has helped students. They're greeting them, they're actually having these conversations, but we've let them know at CAL Prep that's OK. These people have your best interests at heart. And they become a little more accepting.

SS: We talk to our alumni now and they know how to network. It was an unspoken part of our curriculum because we always had so many visitors. But you talk to E. and D., and they'll say, "Oh, yeah, I met this guy in this department. He seems really interesting, so I've been e-mailing back and forth to him. I think he's going to give me an internship." And you're a freshman in college! What [laughing] are you doing? I love it. That's the thing they know how to do.

## A Critical But Not Conflictual Friendship

RW: Did you feel any conflicts between Aspire and UC Berkeley? Bringing those two worlds together?

ST: I never found conflict between the two. Early on, I felt like I have a lot of people [laughter] in my ear about things.

SS: And I have 100 students so . . . [laughing].

ST: But I guess I adapted. Sometimes I was just having a bad day [laughs].

SS: I don't think there was ever conflict. I don't think conflict is the right word for it. I do think that Aspire lives it and breathes it every day and UC Berkeley has a very theoretical bent. How do we take this idea from theory, make it fit, and make that happen? The semester before I started at CAL Prep, I'd taken Alan Schoenfeld's problem-solving course. I was really into the theory of math, getting kids to talk about math and do problem-solving. I want to do all this stuff but I'm under pressure from Aspire to do cycles of inquiry. How do I find time for that and that? I think it just evolved into a perfect medium right now. Like Stacy said, at first it was just a lot of voices . . . And I was hearing some of it from Cal State East Bay (because I was doing my intern credential) so I was constantly trying to figure out how to take these three different perspectives and come up with something that is doable . . . with a group of kids who don't trust me yet. Now I feel there is this stride in the partnership—we are the practitioners and Cal is there as an advisor to help us think about things deeply. That critical friend relationship has been crucial.

ST: Mm hmm.

SS: There is such a mutual respect that nothing is viewed as conflict. Like the advisories (Chapter 5). When Nilo Sami was doing the surveys with kids, I thought that was really interesting. It wasn't critical. It was just, "What does this tell us as practitioners and how can we improve?" And without your support we never would have known.

ST: Never [laughs].

SS: We wouldn't have advisory. Advisory's the best thing ever.

RW: Our attempt to create the program started the conversation, but advisory has evolved very much, you know, by your experiences.

ss: Now we don't do a scripted curriculum. We try to be school mom or school dad. I think it's what fits our kids. Last year's seniors had the same advisor from eighth grade on. That was the advisory experience we wanted it to be. And those kids had the same person for 5 years of their life.

RW: I just had to watch at the graduation, to hear what everybody said about their students. I mean it was obvious each student was cherished and the students loved you back. It was a very moving example of advisories that are working.

ss: When we have parents come to visit and they ask why this school? You guys don't have football, you guys don't have this. "Well, we have this thing called advisory. Your kids are going to hate it the first 2 years." [Laughter]. "They're going to think that they have another mom or another dad breathing down their neck. Year 3, they're going to be stoic because they've got someone in their corner." But the first year it was, "You're not my mom. Why are you calling my mom and telling her about my grades every day? What are you doing?" But then by the end of it, they are: "OMG! You love me!" [Laughs] I'm a big fan of advisory.

## Closing Thoughts

ST: [Effective teaching] is about being open to learning and about giving it time. Don't expect change to happen right away. You've got to take time and stick with it. I find that a lot of educators get really frustrated because things aren't happening as fast as they could. *That's weird because that's the exact same thing that math teachers try to teach their students—resiliency [in the face of obstacles].*

ss: [Laughs] Grit!

ST: Yeah, grit. Sometimes *we* have to take our own advice. I've got to give this time. It's not going to happen in 1, 2, or 3 years. It's going to take 4 years. If that is what it takes, you know, to do a really good job.

ss: Last year [my sixth year] was the first year where I felt confident about what I was doing. I still had rough days, I still second-guessed. But I feel confident that I'm delivering high-quality education. The first year it was, "How am I going to survive today? OMG, I suck at this. I need to stop." Coaching and professional development was critical. [Now] even though I only teach one class this year, I really value that I still meet with my principal to talk about my teaching. And I'm still being pushed to develop—it's not good enough for me to just coast. *If we're not learning, how are we going to expect our kids to learn?*

## References

Carnevale, A. P., Smith, N., & Melton, M. (2011). *STEM*. Washington, DC: Center on Education and the Workforce, Georgetown University.

Finkelstein, N., Fong, A., Tiffany-Morales, J., Shields, P., & Huang, M. (2012). *College-bound in middle school and high school: How math course sequences matter.* Sacramento, CA: The Center for the Future of Teaching and Learning at WestEd.

Gregory, A., & Weinstein, R. S. (2008). The discipline gap and African Americans: Defiance or cooperation in the high school classroom. *Journal of School Psychology, 46*, 455–475. doi:10.1016/j.jsp.2007.09.001

National Research Council. (2011). *Successful K-12 STEM education: Identifying effective approaches in science, technology, engineering, and mathematics.* Washington, DC: Author.

Tucker, J. (2012, November 19) 1,900 in SF class of '14 may not graduate. *San Francisco Chronicle.* Retrieved from http://www.sfgate.com/education/article/1-900-in-SF-class-of-14-may-not-graduate-4051222.php

Tucker, J. (2012, November 30). Students failing algebra rarely recover. *San Francisco Chronicle.* Retrieved from http://www.sfgate.com/education/article/Students-failing-algebra-rarely-recover-4082741.php

Tucker, J. (2012, December 4). Bleak future for males of color unless state acts, report warns. *San Francisco Chronicle.* Retrieved from http://www.sfgate.com/educa-tion/article/Black-boys-see-bleak-future-at-school-4088520.php

# 12 | Titrating from Shallow to Deep Understanding in Chemistry

**ANGELICA STACY AND TATIANA LIM-BREITBART**

*"As a society, we must commit ourselves to the proposition that all students can achieve at high levels in math and science, that we need them to do so for their own futures and for the future of the country, and that we owe it to them to structure and staff our educational system accordingly."* (Commission on Mathematics and Science Education, 2009, p. 1)

NFORTUNATELY, THE STUDENTS WHO CHOOSE science majors in college tend to be majority male and European American, and students from African American and Hispanic groups are notably rare. Given the great need for broader and more diverse representation in the health and engineering fields, both to broaden the scope of inquiry and to provide services to all communities, this lack of diversity needs to be addressed. Moreover, it is vital for all citizens to have the knowledge necessary to make informed decisions regarding health, environment, and quality of life. There is widespread belief among teachers and students alike that success in science in general, and in chemistry specifically, is only achievable by a select group of students. This is a belief that we do not share. Hence, this chapter focuses on the curriculum, supports, and teaching approaches needed to support underrepresented students through high school science courses and facilitate future success in university-level courses. It is our goal to demonstrate that success in science has less to do with the individual student and more to do with curriculum and pedagogy, students' belief about themselves and the subject matter, and the willingness of teachers to focus on outcomes and continually refine their teaching approaches.

This chapter is drawn from an interview conducted by Rhona S. Weinstein and Frank C. Worrell with Tatiana Lim-Breitbart (TL) and Angelica Stacy (AS) on March 23, 2013; the interview was shaped by the two co-authors. Lim-Breitbart is a science teacher who began teaching at the California College Preparatory Academy (CAL Prep) in the 2009–2010 academic year and became the lead science teacher the next year. She completed a bachelor's degree in chemistry and a master's degree in education, specializing in curriculum development at University of California (UC) San Diego prior to coming to UC Berkeley in 2004 to study with Professor Stacy. At UC Berkeley, Lim-Breitbart completed a master's degree in chemistry and assisted in the development of the *Living By Chemistry* high school curriculum (Stacy, 2012), which is used at CAL Prep. Stacy is a Professor of Chemistry and Associate Vice Provost for the Faculty at UC Berkeley. In her long career in chemistry, Professor Stacy has won several national awards for science and teaching and, of particular significance to this chapter, is the author of the *Living By Chemistry* curriculum.

The chapter is divided into three sections. In the first section, we describe how a high school teacher and university professor collaborated on building a curriculum model coupled with expanding their own pedagogical content knowledge to support student learning in chemistry. In the second section, we describe how we built a vertical team to create a pathway to success for underrepresented students. In the third section, we focus on the challenges involved in translating these ideas into practice at the school site and making changes in real time in response to how the ideas are working. We hope to show in all three sections critical features related to student success.

## A Model for Student Success in Chemistry

Chemistry is a gateway course to numerous attractive careers, particularly careers in health-related areas. If all students are to have an opportunity to consider these careers, they need to succeed in high school chemistry. Watering down the chemistry course is not an option because it runs counter to the goal of giving all students an opportunity to pass through the chemistry gateway. However, if chemistry continues to be taught in the manner in which it has always been taught, many students will be frustrated and will not meet the high expectations we have for them. Indeed, neither do the top students under standard practices always gain a working knowledge of the key ideas in chemistry, nor do they necessarily appreciate the relevance of these ideas. Although the goal of having all students take and do well in a content-rich high school chemistry course may at first seem impossible, research has shown that many more students can learn the subject matter if we teachers expand the pedagogies used to teach these subjects.

> TL: It is not about reducing the rigor of the course to get kids to pass; it is about increasing the support for the kids who are not. And that's what has really changed my life and my perspective about working with underrepresented students.

The partnership between the authors of this chapter had its start in the early stages of the development of *Living By Chemistry* (Stacy, 2012), a high school chemistry curriculum developed with funding from the National Science Foundation. A key goal of the curriculum is to provide a set of instructional materials for introductory chemistry at the high school level (typically taken by students in 10th and 11th grades) that is accessible to a broader and more diverse pool of students without sacrificing content. As noted previously, AS is the lead author of the curriculum, and TL was an early tester of the curriculum in her chemistry classes at a large public high school in California.

*Living By Chemistry* consists of six units organized around content. A single contextual theme runs throughout each unit, enhancing the understanding of the chemistry being taught. The context provides a real world foundation for the chemistry concepts and serves to hold the interest of the students. For example, the first unit, called Alchemy, begins with an experiment in which students "turn" a copper penny into a golden penny. The theme of the unit is to determine if this is indeed gold, and if it is not, to question whether it is ever possible to achieve this conversion. Each unit consists of 25 to 30 lessons of 50-minute duration that provide resources for inquiry-based activities to engage students in actively exploring and making sense of the concepts.

A unique aspect of the curriculum is that it provides teacher and student guides, rather than traditional textbooks. Typically, textbooks do not serve the needs of teachers or students. Textbooks do not provide daily lesson plans to support teachers, and the content descriptions are often written for those who already understand as opposed to students learning for the first time. The *Living By Chemistry* teacher guides provide detailed daily lesson plans that have been tested so that teachers can focus their attention on modifications to meet the needs of their students rather than spending time each night designing entire lessons. The lessons include a rich set of activities and engaging questions. The student guides provide a summary of each lesson and practice problems so that students can review the work they did in class. This unique combination of resources supports teachers and students in making a transition from a teacher-centered to a student-centered classroom.

A key premise of *Living By Chemistry* is that students are more likely to be successful if they engage in higher-level thinking skills. Although it might appear more efficient to try to pour knowledge into students' heads, this approach tends to result in shallow understanding and memorization of facts and formulas that are quickly forgotten. Beginning science students need support in finding strategies for deeper learning that rely less on external authorities providing answers and increasingly on students actively engaging in seeking answers on their own and in collaboration with other students. This approach takes time and patience and is dependent on teachers believing that it will eventually lead to greater learning gains and better preparation for college. Despite early frustrations about a slow pace and worries about coverage, student learning tends to accelerate after a slow induction period with this curriculum, with improved learning gains and growth at later stages.

Preliminary data on student learning gains were gathered by administering a pre-test and post-test (with a different set of questions) to several cohorts of students at a large public high school in California who used one of the *Living By Chemistry* units. The tests consisted of open-ended questions that required understanding of the key ideas in the unit. The data suggested that changing the pedagogy to a student-centered, constructivist approach could begin to level the playing field.

TL offered these comments about her early experiences with the curriculum.

> I taught for 2 years before I was introduced to *Living By Chemistry*. In those first 2 years, I recognized that in my large urban school I was working with lots of underrepresented students who were ill-prepared. They were struggling. I was given a textbook package that came with some worksheets and tests. But I didn't really know how to structure the class. It was then in my third year of teaching that the district adopted *Living By Chemistry* in its earliest iteration. Because we were the early adopters, we got lots of special attention from the author and her team. Especially as a new teacher, I immediately found

a big difference in the way that I could teach when I had a curriculum that was focused on what the students were doing, what questions to ask, and how to guide student thinking, as opposed to "here are the facts that you need to teach kids." I could focus more on assessing my kids and understanding how my kids were learning and less on what are we going to do tomorrow.

TL provided important feedback on early versions of the *Living By Chemistry* lessons and ultimately came to UC Berkeley for graduate studies in chemistry and science education under the guidance of AS.

TL: After I met AS in a professional development workshop, and because I felt such big changes in my own thinking, we talked about my possibly going to UC Berkeley to study the chemistry curriculum, to understand it better and to work with it. And then the following year I went to UC Berkeley as a graduate student in science and math education. I also completed a master's degree in chemistry in order to improve my content knowledge. I served as a graduate student instructor multiple times for introductory undergraduate chemistry, including teaching a special section to support underrepresented students. During my time as a graduate student, I got a broad-based understanding from helping to design a new version of the introductory course to writing assessments to supporting other graduate students with their teaching.

AS: Through our work at both the high school and college level, TL and I developed a shared understanding of education research and practice, of the design and construction of activities to engage students in deeper thinking, of the development of assessments worth teaching to, and of the needs of underrepresented and first-generation students. As a faculty member who was intimately involved with the development of CAL Prep, I couldn't have been more excited and proud that TL decided to join the teaching staff at the school

TL: In my first year at CAL Prep, I taught chemistry with *Living By Chemistry* with a focus completely tied to college readiness. Having seen the skills that I desired in the college level students, I focused on academic discourse; students taking ownership for their own understanding; and making them find the information, conduct observations, and determine their own conclusions. While it is a much more time consuming way to learn, it is a better way to learn. It pushes for deep knowledge and deep understanding.

This bilateral relationship between TL and AS is intimate, with shared experiences and a personal connection. At the start of the relationship, TL, the teacher and AS, the curriculum developer engaged with one another. Next, the teacher participated as a graduate student in aiding the university professor in the redesign of the introductory undergraduate chemistry course. Then, the graduate student, TL, returned to teaching with a deep understanding of content, curriculum, and assessment. Because the relationship is not unilateral, there is a willingness to provide and accept feedback to further joint goals and gain understanding of what it takes to support underrepresented students to succeed in science. We anticipate that we will continue to improve *Living By Chemistry* as we refine our understanding of the needs of underrepresented students.

Of course, the curriculum is only one element in successful teaching. Others include content knowledge, pedagogical content knowledge, professional development, and being able to identify the big ideas in the specific discipline. All of these issues are especially critical in working with students who have traditionally been and continue to be underrepresented in the sciences.

TL: There's a huge body of literature that says, at the bare minimum, teachers need to understand their content in order to teach it. We can call that No Child Left Behind (NCLB) compliant. And I was NCLB compliant before I came to the university. I had a bachelor's degree in chemistry. I was prepared to teach high school chemistry. All through college I would take tests and say, "You know, I don't need to know this much to teach high school chemistry. When am I going get to organic chemistry in high school? I don't need to know that." I had this snide attitude about how much I really needed to understand in order to teach high school level chemistry. Then I returned to the university as a graduate student. Being a student after being a teacher is a really unique experience because you get to do all of the things that you both regretted as a student and drove you crazy as a teacher. So I got to do things like go to office hours, ask questions, seek out study groups, all of the things that I wished my students would be doing. And I learned chemistry at an incredibly deeper level.

It was the conversations about the curriculum and my deepening content knowledge that started me thinking about the really important core ideas for my kids to understand. Being able to start differentiating between what is the minutia and what is the big idea revolutionized the way I think about teaching and about chemistry.

So the conversations around the university table weren't about what are we going to teach, they were about how well do we understand this, what part of it really is core, and what part of it is extra. Are we testing the understanding, or are we testing a fact, or are we testing the exception? I think that those conversations about core versus extra deepened my ability to teach.

The focus on trying to understand what you know and need to know has tremendous implications for professional development with subject-matter teachers.

TL: When you do professional development as a teacher, very seldom do you get to think about content. I may get together with chemistry teachers from other schools, but there is no safe space to be able to say, "You know, I really don't think I understand this as well as I thought I did." You are very defensive. So I think getting to that space and finding a place for that with teachers is a professional development line that has not yet been explored. And it changed me the most, being able to sit around with a college professor who could say, "You know, maybe we don't get this as well as we thought we did." And if some college professor says it, then I can acknowledge that I don't understand this too. So it really takes that space and somebody who you view as very, very knowledgeable acknowledging that they don't know it.

The idea of recognizing what you do not know is important not only for teachers in K–12, but at the university as well, where seeking answers around questions in your domain is much more common, although questions are less often focused on teaching.

AS: We were engaged very deeply with a group of people when we were rethinking how to teach introductory chemistry at the university level. We completely redesigned the course and it led to, "Why exactly are we teaching this? What is this good for? And how do we ask questions about the big ideas rather than the exceptions and the minutia?" And we had to admit that we didn't know how to do this, and we ended up not understanding things. We ended up finding things that were incorrect in textbooks because they had generalized when they shouldn't have. As we became less secure in terms of being the know-it-alls, I think we became better teachers.

A common expectation is that things will change steadily with effort. But a linear rate of change is rare when tackling large and complex issues. Building a school where there was none and delivering on a promise of high success rates for students accustomed to failure is a case in point. Much groundwork needs to be laid to build thoughtful and aligned systems for (1) classroom management, safety, and discipline that is not punitive; (2) a school culture that includes teachers, students, parents, and community working toward the same goals and aspirations for students; and (3) curricula that promote deep learning and support students in meeting high expectations. It takes time for all involved to develop a shared understanding of expectations for students, for teachers, for administrators, for partners, and for the school. What is different about CAL Prep is that thoughtful reflection has put robust systems in place that align well with one another.

However, it took several years to get to the point where growth was noticeable, and the recognition that substantive change takes a substantial time is an important aspect of engaging in school reform.

TL: The growth at CAL Prep has not been linear; it has been exponential. I feel that CAL Prep has grown a lot more in the last 4 years than it did in its first 3 years, and a lot of that has to do with reduction in staff turnover. For example, I joined, and in my first year, the science teacher left. I got to hire somebody and she has been with me ever since. This year we lost our principal, but every other person on our lead team stayed. With our new principal, the transition was very smooth. When you have so little turnover, your conversations continue as opposed to restarting. [The work of staff] has changed dramatically from putting out fires to deeper conversations.

AS: It is a general observation about change. It does require this kind of effort to get to a certain stage. You almost want to abandon what you are doing along the way because it seems like you are not getting anywhere, because you are thinking change should be linear. The same thing happens in the classroom. Inquiry is really time-consuming. But then you see that when you actually want to focus on just pulling the pieces together, the students are ready for it.

A critical component to realizing growth in student success in science classes at CAL Prep is a stable and committed vertical science team that grew out of the partnership between TL and AS with support from UC Berkeley, Aspire, and CAL Prep leadership (see Figure 12.1). Each partner brings ideas and inspiration for the overarching goal of student success in science. The vertical science team includes professors, staff, and students

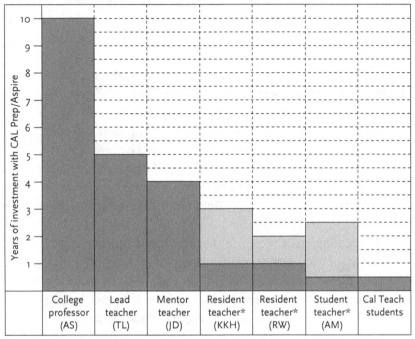

FIGURE 12.1. Vertical science team at the California College Preparatory Academy (CAL Prep). All student teachers are currently teaching in science classrooms, and both resident teachers are currently teaching science within Aspire. The team is vertical in terms of expertise and also in years of investment with the development of CAL Prep. At the top of the vertical ladder, the college professor (AS) has been involved with CAL Prep since its inception. She has served as an expert in secondary and postsecondary education since the earliest stages of ideation at the University of California, Berkeley. The lead teacher (TL) began teaching at CAL Prep when they first offered chemistry to the first graduating class during their 11th-grade year. The mentor teacher (JD) has taught biology, anatomy and physiology, integrated science, and marine biology. Given the small size of the school, it can only support two main science teachers: an expert in physical science (TL) and in life science (JD). In addition, both TL and JD have mentored teaching credential candidates. Aspire has started its own teacher credentialing program using a model similar to medical residency (http://aspirepublicschools.org/join/atr/). TL and JD each mentored a resident in different years. Both of their former residents are currently teaching in Aspire. TL has also mentored a student teacher through the Cal Teach (http://calteach.berkeley.edu/) credential program (AM). At the bottom of the vertical ladder, undergraduates considering science and math teaching careers are invited through Cal Teach to spend a semester supporting the CAL Prep science classes.

from UC Berkeley, teachers at CAL Prep, and science coaches from Aspire. UC Berkeley also provides opportunities for CAL Prep students, materials for chemistry experiments, and connections with professors. The university has written grants to buy equipment and chemicals and to send teachers to meetings such as the National Science Teachers Association meeting. We also lend equipment and invite students to come to campus to use our laboratory facilities and audit classes. Professors are willing to connect with teachers and engage in discussions of what it means to be ready for college.

> TL: As teachers, we are constantly trying to make our kids college-ready, but what college-ready means is vastly different, depending on what college they are going to go to. The more intimate partnerships that high school teachers can get [with their college counterparts] will give them at least a sense of what college professors want of kids when they walk in the door. I do not have a deep content knowledge of physics, but I'm teaching it, and I've passed the test to make me NCLB compliant. But I had a terrific opportunity to meet with a physics professor for 2 hours at the university and I just asked, "If I could prepare these kids to come into your course, what would you want?" It was a great opportunity for the professor to be able to say, "Please prepare the kids in this way." So I think the more partnerships that teachers can have with universities, the better teachers will be able to understand what college readiness might mean.

Successful vertical teaming means that the learning is bidirectional. Thus, although CAL Prep teachers benefit from interacting with UC Berkeley faculty, the faculty also learn from their engagement with CAL Prep teachers.

> AS: And the flip side of that is I've benefited a lot from hearing Tatiana's stories when she was in San Diego and at CAL Prep and from many other high school teachers, hearing about the reality of the individual students, which often gets lost in the introductory science classes. The university classes tend to be quite large and you don't have much time to talk to students. So you don't understand why the individual student or even a class as a whole might not have performed so well on an assessment. You are not even aware of how bad that assessment might have been. And, you just have this very distant view, "Well, they are just not studying hard enough," or "They are just not good enough." And so the reality of actually understanding the

student in more detail, even if it is through the eyes of the teacher, really changes what the university should be doing, could be doing.

I think we have a lot to learn about how to support students, how to engage students so that they don't drop out after the first midterm, which too many students do. They just go, "Oh! This is what this is about? I'm outta here." And that's really sad for our society that we have only certain students who have enough support around them that they make it through, and all these other students are just walking away because we are not engaging them and not supporting them. And we don't even realize why.

Another key aspect of being on a team is the commitment of those involved for the long haul. There is a willingness to reflect, make thoughtful suggestions, admit when things have not worked well, and make continual improvements. It would have been all too easy to give up early on and lower goals and expectations.

TL: Aspire provides a science coach and day-to-day support. They are providing a model for teacher evaluation in a supportive way with professional development. UC Berkeley thinks longer term. They provided support to go to the National Science Teachers Association meeting so that we can see what the conference is about. They have already found funding for us to go next year. They are encouraging us to present some data from the school. Our science coach from Aspire is also going, so we will have the opportunity to discuss the Next Generation Science Standards. This support pushes our own learning. Both UC Berkeley and Aspire are providing services to make me feel supported in a multitude of ways.

Growth also requires consistency of personnel—low turnover—and a strong belief that students can be successful and steady adherence to that vision despite challenges and setbacks along the way.

TL: You can't do refinement if you are constantly turning over. Many schools don't achieve growth because there is a constant influx of new people with new ideas. When you have less turnover, it is easier to enculturate the new teachers, so that they can build and grow the existing culture as opposed to bringing in a different culture. Our student turnover has decreased by a lot as well, except of course, we bring in new ninth graders each year.

AS: Stability of the partnership is very noticeable on the UC Berkeley side. Most of the faculty and staff who began dreaming about a school more than 10 years ago are still deeply engaged. We meet monthly in partnership with Aspire and CAL Prep to update and reflect on progress, and to discuss next steps and set plans in motion.

In conclusion, we have a large vertical science team that runs from undergraduate students, through the high school, through teacher training, through a master teacher, all the way up to the college level. That vertical team is no small feat. It has no gaps right now. All the relationships are close.

## Testing and Refining Ideas

The partnership continues to work toward a higher level. In some sense, we are never arriving and always feel we can do more. As TL described it, it does take the going back and saying, "OK, what's working, what's not working." At all levels, we are testing and refining ideas in an iterative process. The students are doing this in their science classes as a means of learning science. The teachers are doing this in refining instruction. The principal is doing this in setting up coherent processes and policies agreed upon by all. We are doing this in our partnership as we identify new ways in which the university can provide support. We are all thinking like scientists approaching a challenging problem. It is very much about the process. Here we offer a summary of the outcomes of several "experiments" as a means of conveying our growing understanding. We relate three stories about (1) self-assessment, (2) chemistry in the ninth grade, and (3) student science coaches.

**Importance of Self-Assessment.** At the end of the third quarter of the first chemistry class at CAL Prep offered for students in 11th grade, students take a pre-California Standards Test (CST) examination (exam) given to all students at Aspire Schools. When the CAL Prep chemistry students took the pre-CST exam, this was a stark reality check because the students did not do well on a fact-based, multiple-choice exam for which they had little practice. Most of the students scored in the 30% to 40% range, which is equivalent to guessing.

So for the next 4 weeks, we turned off *Living By Chemistry* and did more consolidation of learning. TL still tried to focus on students taking ownership of their own learning. She instituted peer coaching, in which she would coach individual students to be experts in one specific content area, and then the students did rotations to coach each other. Everybody became an expert. It was still student-centered learning but more focused on the facts of chemistry to match the assessment. That year, 64% of the students scored *advanced* or *proficient,* one student scored *below basic,* and none scored *far below basic.* The one student who scored below basic was a student with an individualized education plan who really struggled with reading and test taking. Because this student had been scoring far below basic on previous tests, scoring at the below basic level reflected growth for her.

With three quarters of conceptual work behind them from the *Living By Chemistry* curriculum, TL found that the students in the CAL Prep class were learning the facts faster, presumably because they had a basic understanding and had built trust among one another. Moreover, it was a good way for the students to do some self-assessment, and it was rewarding for them to realize how much they did understand. In this student-centered learning environment, the students had time to reflect on what they did and did not know.

TL: While I try to incorporate the content of those standards, I'm not trying to prep my kids to do well on the CST. That is not my goal. The big "Aha" moment that I had from that first year was that you have to give student-centered opportunities for them to make observations and try to figure things out. But then you also have to give them opportunities to consolidate, to say, "I do get this," and to build student confidence. Without confidence, they are unable to tackle the challenges.

Such self-assessment is a critical skill for success in college.

AS: Back to the university environment, I am finding that the low performance in introductory chemistry is associated with the students who are not doing that consolidation. They are seeing every concept as an independent idea to memorize. They think time on task is the measure of how well they are going to do. They are not looking for patterns. They are not trying to consolidate and then explain their understanding in their own words. So I would agree with TL that the ability to self-assess what you do and do not know is critical for success in science.

**Chemistry in Ninth Grade.** A difficult issue for a small school such as CAL Prep is finding efficient ways of scheduling classes. To this end, the school decided to offer the chemistry class to 9th graders as well. The rationale was that this change would minimize the number of classes offered by a small and overburdened teaching staff; the teacher would have a single "prep" for both the 9th and 11th grade classes, and then the following year, chemistry would not be offered. Because the 11th graders had performed well in chemistry the previous year, we expected that this class would work for the 9th graders. In addition, other Aspire schools were teaching chemistry in the 9th grade and we also thought that if students started taking science classes earlier in high school, they would have more opportunities to take laboratory and college courses.

Unfortunately, chemistry at the ninth grade was somewhat of a disaster. It was not because the students did not try or that they were not working hard. Rather, it was related to the additional knowledge required for learning chemistry. Chemistry is a balance between a conceptual understanding of things that cannot be seen and quantitative understanding. The quantitative understanding in chemistry begins with adding two negative numbers together to get a larger negative number, or adding a positive and negative number together. These simple processes of adding negative and positive numbers are mathematical concepts, and with the involvement of mathematics (math), math anxiety surfaced in the class. Thus, the ninth graders who had any sort of anxiety about math transferred their anxiety to chemistry.

In addition, some of the students could not yet do mental math, such as multiplying by two in their heads, which is critical in chemistry, especially when dealing with simple proportions. For example, if the temperature of a gas doubles, what happens to the volume occupied by the gas? We found that if the students did not understand the math, they believed that they did not understand the chemistry concept even if they did understand that gases expand as the temperature increases. The connection between the conceptual and the quantitative, even at the most basic level, resulted in math-phobic responses and a belief that chemistry was beyond their understanding.

TL: The ninth-grade students had taken many, many, many years of math. They are walking into a chemistry class for the first time. I believe that if they had more opportunities before entering chemistry to quantify simple measurements and observations, they would be in better shape. In other words, we need to start earlier connecting simple math with observations.

Two years later, this ninth-grade cohort, who had a very difficult experience with chemistry, took physics. Many of them believed that they could not succeed in math or science.

TL: This year with physics, I introduced a single problem solving method to alleviate some of the stress with the math. We talk explicitly about the algebra-type problem solving and the conceptual pieces. We bring them together to support one another, but I try to not do both simultaneously.

The ninth-grade cohort who began with chemistry performed well in physics as 11th graders, and anecdotally, the students reported liking physics better and feeling more successful in terms of their understanding. It was evident that the students liked physics because they achieved a greater level of success. The students who failed chemistry in 9th grade will repeat chemistry as seniors, at which point we hope they will successfully complete the course. We will not let them give up.

TL: So I am going to get a second opportunity to prove to those kids that they can do this. They can understand this better than they gave themselves credit for, and they do have the ability.

A key message here is that both teachers and students need to press on and overcome obstacles. In retrospect, offering chemistry in the ninth grade was too early for many of our students. But hopefully, these students will learn that if they work at it, they can achieve.

**Student Science Coaches.** CAL Prep offers what is called eighth-period support, which is different than all the other periods in the day. Some students can go to study hall, and there are a variety of support and elective courses that they can take. If students are passing all their courses, they can choose an elective course during this period. Teachers also identify students for support courses. The support course for science is designed to assist students who are struggling with self-confidence.

TL: In this course, I preview the week's material and prepare the students to be coaches. I do not even call it a chemistry support class. I call it a coach's course. When the student coaches go to class, they are the ones responsible for making sure that their groups understand the concepts. The coaches are the ones responsible for assessing everyone else's learning and so it builds their self-confidence.

Also, students who normally see the coaches as the dumb kids get to see them as, "Oh, you have the answers." So it changes the mindset not only of the kids who are doing the problems, but also the mindset of the kids looking at them. And the way kids look at each other makes a big difference in their self-confidence.

When you take the students who normally get As and you force them to get the answers from the kids who normally get Fs, it is possible to change everyone's mindset little by little. The *Living By Chemistry* curriculum teacher guides make it easy to support student coaches because they are thorough guides for daily lessons. This outcome is an unintentional, but wonderful use of these guides, that they can be used to cultivate confidence in students.

## Lessons Learned

There are several important lessons that we learned in our examination of high school chemistry at CAL Prep. From the perspective of the teacher, the importance of support—in conveying the curriculum and in thinking about what is important to teach and how to teach it—is perhaps most critical. As we have tried to show, textbooks and curricula are not universally useful, and it is important for teachers to have curricula that facilitate rather than impede both (1) teachers' capacity to teach courses that are perceived to be difficult and (2) teachers' attempts to reach the most underprepared students. But, as also shown in this chapter, even a well-constructed curriculum with support from the curriculum's author does not guarantee success. Professional development for teachers needs to provide ongoing support in *thinking* about teaching—support in deconstructing successes and recovering from failures. Also, the vertical team involving students, teacher, coach, and professor speaks to the complexity of the partnerships required to engage and succeed in meaningful curricular and pedagogical reform.

In addition, there are lessons to be learned that have direct implications for the students who are being served by CAL Prep and other reform-minded schools. What other information do students need to know to be able to take a course in chemistry or in any other science subject? How do we support students who are the least prepared and create a space for them to contribute to the learning of their classmates while building their competence and self-efficacy for learning? The answers to these questions can also be found in the interface of supportive curriculum, partnership structures for teaching, and the willingness to try things out, keeping what works and discarding or refining what does not. The students who did not pass chemistry in 9th grade will repeat chemistry in 12th grade, building on their successful experience with physics. They will learn, as the teacher did, that success sometimes only comes with subsequent attempts.

Neither effective science teaching nor school reform is easy, and the most important lesson here is that simple solutions to these concerns are naive and will not stand the test of time. Introductory science courses at the university are gateway courses to science majors, but for many students who are underrepresented in tertiary education environments, these courses in the middle and high school years serve as gateway courses to higher education. It is our task to help these students learn how to successfully pass through these gates.

## References

Commission on Mathematics and Science Education (2009). The opportunity equation: Transforming Mathematics and Science Education for citizenship and the global economy. Retrieved from https://www.carnegie.org/media/filer_public/80/c8/80c8a7bc-c7ab-4f49-847d-1e2966f4dd97/ccny_report_2009_opportunityequation.pdf

Stacy, A. M. (2012). *Living by Chemistry: An introduction for teachers* (1st ed.). New York, NY: Bedford, Freeman, and Worth.

# 13 | Building a *Supportive* College-Preparatory Culture

**MEGAN REED AND MICHELLE Y. CORTEZ**

*"CAL Prep is a great and strong school that sets every student up for success and never failure. Every year it improves more and more for future generations."* (Maribel Garcia, graduating senior at California College Preparatory Academy, in Ness, 2012)

ALIFORNIA COLLEGE PREPARATORY ACADEMY (CAL Prep) is and always has been a petri dish in which we are cultivating new things every day. We meet and talk a lot at CAL Prep, but we are always eager to move past discussion and into action, ever mindful that any idea we incorporate needs to be tailored to our site and tended as it grows. I (Reed) joined CAL Prep in Year 3 as the school's first Dean of Students. I had previously worked as a teacher for Aspire, with special responsibilities for teacher–student advisories. At CAL Prep, in Year 4, I became a first-time principal, serving 4 years in that role through the school's second graduating class of 2011–2012. I (Cortez) also joined CAL Prep in Year 3, first serving as the lead teacher for Advancement Via Individual Determination (AVID), a college-readiness program implemented for all students (Mehan, Villanueva, Hubbard, & Lintz, 1996). I served in many roles at CAL Prep: first as an eighth-grade English teacher and college-readiness lead teacher, then as the Wrap-Around Services Coordinator, and finally as Dean of Student Life. Given the success of our support framework, I was invited to split my time between CAL Prep and the Aspire Home Office, where I served as Secondary Supports Specialist. Both of us worked at CAL Prep for 5 years through 2011–2012, at which time Reed moved out-of-state to another principal position and Cortez became a first-time principal for another Aspire high school.

From the very first day of our collaborative work, the need for student supports emerged high on our agenda. A rigorous curriculum, while critical, was not enough. There was tremendous need for both catch-up and acceleration of learning to better prepare our students for college entry and successful college completion. In the context of prior school failures and tough life challenges, combining catch-up and acceleration for a diversity of learners proved to be an enormous challenge.

One principle was clear at the start. Our support system at CAL Prep was always *evolving*—in response to changing student needs, to the school's growing capacity to meet these needs, to the data we examined, and to the research literature on comprehensive supports that was available. Ours was a learning culture or petri dish as Reed (2009) described it above: we were learning along the way just as our students were. Importantly, as Cortez also underscored, with each new idea, we were tailoring programs to our own site and improving at every turn (Cortez, 2011). We were fortunate to build a stable leadership team and strong administrator–faculty collaboration. With Weinstein as principal investigator, our partnership garnered a grant from our intermediary organization, the Woodrow Wilson National Fellowship Foundation (WWNFF), to fund our joint developmental work on student supports (Weinstein, 2011). Our thinking was challenged by presenting this work in a number of venues, including professional development sessions for teachers at CAL Prep, conferences at the University of California (UC) Berkeley, annual meetings of the American Educational Research Association, and Early College gatherings at WWNFF in Princeton, New Jersey.

The results of our collaborative work on student supports are presented in two distinct but interrelated chapters. In this chapter, we emphasize practice and the perspective of a principal and a supports coordinator who built the student support system from the ground up. We examine (1) stages in the evolution of student supports at CAL Prep, (2) key processes and component parts that we used to build student supports, and (3) examples of supports in place during a typical week. In Chapter 14, Weinstein and Bialis-White present a conceptual framework, driven by both research and practice, which they call "SMART Supports." This framework illuminates the set of underlying principles that guide support planning toward the seamless interweaving of rigor and help in a college-preparatory high school education.

## An *Evolving* Support System

As reported in Chapter 9, there were many changes at CAL Prep over the 7 years studied in this book—in grade levels served, demographics, staffing and leadership, and physical location. In 2005, CAL Prep started with a sixth grade, growing a grade each year with the plan of serving Grades 6 through 12. As we write this chapter, the school currently serves students in Grades 9 through 12. During this time, the student and family demographic profiles changed from majority African American to majority Latino (at 55%), the English language learner population increased (to 16%), and the percentage of students receiving a free or reduced lunch dropped to 48%.[1] The percentage of families who have not completed college is 79% and number of neighborhoods from which students travel to school (approximately eight) has stayed relatively constant.

CAL Prep's mission to close the achievement gap by preparing underserved students for college success necessitated developing not only a robust support system at the school site but also a dynamic one. These supports needed to be structured, yet flexible, to accommodate current and anticipated changes at the school site. As with any program, the supports at CAL Prep changed over time as the school matured. In looking at CAL Prep's history, there were phases that the school went through to get to a place where the robust support system could be developed to the point it is now.

Following is a broad overview of this journey over time. We identify the themes that best characterized each year of targeted efforts and the data that fueled the development of additional supports for the school community each year.

### Years 1 and 2: From Rigor to Relationships

When CAL Prep first started in 2005, it did so as a middle school with a group of adventurous and trusting families who were willing to help build the ship as it sailed. Students who came to CAL Prep hailed from different regions, districts, as well as backgrounds and they varied greatly in academic levels. For the most part, students were multiple years behind in reading and mathematics (math) and had limited "student skills," including the capacity to sit through an entire class, take notes, do homework, and stay on task. The work, then, was to ensure that students learned these

---

[1] Data are from http://api.cde.ca.govAcnt2011/2011GrthDem.aspx?allcds=01-10017-0118489

skills and were able to handle the rigor of a college-preparatory curriculum. Consequently, we began with an emphasis on high curricular and behavioral standards. But, as documented in Chapter 4, demanding rigor without strong relationships with students proved ineffective. Academic failure was pervasive and behavioral concerns were rampant. A shift was needed, away from behavior management toward student engagement, and away from what unintentionally became a detention-heavy climate toward the building of a positive school culture.

We embraced a theory of action premised on the notion that students become engaged when they experience some success. Given their earlier school experiences (generally negative with very low expectations), academic success was facilitated by extra adult attention (e.g., in small groups, one-one-one time with teachers, and advisories) and by involvement in extracurricular activities to provide an arena of success as students gained strength in academics. One of our first efforts in providing students with a college experience was to engage students in summer programs, both academic and nonacademic, that were held on the UC Berkeley campus. We also adopted a reading intervention program for students with poor reading skills.

In looking at student discipline and attrition data as well as student and family satisfaction data, it became clear that students needed to feel more connected to staff and each other. In response to this, a new advisory program was launched, giving voice to the vision of students and teachers (see Chapter 5). Furthermore, in light of poor homework completion rates, we introduced an after-school homework hall that provided support and a quiet place for students to successfully complete their homework assignments, thereby ending a cycle of repeated failure. Undergraduate tutors, mental health interns (from counselor education and clinical psychology), and college experiences such as attendance at athletic and cultural events were also added to the program.

## Year 3: Supporting Early Intervention

In the third year, with a ninth grade added, we invested in additional staff positions—a Dean of Students—who focused on developing a positive culture, proactively managing the discipline processes, supporting advisories, and enriching after-school opportunities. In this role, the Dean (Reed) developed *positive* referrals for appropriate behavior and implemented early, supportive interventions around disciplinary infractions, so as to reengage students in instruction instead of pushing out through detentions and suspensions. We reworked advisories to prioritize the advocacy role of teachers, rather than the curricular units, by organizing multiyear (single-, single-grade) advisories with the same leader, who followed stu entry to graduation. In addition, the school added an AVID program to support the development of a college-going culture and the s teaching of college-readiness skills in students (Mehan et al., 1996)

## Years 4 and 5: Character-Driven Culture and Whole-Student Development

In its fourth year, in a new school site with Reed as principal, CAL Prep introduced the character system of cooperation, assertiveness, responsibility, empathy, and self-control (CARES)—drawn from the Responsive Classroom (n.d.). This program, developed by the Northeast Foundation for Children, focuses on teaching social-emotional skills to elementary school students and has shown positive effects on achievement. This addition allowed us to align schoolwide initiatives with the development of these traits in students. In essence, it enabled everyone (students, parents, and teachers) to be on the same page, which is a critical component to feeling a part of a strong and positive community.

Prior to having a college counselor position, CAL Prep was also lucky enough to add the Berkeley United in Literacy Development, or BUILD, program to its course offerings (n.d.). This program includes a business entrepreneurship class offered to students in their freshman year alongside college counseling, Scholastic Aptitude Test (SAT) preparation, and homework support in the following 3 years. We also extended the school day in Year 4 to allow room for additional eighth-period interventions, beyond its voluntary use for homework. A weekly newsletter, the "Grizzly Growl," prepared by the principal and sent to teachers, more clearly communicated the mission of the school and helped develop a sense of community, responding to the needs of teachers for greater support (see Chapter 7). The after-school program expanded to include sports and debate teams.

As a part of transitioning fully to a high school, CAL Prep's focus became more keenly directed toward college readiness and college persistence. When looking at the CARES values at the before-school planning workshop, the staff realized there was a need to integrate cognitive skills with the social-emotional skills. Thus, CARES transitioned to CARRIES (to and through college)—Cooperative Citizen, Assertive Activist, Rigorous Problem Solver, Inquisitive Scholar, Empathetic Contributor, and Self-Controlled Success (see Figure 13.1). In order to better meet the growing needs of our students, Cortez transitioned into the role of Wrap-Around Services Coordinator. She

UNDERSTANDING AND PRACTICING THE FOLLOWING QUALITIES WILL BE THE FRAMEWORK THAT CARRIES YOU TO COLLEGE AND BEYOND …

| C | A | R | R | I | E | S |
|---|---|---|---|---|---|---|
| Cooperative Citizen | Assertive Activist | Rigorous Problem Solver | Responsible Role Model | Inquisitive Scholar | Empathetic Contributor | Self Controlled Success |
| Makes good choices for self and community, even when others may not make the right choices or notice.

Understands how actions or lack of actions affect oneself, others, and the community at large.

Demonstrates skills in resolving conflicts through positive, non-violent, alternative actions.

Contributes and functions in various group roles. | Speaks with confidence within a group and to an audience.

Sees a need in the community and uses effective leadership skills to find an appropriate way and time to meet that need.

Strong academic identity and sense of self; understands how learning takes place and interacts with social/cultural identity. | Identifies, assesses, analyzes, integrates, and uses complex and diverse resources and information.

Develops solutions to problems and formulates recommendations based on justifiable rationale.

Applies concepts to new material noting the inter-connectedness and/or unique aspects among themes, disciplines, or historical periods. | Maintains supplies, resources, and coursework with integrity

Prioritizes and uses time effectively remaining on task and following through to complete all steps in a task.

Plans for the future by setting priorities and achievable goals. | Actively uses resources (notes, reference materials, interviews, etc.) to find answers and satisfy curiosities.

Demonstrates interest in diverse cultures that fosters knowledge of individual differences.

Curious and creative navigation through uncertainty utilizing individual and group study skills to consider multiple perspectives.

Cultivates deep interest in ideas, people, and processes outside the focus field of study. | Contributes time, energy and talents to improve the quality of life in their home, school, community, state, nation, and world.

Shows understanding and/or appreciation for someone who is different than you.

Puts someone else's needs before your own. | Speaks using appropriate words and tone at all times, code-switching as necessary.

Persistently pursues challenging tasks, self-monitoring progress, and adapting, improving as necessary.

Works to highest potential at all times, often doing more than the required work. |

FIGURE 13.1. California College Preparatory Academy values and responsibility standards. These expected schoolwide learning results, or ESLRs, continue to shape school culture, professional development, and school-wide programs and activities like exhibitions and community service in the years to come.

coordinated college-readiness supports during the day, after school, and off campus (including a writing center, tutoring, special education, psychological counseling, health information, and college preparation).

Cortez began a team for Response to Intervention (RTI; n.d.), which planned interventions for students at three tiers (schoolwide, targeted, and intensive; see Figure 13.2). Staff development work was deepened through weekly meetings of the entire staff (professional development), department meetings (facilitated by lead teachers using a cycle of inquiry to evaluate and differentiate instruction), grade-level teams (to plan advisory lessons and exhibition support), supports team, and lead team (with the support coordinator a vital presence). An additional reading intervention was added in the form of a library, to more deeply engage students in literacy (see Chapter 8).

### Years 6 and 7: Rigor, Support, and Differentiation

Now that CAL Prep was a full high school (Grades 9–12), years 6 and 7 were years of honing and improving. We increased supports, training, and expectations for advisories; refined the "student of concern" process through which people referred students to the RTI team; fully realized eighth-period interventions, while refashioning what the *support period portion* looked like; and started office hours. We also focused schoolwide on engaging students in instruction, differentiating instruction, and continuing to build community between all stakeholders. We emphasized *supportive teaching* in the classroom (Reed, 2010, 2011) by integrating into classes higher level inquiry, organization for student engagement, and social-emotional responsiveness, drawing from the work of Conley (2010) and Pianta and colleagues (e.g., Pianta & Hamre, 2009).

## The Process of Developing Student Supports

Whereas the previous section depicts clear shifts over time in the development of the student support system, here we illuminate the processes we engaged in yearly and the varied component parts we drew on to design student support at CAL Prep. In order to build and revise this structure of supports, CAL Prep went through the following steps, each of which will be described in depth below. Every year, we examine data from the previous year and assess needs, redefine our problem statement, and develop the vision for the forthcoming year with a specific emphasis on supports. In this way, we are able to look at big-picture drivers (e.g., school structure), how these play out in our context, and what features might need to be changed.

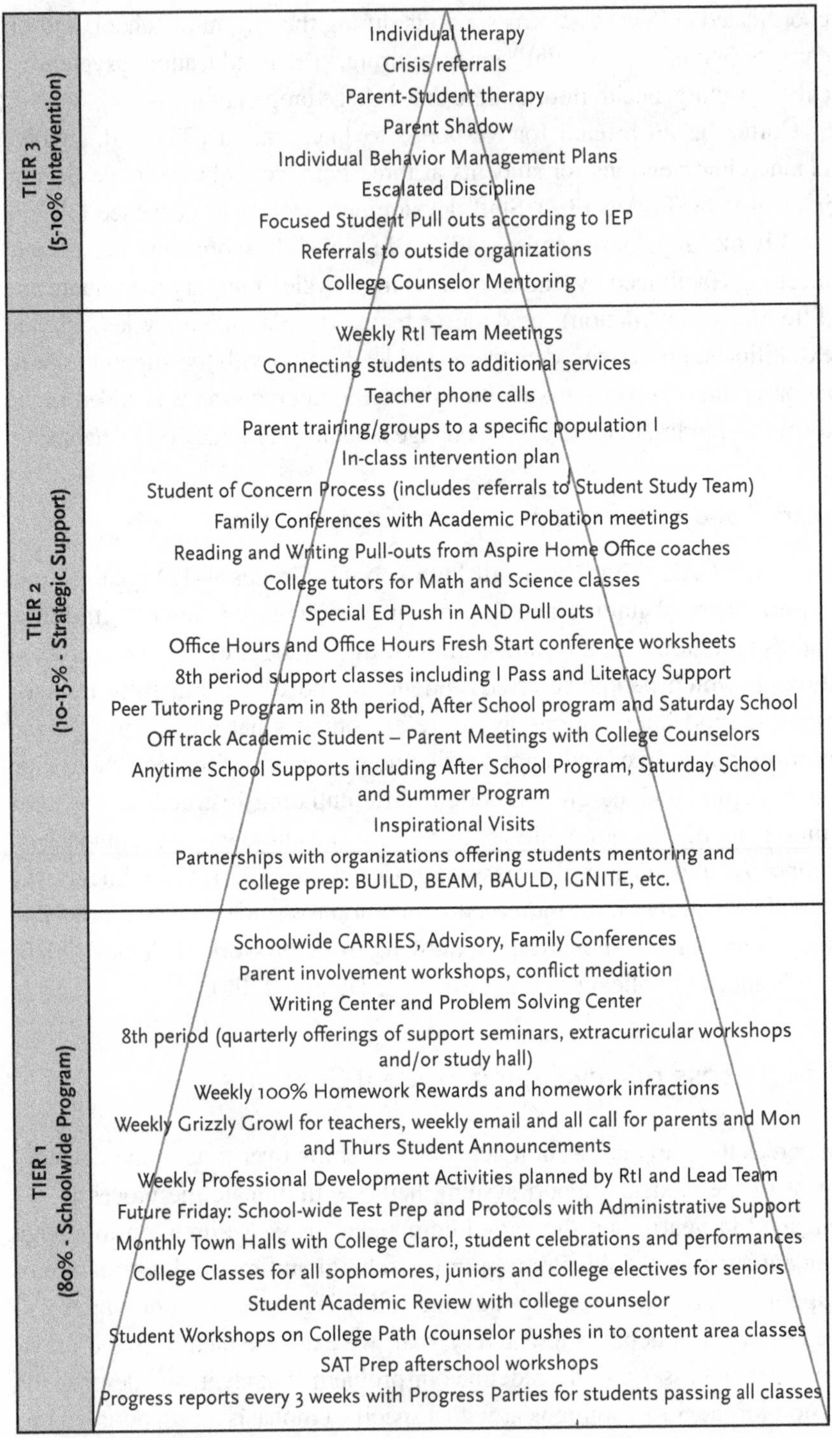

**TIER 3**
**(5-10% Intervention)**

Individual therapy
Crisis referrals
Parent-Student therapy
Parent Shadow
Individual Behavior Management Plans
Escalated Discipline
Focused Student Pull outs according to IEP
Referrals to outside organizations
College Counselor Mentoring

**TIER 2**
**(10-15% - Strategic Support)**

Weekly RtI Team Meetings
Connecting students to additional services
Teacher phone calls
Parent training/groups to a specific population I
In-class intervention plan
Student of Concern Process (includes referrals to Student Study Team)
Family Conferences with Academic Probation meetings
Reading and Writing Pull-outs from Aspire Home Office coaches
College tutors for Math and Science classes
Special Ed Push in AND Pull outs
Office Hours and Office Hours Fresh Start conference worksheets
8th period support classes including I Pass and Literacy Support
Peer Tutoring Program in 8th period, After School program and Saturday School
Off track Academic Student – Parent Meetings with College Counselors
Anytime School Supports including After School Program, Saturday School and Summer Program
Inspirational Visits
Partnerships with organizations offering students mentoring and college prep: BUILD, BEAM, BAULD, IGNITE, etc.

**TIER 1**
**(80% - Schoolwide Program)**

Schoolwide CARRIES, Advisory, Family Conferences
Parent involvement workshops, conflict mediation
Writing Center and Problem Solving Center
8th period (quarterly offerings of support seminars, extracurricular workshops and/or study hall)
Weekly 100% Homework Rewards and homework infractions
Weekly Grizzly Growl for teachers, weekly email and all call for parents and Mon and Thurs Student Announcements
Weekly Professional Development Activities planned by RtI and Lead Team
Future Friday: School-wide Test Prep and Protocols with Administrative Support
Monthly Town Halls with College Claro!, student celebrations and performances
College Classes for all sophomores, juniors and college electives for seniors
Student Academic Review with college counselor
Student Workshops on College Path (counselor pushes in to content area classes
SAT Prep afterschool workshops
Progress reports every 3 weeks with Progress Parties for students passing all classes

FIGURE 13.2. California College Preparatory Academy's Response to Intervention supports inventory.

This review also allows the school to maximize the human capital of the staff with tailored professional development activities, while actively engaging families and getting buy-in from students. We are also deliberate in rolling out the supports and in assessing them throughout the year, both to inform changes on the ground and to provide guidance for the following year.

## Gathering Data and Assessing Needs

In order to develop the most successful targeted supports at CAL Prep, we first gather both quantitative and qualitative data from multiple stakeholders and sources to identify the areas of greatest academic and social-emotional needs for families and students. All data are inspected through the lenses of gender, ethnicity, class, grade level, trimester, and home room. Quantitative data primarily include interim and final grades, state test scores from the previous years, Preliminary SAT (PSAT) and SAT scores, participation data (taken from observations), counseling referrals, attendance data, discipline data, attrition data, college acceptance data, and college retention data.

We also gather qualitative data from all types of students and families. We believe it is important to gather data across multiple ethnic groups, families of students who have attended the school for varying periods, students and families who are satisfied and dissatisfied with the school, students from different neighborhoods, and students from different grade levels. The qualitative data are gathered in several ways. We administer formal student surveys where students are asked open-ended response questions about their own well-being, their perceptions of the school, their perception of their own readiness for college, and their needs for support. These questions are also asked of students on informal, in-person surveys, and students reflect on their experience and their needs in their advisories. Staff are asked about specific areas of student performance, behavior, and well-being. In addition, graduates of the school are interviewed (via Facebook or in person). Ideally, every member of the staff is involved in efforts to gather qualitative data as they engage in listening conversations with students. It is important for school leadership to provide a place such as an RTI team, administrative or teacher meetings, or staff professional development time where these data can be shared.

## Defining a Mini-Mission Statement

CAL Prep starts to look at data from the above sources in February to begin forming a mini-mission statement for the coming academic year.

This mission statement ensures that there is a single, defined target that will focus the scope of the work in developing supports. For example, in 2010, the initial mission statement was "We need to be sure that all of our students are supported to meet the demands of our rigorous high school curriculum. We need to be a 'college for certain' school." As the central office received information from Aspire graduates about their level of preparation for rigor and social life in college, examined students' grades in our college level and Advanced Placement courses, and monitored Aspire graduates' persistence rates, the mini-mission statement changed to "We need to support our diverse students to be prepared to meet the demands of a rigorous college curriculum and challenging college life. We need to be a 'Graduate from College, Yes We Can!' school." This statement reflected a higher bar that would guide our supports to the right target. Key elements in this shift in mission were first, ensuring that staff acknowledged the diversity of the student population, and second, that curriculum and supports focused on achieving success in college preparation (as measured on college-readiness tests) in addition to success in meeting high school standards (as reflected on state testing). Also, most importantly, the second statement focuses on *college graduation*, not *college acceptance*.

## Articulating Vision for the Year

After we define the target (and single-sentence focus points) in the mini-mission statement, we "unpack" the mission statement into its component parts, choosing the most important and most "doable" tasks for the coming year. These become the focus areas that will govern *all* of the actions of the school, including the supports. One set of components CAL Prep focused on in pursuit of the mission were as follows:

- Engaging every student in instruction
- Inspiring curiosity in every student
- Increasing students' sense of belonging to a community
- Differentiating instruction to meet students where they are
- Providing interventions at multiple points during the day

As articulated, these points are not yet actionable or measurable, but further work leads to at least one or two actionable steps that can be assigned per focus point. When making the actionable steps, it is important to link the steps back to the area of the vision or focus point. It is also important to choose a small number of precise enough actions that they can be implemented successfully within the year.

## Looking at the Big Picture—Structures and Schedules

When developing supports, one cannot be afraid of change and flexibility on a large scale—it is necessary to think both in and out of the box and then find a comfortable middle ground. Different school types will have differing amounts of freedom with bell schedules, calendars, use of space, transportation, and structure of the day, but it is necessary to embrace the least number of restrictions and then be creative when considering what supports can and should look like. At CAL Prep, the initial limitations in developing supports included the number of classrooms, the number of periods available to meet the diverse needs of students, and the number of staff available. These limitations were addressed by creative scheduling, use of space, and staffing. The eighth period and office hours are two ways in which CAL Prep circumvented limitations of schedule and structures.

**Eighth Period.** The eighth period is most closely linked to the vision points of differentiating instruction to meet students where they are and providing interventions at multiple points during the day. During this period 3 days a week, each student is assigned either to intervention (support seminars by subject matter), study hall (support period), counseling groups, enrichment programs or leadership groups (honors seminars), or college classes off-campus. Two days a week, each student is enrolled in an advisory group during this period. Each student's schedule for eighth period is individualized and flexible. The study hall portion, which can have up to 50 to 60 students, is leanly staffed with two staff members, and students are socialized to do their work and meet expectations of reduced noise and productivity. This level of staffing allows teachers to all do intervention and enrichment and to guide tutors, allows counselors to meet with groups, and allows administrators to run leadership groups.

**Office Hours**. Many students who are far enough behind to be scheduled for eighth-period intervention are still in need of individualized assistance from a teacher, which most closely relates to our vision points of engaging all students and differentiating instruction. When our leadership team initially looked at this problem, the major constraints lay in the fact that students and teachers do not have the same unscheduled periods outside of lunch and recess (which teachers already use for intervention). The use of office hours circumvents this problem by having teachers on their preparation (prep) period work with students, who are pulled out of other classes.

First, each teacher is assigned several "office hours" slots per week that last for 20 minutes in two separate "prep" periods. The teacher is also assigned a place to hold office hours, ranging from a table in the cafeteria to a desk in an open classroom. When students want to sign up for office hours, they first get permission from the teacher of the class in which they will miss the 20 minutes of instruction, and then they sign up for an office hours slot with the teacher on prep period. The teacher on prep waits for the student at the assigned time and the student must arrive in a timely manner with an excused pass from the instructor. The student comes with one or several specific questions that they discuss with the teacher and then return to class. The obvious difficulty with this process is that the student does miss work in the other class. To minimize the impact, office hours are scheduled during the "do now" assignment or independent-practice phases of classes, but this solution does have a negative impact on some students. Another way of structuring office hours with less negative impact but a similarly responsive approach is to assign a tutor, special education teacher, aide, or another teacher to see students in the same class in which they need the extra support.

## Utilizing All Human Capital

Every person on a campus is an asset and the work of administrative leadership is to see how to best utilize the gifts, talents, and time of each adult on campus to meet the needs of all students. In this process, it is essential to look at data to determine the assets and limitations of each individual's content knowledge, relationship–capital with students and families, working style, talents outside the classroom, and ability to juggle multiple tasks without sacrificing quality. Professional development is a powerful tool, and there is no doubt that all teachers and staff members take great pride every year in working toward excellence at their jobs—be it classroom instruction, office management, or building and enforcing school culture. Most of the professional development in a school should, in fact, be targeted to assist people in maximizing their potential and allowing staff to build on their strengths.

At CAL Prep, for example, the Dean of Student Life (Cortez) started a peer tutoring and mentoring program that suited her expertise as a former AVID teacher and was woven into the eighth-period supports. A second example involves the algebra teacher, who has immense relationship capital with students and families as well as the ability to juggle several tasks without diminishing the quality of classroom instruction. She, therefore, was assigned to support senior life activities as a part of her duties in working on supports for students. A third example involves advisories, one of the areas in which teachers support students outside the classroom in both a non–subject-specific and social-emotional role. The current advisory model is described briefly below.

**Advisory.** Advisory at CAL Prep takes place 2 days a week, is a single-gender and single-grade activity, and serves 10 to 18 students in a group. It is most deeply aligned with the vision point of increasing students' sense of belonging to a community. Although *every* staff member on campus has an advisory, the type of advisory on which a staff member is asked to serve may vary. For example, someone who has demonstrated less strength in building relationships with students might have a 10-person (rather than 18-person) group, or be partnered with another teacher to run their advisory. It is important to underscore that every adult on campus is used as an advisor and that professional development and lessons are differentiated, depending on the assets and weaknesses that the individuals have as advisors. Also, professional development for advisories looks very different from some of the professional development that is conducted for classroom teachers.

**Response to Intervention Team.** Another way of utilizing staff members' assets in meeting students' needs is the RTI team, which includes members who have diverse perspectives to offer on student success and struggle. The RTI team at CAL Prep includes the social-emotional counselor, the special education director, principal, a teacher, the after-school director, and the school psychologist. Other schools have also included a dean of students, two teachers (to represent younger and older students), and an office manager (who was particularly influential with the students).

Ideally, the RTI team looks at data on student achievement and well-being for individuals and groups of students on a regular basis. Using these data, the team identifies individual students and groups of students who are struggling. The team then creates plans for individual students as well as structures and systems that will assist the students in being more successful academically and socioemotionally. The team either implements these plans or assigns others to implement them. Most importantly, the team goes through a weekly cycle of reviewing data for these students to monitor the success of the interventions. When looking at student data, it is important to recognize that even small, positive changes are signs of success and that larger change may take several weeks or months to come to light.

**Using Time Outside of the Regular School Day.** In addition to using time creatively during the regular school day, CAL Prep looked to maximize time outside of the regular school day as an opportunity to provide supports. Two essential programs that operate outside of the school day are Saturday School and after-school activities.

*Saturday School.* Initially, Saturday School was designed as a way for students with multiple absences (more than three in a quarter) to make up a day of absence on their record. Saturday School staff noticed that multiple students starting "opting in" to Saturday School as an opportunity to secure help and/or work in a quiet environment. As a result of this, leadership changed the staffing for Saturday School from stipended monthly positions to staff that worked fewer hours each day or for a half day one time per week in order to accommodate Saturday School hours.

*After-school Program.* After-school programs are challenging to develop in small schools because there are fewer students to form teams and fewer staff members to act as leaders. Moreover, as noted in Chapter 5, students want extracurricular activities. CAL Prep's after-school program has transitioned to a primarily athletic and academic focus and includes peer tutoring, tutor tutoring, debate, basketball, and soccer.

**Adults from Outside the School Campus.** CAL Prep's partnership with UC Berkeley affords it the unique opportunity to have access to many adults from outside the school. In other schools, this might look like forging a partnership with local community organizations, community colleges, mentoring agencies, or internship programs with local businesses. This access to multiple trusted adults allows CAL Prep to have other adults mentor and enrich students' experiences. At some point, we realized that although everyone on campus reiterates daily to students that each one of them can be successful in college and beyond, students will tell us things like "my coach [outside school] tells me I can go to college, so I am going!" At first, staff felt parent-like frustration at the fact that messages seemed to matter more when they came via others rather than our daily reminders. But then we embraced the idea that messages feel unique from people who are outside of the daily norm. We also saw that we had an incredible untapped resource in the teaching and non-teaching staff at UC Berkeley, who can provide experiences to students that are well outside of what we could offer on our school campus.

In response, the CAL Prep leadership and UC Berkeley partners set up the "Inspirational Visits" program. To plan an inspirational visit, the UC Berkeley representative from the Center for Educational Partnerships sends mass e-mails and spreads the word via professors and staff who are involved in the CAL Prep–UC Berkeley faculty meetings that we are looking for individuals willing to host a visit for some of our students. Interested parties respond with dates, times, and possible schedule for the (usually) half-day visit. Leadership and teachers then chose students for whom the trip could be a good fit. This fit is done on a case-by-case basis—students can be honor roll and very interested in career choices similar to the trip or struggling academically or socioemotionally and in need of some inspiration. The trips for students have ranged from getting to eat lunch at the faculty club to visiting the African American museum with an art history professor to visiting sports facilities on campus.

## Engaging with and Supporting Families

When considering supports, it is important to factor in supporting families as well as students. Families who have students at or approaching transitional points (entering elementary, middle, or high school, as well as college) are especially in need of support and guidance about the transition. This support is key because it helps families know how to interpret and process students' reaction to these transitions as well as plan for all the financial, academic, and emotional needs in the months and years to come. Engaging families is most closely tied with engaging every student and making students (and families) feel a part of the community.

**Saturday School Support Sessions.** During the Saturday Schools for students, families are given the option to drop in for a cup of coffee and conversation with other families to build relationships and offer support family member to family member.

**Evening Counseling Group.** The largest transition for CAL Prep families comes in the senior year when students are preparing for college. This transition is huge for any family, but it is especially challenging when no one in the family has attended college previously. To support families through this transition, we offer monthly sessions with our counselor where families engage in facilitated conversations to process their own emotions about the transition and obtain help from each other and the counselor about how to support their own students.

**College-Readiness Nights.** Starting in freshman year, CAL Prep's college counseling office provides informational sessions monthly about college-readiness topics, including financial aid, college selection, college admission requirements, and the college transition process. In addition to supporting families themselves, it is important that families are made aware of and fully understand the supports offered to students. These sessions allow families to encourage students to take advantage of the supports and to talk with their children about how the supports are helping them (see Chapter 7). In order to do this, CAL Prep engages with families on a regular basis to provide more information about all of the schools' programs including supports. Families are invited to three Saturday Schools a year where several workshops and informational sessions are offered on different topics depending on the time of year and needs of families and students. In addition, families receive a calendar for the upcoming month as well as weekly e-mails with any updates and homework assignments.

## Providing Professional Development

As with all work in a school, strong professional development is critical to implementing initiatives well. The CAL Prep staff receive professional development in all areas of practice via professional development meetings on early-release Fridays, weekly department meetings with lead teachers, and weekly leadership team meetings. Professional development, particularly related to supports, is provided in weekly model advisory sessions, RTI team-run monthly development on differentiation, monthly consultancies about individual students who are struggling to make progress, regular use of data to identify students who need support, and practice sessions for family conferences and family phone calls. In addition to this whole-group development, teachers also receive weekly feedback on lesson plans, biweekly or triweekly observations, professional learning plans, and data meetings after interim assessments. Each of these individualized sessions has a section where teachers receive support in working with struggling or high-achievement students, building relationships with students, and using varied and effective teaching practice to reach all students.

## Engaging Students

The final element of building a successful supports program is engaging and getting buy-in from students. Generating excitement for and establishing the purpose for and usefulness of supports is essential, especially when working with older students. In order to establish an understanding about the usefulness and purpose of the interventions, the interventions and everything that we do at CAL Prep are tied to the common core characteristics—CARRIES (see Figure 13.1). Students are taught what these characteristics are and what they look like at school, home, college, and the workplace. All of our cultural elements such as awards, corrections, and supports are aligned to these skills so that students can understand how all the things they are asked to do are related and how each leads to college and career success.

The other element that CAL Prep relies on for buy-in is purposeful advertisement that leads to excitement. Individuals in charge of certain supports display as much attractive environmental print around that support as possible to ensure students know about the support, its purpose, and its goal. Recognition for students who take part in, excel in, or try any of the supports is also advertised in weekly announcements and in print, and there are also rewards. One type of reward is that the college counselors draw two names of attendees to the college nights to win free dress (a non-uniform day) for the next day. Another reward was a picnic provided to a counseling group for supporting each other to raise their grades. Also, for as many supports as possible (e.g., advisory, after-school programs), the lead staff make or purchase spirit items such as T-shirts, buttons, bumper stickers, and pencils, so that students can "show off" their membership in that group.

## Implementation: A Week in the Life of California College Preparatory Academy Supports

Here, we offer a brief perspective of what our SMART support system feels like on the ground and how we make it work at CAL Prep. In the resource guide that we prepare for students and their families, we make clear our expectation that *all* students need support:

> Succeeding in CAL Prep's quest for "College for Certain" is no easy task. You have to stay organized, study efficiently, think deeply, test well, demonstrate understanding in writing, and solve all kinds of

problems (with school, friends, family, and just life in general). No matter whether you are a high-achieving or struggling student, we want to make sure you receive the right kind of support to match your challenges. That's why CAL Prep has a whole team of staff members to support the success of *every* student at CAL Prep. This is a school that *cares* about you. Ask and you shall receive the help you desire . . . but *be specific* in asking for appropriate supports and use each support *wisely*.

This resource guide lists the wide array of support programs (from progress reports every three weeks to electives as examples), noting the challenges that students might face, questions that they should ask themselves, and the lead staff member to see for that specific support.

Students can access on-demand supports when they need them. However, on-demand by student choice is always paired with "*as needed*" with regular review of student data (grades, attendance reports) by teachers, advisors, and the RTI team, if a referral is made. CAL Prep supports for academic success fall into three tiers of interventions, with 80% of the efforts placed on schoolwide programs, 10% to 15% on differentiated strategic support such as an in-class intervention plan, and 5% to 10% on intensive intervention such as individual therapy (see Figure 13.2).

Figure 13.3 shows supports as students might experience them, through School-Day Structures (announcements), Classroom Rigor (A–G requirements, college classes), On-Demand Supports (office hours, counselors), and Student Life (progress parties, spirit day). Students are greeted as they arrive with a smile from teachers who stand at the school's threshold to welcome them. As students travel through course of a day, week, or quarter, regular structures are consistent. These are introduced in August, reinforced in environmental print and announcements, and, if necessary in advisory. As students travel from class to class, their teachers push them toward rigorous discourse, which we define as "purposeful learning and instruction directed toward objectively high standards and discourse of ideas supported by *evidence*."

In August, our beginning-of-the-year boot camp for students includes rigor rotations where content teachers introduce schoolwide norms for turn-and-talk, student-led discussions, and group work. Students earn CARRIES-positive referrals emphasizing college-ready skills and benefit from hidden rigor accelerators that help teachers (e.g., lesson-plan feedback, observations, teacher Professional Learning Plan focus points). Finally, administrative leadership actualizes these supports in daily practice

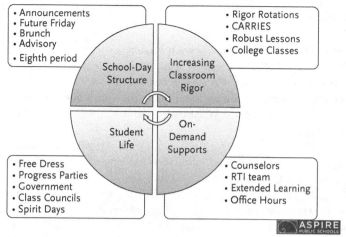

- Announcements
- Future Friday
- Brunch
- Advisory
- Eighth period

School-Day Structure

Increasing Classroom Rigor

- Rigor Rotations
- CARRIES
- Robust Lessons
- College Classes

Student Life

On-Demand Supports

- Free Dress
- Progress Parties
- Government
- Class Councils
- Spirit Days

- Counselors
- RTI team
- Extended Learning
- Office Hours

ASPIRE
PUBLIC SCHOOLS

FIGURE 13.3. An overview of SMART supports—what SMART supports look and feel like from a student perspective. RTI = Response to Intervention.

by overseeing the work of multiple teams, observing in classrooms, talking with parents and students, and planning professional development.

## Conclusion

We meet and talk a lot at CAL Prep, but we are always eager to move past discussion to action, ever mindful that any idea we incorporate needs to be tailored to our site and tended as it grows. At CAL Prep, we make interventions our own, ever mindful that our efforts need to be coordinated and complimentary. Tweaking our program makes us SMARTer (see Chapter 14), reflecting the name for our support framework. Language shapes experience, and we often get playful when it comes to thinking through how we introduce a new element to our staff and students. Our staff of 22 work hard, get their hands dirty, give and receive feedback, make changes, get back to work, become a little more resourceful as time goes on, and take on more challenge and complexity. Our experience underscores our site's need to grow, modify, and rethink roles and language from year to year. Each support in and of itself is not the critical element. Rather, it is the conceptual framework—that is, how we think about the support system—which fuels assessment, design, implementation, and revision of the supports needed by a diverse student body to reach their highest potential. Take it away and make it all yours.

# References

BUILD. (n.d.). Retrieved from http://www.build.org/

Conley, D. (2010). *College and career ready: helping all students succeed beyond high school*. San Francisco, CA: Jossey-Bass.

Cortez, M. (2011, March). *Growing smart supports: A week in the life of CAL Prep supports*. Presentation at the Woodrow Wilson National Fellowship Foundation, Princeton, NJ.

Mehan, H., Villanueva, I., Hubbard, L., & Lintz, A. (1996). *Constructing school success: The consequences of untracking low-achieving students*. New York, NY: Cambridge University Press.

Pianta, R. C., & Hamre, B. K. (2009). Conceptualization, measurement, and improvement of classroom processes: Standardized observation can leverage capacity. *Educational Researcher, 38*, 109–119. doi:10.3102/0013189X09332374

Reed, M. (2009, September). *On supports*. Presentation at a symposium on "Engaged scholarship at CAL Prep," Tang Education Center, University of California, Berkeley.

Reed, M. (2010, March). *State of supportive teaching at CAL Prep*. Presentation at the Woodrow Wilson National Fellowship Foundation, Princeton, NJ.

Reed, M. (2011, April). State of supportive teaching at CAL Prep. In L. Jaeger (Chair), *Thinking outside the box: Which student supports are necessary in high expectation secondary schools*? Symposium presented at the annual meeting of the American Educational Research Association, New Orleans, LA.

Responsive Classroom. (n.d.). Retrieved from https://www.responsiveclassroom.org/

RTI Action Network. (n.d.). Retrieved from http://www.rtinetwork.org/

Weinstein, R. S. (2011, February). *Toward a comprehensive support structure for early college students*. Final report to the Woodrow Wilson National Fellowship Foundation, Princeton, NJ.

# IV|Lessons Learned

# 14 | A Model for Interweaving Rigor and Support

## RHONA S. WEINSTEIN AND LIONEL H. BIALIS-WHITE

*"The teachers expect more, and the more they expect, the more they were there to help."* (Maria Torres, senior at California College Preparatory Academy, in Ness, 2011)

C RITICAL TO THE SUCCESS OF nontracked secondary schools where all students participate in a college-preparatory curriculum is the provision of support that enables a diversity of students to achieve academic proficiency and college readiness. Research on expectancy effects underscores that it is not only beliefs that are pivotal, in this case about college-going capacity, but also the mediating practices that develop student potential and confirm such expectations in reality (Weinstein, 2002b). With high academic expectations and access to a rigorous education as givens, reform must push further to ensure successful mastery to and through college by addressing obstacles along the way. Many of these obstacles are found in the design of schools, the quality of instruction, or school culture. Successfully overcoming these barriers requires systemic change and capacity-building as well as differentiated supports delivered without stigma and the sacrifice of academic challenge. Indeed, the deep resistance to detracking secondary schools rests in part upon this seemingly insurmountable hurdle—how to interweave rigor and support while teaching a heterogeneous population of students with varied needs.

The nature of student supports was frequently debated in our partnership meetings and was the first topic the University of California (UC) Berkeley and Aspire brought for discussion to the twice-yearly national

facilitated by the Woodrow Wilson National Fellowship
dation (WWNFF) for Early College Secondary Schools. As a result of
ese discussions, engaging all students in such a support system became
the fourth of five core principles of the Early College Initiative. But what
was meant by a "*comprehensive support system* that develops academic
and social skills as well as the behaviors and conditions necessary for college completion," and how was it best implemented (Early College High
School Initiative Core Principles, 2008, p. 2)?

The work reported in this chapter was funded by a grant from WWNFF
to the first author. Among the interrelated projects we pursued were two
independent literature reviews on student support, as applied to schools in
general (Grubb & Anyon, 2010) and to academically accelerated schools
such as early college high schools (Weinstein, 2011). We also worked with
the principal and teachers around the development of the support system
at California College Preparatory Academy (CAL Prep), and we collaborated in a survey study of student supports, completed by principals in 26
early college school sites across the country (Jaeger & Venezia, 2010).

Historically, student support services have been provided by multiple
specialties, such as school psychology and special education, guidance and
counseling, health, mental health, and social work as well as the domain
of extracurricular, after-school, and summer programs. Supports are also
embedded within numerous school reform models as well as provided by
community-based settings that link with schools to expand offerings to
students (Moore, 2014). The provision of support for learning, however,
has had uneven, sometimes pernicious, and marginalized history in the
schools (Sedlak, 1997; Tyack, 1992). Among many critiques are the fragmentation of efforts, segregation of students, and difficulties in integrating
supports with the school mission. As we press ahead with a *college-for-all
agenda*—in the face of enormous disparities in children's opportunities to
learn—it is crucial to interweave our more challenging expectations with
timely and effective student support. Moreover, with rising inequality and
an increasingly underfunded societal safety net, the availability of supports inside schools becomes ever more urgent (Aber & Chaudry, 2010).
Adelman and Taylor (2010) chide federal efforts for continuing to ignore
the enabling function of schools in its reform initiatives.

Whereas Chapter 13 provides an on-the-ground perspective of principal
and supports coordinator in growing and implementing what we call a
*supportive college-preparatory culture* at CAL Prep, this chapter presents
a research- and practice-driven conceptual framework for such a student
support system. To better meet the needs of underprepared students in

high-expectation secondary schools, this is a support system that is comprehensive, instructionally aligned, sensitive to developmental and cultural needs, coordinated, and integrative. Although we specifically address high-expectation secondary school settings for underserved students, the national goal of college for all students suggests that such supports are essential for all schools.

In this chapter, we briefly visit the history of school-based support services. We highlight early developments, with its unintended consequences, and describe promising advances, which in practice still fall short of full integration with instruction. Drawing on this work, we encourage prioritizing school redesign and nurturing a fuller, more challenging, and more coherent student development—importantly spearheaded by principals and teachers. Focused on building more rigorous and supportive schools, as well as more responsive teaching, our conceptualization of SMART supports includes five principles that progressively guide and integrate tiered supports across six domains of youth development, preparing students to be to be ready for college and be successful there. We give examples of such integration and discuss implications for research, practice, and policy.

## Student Supports in Historical Context

### Early Roots and Unintended Consequences

Services for children, as distinct from adults, were largely developed between the 1890s and World War I in the early 20th century, with the Visiting Teacher and Dewey-inspired Gary schools as examples (Levine & Levine, 1970). The goal was to strengthen institutional settings to better serve children rather than to change perceived deficiencies within the child—a systemic and preventive conceptualization that did not prevail. In the early 20th century, immigration and compulsory secondary education brought a greater diversity of students into classrooms, highlighting individual differences in school readiness. With this influx came the call for support services and a broadened purpose for schools as community hubs, where the needs of students and families could be better met (Sedlak, 1997). Social and educational services did not have secure financial footing in schools until the 1960s, when federal and state government mandates played an increasing role in addressing the unmet needs of children. Early examples include the Elementary and Secondary Education

Act of 1965 for disadvantaged students and Public Law 94-142 (1975) for children with special needs (Thomas & Brady, 2005).

Although legislation increased professional resources in schools, it failed to prepare teachers to more effectively reach a diverse population of students in the classroom. Teachers typically "referred out" those children deemed unable to learn. As helping services became increasingly professionalized, many fields aligned with the medical model, adopting an individual- and deficit-oriented approach, rather than the earlier educational and preventive perspective. Students were sorted into parallel systems of supports that became reified through laws, categorical funding streams, and turf-protective experts (Weinstein, 1996, 2002a).

In broad strokes, these parallel systems fragmented service delivery, undercut prevention, slowed the helping process, stigmatized groups of students, and limited opportunity to learn—especially for access to a college-preparatory curriculum. For example, remedial classes kept many students from a challenging curriculum, with poor and minority youth overrepresented in special education classes and underrepresented in higher academic tracks (Oakes, 1985). Suspensions for behavioral infractions and zero-tolerance policies drove students of color away from school rather than reintegrating them back into classrooms (Carter, Skiba, Arrendondo, & Pollock, 2014; Gregory, Skiba, & Noguera, 2010). Differential college advising discouraged too many minority students from applying to higher education, especially to selective 4-year colleges where attendance has been documented to increase minorities' chances of successfully graduating (Bowen, Chingos, & McPherson, 2009).

Not only did support practices inadvertently contribute to differential pathways but the availability of supports proved starkly uneven among schools, disadvantaging low-income and minority students who attended schools with fewer resources. For example, extracurricular activities have been found to "provide a protective context in terms of involvement in risky behaviors and a promotive context in terms of academic performance" (Eccles, Barber, Stone, & Hunt, 2003, p. 872). But differential access to these enriched experiences creates an opportunity divide that limits the development of low-income youth (Oakes & Saunders, 2008). Furthermore, opportunities to prepare for college are not fairly distributed through schools, resulting in what Oakes and colleagues (2006) have called a counseling roadblock to college. Enrichment in after-school and summer programs as well as intensive college preparation too often prove hit-and-miss and when purchased from an outside market as add-ons, they increase fragmentation.

## Push for Change

Given this history of uneven, unequal, and fragmented support services, many have called for a paradigm shift in how student supports are conceptualized and implemented, including a press for school-integrated services (Adelman & Taylor, 2010, 2015) and for the new practice field of integrated student supports (Moore, 2014). As federal laws for services to disadvantaged and special needs children have been reauthorized, these laws have pushed for inclusion (mainstreaming children in regular classrooms, higher standards for all), for a continuum of services to include prevention, and for greater accountability for equity of results in student achievement (Fuchs, Fuchs, & Stecker, 2010; Thomas & Brady, 2005). Promising developments include models that reflect (1) tiered interventions, (2) interwoven learning and healthy development goals, (3) a classroom- and school-level focus, and (4) comprehensive and integrative services.

**Tiered Interventions.** Response to Intervention (RTI) is an alternative to the ability–achievement discrepancy or the wait-to-fail model that was previously used to identify students for special education services, resulting in the overselection of ethnic minorities (e.g., Fletcher & Vaughn, 2009). Integrated into federal policy, RTI adopts a tiered approach to distinguish between failures in instruction (requiring revisions in teaching) and skill deficits in students (requiring individualized approaches). Drawing upon Caplan's (1964) classic public health distinctions among primary, secondary, and tertiary prevention, schoolwide primary prevention is prioritized *before* individualized and more intensive interventions. This pyramid model begins with the widest band of interventions directed universally toward all students and then targets smaller bands of students who receive early/secondary interventions and tertiary/intensive treatment. Critical ingredients include monitoring student performance on academic benchmarks, timely interventions, and changes in intervention level, based on student response.

**Interwoven Learning and Healthy Development Goals.** Given growing evidence that successful academic learning rests upon more than the development of cognitive capacities, there is increasing consensus that the divide between academic learning and healthy development must be bridged in schools (Caprara, Barbaranelli, Pastorelli, Bandura, & Zimbardo, 2000). Atkins and colleagues (2010) underscored that this integration will happen only when "the goal of mental health includes effective schooling and the goal of effective schools includes the healthy functioning of students"

(p. 40). As examples, a recent meta-analysis pointed to achievement gains as a result of school-based programs of social and emotional learning (Durlak, Weissberg, Dymnicki, Taylor, & Schellinger, 2011). In addition, a randomized trial demonstrated the effectiveness of a combined social-emotional and literacy program (4 Rs: Reading, Writing, Respect, and Resolution) on achievement and other competencies in elementary school (Brown, Jones, LaRusso, & Aber, 2010). Responding to such evidence, Galassi and Akos (2004) call for the school counselor of the 21st century to become a developmental advocate for students.

**School and Classroom Focus.** Moving away from narrowly targeted remedial, intensive, and pull-out approaches so detrimental for children of poverty, Cappella and colleagues (2008) described an ecological and school-based mental health model that redirects attention to the core mission of schools to promote learning and support classroom teaching. The model emphasizes mobilizing resources, universal programs, and maintaining children in their primary learning environments. In such models, mental health workers serve as educational enhancers and adapt efforts to meet the needs of each school (Atkins et al., 2010).

**Comprehensive and Integrative Services.** Among many visions are *school-based* health and mental health clinics, seen as vital, given the inequity in children's access to healthcare (Dryfoos, Quinn, & Barkin, 2005). The Harlem Children's Zone, a model supported by recent federal initiatives, combines layers of supports (health clinics, social services, after-school programs, and community-building) that wraparound families from birth to college graduation, along with enrollment in "no excuses" charter schools (Dobbie & Fryer, 2010). Full-service community schools incorporate an array of supports provided by local agencies and universities to extend the reach of underresourced schools and include reform models such as the Comer School Development Program and School of the 21st Century (Harkavy, Hartley, Axelroth Hodges, & Weeks, 2013; Moore, 2014).

In their comprehensive mental health model, Adelman and Taylor (2010, 2015) argued for a *school-integrated* thrust—not just school-linked or school-based efforts—where the supports that target learning barriers intersect coequally with instruction and management. Their three-component model enables a coordinated and tiered continuum of interconnected systems of interventions, from prevention to treatment, with the six domains for support defined by the activities of mental health providers. These include classroom-based consultation, crisis intervention, transition support, student and family assistance, community outreach, and home involvement in schools. Grubb and Anyon (2010) similarly proposed a tripartite and integrative solution, but one that first targets school reform but then includes the addition of school-based health/mental health clinics and after-school programs, with examples of joint planning that coordinates with instruction.

## Gaps in Conceptualization

Although these contemporary approaches reflect clear advances, in practice they still fall short of integrative instruction and support. First, despite the press for integrative schoolwide supports, in reality, support providers rarely have a regular seat at the table, inherently limiting their contributions to preventive schoolwide planning. Second, the involvement of many support providers typically begins *after* trouble appears or with the needs of individual children. This late entry, deficit approach, and individual lens serve to prioritize treatment over preventive schoolwide approaches, risking marginalized and fragmented services (Elias, 2011). Third, coming from single disciplines, silos within schools and districts, or outside agencies, providers cannot integrate *all* programming within a *single* model, omitting critical domains of growth (such as college and extracurricular preparation) as well as joint accountability for the longer-term attainment goals. Finally, single discipline approaches do not systematically address the core features of schooling or universal barriers that limit the achievement trajectories of low-income and underrepresented minority youth.

Although there is a growing evidence base about specific reform models or about distinct supports such as effective tutoring and after-school programs, there is little research yet to guide the field toward the supports that are critical for whom, for what outcomes, and when (Moore, 2014). An interesting study by Dobbie and Fryer (2011) on the Harlem Children's Zone project suggests that it is the opportunity for *high-quality schools*, not the support programs, that increases the achievement of low-income students. This finding raises the empirical question about wherein lies the most powerful intervention. In their work with low-income populations, Aber and colleagues (2006) also underscored an approach focused on building the best model of curriculum and instruction that can be combined with synergistic, not merely additive, non-instructional intervention (e.g., social-emotional learning). It is this gap between the development of high-quality schools and *synergistic* student supports—importantly targeting specific attainment goals—that must be bridged. Although we draw from these advances, we suggest a critical reframing that enables a greater integration of instruction and support.

## Toward SMART Supports

More than 30 years ago, in a review of disparities in children's mental health services, we urged that children's services should "ultimately strengthen the capacity of schools to guide children's development" (Namir & Weinstein, 1982, p. 66). Such disparities in access to health and mental health services have only increased, and ironically, recent recommendations call for greater investment in protective factors, such as the construction of positive school environments that engage minority youth (Alegria, Green, McLaughlin, & Loder, 2015). The deficiency view (e.g., removing barriers to learning) of past support services worked to separate providers and teachers as well as to remove services away from the core responsibilities of schools (Grubb & Anyon, 2010). This divide has increased fragmentation as well as the expenditure of resources on what Grubb (2008) labeled "second-chance programs . . . rather than applying them to the improvement of first-chance institutions like high schools" (p. 43).

Thus, we began with a focus on improving the qualities of first-chance institutions—the school. The paradigm shift lies in *reframed* schools, which support a fuller, more rigorous, and more coherent student development for *all* students. The reframing requires a shift from an at-risk student to an at-risk setting perspective, where school features, those that create discontinuities, awkward transitions, and unmet needs, are modified to better serve students. This framework directs supports toward specific learning and development goals, but importantly it is neither defined nor limited by the activities of support disciplines or the attributes of supports (e.g., Savitz-Romer, Jager-Hyman, & Coles, 2009). It calls for a *multidisciplinary* perspective, the incorporated expertise of *all* support disciplines, and an integrative commitment to *all* aspects of youth development. Adapting Adelman and Taylor's (2010) definition, we define supports for both learning and positive development as those policies, resources, programs, and practices that, in a coordinated and integrative way, address the intellectual, physical, psychological, and social needs of children and youth so that all students can successfully complete a challenging educational curriculum, including a 2- to 4-year postsecondary program, preparing them for productive lives.

Such capacity-building around student supports requires school-driven leadership by principals and teachers, much like Bryk and colleagues (2010) have underscored in organizing schools for improvement. Educators are as much enablers as are support professionals and they have the most concentrated contact with students. With training, they are in the best position to consider alignment and progression in programming as well as to identify learning, health, and mental health concerns. Spearheaded and monitored by principals and teachers, parallel systems can be integrated into one coherent whole, with support for students at its very heart. Just how many students can be effectively reached by such reframed schools—before more intensive individualized approaches are needed—remains an important question for future research (see Fuchs et al., 2010).

## SMART Support Principles

We identify five underlying principles foundational to the design of a student support system that is comprehensive, instructionally aligned, developmental in nature, culturally sensitive, coordinated and integrative. These principles are described as SMART Supports (see Figure 14.1).

**S: Schoolwide, Strengths-Focused, Stigma-Free, with Second-Chances.** Support is delivered primarily schoolwide and is built into school design, culture, curriculum, and instruction as a first-level intervention.

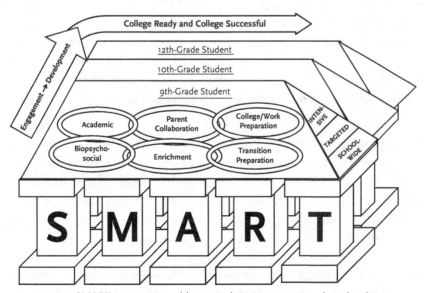

FIGURE 14.1. SMART supports to address six domains across student development.

Furthermore, the schoolwide approach is strengths-based, building a positive climate that focuses on leveraging strengths at all levels to nurture the potential of all students. As support is utilized by all students and teachers alike, it is normative and stigma-free, with second chances made available in programming.

**M: Multidomain and Multicultural Youth Development.** Supports are provided to enable students to engage deeply in an intellectually challenging and relevant college-preparatory academic program. Beyond academics, prioritizing a fuller development means the promotion of the biological, psychological, and social development of students (e.g., Greenberg et al., 2003). Thus, school design must better meet adolescent needs for forging competence, identity, relatedness, autonomy, and self-regulation (Roth & Brooks-Gunn, 2000). Sensitive to culture, school design must also meet the needs of minority students for belonging as well as for the development of an integrated academic and ethnic identity (APA Task Force, 2008; McKown & Strambler, 2008; Nasir, 2012) through the use of practices such as culturally relevant pedagogy (Ladson-Billings, 1995).

Other crucial domains for development include opportunities for extracurricular enrichment, creating a life narrative and preparing for college and/or work, and learning coping skills that strengthen adjustment during transitions. Finally, maintaining connection, brokering separation, as well as aligning home and school priorities are also among the tasks of adolescence. School programs need to support a student–family collaborative partnership around academic socialization (expectations, learning strategies, preparing for the future), which in a meta-analysis of 50 studies of parent involvement in middle and high school proved the strongest predictive factor of student achievement (Hill & Tyson, 2009). Preparing for a college path requires an enormous and consistent effort that strains all families, an effect that is compounded for first-generation college families.

**A: Alignment and Adaptability.** By alignment, supports can be seen in targeted efforts to repair many discontinuities or mismatches present between levels of schooling and domains of development, as well as among disciplines, programs, and grade levels within schools. Course requirements, curriculum, and instruction also need to be aligned with college eligibility and college readiness. Teaching cognitive strategies (such as problem formulation, research, interpretation, communication, and precision) and scaffolding student-led rather than teacher-directed learning eases the transition between high school and college (Conley, 2010). The capacity to reason, consider alternatives, examine evidence, and problem solve—habits of mind needed in college level work—are skills that are also critical to social-emotional development. These intellectual skills protect students from risky behaviors and help them adapt to new environments across the life span. In embracing alignment, supports in one domain enhance rather than contradict efforts in other domains and promote student adjustment across transitions.

The "A" also refers to support for the development of adaptability, a key feature of resilience. Adaptability here refers to the capacity for both student and school to change in the face of new circumstances by adopting a growth mindset, using data and resources, and making midcourse corrections (Dweck, 2006; Masten & Coatsworth, 1998). For students, the flux might include learning challenges, developmental changes, and environmental transitions as well as non-normative transitions such as illness and bereavement. For schools, a shifting student population, new staff, and changing societal and fiscal tides require readjustment as well.

**R: Relationships, Responsive, and Research-informed.** Learning is socially mediated and guided through the development of strong relationships among teachers, peers, and parents (Smetana, Campione-Barr, & Metzger, 2006). Study of the transition to CAL Prep (Chapter 6) highlighted the importance of *supportive* teachers as a contributing factor to students' sense of belonging in the school, especially for those students whose needs were not met at home. Pianta and colleagues (e.g., Allen, Pianta, Gregory, Mikami, & Lin, 2011) have shown how teaching can be supportive in its sensitivity to student developmental and ethnic-cultural needs (regard for student perspectives), as well as rigorous in its conceptual reach (concept development) and facilitative in its engagement of students (productivity). These responsive teaching practices are measurable, amenable to improvement through coaching, and promote student achievement at both elementary and secondary levels. Responsiveness to changing developmental needs also requires progression of challenge, with diminished scaffolding and more independence of action—for example, in choice, self-monitoring, and self-correction. Finally, support practices are research-driven, drawing on evidence-based strategies, using school data to assess student benchmarks and progress, and evaluating the effectiveness of programs and practices (Forman, Olin, Hoagwood, Crowe, & Saka, 2009).

**T: Time and Tiered Intervention.** The "T" refers to time, which is increased as well as harnessed, and to three tiers of intervention (Fletcher & Vaughn, 2009). Time is extended to include a longer school day, longer school year, and double periods in order to address the underpreparedness of the students, provide an accelerated academic program, and bridge the divide in after-school and summer programs that disadvantages students with lesser economic means. Support is timed early to promote positive development and prevent maladaptive functioning—beginning with universal approaches and moving toward fluid use of targeted and intensive interventions for subsets of students (i.e., use of the second and third tier of intervention). Support is also timely (i.e., offered when needed), timed with school milestones such as quarters (through the regular appraisal of student functioning in order to inform next-stage supportive interventions), and time-effective.

Figure 14.1 also highlights the interlocking and aligned domains in which supports are provided, the three tiers of intervention (schoolwide, targeted, and intensive), and the progressive development of supports across grade levels. As described above, we suggest six *interactive* domains of student development that supportive programming must address. These include (1) academic development; (2) biological, psychological, and social development; (3) extracurricular enrichment; (4) life journey planning and preparation for college and/or work; (5) coping skills for transitions; and (6) parental collaboration and partnership.

## A Delivery System for Student Supports

Planning for student supports is guided by the SMART principles and systematically addresses the six domains of student development. It begins schoolwide with a comprehensive, coherent, and coordinated effort to build in school features and teaching capacity that promote student development across all the domains. In addition to academic goals (including catch-up and remediation), supports include programming for social-emotional development, health, mental health and enrichment (clubs, after-school and summer activities), college preparation (guidance), and parent–youth collaboration. Furthermore, efforts are make to align the efforts across domains and progression across school years in growing challenge and autonomy for students. Thus, the best practices of *all support fields* are integrated into instructional planning for all students. Finally, using the framework of RTI, there are tiered levels of intervention, with opportunities to progress to more targeted and intensive interventions for groups and individuals as needed.

Six features of school organization appear especially critical in developing an instructionally aligned student support system. These include (1) a shared mission and accompanying framework that guides the development of a rigorous and supportive school for students and teachers alike; (2) a support coordinator present at the school leadership table, with access to support resources; (3) the regular monitoring of data (school, classroom, group, individual) and use of empirically validated interventions to inform programs and practice; (4) a collaborative team approach, led by principals and teachers, that translates analysis into intervention and evaluation into revision; (5) professional development and coaching for principals, teachers, and support staff, that builds capacity around rigor and responsive practice; and (6) a collaboration with a district (or district and university) that encourages innovation (in structures, resources, and scheduling) to better serve students. Thus, what we are describing is a learning community, engaged in a multilevel cycle of inquiry and action, targeting continuous improvement of programs and practices (McLaughlin & Talbert, 2006). It is a community learning by design, as we had originally envisioned for CAL Prep.

## Examples of Integrative Student Supports in Action

Moving beyond a laundry list of distinct student supports, we provide three examples of the integration we achieved in practice. Our theory of action is evident in Figure 14.1. The conceptual framework (SMART Supports principles) serves as the pillars that guide the building of rigorous and supportive learning opportunities, both schoolwide and targeted, across six domains of student development and across school years. It is engagement in these progressive learning opportunities that prepares students to become ready for college and successful there, indicated by having met required subject-matter proficiencies and developed curiosity, habits of mind and character, and an academic identity and sense of belonging to a community of scholars. This method of interweaving rigor and support makes possible an educational journey where school culture, curriculum, and progressive challenge are aligned to meet a common goal.

### A College-Going and College-Successful Culture

Beyond the display of college banners, the supportive college preparatory culture we have created at CAL Prep is explicit, strengths-based, responsive, and inclusive. CAL Prep students are immersed in a culture with clear mission and "can do" expectations that convey "College for Certain" and "Graduate from College, Yes We Can!" Importantly, we specified the habits of mind *and* character to be developed that would carry students to and through college, as well as through life. The attributes of the CARRIES framework described in Chapter 13, speak to the kind of intellectual inquiry (inquisitive scholar, rigorous problem solvers), personal and community relationships (responsible role model, empathic contributor, cooperative citizen), and coping skills (assertive activist, self-controlled success) that we expect of students at CAL Prep. These skills are strengths-focused and underscore that both intellectual and social-emotional development are school priorities. Also, self-monitoring (self-controlled success) is prioritized; this is deemed critical to student ownership of their learning, recovery from failure, and improvement, as well as adaptability to transition challenges. These attributes reflect a shared vision for student goals, set behavioral norms, and instill a common language that unites teachers and students. They are developed in classes, advisories, exhibitions, and disciplinary interactions, providing a tangible model for students to adopt.

Many school features create a positive, responsive, and can-do culture. These include continuity of advisor and advisory group across 4 years, a dean of students focused on positive disciplinary interventions (positive referrals, awards for excellence and improvement), and teacher involvement across domains of student development (such as in planning for tutors, leading field trips, and creating school rituals). These features deepen teacher–student and peer relationships, allow students to become known, and enable their needs to be addressed. As the opening quotation for this chapter attests, although more was expected of students, the teachers were there to help. In responding to the yearning of students of color (e.g., "to learn about my history"; "to gain a better understanding of the reality of the world I live in"; and "what makes a Chicano, Chicano?"), we also worked hard to reflect ethnic and cultural diversity in what and how we taught (see Chapter 13). To herald the clear message that students of color belong on college campuses, we added school-based mini-seminars in African American and Chicano literature led by UC Berkeley faculty or graduate students; the university summer programs in Alvin Ailey (dance) and diversity in staffing at the school and from the university served as other examples. Our culture was adult-rich and peer-rich, increasing the opportunities to reach a diversity of students and create an inclusive family around shared goals.

Rather than set a ceiling on the level of challenge, such as in tracking, we immersed all students in challenging curricula and made available opportunities for catch-up and remediation. Our school culture also conveyed every day what Carol Dweck (2006) has described as a *growth mindset*. This is a belief that intelligence can be developed and failure can be overcome—with instruction, effort, and strategy choice. As one student put it so artfully, aware of the needed steps and hopeful, "If you are going to go to college, you need to understand what you're good at and what you need to work on, because you probably just have to learn some *new ways* to get the things that you are not good at *yet*."

## A Package-Deal and *Balanced* Curriculum

In their review of the special features of early college high schools, Rosenbaum and Becker (2011, p. 15) described what they observed as a method of "preparation through acceleration," which was used to ease the transition to college for disadvantaged and first-generation college youth. Instead of relying on student initiative, these schools provide a package-deal curriculum that includes college-readiness skills, keeps students on track with regular and mandatory guidance, and manages the college application process. This approach is similar in part to what Dupey and colleagues (2006) have called *intrusive advising*—a likely advance given evidence that students without sufficient college knowledge may not seek help.

Our package-deal curriculum reflected rigorous and aligned preparation, but importantly extended across the six domains of student development, resulting in an opportunity-rich education. This packaging of critical features—infused with multifaceted support—enabled more effective use of time and mandated rather than invited engagement (Edmunds, Willse, Arshavsky, & Dallas, 2013). Working to avoid the curricular, developmental, and cultural mismatches in school design that challenge student adjustment as they transition between educational levels, we created one clear pathway to college preparedness, importantly one with teeth. Accountability, however, was positive and mutual. Students were required to successfully complete this program and reach multiple milestones, among them one acceptance at a 4-year college, in order to graduate from high school. We held ourselves accountable for providing varied and sufficient support, with opportunities for second chances.

All our students were engaged in a standards-based and nontracked college-preparatory program, which included the successful completion (with a grade of C or higher) of the A–G course sequence required for 4-year college eligibility in California, layered with the yearly requirement of student exhibitions or capstone projects. These reflected an authentic and integrative assessment of problem-based learning, spanning topics such as media literacy, college and career planning, a science inquiry, and a senior portfolio. Also, as an early college secondary school, our accelerated curriculum included the successful completion of five community college classes, bridging the divide between high school and college. Equally critical, ample opportunities for catch-up, remediation, and second chances were made available through program features such as extended time (day, year, and double periods), niches for differentiated supports (a daily support period for homework, tutoring, and small-group interventions, as well as a writing center and teacher office hours), and course credit recovery after failure. Special education personnel provided more intensive remedial work through Individualized Education Programs, with accompanying evidence-based interventions.

Applying a developmental lens, college preparation was also a multi-year journey. With the efforts of our college counselor, this preparation was programmed into classes, advisories, and Saturday School for all students (College Tools for Schools [n.d.], http://collegetools.berkeley.edu). Among the tasks were (1) identification of subject-matter and career interests; (2) knowledge about college preparation, selectivity, and selection; (3) meeting college eligibility requirements (required courses, college-readiness skills, and examinations such as the SAT and American College Test(ing) [ACT]); and (4) applications for college and financial aid (including essays, supporting letters, financial forms, and scholarships). Family–teacher conferences, Saturday Schools, and parent classes also created opportunities for parents and students to partner around the tasks of college preparation, as well as better align school and home efforts. More targeted interventions were offered, for example, for undocumented students regarding financial aid. Our package-deal curriculum also included opportunities for strengthening biopsychosocial development (such as in CARRIES skills or healthy lunches and nurturing a school garden), coping strategies to master transitions (such as self-regulation and persistence [Duckworth & Seligman, 2005] and quarterly *student-led* family–school conferences), and enrichment (in extracurricular activities as well as after-school and summer programs). In developing these aspects of our curriculum, we encouraged the same habits of mind across multiple facets of development.

The school infrastructure supported this program through its regularized examination of student data, which informed instructional and programmatic revision as well as more differentiated and *tiered* interventions.

Staff, representing special education, college preparation, mental health counseling, and after-school services, worked under the supervision of the supports coordinator, a teacher. They contributed first to strengthening schoolwide efforts (e.g., timeline and content for college preparation, advisory units on health/mental health and social-emotional skills, differentiated instruction, college application process for parents) and then to group and individual sessions with students and parents. Data-driven weekly team meetings (subject-matter, grade-level, and school leadership), coupled with aligned professional development and coaching, enabled timely responsiveness to student needs. As one example, CAL Prep adopted the teacher effectiveness rubric developed by the College Ready Promise (n.d.) to support growth in teaching quality. Its focus is on strengthening rigor in instruction and classroom discourse, use of data to inform lesson design, and the emotional safety of a learning culture. In these ways, the school aligned curricular objectives with intensive teacher preparation and support.

## Progressive Challenge, Autonomy, and Individuation

A final example concerns progressive programming across the 4 years of high school. Progressive challenge drives growth, meets adolescent developmental needs for increased autonomy and individuation, and reduces the adjustment difficulties inherent in transitions between educational levels. At CAL Prep, we provided students with progressive exposure to college experiences. We began with activities on the UC Berkeley campus (such as the ropes course for trust-building, as well as sports and arts events), inspirational visits with faculty (in laboratories and lunches), summer program classes, and mini-seminars at CAL Prep (led by faculty or graduate students). We then introduced college classes, taught on the school site or on college campuses, with the requirement of five credit-bearing community college courses for high school graduation, and students were also able to audit freshman seminars at UC Berkeley. Undergraduates tutored, served as classroom assistants, and mentored college preparation.

A culminating event in senior year was participation in College Week on the UC Berkeley campus. This introduced CAL Prep students to 5 days of seminars and laboratories (taught by faculty over one to three sessions) and to the residence halls, where lunches were taken. Among the mini-courses offered in 2012 were Library Skills, Crime Lab Chemistry, the Internal Structure of Engineering Materials, Archaeology Today, Identity and Achievement, and Growing up Chicano/Latino from a Literary Perspective. Students independently negotiated seminar attendance in different buildings as well as the completion of reading and writing assignments for multiple classes. Back at CAL Prep, students reflected on how well they had handled the varied challenges of college week, with an eye to the improvements needed in their full-time transition to college. Other examples of progression include the yearly public and peer-rated student exhibitions or capstone projects, with increasing intellectual challenge and greater student independence, and student-led family–school conferences that progressively strengthened student initiative, self-monitoring, and responsibility for their growth.

Especially for a school with a close-knit culture and a packaged curriculum, our enrichment program provided an important niche for progression in student choice, autonomy, and individuation—critical to identity development and eventual individuation from family and high school. Although we recognize different cultural views on identity (individual vs. interdependent) and on the degree of family separation that is judged normative, the very act of college-going requires individuation. At CAL Prep, students participated in art classes; student government; after-school sports and debate teams; field trips involving museums, sailing, and college tours; and in summer programs on the university campus. Investments such as these were crucial in fueling student aspirations for college, career, and life.

Through summer programs on the UC Berkeley campus, students embraced new subject matter (e.g., "I learned about [developing] HTML codes and websites"), developed in positive ways (e.g., "I used to be really quiet but I learned how to be more open and myself"), and realized their dreams ("It was the first place in my life [Alvin Ailey dance program] where I felt like I could just be myself"). These lessons generalized to the next school year, and parents were appreciative of the changes they saw in their children. One parent reported that her son "learned about the UC system and aspired to be a professional in the real world of science." Another parent shared that her daughter "had become a better student . . . having a male teacher of her own race was a very culturally valuable experience for her."

In field trips such as sailing on the San Francisco Bay, students acknowledged that these were new events for them ("It was a lot of fun for me because our family doesn't get to go places") and that they were challenged ("I've never done anything so daring in my life"). Importantly, these shared experiences strengthened their relationships with peers ("By being on the field trip, I changed because I trusted my friends as well as with teachers ("The best part was seeing everybody outside of school—the teachers even wore jeans"). And bottom students "got to enjoy the world instead of just school. We need . from all the hard work we have to do."

These activities enabled students to move from novice to expert, develop autonomy and close bonds with peers and mentors over shared interests, recover from defeats in rigorous academics, and gain new interests. Seeing oneself as successful in new and multiple contexts proved critical for envisioning college-going and adaptation. Furthermore, having a special talent, an indication of student motivation, is an important criterion in college admissions. Ultimately, with engagement in *all* these learning opportunities, students began to define their identities. Then 10th grader Alana Banks (2009), in her presentation to faculty at UC Berkeley, described her changed goals in these words: "Before I got to CAL Prep, I never thought about science. Now I think of myself as a scientist." This reported transformation, fueled in part by an inspirational talk from a university cancer researcher, reflects not only her appreciation of the subject matter but also her aspiration to become a scientist, her newly emerging academic identity. For vastly underprepared students, this awakening is an especially important step.

## Conclusion

Roderick and colleagues (2009) underscore the troubling *aspiration–attainment gap* created by the rise of college expectations of low-income and minority students who are without access to a college-preparatory education and supports for successful completion. Schools have found it challenging to provide high levels of intellectual rigor for *all* students—especially those underprepared by previous schooling and who face difficult life circumstances. Of similar challenge, integrating student supports into the core mission of schooling—now a *more inclusive mission* for a greater diversity of students—continues to be an intractable problem.

In short, we offer a model of the integration of rigor and support for all. That is, five (SMART) supports provide anchor points for how to structure and allocate resources to promote six domains of student development. Furthermore, we applied multidisciplinary knowledge to align school features, culture, curricular–instructional capacity, and strategic interventions to help a diversity of students develop the competencies that underlie college and life success. These included not only academic and social-emotional competencies but also the development of talents, identity, and autonomy, and a road map for as well as a partnership with parents for college-going. With a schoolwide focus, package-deal offerings, and the press for engagement, we were able to nurture, remediate, and accelerate, keeping students on the college track (Edmunds, Willse, Arshavksy, & Dallas, 2013; Rosenbaum & Becker, 2011). Edmunds and colleagues (2013) provided evidence for this engagement press. Early college students, as compared to control students, reported better relationship with teachers, more rigorous and relevant instruction, more academic and affective support, and higher expectations—all setting opportunities that, in their words, mandate student engagement.

What recommendations for practice, policy, and research follow from this conceptualization of student supports? First, this framework requires new roles for teachers, principals, and support providers, in a school culture organized around the improvement of practice and with partnerships between educational levels. Importantly, teachers serve as the primary enhancers of a fuller whole-student development. In our efforts to better meet student needs, teacher time in classroom instruction was blended with contributions as a supports coordinator, dean of students, or teaching coach, offering a teacher ladder for differentiated responsibilities. Furthermore, principals need be trained in schoolwide design, differentiation, data literacy, and evaluation of supports as well as capacity-building around integrated rigor and support. Gregory and colleagues (2007) have demonstrated how critical administrative leadership is for the usage and effectiveness of evidence-based programs in the classroom. Although student supports were found in some combination in the 26 college high schools surveyed by Jaeger and Venezia (2010), only 30% of principals could articulate a philosophy for student supports, which when described, was likely to be a medical model or a behavior modification approach. Finally, the work of the support professions must shift, in larger part, to programmatic contributions that strengthen school capacity to promote positive youth development—a role change with implications for training, professional development, and resource use by the district.

Second, with regard to policy, this framework broadens the range of support resources that must be adequately and securely funded in schools. Support resources include the extended school day for students, with after-school activities, field trips, and summer programs under the supervision of teachers and principal. They include access to health, mental health, special education, and college-preparation providers, whose contributions are built into schoolwide programs as well as into individual work with students and families. Also, support resources include new administrative roles for teachers; access to evidence-based practices and professional development; and regularized weekly teamwork that integrates data examination, program revision, and differentiation of interventions. Funding streams need to allow support resources to be used more flexibly by schools in line with their specific needs (Cappella et al., 2008).

Although we, at CAL Prep, aimed to provide all our programs with state-allotted funds, we averaged about $1,000 more per student for enrichment (after-school activities, field trips, and summer programs), which we raised through grants and philanthropy. Investment in stronger schools, which in their design and practice are both challenging and supportive to students, will likely prove cost effective in the long term. A study by Vargas (2013) highlights the economic payoff for states if schools could close the college-readiness and college-completion gaps that disadvantage low-income students. The growing literature on cost-benefit analyses of prevention programs and integrated student supports have demonstrated promising returns on investments (Kuklinski, Briney, Hawkins, & Catalano, 2011; Moore, 2014).

Third, research is a critical partner in the improvement of student supports. Research has delineated the features of positive settings for youth development (Seidman, 2011), rigorous and supportive classroom practices (Pianta & Hamre, 2009), critical thinking and its assessment (Conley, 2010), and effective social-emotional learning interventions (Durlak et al., 2011). These empirically validated programs and practices are ripe for adoption by schools, but careful choices need to be made in order to align programs toward a unified school mission. Tensions between program fidelity and schools' need for adaptation persist. With a commitment to broadened schooling outcomes, future research must also identify critical skills within each domain and develop brief assessment tools, grade-level standards, and curricula that would promote a fuller student development. Future research must also test which models are most effective in helping underprepared students, especially low-income and underrepresented ethnic minority ones, become ready for college—and successful there.

Finally, a glaring gap in the work on supports is attention to coherent alignment of strategies across youth development domains and a progressive or developmental approach across school years. What can be said about optimal versus sufficient or too much support? How might supports developmentally unfold across grade levels to promote increasing student autonomy? Could such systematic supports create an environment that is too sheltering, making it difficult for students to make successful transitions? This work is still in its infancy. As Berger and colleagues (2010) underscored,

> The ECSs [early college schools] are also aware that although the supports they provide are critical in the short term, the larger goal is to help students to be independent self-advocates who recognize when they need assistance and who know where to turn to find the kind of support they need. (p. 342)

To date, there is surprisingly little evidence of developmental progression in support programs or practices across the six domains of youth development. At the elementary level, Butterworth and Weinstein (1996) described five schoolwide programs (jobs, businesses, government, ecological trips, and graduation milestone events), where by design, each grade level plays increasingly demanding roles, mentored by older students. The LifeMap counseling program (Shugart & Romano, 2006) offers a scope and sequence for students adjusting to community college and beyond. Conley (2010) underscored the use, each successive year of high school, of assignments and grading schemes that more closely approximate college expectations. Students need to stretch their capacities, feel the disequilibrium that comes with higher-level demands, adapt and/or fail, and recover. This issue merits further research.

To conclude, we highlighted a conceptual framework (with principles, domains, tiers of intervention, and a delivery system) and a process of intensive staff work rather than providing a prescription for specific supports (e.g., tutoring), directed toward actualizing high and accelerated expectations for all youth. As a principle-based approach, the framework can be adapted to other secondary schools (large and small) in ways that are sensitive to the ecology of specific sites and different populations. It can also be used at the elementary level where life goals and college aspirations begin to be shaped and where program coherence needs to be addressed (Newman, Smith, Allensworth, & Bryk, 2001). Teachers and support professionals work together, with data about program outcomes and the progress of students, to strengthen the capacity of schools to enhance the positive development of a diversity of students. This is what Seymour Sarason (2004) has called a context for productive learning—an engaging, challenging, and supportive school for students and educators alike.

# References

Aber, L., Burnley, K., Cohen, D. K., Featherman, D. L., Phillips, D., Raudenbush, S., & Rowan, B. (2006). *Beyond school reform: Improving the educational outcomes of low-income children.* Report to the Spencer Foundation, Center for Advancing Research and Solutions for Society (CARSS), University of Michigan. Retrieved from http://carss.umich.edu/content/2010/11/SpencerReport081506.pdf

Aber, L., & Chaudry, A. (2010). *Low-income children, their families and the Great Recession: What's next in policy?* Washington, DC: The Urban Institute. Retrieved from http://www.urban.org/url.cfm?ID=412069

Adelman, H. S., & Taylor, L. (2010). *Mental health in schools: Engaging learners, preventing problems, and improving schools.* Thousand Oaks, CA: Corwin.

Adelman, H. S., & Taylor, L. (2015, January). Developing a unified, comprehensive, and equitable system. Retrieved from http://smhp.psych.ucla.edu/

Alegria, M., Green, J. G., McLaughlin, K. A., & Loder, S. (2015, March). *Disparities in child and adolescent mental health services in the U.S.* A William T. Grant Foundation Inequality Paper. Retrieved from http://blog.wtgrantfoundation.org/post/114541733572/new-report-disparities-in-child-and-adolescent

Allen, J. P., Pianta, R. C., Gregory, A., Mikami, A. Y., & Lin, J. (2011). An interaction-based approach to enhancing secondary school instruction and achievement. *Science, 333,* 1034–1037. doi:10.1126/science.1207998

American Psychological Association [APA] Task Force. (2008). *Resiliency and strength in black children and adolescents.* Washington, DC: American Psychological Association. Retrieved from http://www.apa.org/pi/cyf/resilience.html

Atkins, M. S., Hoagwood, K. E., Kutash, K. K., & Seidman, E. (2010). Toward the integration of educational and mental health in schools. *Administration and Policy in Mental Health and Mental Health Services Research, 37,* 40–47. doi:10.1007/s10488-010-0299-7

Banks, A. (2009, September 14). How CAL Prep changed me. Presented at a symposium on *Engaged scholarship at CAL Prep,* Tang Education Center, University of California, Berkeley, CA.

Berger, A., Adelman, N., & Cole, S. (2010). The early college high school initiative: An overview of five evaluation years. *Peabody Journal of Education, 85,* 333–347. doi:10.1080/0161956X.2010.491697

Bowen, W. G., Chingos, M. M., & McPherson, M. S. (2009). *Crossing the finish line: Completing college at America's public universities.* Princeton, NJ: Princeton University Press.

Brown, J. L., Jones, S. M., LaRusso, M. D., & Aber, J. L. (2010). Improving classroom quality: Teacher influences and experimental impacts of the 4Rs Program. *Journal of Educational Psychology, 102,* 153–167. doi:10.1037/a0018160

Bryk, A. S., Bender Sebring, P., Allensworth, E., Luppescu, S., & Easton, J. Q. (2010). *Organizing schools for improvement: Lessons from Chicago.* Chicago, IL: The University of Chicago Press.

Butterworth, B., & Weinstein, R. S. (1996). Enhancing motivational opportunity in elementary school. *Elementary School Journal, 97,* 57–80. doi:10.1086/461849

Caplan, G. (1964). *Principles of preventive psychiatry.* New York, NY: Basic Books.

Cappella. E., Frazier, S. L., Atkins, M. S., Schoenwald, S. K., & Glisson, C. (2008). Enhancing schools' capacity to support children in poverty: An ecological model of school-based mental health services. *Administration and Policy in Mental Health and Mental Health Services Research, 35*, 395–409. doi:1007/s10488-088-0182-y

Caprara, G. V., Barbaranelli, C., Pastorelli, C., Bandura, A., & Zimbardo, P. G. (2000). Prosocial foundations of children's academic achievement. *Psychological Science, 11*, 302–306. doi:10.1111/1467-9280.00260

Carter, P., Skiba, R., Arrendondo, M., & Pollock, M. (2014, December). *You can't fix what you don't look at: Acknowledging race in addressing racial discipline disparities.* Retrieved from http://www.indiana.edu/~atlantic/wp-content/uploads/2014/12/Acknowledging-Race_121514.pdf

College Ready Promise. (n.d.). Retrieved from http://thecollegereadypromise.org/

College Tools for Schools. (n.d.). *A toolkit for California high schools.* Retrieved from http://collegetools.berkeley.edu

Conley, D. T. (2010). *College and career ready: Helping all students succeed beyond high school.* San Francisco, CA: Jossey-Bass.

Dobbie, W., & Fryer, R. G., Jr. (2011). Are high-quality schools enough to increase achievement among the poor? Evidence from the Harlem's Children's Zone. *American Economic Journal: Applied Economics, 3*, 158–187. doi:10.1257/app.3.3.158

Dryfoos, J. G., Quinn, J., & Barkin, C. (Eds.). (2005). *Community schools in action: Lessons from a decade of practice.* Oxford, UK: Oxford University Press.

Duckworth, A. S., & Seligman, M. E. P. (2005). Self-discipline outdoes IQ in predicting academic performance of adolescents. *Psychological Science, 16*, 939–944. doi:10.1111/j.1467-9280.2005.01641.x

Dupey, P., Maples, M. F., & Oaks, K. (2006). Multiple pathways to enhancing retention and success of students of color. In G. R. Walz, J. C. Bleuer & R. K. Yep (Eds.), *2006 ACA annual convention, 2006, US* (pp. 89–93). Alexandria, VA: American Counseling Association.

Durlak, J. A., Weissberg, R. P., Dymnicki, A. B., Taylor, R. D., & Schellinger, K. B. (2011). The impact of enhancing students' social and emotional learning: A meta-analysis of school-based universal interventions. *Child Development, 82*, 405–432. doi:10.1111/j.1467-8624.2010.01564.x

Dweck, C. S. (2006). *Mindset: The psychology of success.* New York, NY: Random House.

Early College High School Initiative Core Principles. (2008, October 28). Retrieved from http://www.txechs.com/downloads/48_echsi_core_principles.pdf

Eccles, J. S., Barber, B. L., Stone, M., & Hunt, J. (2003). Extracurricular activities and adolescent development. *Journal of Social Issues, 59*, 865–889. doi:10.1046/j.0022-4537.2003.00095.x

Edmunds, J. A., Willse, J., Arshavsky, N., & Dallas, A. (2013). Mandated engagement: The impact of early college high schools. *Teachers College Record, 115*, 1–31.

Elias, M. J. (2011). How and why to use RtI to promote universal school-wide mental health and prevention-related interventions at a policy-systems level. *The Community Psychologist, 44*, 30–31.

Fletcher, J. M., & Vaughn, S. (2009). Response to intervention: Preventing and remediating academic difficulties. *Child Development Perspectives*, *3*, 30–37. doi:10.1111/j.1750-8606.2008.00072.x

Forman, S. G., Olin, S. S., Hoagwood, K. E., Crowe, M. & Saka, N. (2009). Evidence-based interventions in schools: Developers' views of implementation barriers and facilitators. *School Mental Health*, *1*, 26–36. doi:10.1007/s12310-008-9002-5

Fuchs, D., Fuchs, L. S., & Stecker, P. M. (2010). The blurring of special education in a new continuum of general education placements and services. *Exceptional Children*, *76*, 301–323.

Galassi, J. P., & Akos, P. (2004). Developmental advocacy: Twenty-first century school counseling. *Journal of Counseling & Development*, *82*, 146–157. doi:10.1002/j.1556-6678.2004.tb00296.x

Gregory, A., Skiba, R. J., & Noguera, P. A. (2010). The achievement gap and the discipline gap: Two sides of the same coin? *Educational Researcher*, *39*, 59–68. doi:10.3102/0013189X09357621

Greenberg, M. T., Weissberg, R. P., O'Brien M. U., Zins, J. E., Fredericks L., Resnik, H., & Elias, M. J. (2003). Enhancing school-based prevention and youth development through coordinated social, emotional, and academic learning. *American Psychologist*, *58*, 466–474. doi:10.1037/0003-066X.58.6-7.466

Grubb, W. N. (2008). Dreams and leaks, reforms and band-aids: The transition from high school to postsecondary education. In D. Blanck (Ed.). *Conditions of education in California 2008* (pp. 35–47). Berkeley, CA: Policy Analysis for California Education.

Grubb, N. W., & Anyon, Y. (2010). *A trio of changes supporting students: Integrating school reforms and support services*. Princeton, NJ: Woodrow Wilson National Fellowship Foundation, Early College High School Initiative.

Harkavy, I., Hartley, M., Axelroth Hodges, R., & Weeks, J. (2013). The promise of University-Assisted Community Schools to transform American schooling: A report from the field, 1985-2012. *Peabody Journal of Education*, *88*, 525–540, doi:10.1080/0161956X.2013.834789

Hill, N. E., & Tyson, D. F. (2009). Parental involvement in middle school: A meta-analytic assessment of the strategies that promote achievement. *Developmental Psychology*, *45*, 740–763.

Jaeger, L., & Venezia, A. (2010, November). *Offering student supports in high rigor, high need second schools partnered with postsecondary institutions: The case of Early College high schools*. Paper presented at the annual meeting of the Association for the Study of Higher Education, Indianapolis, IN.

Kuklinski, M. R., Briney, J. S., Hawkins, J. D., & Catalano, R. F. (2011). Cost-benefit analysis of communities that care outcomes at eighth grade. *Prevention Science*, *13*,150–161. doi:10.1007/s11121-011-0259-9

Ladson-Billings, G. (1995). But that's just good teaching! The case for culturally relevant pedagogy. *Theory into Practice*, *34*, 159–165. doi:10.1080/00405849509543675

Levine, M. & Levine, A. (1970). *A social history of helping services: Clinic, court, school and community*. New York, NY: Appleton Century Crofts.

Masten, A. S., & Coatsworth, J. D. (1998). The development of competence in favorable and unfavorable environments: Lessons from research on successful children. *American Psychologist, 53*, 205–220. doi:10.1037/0003-066X.53.2.205

McKown, C., & Strambler, M. J. (2008). Social influences on the ethnic achievement gap. In S. M. Quintana & C. McKown (Eds.). *Handbook of race, racism, and the developing child* (pp. 366–396). John Wiley & Sons.

McLaughlin, M. W., & Talbert, J. E. (2006). *Building school-based teacher learning communities: Professional strategies to improve student achievement.* New York, NY: Teachers College Press.

Moore, K. A. (2014). Making the grade: Assessing the evidence for integrated student supports. *Child Trends.* Retrieved from http://www.childtrends.org/?publications=making-the-grade-assessing-the-evidence-for-integrated-student-supports

Namir, S., & Weinstein, R. S. (1982). Children: Facilitating new directions. In L. Snowden (Ed.). *Reaching the underserved: Mental health needs of neglected populations* (pp. 43–73). Beverly Hills, CA: Sage.

Nasir, N. S. (2012). *Racialized identities: Race and achievement among African American youth.* Stanford, CA: Stanford University Press.

Newman, F. M., Smith, B., Allensworth, E., & Bryk, A. S. (2001). Instructional program coherence: What it is and why it should guide school improvement policy. *Educational Evaluation and Policy Analysis, 23*, 297–321. doi:10.3102/01623737023004297

Ness, C. (2011, May). *CAL Prep's first graduates – all of them – get into college.* Retrieved from http://newscenter.berkeley.edu/2011/05/06/cal-preps-first-graduating-class/

Oakes, J. (1985). *Keeping track: How schools structure inequality.* New Haven, CT: Yale University Press.

Oakes, J., Rogers, J., Silver, D., Valladares, S., Terriquez, V., McDonough, P., & Lipton, M. (2006). *Removing the roadblocks: Fair college opportunities for all California students.* UC/ACCORD and UCLA/IDEA. Retrieved from http://inpathways.net/Removing_Roadblocks_to_College_%28Oakes_et_al__07%29.pdf

Oakes, J., & Saunders, M. (2008). *Beyond tracking: Multiple pathways to college, career, and civic participation.* Cambridge, MA: Harvard Education Press.

Pianta, R. C., & Hamre, B. K. (2009). Conceptualization, measurement, and improvement of classroom processes: Standardized observation can leverage capacity. *Educational Researcher, 38*, 109–119. doi:10.3102/0013189X09332374

Roderick, M., Nagaoka, J., & Coca, V. (2009). College readiness for all: The challenge for urban high schools. *The Future of Children, 19*, 185–210. doi:10.1353/foc.0.0024

Rosenbaum, J. E., & Becker, K. I. (2011). The early college challenge: Navigating disadvantaged students' transition to college. *American Educator, 35*, 14–20.

Roth, J., & Brooks-Gunn, J. (2000). What do adolescents need for healthy development? Implications for youth policy. *Social Policy Report, 15*, 3–19.

Sarason, S. B. (2004). *And what do you mean by learning?* Portsmouth, NH: Heinemann.

Savitz-Romer, M., Jager-Hyman, J., and Coles, A. (2009). *Removing roadblocks to rigor: Linking academic and social supports to ensure college readiness and success.* Washington, DC: Institute for Higher Education Policy. Retrieved from http://www.ihep.org/research/publications/removing-roadblocks-rigor-linking-academic-and-social-supports-ensure-colleg-0

Sedlak, M. W. (1997). The uneasy alliance of mental health services and the schools: An historical perspective. *American Journal of Orthopsychiatry, 67,* 349–361. doi:10.1037/h0080238

Seidman, E. (2011). An emerging action science of social settings. *American Journal of Community Psychology, 50,* 1–16. doi:10.1007/s10464-011-9469-3.

Shugart, S., & Romano, J. C. (2006). LifeMap: A learning centered system for student success. *Community College Journal of Research and Practice, 30,* 141–143. doi:10.1080/10668920500433116

Smetana, J. G., Campione-Barr, N., & Metzger, A. (2006). Adolescent development in interpersonal and societal contexts. *Annual Review of Psychology, 57,* 255–284. doi:10.1146/annurev.psych.57.102904.190124

Thomas, J. Y., & Brady, K. P. (2005). Chapter 3: The Elementary and Secondary Education Act at 40: Equity, accountability, and the evolving federal role in public education. *Review of Educational Research, 29,* 51–67. doi:10.3102/0091732X029001051

Tyack, D. B. (1992). Health and social services in public schools: Historical perspectives. *The Future of Children, 2,* 19–31. doi:10.2307/1602459

Vargas, J. (2013, March). *The economic payoff for closing college-readiness and completion gaps.* Retrieved from http://www.jff.org/publications/economic-payoff-closing-college-readiness-and-completion-gaps

Weinstein, R. S. (1996). High standards in a tracked system of schooling: For which students and with what educational supports? *Educational Researcher, 25,* 16–19. doi:10.3102/0013189X025008016

Weinstein, R. S. (2002a). Overcoming inequality in schooling: A call to action for community psychology. *American Journal of Community Psychology, 30,* 21–42. doi:10.1023/A:1014311816571

Weinstein, R. S. (2002b). *Reaching higher: The power of expectations in schooling.* Cambridge, MA: Harvard University Press.

Weinstein, R. S. (2011, February). *Toward a comprehensive support structure for early college students.* Final report to the Woodrow Wilson National Fellowship Foundation, Princeton, NJ.

# 15 | Talent Development: The Forging of an Academic Identity

**FRANK C. WORRELL**

*"I grew up in Richmond, and . . . a lot of people there don't know about college or like they just don't care about it. So there is always like that distraction of like two different paths that I could have chosen, and sometimes it was hard to stay away from like the bad paths. But I overcame it . . . and it just made me want to do even better, to do something better with my life."* (Graduating Senior, California College Preparatory Academy, 2011)

A SUBSTANTIAL NUMBER OF SCHOOL REFORM initiatives focus on decreasing the achievement gap and preparing students to enter college, in the hope that by sending more underrepresented students to college, we can counteract the pernicious effects of the achievement gap and, by extension, the concomitant occupational and income gaps among ethnic, racial, and socioeconomic groups. California College Preparatory Academy (CAL Prep) was founded on the basis of one of these initiatives, the early college model. The early college model requires students to complete a substantial number of college credits—up to attaining an Associate's degree—while still in high school. The model is predicated in part on the notion that students from underrepresented backgrounds do not complete college because 4 years is too long a time for these students to delay entering the workforce, given familial resources and societal pressures. Thus, allowing these students to complete their first 2 years of college while in high school should result in greater numbers of them completing 4-year degrees, because they will have to spend only 2 years in college.

However, the early college model, like many of school reforms, requires only changing the way schools operate, which although important, ignores the role and responsibility of the individual learner, particularly those from low-income and minority backgrounds who are underrepresented in colleges and universities. Learning is potentiated by both the social context (e.g., teacher, classroom, school, home) and the individual differences that the learner brings. Thus, schooling is a *psychosocial* enterprise that is closely tied to fundamental questions of identity: who am I, who am I in this context, do I belong here, and what do others think about me? It is not surprising, then, that the two leading explanations for the achievement gap—that is cultural ecological theory (Ogbu, 2008) and stereotype threat (C. M. Steele, 1997)—are psychosocial theories whose mechanisms involve the integration of personal and cultural identities. There is a substantial literature indicating that ethnic minority students, including African Americans, Asian Americans, and Latinos, obtain higher scores on measures assessing group belonging than their European American peers (e.g., Worrell, 2007). Ethnocultural identities are of particular importance to members of ethnic minority groups, especially in societal contexts where these groups are discriminated against (Phinney, 1990).

As reported in earlier chapters in this volume, there were resonances of the clash between cultural and academic identities at CAL Prep: complaints by students that the schoolwork being asked of them was too demanding; student requests that teachers address issues of race and culture; and the disproportionate attrition of African American students. In Chapter 14, Weinstein and Bialis-White highlighted the importance of a comprehensive model of supports across six domains: academic, biopsychosocial, parent collaboration, enrichment, college work/readiness, and transition preparation. A common thread across all of these support systems is the integration of multiple identities. A comprehensive model must incorporate multiple aspects of individuals and their contexts, including the roles of parents. Also, academic and other enrichment opportunities must prepare students for the contexts of college and work, contexts in which they will be underrepresented and possibly underestimated and misunderstood. The following section provides a model for framing the approach that CAL Prep took.

# From Closing the Achievement Gap
# to Developing Academic Talent

Although the achievement gap has dominated the discourse on school reform for several decades, it can be argued that this singular focus on closing the gap has been misguided to some extent. Individual differences are to be expected in any field of endeavor, including education. The more pressing concern is what the individual differences represent. In the National Assessment of Educational Progress' annual ranking of student performance, students are placed into four groups: *below basic, basic, proficient,* or *advanced.* One reason for the salience of the achievement gap is that whereas 30% to 40% of all US students obtain scores in the Proficient or Advanced range in reading and mathematics (Aud et al., 2012), only 13% to 20% of African Americans, Native Americans, and Latinos obtain scores in these ranges (Aud, Fox, & KewalRamani, 2010; Plucker, Hardesty, & Burroughs, 2013). The achievement gap would be far less prominent in educational discourse if (1) the lower end of the gap was the proficient range and (2) students in all groups had the skills to attend and succeed in any type of tertiary education program that they chose, ranging from the vocational to the liberal arts.

A different lens through which one can examine the education of youth who are underrepresented in tertiary education is the lens of *talent development.* More closely associated with gifted and talented education programs than with underachievement and school failure, the talent development paradigm subsumes several prominent models related to outstanding student performance (e.g., Dai & Chen, 2013; Subotnik, Olszewski-Kubilius, & Worrell, 2011). Early discussions of talent development were premised on the Johns Hopkins' talent search model (e.g., Stanley, 1973), which promotes the use of above-level testing to identify students at the top of the achievement distribution for accelerated academic experiences. This policy resulted in the underrepresentation of students of color in gifted programs (e.g., Worrell, 2003). More recent discussions of talent development (e.g., Weinstein, 2002, 2008) do not limit the model to students who are already outstanding academically. As Dai and Chen (2013, p. 156) noted, the goal of talent development is "to cultivate a broader, more diverse range of strengths and interests and to help students achieve excellence in their chosen areas." Similarly, Subotnik and colleagues posited that in the early stages of talent development, potential is the important variable, and that the goal of talent development programs is to transform potential into competence, competence into expertise, and, at the highest levels, expertise into eminence. When described in these terms, this paradigm seems to be a more appropriate one for working with underrepresented students, and perhaps all students, than models focused on closing the achievement gap.

Subotnik and colleagues (2011, p. 29) integrated the literature on talent development into what they called "a mega-model." In addition to domain-specific ability, they identified several critical correlates of outstanding performance, including (1) opportunities (provided and utilized), (2) psychosocial factors such as task commitment and cultural identities, and (3) appropriate support for the development of talent. These authors argue that achievement is a result of the interaction of these factors. A brief overview of these constructs follows.

## Opportunity

The literature on individuals who make outstanding contributions to society is replete with examples of opportunities that were provided at critical moments in development. For example, Gladwell (2008) highlighted Bill Gates' exposure to computers in high school and Bill Joy's access to the computer mainframe when he was an undergraduate. Syed (2010) credited his parents' decision to buy a table tennis board that was able to be available year-round in the garage as well as the national coach living in the same neighborhood and choosing to give lessons to local youth with his and his brother's junior national championships.

Opportunities can range from attending well-resourced schools with highly qualified teachers to belonging to families that have the resources to provide numerous supplemental educational opportunities. Family resources are also markers of differences in educational capital opportunities that have potent implications for student achievement. Consider the difference between two fourth graders studying ancient Egypt, one who has visited the pyramids in Egypt and one who has never been more than 20 miles from his home; these students will not only bring vastly different lenses to bear on the subject matter but also will have different visions of the possibilities for the future.

As opportunities are frequently tied to the social and financial capital of parents and well-resourced schools in suburban districts, the chance for students who are underrepresented in college to attend schools with competent and caring teachers who believe that these students have what it takes to enter and succeed in college provides a critical opportunity. CAL Prep was intended to be such an opportunity for all of its students with the goal of altering their educational trajectories. However, it is important to note that *providing* opportunities is not sufficient. Individuals must also recognize and be willing to take advantage of the opportunities that come their way; *taking advantage* of educational opportunities is one of the contexts in which psychosocial factors become important.

## Psychosocial Factors

The importance of psychosocial factors (e.g., academic self-concept, self-efficacy, and achievement motivation) to academic success is well established in the education literature. However, as with many other variables, psychosocial factors are subject to Matthew effects (Ceci & Papierno, 2005), with the richer students benefiting more than their poorer peers. Students who do not have consistent histories of academic success are often less likely to persist when things become difficult for a variety of reasons, such as believing that ability is fixed (Dweck, 2006) or preferring to be thought of as lazy rather than stupid in the face of failure (Covington, 1992). Dweck's conceptualization of abilities as fixed or malleable brings together many of the psychosocial constructs into a theoretical model, including mastery versus performance orientations, the role of effort, and the interpretation of lack of success. However, the superordinate psychosocial construct that brings these variables together is the concept of an academic identity.

## Academic Identity

In the context of schooling, an academic identity has several components. First is the belief that a person is a competent, college-bound student. For students who are underrepresented, this belief also includes "despite not being from a group for whom college is the norm." Using a slightly different term, Whiting (2006, p. 48) defined a scholar identity as "one in which culturally diverse males [and females] view themselves as academicians, as studious, as competent and capable, as intelligent or talented in school settings." Similarly, Nasir, McLaughlin, and Jones (2009) operationalized academic identity as viewing school as important, caring about grades, wanting to do well, and considering oneself a good student.

Second, an academic identity is both present- and future-oriented; it includes an expectation of pursuing educational opportunities beyond high school. Worrell and Hale (2001) found that at-risk youth who were hopeful about the future were more likely to complete their high school diplomas than youth who were equally at risk but did not believe that the future would work out.

Third, an academic identity involves a sense of belonging to a learning community—that is, a community determined by academic interests and not by demographic group membership (Horn, 2014; Sosniak, 1995). Learning communities are critically important for students from underrepresented backgrounds for whom the engaged academic path is often the road less traveled (e.g., Graham, 2004; Nasir, 2012).

Fourth, an academic identity involves the willingness to engage in hours of concentrated work. Ericsson, Krampe, and Tesch-Römer (1993) suggested that to become an expert in a domain, one needs to put in about 10,000 hours of *deliberate* practice. In a similar vein, the probability of getting into and succeeding in college is dependent both on putting in a fair amount of deliberate practice in secondary school and being willing to continue to engage in this type of deliberate practice in college.

Finally, academic identities are more likely to develop in "identity-safe classrooms" (D. M. Steele & Cohn-Vargas, 2013, p. 4). In order to encourage low-income and minority students to commit to the work of schooling, educators must be able to convince students from these underrepresented communities that their academic commitment is not incompatible with their racial and ethnic identities and, moreover, that this academic commitment can lead to working toward a more just society for everyone, including the groups that they belong to. D. M. Steele and Cohn-Vargas described identity-safe classrooms as places where students both *belong* and *learn* and point out that these types of classrooms require teachers treating students with respect as well as teachers having the appropriate "respect and authority ... to build intellectually and socially dynamic, caring classrooms focused on learning" (p. 4). Several students echoed this comment in the responses reported in Chapter 5 on advisories, supporting the notion that the forging of an academic identity takes place in supportive and socially complex school environments where traditional stereotypes are known but not supported.

## Student Voices on the Contributions of the California College Preparatory Academy

To examine whether and how CAL Prep succeeded in helping students develop academic identities, I turned to students' perspectives on this issue, drawing from two sources of information from students. The first was based on interviews with students from CAL Prep's first graduating class, who responded to questions on how CAL Prep contributed to their educational journey. Five students are featured—an African American boy, an African American girl, two Latinos, and a Latina. I also drew on interviews with two students—an African American girl and a Latina—from CAL Prep's second graduating class in 2012 who were admitted to the University of California (UC) Berkeley and completed interviews that are published on the UC Berkeley website. Together, these seven students provide a cross-section of genders, ethnicities, and lengths of time attending CAL Prep. Pseudonyms are used for the class interview responses to preserve confidentiality. However, when citing the interviews published on the website, we use the students' names with the website citation, because the interviews are publicly available.

The idea of interviewing the first graduating class was proposed in the spring of 2011 at one of the monthly meetings of the Early College Initiative faculty committee, with the goal of getting the thoughts of and feedback from the graduating class. Interview questions were discussed at one of the monthly faculty meetings, with faculty making suggestions about questions that they thought should be asked. Based on notes from this meeting, the faculty co-directors developed the final set of questions that are presented in Box 15.1. These interviews with the Class of 2011 were conducted in May by a male, European American doctoral student in school psychology.

In analyzing these two sets of interviews for this chapter, I looked for responses reflecting the talent development themes discussed previously, including opportunity, task commitment, support, a sense of community, and the development of an academic identity. The research question was as follows: would students' responses to the questions in Box 15.1 reflect themes linking talent development and identity (these constructs were not being asked about directly)? Below, I have reported on comments from the students in support of CAL Prep's contribution to these themes but also included comments by students about how CAL Prep may have fallen short. I have also described how the school responded to issues that arose.

## Opportunity

JN, a 17-year-old African American girl, provided a heartfelt description of one of the opportunities that CAL Prep had given her.

> JN: I actually had the opportunity to audit a class at the Bancroft Library [UC Berkeley] while I was here. And that was amazing because they

pulled out JFK's binder, from when he was here and gave his speech. Most people don't know that's there. He left the binder, and it was one of his old military binders, and his actual speech that he had edited over while he was sitting there before he gave it. It was just a few months before he was assassinated. It's there. And a lot of people are like, "Well, it's a binder, and a piece of a paper." And I understand that. But it's a piece of history. And Berkeley has that piece of history. We have so much history here.

As JN notes in this comment, what others see as just a piece of paper was for her an amazing opportunity to experience a piece of American history in her backyard. As noted previously, opportunities are among the most potent factors in student success. But opportunities are more than financial resources, even though they are important. From our point of view, CAL

Prep provided opportunities for students to get a rigorous academic program and to have access to a university which values equity and access as much as it does scholarship.

CAL Prep's goal is to prepare students to succeed in college, and the students suggest that the school succeeded to some extent. JN responds to a question about if anything scared her about going to college.

> JN: Not so much. I mean I know that that's something—I'm sure when I get here, there'll be different things, and I'm excited to learn more, to be a part of it, just to have the opportunity to go to college is phenomenal. So I'm not fearful about that at all.

While JN is focused on going to college, other students were focused on more proximal opportunities. WS (17-year-old African American boy) was asked what was his proudest moment at CAL Prep and he chose a moment in the very near future that he had not been sure he would attain—his high school graduation.

> WS: Actually, to be honest, my proudest moment hasn't really happened yet. For me, I honestly believe that my proudest moment will be when I'm sitting there in the stands or wherever I'll be at the day of graduation, and I realize that I'm closing this chapter of my life that's been challenging. It's been rewarding. But the journey has come to an end, and I'm going to be beginning a different chapter, so I think that'll be the proudest moment, to know that I made it, that I didn't give up.

Even students who may not have attended CAL Prep if they had a choice saw the school as an opportunity. Here are the comments of a 17-year-old Latino.

> RK: Well, the main reason why I transferred was because being a private school, the tuition was really expensive. And so we . . . the second year, my sophomore year tuition rose. And I had financial aid, but my parents couldn't contribute their portion of the tuition anymore, so I had to like change schools 'cause it wasn't working out. But when I moved here, like I hadn't really known much about college or anything, like I knew it existed and like that it was good to go, but I didn't really know all the steps to do it and like all the information, and like here at CAL Prep they're really like college ready and

like college bound, like everybody you walk down the halls and say college this and that. And like that really like inspired me and like motivated me to do good 'cause I want to go to a good college and like also be able to afford it.

RK's comments reflect the critical role of secondary schools as communities of learning in not only preparing students for college, but in making students aware of college as a possibility for the future for everyone who has the desire to attend. There is a growing body of research on the importance of middle and high schools increasing students' *college knowledge* so that they can adequately prepare to take advantage of that opportunity when it arises (Burleson, Hallett, & Park, 2008; Hooker & Brand 2010).

However, there were students who felt that CAL Prep could have done more in preparing them for college. One student expressed concerns that taking college classes at a community college—one of the opportunities that the school provided—rather than at the university may not have prepared him to be successful in college, in large part because he saw the community college environment as sheltered in comparison to a 4-year institution. This concern was one that the faculty had discussed as well. The faculty agreed that community colleges were more sheltered than 4-year universities, but in general, saw the less competitive environment as a positive rather than a negative factor. Part of developing an academic identity is being successful, and it was not clear that all of CAL Prep's students could be successful taking classes at 4-year universities while still in high school. Moreover, any grade received at UC Berkeley by a high school student, including an "F," would follow them into the UC and California State University systems. A few of the stronger students were encouraged to take UC Berkeley courses during summer sessions with varying degrees of success.

However, this concern led to the development of College Week for the seniors, which provided another sheltered opportunity for CAL Prep students to take college-level courses on the UC Berkeley campus. Our goal was to facilitate students in having this 1-week experience, where they would have to attend classes in different buildings and at different times with minimal supervision in a context where failure would be a learning experience but not put a blemish on their college record before it had begun. WS's comment below suggests that we succeeded to some extent.

ws: I think that CAL Prep's ability to kind of present me with opportunities like this, with being at Cal for a week and getting a chance to sample what college classes are like, even though it was just like a miniseries that they developed for us, it still, you know, allowed us to understand about, you know, what you have to do to plan out your time and do your readings and reading a course syllabus. Some things that we still get at CAL Prep, but just actually being on campus, I think, was something that CAL Prep was able to do for me. But there are other things as well that has had a big impact on my life, like the college for certain thing and, you know, their stance on really getting individuals into college and to go to college has been a big impact because I know that other institutions may not have stressed it as much as CAL Prep, so the culture of going to college and it being a possibility had an impact on my life and, you know, helped give me that extra push to actually do it.

As these comments by students indicate, CAL Prep did succeed in its goal of opening up the opportunity of college for students—in terms of college knowledge, the expectation to attend college, and preparation for academic college life.

## Task Commitment

This section considers the theme of task commitment, which is more than hard work or persistence; rather, it is a constellation of psychosocial variables that relate to successful outcomes. Renzulli (1986, p. 69) defined task commitment as

> . . . a refined or focused form of motivation. . . . Whereas motivation is usually defined in terms of a general energizing process that triggers responses in organisms, task commitment represents energy brought to bear on a particular problem (task) or specific performance area. The terms that are most frequently used to describe task commitment are perseverance, endurance, hard work, dedicated practice, self-confidence, and a belief in one's ability to carry out important work.

Task commitment is perhaps one of the most underestimated variables in predicting outstanding performance, especially as, in many cases, the amount of work that goes into a final, polished product or performance is not evident. Additionally, there is the view that having to work hard signals a lack of ability (Dweck, 2006). The talent development perspective counters this notion by highlighting the fact that irrespective of one's initial level of ability or talent, task commitment is essential for transforming the potential that one's talent represents into actual accomplishments (Subotnik et al., 2011).

Alana Banks, a former student body president at CAL Prep and a current UC Berkeley student, reflected on the importance of hard work with a reporter from UC Berkeley (Ness, 2012):

> For me, elementary school was a living hell. I was dyslexic and had a speech impediment, so as early as kindergarten I was labeled with "special needs." My sixth grade math teacher [at CAL Prep] realized that I needed help, so she signed me up for after-school tutoring. She realized that I didn't know how to do pre-algebra, let alone my times tables or basic addition and subtraction. For sixth and seventh grade I hated CAL Prep, because it was so hard for me to just get by. Every day I stayed after school, and it felt like I never got a break. When I started eighth grade, I learned how to manage my dyslexia. I became stellar at math— it was my favorite subject.

At CAL Prep, the importance of working hard is integral aspect of the school's philosophy, and one that the students recognized—not just as something that they had to do but in terms of the outcomes that hard work results in. Here is RK's response to the question about his most challenging moment at CAL Prep.

> RK: I guess just like the transition at first, like the getting used to. I kinda felt out of place, like I didn't belong, just like everybody else was like already knew the rhythm of like how things work here and they had their own flow going on. So like having to catch up and like keep up with everybody else was like kinda a struggle, and it made me feel like maybe I wasn't ready, like I wasn't good enough.

The theme of struggling surfaced in many of RK's responses, perhaps because of the fact that he came to CAL Prep in his sophomore year and thus had not had to deal with the higher expectations for academic commitment that CAL Prep presented.

In the next response, RK acknowledges the difficulties that come with being a native Spanish speaker, but also reflects on the pride that comes with working hard and succeeding.

> RK: Well, I've done a lot of things here that I'm proud of, like one of the main things is like English has always been like a struggle for

me, maybe 'cause like the language barrier, I guess. And I had never gotten an A in English until like I came to this school, and I got my first A actually this year in English, and like I was really excited about that.

RK also had to "step up his game" to be able to graduate, as he notes below, and as before, there is a sense of satisfaction and pride that comes with succeeding through hard work and effort.

> RK: Well, I just—like I talked to Mr. L., the counselor, and like talked to him about what I had to do in order to like be on track to graduate because when I transferred here, I was missing a lot of like credits and stuff. So then he just gave me the classes I needed to take in order to make up for the credits. And I took two college courses, Spanish and then Art History, and I did like a packet for a tech class, and then that got me on track. And that kinda helped me like feel like I could do it because I did what everybody had done like in one in year in like a quarter.

The task commitment theme, reflected in students' feeling that school was a "struggle" is reflected in several students' comments, as is the theme of pride in a hard won outcome. In the next two comments, WS begins by describing his struggles with time management and FV (an 18-year-old Latina) talks about her proudest moment at CAL Prep.

> WS: Well, particularly mentioning a struggle, for me—I'm not necessarily known to be the most punctual or timely person, and that has carried on into the senior year, even into now. But what I'm finding that I'm having to do now is make a conscious effort and really think about what time is, and, you know, being a form of respect and putting myself in other people's shoes. So it's a work in progress, but I can say that I'm getting progressively better at being more punctual and taking more responsibility for my timeliness.
>
> FV: [My proudest moment at CAL Prep was] getting on the honor roll. Having 100% homework every week. Yeah, 'cause what they do here is when you have 100% homework for the whole week, you get free dress. But that's when back then when we were wearing uniforms. So I was on that list all the time, so it was like, wow, I was proud of myself.

These comments reflect the understanding of the benefits of task commitment on the part of these students, and they also reflect the types of comments that are echoed by individuals who become outstanding performers in a range of other academic and nonacademic domains. RK's response to what he would say to the students who are still at CAL Prep provides a fitting capstone to this section on task commitment, summarizing quite cogently the notion that ability is malleable and that effort makes talent manifest.

> RK: I would tell them like to just keep trying and to work hard because I know that a lot of the students here are very smart, and I know they can do a lot . . . they can go very far in life, and they should go far in life 'cause they deserve it, 'cause they've all been working hard.

## Support

A previous section discusses the notion of schooling as opportunity. However, even within the same schools, there can be students who teachers expect to succeed and students who teachers expect to fail, and the students in the latter group often do not expect to succeed, either. Thus, it is crucial for schools and teachers to provide the appropriate supports (see Chapter 14) for all students, but particularly for the students who believe least in their ability to succeed. As FV notes, the idea of support in the context of effective schooling is more than believing in the students—support is also reflected in the insistence by teachers that students *can, will,* and *must* engage academically. In responding to the question about what he would like to say to the principal and staff at CAL Prep, FV responds in the following way.

> FV: Thank you for all your hard work. I appreciate you guys pushing me and everything, 'cause I came from a school that—my grades were bad. They were really bad. And at times [here] . . . I would be on the honor roll, and I'm just so happy that you guys were there for me and helped."

This notion of a supportive staff echoes through all of the students' responses in different ways. For example, consider JN's comments about the CAL Prep staff.

JN: Well, a nice thing about CAL Prep is the staff that we have. The faculty is always there for you. So you can go in and sit down with the counselor. You can go in and sit down with the principal, with a teacher. And it's not like you have to go see a specialized person to help you, because they've become like your own family. They've become your surrogate family when you're at school. We joke about it all the time because we're like we spend more time at school with our teachers than we do at home [laughs], because some of us get there at 7:30 in the morning and don't leave till 6:00 in the afternoon. Others of us, teachers are willing to pick them up in the morning to give them rides if they're going to be late. And a teacher may be like, 'I'm leaving home at 6:00. I can pick you up at 6:30.' So they're with that teacher in the morning, and they're there until they go home in the afternoon. Our teachers are really good on just being there to give that helping hand.

The idea of school as family is in keeping with the theme of identity-safe educational environments (D. M. Steele & Cohn-Vargas, 2013) mentioned earlier. Schools that serve students from low-income backgrounds often do more than provide additional support to students. Sometimes, they provide the only support that students receive in aspiring for higher education—not because families do not care, but often because families care too much and do not want to set their youth up for disappointment and failure. Consequently, the role of the school is to provide support not only for the student, but also for the student's family. As Alana Banks reported (Ness, 2012),

My mom discourages me from thinking about college because college costs more than she will ever make in her entire life. But CAL Prep has helped me see that this should not be a barrier to opportunity. Every time finances were a problem, CAL Prep and my other supporters have always supplied. College applications? CAL Prep gave me a fee waiver. College visits? CAL Prep helped me fundraise. It's like, these guys really don't put a price tag on education. CAL Prep has taught my mom that going to college is priceless, and that no matter what I will be fine, financially. So this fall I'm attending Cal, my dream school, and I received a full ride—a real example of self-controlled success.

An important aspect of Alana's comment here is the last sentence in which she owns her self-controlled success, one of the aspects of the school's values discussed in Chapter 13.

An interesting twist on the students' views of CAL Prep staff as supportive was the contrast that many of the students made about the staff at their previous schools. Whereas CAL Prep staff were perceived as supportive and caring, staff at the students' previous schools were often portrayed as just the opposite.

> FV: My most challenging [moment at CAL Prep] probably has to be the tests, 'cause I don't perform as well as I want to on tests, but I get through them. And I get the little extra help. I go to the office hours for my teachers and yeah.
>
> INTERVIEWER: Was it hard at first to know what to do to get help?
>
> FV: Yeah. 'Cause I came from a school where a lot of the teachers did not care at all. And it's like, oh, should I ask? Should I raise my hand? Or - so I just finally came over that fear, and I just went to ask for help.

Moreover, as evident in the responses, the theme of support emerged in response not only to the question about what they would like to say to the teachers, but also in response to the question on their most challenging moments at CAL Prep. The students all seemed to recognize that the CAL Prep staff were there to help them in their moments of need. The student MJ also acknowledges the support that CAL Prep staff provided for the college classes that he took.

> INTERVIEWER: What about your most challenging or your lowest moment at CAL Prep?
>
> MJ: I would say my freshman year, when I had to take the first college courses, especially the 201A and 201B, because I'm doing a lot of writing and doing essays, and that wasn't my strength, so that was like the hardest thing to do.
>
> INTERVIEWER: How did you turn it around?
>
> MJ: My professor's very chill, very laid back and very helpful. He helped me a lot on how to do the outlines and make them so it wasn't so hard to do the essay, and then my English teacher, Miss D., also did the same thing with the outlines and like breaking it down and adding more examples. So that way when I went back to do the essay, it was easier to do.

Maribel Garcia graduated from CAL Prep and went on to UC Berkeley. She reports (Ness, 2012),

> I was the first student Cal Prep ever had that became pregnant and stayed during my pregnancy and after to finish my high school education. I was surrounded by so many people who helped me overcome my obstacles because they did not want to see me fail; it just wasn't an option. And they were right; it's not and never will be an option. Cal Prep has taught me to fight for what I really want, and I'm doing it. I fought and struggled to make it to UC Berkeley, and I'll be there this fall.

As can be seen, the notion of support is not tied to "dumbing down" the curriculum or giving the students less to do. Rather, it is tied to (1) making learning explicit, (2) providing structures and processes that facilitate the student doing the work that needs to be done, (3) motivating and inspiring students to keep trying, and (4) highlighting the CAL Prep mantra of "Yes, we can." Consider what RK says when asked about the biggest impact that CAL Prep has had on him:

> RK: I think that it would be just like all the support that the teachers give you . . . like they really encouraged you when they talk to you about their college experience, and that just really helps me like stay focused and like really work hard 'cause like I know it can be done and I can do it too . . . I think they give you like a lot of the information that you need. Mr. L. really like gets on you about what you have to do and what you have to take in order to be on track, and Miss R. is always like pumping you up and motivating you. And like you can tell that she genuinely cares for everybody.

Although there are large numbers of underrepresented students who do not attend college, there are also large numbers who begin to attend college and do not continue after one to three semesters. Thus, one of the goals of successful preparation in high school is to provide students with the ability to function with the independence necessary to succeed in a college environment. Thus, students were asked if they thought that CAL Prep had prepared them to be successful in college. JN's response speaks to how CAL Prep supported this type of independence.

> JN: Yes. They definitely have. They've taught us how to find our resources and how to use the resources once we find them, and to not

be afraid to ask questions, and to approach authorities to ask them for help. Our teachers are really good about, you know, when you first come into a school, they're really big on, "OK, this is who I am. This is what you call me. This is my name, such and such and such."

The ability to navigate the college environment is critical. It is one that the Early College Initiative committee has observed first hand and had to intervene in as the committee monitors the students in their first year of college.

In response to what CAL Prep could have done better, MJ, a Latino immigrant student, had indicated in an earlier comment that attending community college may not have prepared him adequately for attending a 4-year institution. In the following comment, he reverses himself, as he reflects on his community college experience.

MJ: Well, I failed a couple college courses [offered at CAL Prep], so I had to take them on my own. And that was a different experience because I had to take them with college students at BCC [Berkeley City College] instead of with my classmates. So that's helped me better be independent and know how to like be responsible for my own work, and talking to my teachers and putting myself out there, where I'm not comfortable with, since all these people are like 20 years and older than me.

MJ's reflection is particularly poignant, because it speaks to the notion of continuing to try after experiencing failure, an important and critical element in the talent development paradigm (Subotnik et al., 2011). MJ then goes on to thank the CAL Prep principal and teachers for their support in helping him graduate.

MJ: To the principal, um, I would just say thank you for pushing me as hard as you did. Um, to the staff I will say the same thing, plus um, helping me with everything I've had to go through and always being there for me and not like shutting the door or not picking up the phone when I needed help. Like everything I've done is because of them. The staff.

As noted earlier, the theme of support seems to be intimately connected to the theme of work in the students' minds. In the next comment, FV returns to both of those themes in response to questions on the way in which CAL Prep could have done more and in response to what outside of CAL Prep helped her get ready for college.

> INTERVIEWER: Now, do you think there are some ways that CAL Prep could have done better?
>
> FV: Better? I don't think so. They're preparing you, giving you a good . . . uh—the teachers are really on it. They say, "OK, you have to turn in your homework. Come on. This is detention." . . . If you don't do it, there's a consequence, so you have to do it, and that like motivates you won't get left behind.
>
> INTERVIEWER: "So what outside of CAL Prep has helped you get ready for college?"
>
> FV: Giving us projects over the weekend, or giving us extra homework over the weekend so you know when you come Monday morning, you're prepared, ready to talk about the article we read or extra things we have to do over the weekend to finish the whole week.

These comments suggest that task commitment on the part of the students is in response to task commitment on the part of teachers. Also, they point out that, at least in retrospect, students appreciate teachers who hold them to high expectations with appropriate supports, even if they are not necessarily as appreciative at the moment when they are being pushed. My research on academically talented youth has shown that although academically talented students' academic self-concepts decrease in more competitive environments as predicted by big-fish–little-pond effect (Marsh & Hau, 2003), the impact on perceived ability is substantially greater (Worrell & Young, 2012). Believing in the ability to succeed after failure on the basis of hard work may be a critical in helping students who are not considered academically talented persist and succeed as they enter more selective tertiary education environments.

## Community

The theme of family was lifted up by JN in a previous comment, and it is quite appropriate in the context of CAL Prep. However, a more appropriate term may be "community," another term for a place where one belongs. One of the important ideas in the development of CAL Prep was the idea of creating a community of learners, a term taken from the gifted and talented literature. Sosniak (1999) identified three phases in the development of talent: "(a) informal but regular exposure to the skills and activities in a field, (b) more formal and systematic instruction in the talent domain beginning in adolescence, and (c) an introduction to the talent community modeling the highest standards of the field" (p. 168). Sosniak's analysis was incomplete, however. I would argue that there were relevant communities of learning at each phase of talent development, and that participation in the community from the previous phase helps to set the stage for participation in a later phase. Thus, CAL Prep was intended to be a community of learning that sets the stage for participation in the community of learners that constitute a university or college.

In the next comment, JN talks about the development that took place in the CAL Prep community from its early years when she was in seventh grade through her current status as a senior, recognizing that the shared experiences—both good and bad—contributed to the sense of community.

> JN: I've been at CAL Prep since it first opened its doors 6 years ago, so I'm one of the people who have been there for the long haul. I've seen us when we started out and didn't have desks yet. We had these long picnic tables that were covered in butcher paper. And we all sat around them in chairs because we didn't have desks yet, and we didn't have all new textbooks. And throughout the year we grew as a school. So now, of course, we have all these nice desks, and these really nice Promethean boards, and all these wonderful things. But it was a process to get there, and to be able to be a part of it has been a really big thing for the students who are currently at CAL Prep because we feel like we've earned everything that we've gotten along the way, and it's developed a real sense of community.

JN also recognizes the loss that will come from the disbanding of the CAL Prep community that she was a part of as she moves from high school into college.

> JN: At the same time, as excited as I am to graduate, it's one of those really bittersweet moments, because I've been with these people for 6 years. I've known most of the teachers since they got there, and I took many of them on their first tours of CAL Prep, so [laughs] it's really like being part of a family. And I've watched the family grow and change, and now I'm leaving, after 6 years, and that's a really big change for all of us who have been there, because we're just like, you know, we're used to coming in and seeing the same faces every day,

and being able to talk to whoever we want to whenever we want to, and now we have to say goodbye. It hasn't hit us all yet. You know, we haven't shed any tears, and we all say we're not going to shed any on graduation day. But we know that's not true. We will definitely have waterworks."

In response to the question about "what would you like to say to the students," MJ indicated that he did not have anything to say to the student body at large but did want to thank his cohort "for the family relationship that we have built together, for always being there, for always helping everyone out when we needed help." The interviewer then asked MJ if he thought that he was going to stay in contact with his graduating class.

> MJ: We're trying to. We're planning on, on it. I'm going to Chico with three other of my classmates, so I won't be that alone, which I'm happy about. For the rest, we're planning to do this road trip for Christmas. But like I don't know if it's really going to happen. We'll need to come up with some type of money to like get down there, 'cause we're going from Chico to Riverside.

Despite not having anything to say to the student body as a whole, in response to the last question, MJ indicated that he hoped to come back to CAL Prep and assist as he can.

> MJ: So my plans are to come back at some point and help. I also like the vision that Aspire [the charter school district] has on helping students go to college . . . Especially because I've been to the other schools down in Oakland, and I've seen how Aspire changes the students' perspective. I also have friends that go to a non-Aspire school, and how I compare them to my life at school and their life, and how mine is basically better than theirs in terms of student support and my college counselor's support. So I would definitely come back and help.

As stated in Chapter 1, CAL Prep started as an early college secondary school, with students in Grades 6 and 7. One rationale for this decision was that it was going to be important to use the full 7 years of secondary school to prepare students to succeed at selective colleges. Clearly, the sense of community that some of the students in this cohort reported was related to their joint secondary school journey, as JN states.

JN: I've been with my classmates for 6 years. A lot of times students in a conventional high school are with a group of students, what'll happen is you rotate between classrooms. That doesn't happen with us. I have been with the same 17 students for at least the past 3 years, so . . . those who have been there for the full 6 years and those who have been there for the full 3 years, we know each other. Inside and out. We've been together. We've built a sense of community . . . I love law, and my classmates are actually joining with me. They're like we all have designated roles for what we've ·going to be when we grow up. So we can call on each other. We've already made this little networking community, which is great. And it's just a lot of fun. We have one student who wants to be a neurosurgeon. So we know if we ever need neurosurgery help, we can go to them [laughs]. We have someone else who is like they are going to go into architecture and art. So were like, OK, wonderful! We have someone for that. We've really built this sense of community. It's just great.

## An Academic Identity

Although task commitment and pride in accomplishments speak to the students' development of an academic identity, they do not fully reflect the students' journeys toward this identity. The social role of the school as a supportive and family-oriented community of learning was also crucial, especially in the face of other social contexts that were pushing students in a different direction. As RK pointed out in the quote opening the chapter, there were many things outside of CAL Prep that were potential obstacles on his path to college, including a lack of role models and of college as an expected future in his community. FV makes a similar claim highlighting not just the neighborhood, but the importance of financial resources that are not available to her and others like her.

FV: 'Cause other people like come from richer neighborhoods or came—they have money. I didn't. So it's harder to pay for the applications. It's harder to take the tests. It's harder to pay for the whole entire school education. And coming from my background, it's hard 'cause not as many Latinos or Latinas get that education. Most don't just not even think about school. I really want to go to school and make my family proud.

In WS's comments about obstacles to be overcome, he focuses on the psychosocial factor of persistence as a key in his academic journey.

ws: Well, honestly, not giving up has been it. I mean I've been faced with some challenging circumstances, and I mean the statistics are out there. I'm an African American male in an urban environment. Dropout rates are crazy. But I'm here to say that I'm a senior and I'm just that much closer to graduating. So the fact that I persisted through challenging circumstances will be, you know, would be an example of me turning it around and just not giving up.

But although an academic identity may be related to where students have come from and what they have overcome, it is primarily about where they see themselves going. As WS notes, college is the destination, and as his comment indicates, he seems surprised that he is excited about going to college to study and meet others who are interested in the same intellectual pursuits.

ws: So many things about college excites me. Of course, I'm excited about engaging with individuals who are more knowledgeable about the fields that I want to study, so talking to professors, being in lecture halls. I'm excited about that, believe it or not. I'm excited about those schooling. But, on the flip side, I'm also excited about meeting new people. I'm going with two of my cousins, but outside of that I'm excited about talking to other individuals and really getting to know other people and so the social aspect, going out should be fun. So I'm looking forward to that.

The Early College Initiative at UC Berkeley has been a campuswide endeavor as described in Chapters 1 to 3, with participation and support from many departments and the administration. Chancellor Birgeneau's leadership proved to be as important to one of the students in the first CAL Prep class as it was to the campus community, as JN notes in this statement.

JN: Overall I'm proud of the school, to see where we came from to where we are now. I have to say one thing that I will always remember was when the school first opened, we had our big opening ceremony. And Chancellor Birgeneau was there, and that was just such a wonderful thing. And the fact that he was there—he gave a speech, and then I gave a speech [laughs] after him, and I remember it because I had on my Cal Berkeley socks, and I'm this little 7th-grader, who's taking him on a tour, talking about, "I'm gonna be at Berkeley." And now to actually be coming to Berkeley is just such a phenomenal thing.

## Conclusion

In the late 1900s, educational reformers condemned the routing of poor and underrepresented minority students into vocational and other courses that did not allow them to gain the necessary skills to enter college or to obtain higher-paying jobs (e.g., Arum & Shavit, 1995; Oakes, 1983). Contemporary researchers are also concerned about the failure of some colleges and universities to increase skill levels in writing and critical thinking of students several years after matriculation (e.g., Arum & Roksa, 2011). Moreover, of the underrepresented students who do enter college, nearly one third drop out after their first year and 50% or more never graduate (Aud et al., 2012). In sum, it is becoming increasingly clear that simply sending more students to college may have no meaningful impact on increasing the number of well-educated members of society if these newly matriculated students do not have the appropriate preparation to *succeed in* and *graduate from* college.

At the heart of every learning enterprise are the students, and the comments by the students in this chapter reflect their growth as students and their integration of academic and ethnocultural identities that will serve them in good stead in their college journeys. As the attrition data in Chapter 9 indicate, we were successful with some students and not with others for reasons that are still not fully understood. As stated earlier, one goal of interviewing students was to obtain feedback to help us to continue to work on and refine the CAL Prep partnership, which remains a work in progress. As WS notes below, he thinks that there are ways in which we succeeded and there are areas in which CAL Prep needs to grow.

WS: I would say that [CAL Prep] prepared me in some ways, and then in some ways maybe not so much. I mean it's a fairly new school in comparison to other schools in the area that really aren't necessarily even doing as good a job as CAL Prep is doing, but I would say that on the front of academics, CAL Prep is doing a good job in preparing students to, you know, perform on standardized tests, as we have done, and going to college, with the expectation that it's going to be rigorous and preparing us with the skill set that we need to, you know, deal with the level of rigor.

But in ways that I think about college as in a space for individuals to come and to be activists and, you know, speak to change and be really critical of society and the institution itself, I'm not sure that CAL Prep has done the best job at doing that for its students because of the pressures and the weight of making sure that students perform well academically. And so I would say that, you know, CAL Prep is doing well, but there is room for growth and creating a space where your graduates are going out into the world and they are equipped with the skills that they need to be critical of society, and I think that's what they're going to need, especially considering that these, you know, individuals that are graduating from CAL Prep are, you know, considered to be underrepresented individuals. They're going to need to have that skill set in order to be successful, in order to really, you know, like I said before, effect change, which is definitely needed.

In this final quote, WS's critique of CAL Prep is ironically complimentary. Although he is criticizing the school for not inculcating a critical mindset, his comment speaks to the fact that he has developed such a mindset and is willing to communicate his criticism back to the school. Thus, although he may see this as a deficit of CAL Prep, his very critique speaks to the success of CAL Prep in helping to create an academic identity in its students that integrates academic performance with concerns about equity and social justice. If all of the students recognize that academic achievement takes place in a socio-historical context that must be a part of how they understand issues (see Chapter 10), CAL Prep has done very well by its graduates to date and looks forward to continuing to promote critical academic identities into the future. As a postscript, Alana Banks (quoted above) was a vocal participant in the "Black Lives Matter" protest marches in Oakland, California, in December of 2014.

# References

Arum, R., & Roksa, J. (2011). *Academically adrift: Limited learning on college campuses.* Chicago, IL: The University of Chicago Press.

Arum, R. & Shavit, Y. (1995). Secondary vocational education and the transition from school to work. *Sociology of Education, 68,* 187–204.

Aud, S., Fox, M., & KewalRamani, A. (2010). *Status and trends in the education of racial and ethnic groups* (NCES 2010-015). U.S. Department of Education, National Center for Education Statistics. Washington, DC: U.S. Government Printing Office.

Aud, S., Hussar, W., Johnson, F., Kena, G., Roth, E., Manning, E.,.....Yohn, C. (2012). *The condition of education 2012* (NCES 2012-045). U.S. Department of Education, National Center for Education Statistics. Washington, DC: U.S. Government Printing Office.

Burleson, D. A., Hallett, R. E., & Park, D. K. (2008). College knowledge: An assessment of urban student's awareness of college processes. *College and University, 84,* 10–17.

Ceci, S. J., & Papierno P. B. (2005). The rhetoric and reality of gap closing: When the "have-nots" gain but he "haves" gain even more. *American Psychologist, 60,* 149–160. doi:10.1037/0003-066X.60.2.149

Covington, M. V. (1992). *Making the grade: A self-worth perspective on motivation and school reform.* Cambridge, UK: Cambridge University Press.

Dai, D. Y., & Chen, F. (2013). Three paradigms of gifted education: In search of conceptual clarity in research and practice. *Gifted Child Quarterly, 57,* 151–168. doi:10.1177/0016986213490020

Dweck, C. S. (2006). *Mindset: The psychology of success.* New York, NY: Ballantine.

Ericsson, K. A., Krampe, R. T., & Tesch-Römer, C. (1993). The role of deliberate practice in the acquisition of expert performance. *Psychological Review, 100,* 363–406. doi:10.1037/0033-295X.100.3.363

Gladwell, M. (2008). *Outliers: The story of success.* New York, NY: Little, Brown, & Company.

Graham, S. (2004). "I can, but do I want to?" Achievement values in ethnic minority children and adolescents. In G. Philogène (Ed.), *Racial identity in context: The legacy of Kenneth B. Clark* (pp. 125–147). Washington, DC: American Psychological Association.

Hooker, S., & Brand, B. (2010). College knowledge: A critical component of college and career readiness. *New Directions for Youth Development, 127,* 75–85.

Horn, C. (2014). The young scholars model. In C. M. Adams & K. L. Chandler (Eds.), *Effective program models for gifted students from underserved populations* (pp. 45–60). Waco, TX: Prufrock Press.

Marsh, H. W., & Hau, K. (2003). Big-fish-little-pond effect on academic self-concept: A cross-cultural (26-country) test of the negative effects of academically selective schools. *American Psychologist, 58,* 364–376. doi:10.1037/0003-066X.58.5.364

Nasir, N. S. (2012). *Racialized identities: Race and achievement among African American youth.* Stanford, CA: Stanford University Press.

Nasir, N. S., McLaughin, M. W., & Jones. A. (2009). What does it mean to be African American? Constructions of race and academic identity in an urban public high school. *American Educational Research Journal, 46*, 73–114. doi:10.3102/0002831208323279

Ness, C. (2012, May). *Against formidable odds, four from CAL Prep are entering Berkeley this fall.* Retrieved from http://newscenter.berkeley.edu/2012/06/04/31377/

Oakes, J. (1983). Limiting opportunity: Student race and curricular difference in secondary vocational education. *American Journal of Education, 91*, 328–355.

Ogbu, J. U. (Ed.). (2008). *Minority status, oppositional culture, and schooling.* New York, NY: Routledge.

Phinney, J. S. (1990). Ethnic identity in adolescents and adults: A review and integration. *Psychological Bulletin, 108*, 499–514. doi:10.1037/0033-2909.108.3.499

Plucker, J. A., Hardesty, J., & Burroughs, N. (2013). *Talent on the sidelines: Excellence gaps and America's persistent talent underclass.* Storrs, CT: Center for Education Policy Analysis, Neag School of Education, University of Connecticut.

Renzulli, J. S. (1986). The three-ring conception of giftedness. A developmental model for promoting creative productivity. In R. J. Sternberg & J. E. Davidson (Eds.) *Conceptions of giftedness* (pp. 52–92). New York, NY: Cambridge University Press.

Sosniak, L. A. (1995). Inviting adolescents into academic communities: An alternative perspective on systemic reform. *Theory into Practice, 34*, 35–42. doi:10.1080/00405849509543655

Sosniak, L. A. (1999). An everyday curriculum for the development of talent. *The Journal of Secondary Gifted Education, 10*, 166–172.

Stanley, J. C. (1973). Accelerating the educational progress of intellectually gifted youths. *Educational Psychologist, 10*, 133–146. doi:10.1080/00461527309529108

Steele, C. M. (1997). A threat in the air: How stereotypes shape intellectual identity and performance. *American Psychologist 52*, 613–629. doi:10.1037/0003-066X.52.6.613

Steele, D. M., & Cohn-Vargas, B. (2013). *Identity safe classrooms: Places to belong and learn.* Thousand Oaks, CA: Corwin.

Subotnik, R. F., Olszewski-Kubilius, P., & Worrell, F. C. (2011). Rethinking giftedness and gifted education: A proposed direction forward based on psychological science. *Psychological Science in the Public Interest, 12*, 3–54. doi:10.1177/1529100611418056

Syed, M. (2010). *Bounce: Mozart, Federer, Picasso, Beckham, and the science of success.* New York, NY: HarperCollins Publishers.

Weinstein, R. S. (2002). *Reaching higher: The power of expectations in schooling.* Cambridge. MA: Harvard University Press.

Weinstein, R. S. (2008). Schools that actualize high expectations for all youth: Theory for setting change and setting creation. In M. Shinn & H. Yoshikawa (Eds.), *Toward positive youth development: Transforming school and community programs* (pp. 81–101). New York, NY: Oxford University Press.

Whiting, G. W. (2006). Enhancing culturally diverse males' scholar identity: Suggestions for educators of gifted students. *Gifted Child Today, 29*(3), 46–50.

Worrell, F. C. (2003). Why are there so few African Americans in gifted programs? In C. C Yeakey & R. D. Henderson (Eds.), *Surmounting the odds: Education, opportunity, and society in the new millennium* (pp. 423–454). Greenwich, CT: Information Age, Inc.

Worrell, F. C. (2007). Ethnic identity, academic achievement, and global self-concept in four groups of academically talented adolescents. *Gifted Child Quarterly, 51*, 23–38. doi:10.1177/0016986206296655

Worrell, F. C. (2011). Promising practices in serving academically talented youth in urban settings. *Gifted Child Today, 34*(1), 44–49.

Worrell, F. C., & Hale, R. L. (2001). The relationship of hope in the future and perceived school climate to school completion. *School Psychology Quarterly, 16*, 370–388. doi:10.1521/scpq.16.4.370.19896

Worrell, F. C., & Young, A. E. (2012, November). *Revisiting the big-fish-little-pond-effect in academically talented students.* Poster presented at the annual meeting of the National Association for Gifted Children, Denver, CO.

# 16 | From Parallel Tracks to Intertwined Efforts: Aspire Public Schools Reflects

**ELISE DARWISH AND TATIANA EPANCHIN-TROYAN**

*"[CAL Prep] is the only school of our secondaries that has this kind of [college] affiliation. This is their public university, they have access, and that's normal. And I think that's a really powerful thing for communities . . . to have an enduring partnership that is evolving to meet the next challenge that rises, that's an incredible gift. There is a natural curiosity that stays part of our collaborative effort, that asks how do we get it better next time?"* (Kimi Kean, Bay Area Superintendent, Aspire Public Schools, 2014–present)

ALTHOUGH CALIFORNIA COLLEGE PREPARATORY ACADEMY (CAL Prep) opened in 2005, the first discussion about the partnership with the University of California (UC) Berkeley took place in February, 2003. I (Darwish) served as the first regional superintendent of schools for Aspire Public Schools and hence worked closely with CAL Prep from the planning days through the first 2 years of the school's operation (2003–2007). Currently, I am Chief Academic Officer for Aspire Public Schools. I vividly remember deep conversations about our vision for CAL Prep taking place in an empty banquet hall during a workshop about early college high schools held by the Woodrow Wilson National Fellowship Foundation. At the time, early college high schools were cropping up all over the country as a way to provide college experiences to high school students—thus making the transition to college easier.

Aspire Public Schools was interested in opening a new high school in partnership with a university, so that we could offer students a college experience that would match the rigor of a prestigious university. UC Berkeley seemed to be a natural choice for us because of their desire to serve first-generation college students just as we did. After numerous meetings with different committees at the university to identify ways in which we both saw the partnership as beneficial, we hammered out all the details of the memorandum of understanding between the UC Berkeley and Aspire Public Schools in that banquet hall. At the time, we poured over every word to make sure it was clear who made which decisions. Who picked the curriculum? When could we use the UC Berkeley insignia? Who ran payroll? Who held the charter? It was a new kind of partnership for us and for the University, and we all wanted to get it right. In hindsight, what we should have written was

> Each team will do what they're best at doing. When there's not agreement, we'll talk it through. We'll both focus on serving our students.

This *implicit understanding* of our relationship and mission is why CAL Prep succeeds.

At the time of our meetings with UC Berkeley, Aspire operated 12 schools across California. Although we had much to learn, we understood the operations of running a school. Our educational program had been established and our student achievement results as measured by the state tests were outperforming district schools, particularly in our elementary schools. Our secondary model was still forming as we only had two secondary schools, Grades 6–12, one in Stockton and the other in Oakland. Since then, the Aspire system has expanded to include 38 schools, and we are the highest-performing large public school system serving students, at least two thirds of which are from low-income families, in California. A lot of what we have learned came from our partnership with UC Berkeley.

The opening of CAL Prep was bumpier than most of our school openings. Unlike at most of our other Aspire schools, the students at CAL Prep came from all over the county, which meant we did not have a cohesive or geographically coherent family population. The Aspire name had also attracted siblings of the co-located elementary school we ran. The UC Berkeley affiliation, as well as its design as a regional school, had attracted families from all over the county. All of the other schools we had started were primarily neighborhood schools, with students knowing each other and sharing a common school experience. With students coming from so many backgrounds, the establishment of a strong school culture was paramount to bringing together this student community. This initial challenge, combined with our nascent partnership with UC Berkeley, meant that the school's start-up year was a steep learning curve for both partners as we furiously worked to meet the vision we had established together.

## Two Organizational Cultures

As we began working together, the differences in our organizations became clear. Despite having been around for 16 years, Aspire is a start-up organization and has a strong start-up culture of getting work done. When we see something that needs to be done, we do it as quickly as we can. We share an intense sense of urgency because the needs of schools, principals, teachers, and students are constant and immediate. We are not impulsive, but people in a start-up mode do not take a lot of time to discuss all of the options or do extensive research. The UC Berkeley is an established and respected research university. The work is deep and careful. As Rhona Weinstein explained, this is one of the theories on why institutions of higher education have lasted so long. The professors and students keep a deep focus on their purpose and are not immediately reactive to changing circumstances. A useful analogy might be this: while Aspire is playing Pac Man, UC Berkeley is playing chess. Both games can provide hours of entertainment, but the skills are very different.

These two styles were evident as we began to address our issues around student culture. Aspire's approach was to establish tight procedures for everything from passing between classes to going to the bathroom. The principal took on the role of monitoring and correcting students' short-term behavior so teachers could teach. The school leadership did not hold a lot of discussions or meetings about how to structure the systems; they just implemented them. The UC Berkeley team wanted to take a deeper dive into (1) understanding the needs of the students and their backgrounds and (2) building a community. They created surveys to send out to families, began methodically researching problems, arranged meetings with the staff and our joint committee, and shared research about the soft habits of mind needed to succeed in the long term. Theirs was a long-term view on student culture in the school.

At the time, both parties seemed willing to accept the actions of the partner but not engage in each other's work. We worked on parallel tracks toward the same goal. Both perspectives were needed to make sense of the challenges in front of us. We also recognized that we needed an immediate sense of safety and routine to establish a calm sense of learning for the students and the teachers in the school. We also needed a long-term view on how to build our students' internal skills as well as share our lessons learned and work with others outside the school. Both organizations approached the problem leveraging their own expertise, but each found the other's approach puzzling.

The work of each organization began to intertwine more when we began to look at the academic levels of our students. When we first began diagnosing our students' academic proficiency, the results were not heartening. At the end of the first year, only 14% of CAL Prep students scored *proficient* on the English Language Arts section of the state test. As a relatively new charter management organization, Aspire's existence and potential growth was largely dependent on showing our students' success on the California Standards Test, the only external measure that funders, sponsoring districts, and parents could use to compare our performance. Although we truly wanted to prepare students to be strong readers and writers, our measurement of progress rested largely on the state tests.

UC Berkeley shared the desire to help students become better readers and writers, but their measures of success were not the same as ours. Their view was a deeper and more long-term one with a focus on learning ways to have a future impact on school systems. They wanted students to do well on the test just as Aspire wanted students to learn at a deeper level, but they did not share Aspire's concern or sense of urgency about the annual test scores.

Luckily in this case, the means to increase student test scores and foster better reading comprehension was a common solution. The former Dean of the School of Education, David Pearson, is an expert in reading instruction. He agreed to help launch a study into evaluating and implementing READ 180, a reading software program already running in one of our other secondary schools. Pearson's study ultimately informed our thinking about student reading and allowed us to do the work of teaching while Berkeley studied the work in order to inform our thinking about instruction and content. This study also led to the library intervention project, spearheaded by Goodin and Pearson (Chapter 8). This was a great example of a joint undertaking in service to the students that took the deep research expertise at UC Berkeley and the operational knowledge of undertaking a classroom study by Aspire. Ultimately, our work together was successful as students' reading scores grew and we learned much about our implementation of the program. Our most recent state assessments show 61% of our students are proficient or above in English Language Arts.

In the beginning years of opening a school, there's much work to do to get the school running successfully. In the early years of CAL Prep, each of the two partners (Aspire and UC Berkeley) gave the other a wide berth to do its work and believed that as long as the CAL Prep continued to improve and the work was good for students, both sides were pretty willing to work in a similar space on different aspects of the work.

Some choices were easy for us. It was not difficult for us to choose the founding principal for CAL Prep together. After an extensive search, we found an experienced individual pursuing his doctorate at UC Berkeley in the same program as one of our most successful principals. The two principals were going to co-locate schools in the same building, so the person seemed like a natural fit. He was both a fit for Aspire and a member of the UC Berkeley community. As well, when both teams agreed that we needed an experienced mathematics (math) teacher, we talked to a successful teacher at a different Aspire school. His experience with Aspire in another Oakland neighborhood made him a perfect candidate for the open position at CAL Prep. He believed in Aspire and was willing to leave his school team to support students at CAL Prep. His hard work and commitment to students were key in making the school the high-performing place it is. Subsequently, a principal who had a tremendous impact at CAL Prep came from another Aspire secondary school.

## Emerging Strain: Model School or Model District

The strain came later in the evolution of the school, when decisions were made for the good of all Aspire schools and not only CAL Prep. The most stressful times in which we experienced conflicts arose when key decisions had to be made that affected both partners. Aspire currently runs 38 schools. Our mission is that every student is prepared to earn a college degree. We made a decision early in our history to serve students directly rather than devoting our energies to influence districts or other educators to change. We knew every school district had "lighthouse" schools, which showed great success. However, this success rarely seemed to have an impact on other schools, especially schools serving underserved children. Our goal was to develop quality schools and the organization to a large enough scale that our success would be in direct competition with the local school district. That is, we believed we could better serve failing students directly rather than through the sharing of best practices. To us, this meant all of our schools had to be successful. In contrast, when

UC Berkeley began the partnership with us, it wanted to co-construct one high-performing school that could serve as a flagship to inform others about how to best serve students, particularly first-generation college students. In addition, it understood the complexities of running a school and believed that the research would be richer if it was done in a real-life setting. Usually these goals were compatible—what was best for the school usually aligned with what was best for Aspire. But in this situation, the goals were mutually exclusive, and it created tension in the partnership.

Our needs clashed when CAL Prep began creating the talent we needed at other schools or in our home office. Several individuals have left CAL Prep but stayed in the Aspire system. The founding principal became our Dean of Student Services. A very successful humanities teacher left CAL Prep to lead our teacher effectiveness work. Last year when one of our high schools did not have a principal, CAL Prep's dean took over. Each time we'd talk to the UC Berkeley team about a transition, their frustration was clear: "We've invested a lot of energy in the human capital of these individuals and built strong relationships. Why are you taking them away?" Both of us have made a series of trade-offs, and we expect that the tension between what is good for the school and good for all our schools will never go away. At the heart of the matter, working in urban schools is hard. The teaching talent pool is not currently deep enough to meet the needs of all schools. Both Aspire and UC Berkeley want to serve students in a great way. The means to the ends are just different.

## Change in Bay Area Superintendents: California College Preparatory Academy in 2010

I (Epanchin-Troyan) served as the Aspire Bay Area Superintendent from 2010–2014 with oversight for CAL Prep. I followed Gloria Lee, a member of the Aspire founding team who had just completed 3 years as the Bay Area Superintendent (after Darwish) and moved to a position at the NewSchools Venture Fund. As a former teacher and principal within Aspire, I brought strength around helping principals develop instructional leadership expertise.

CAL Prep was in its sixth year—its first year as a Grade 9–12 high school and first graduating class. I did not have any concerns coming in about the partnership, partly because I had not played this role before. However, I did feel a tension about the fact that CAL Prep is only one tenth of my work—really more like one twelfth if you count the work that I do for Home Office and our charter district. Tension is perhaps too strong a word. I spend three Mondays a month in the afternoon for what we say is going to be an hour, but typically is longer, and these are three hours that I do not put into my other nine schools. Because I still provide the CAL Prep principal the same amount of coaching as I provide to other principals, this is additional time for CAL Prep because of the partnership. On the other hand, we came up with the idea about doing the College Week at one of these meetings. Good things come out of these meetings, so it is not wasted time.

I also ask myself the following questions: Are we meeting the needs of the UC Berkeley partnership? Are we aligned? Are we working toward the same outcome? Do we believe the same things about kids and what is possible for them? Ultimately, I think that we are aligned. The work we do each and every day is quite different from what university faculty members do every single day. What I am doing as a teacher, who is dealing with a student who is homeless, who has mental health issues, and who is texting me at 10:30 at night, could feel really far removed at times from this UC Berkeley partnership or from the realities of what has allowed CAL Prep to become CAL Prep. Ultimately, I see our work as concentric layers. We are all working for the same outcomes, but at different levels. I do not see the levels as really being hierarchical in any way, just on different planes in support of the same goal. In my opinion, more and more of our youth should be ready for college, and it is also important to debunk the myth that children of color who are poor cannot learn. The more people who can be involved in carrying that torch, regardless of the plane they are working on, the better for the world.

## Growing Our Own

When I first walked into CAL Prep in August of 2010 (Year 6), I found an extraordinary leader there, who ultimately served as principal for 4 years and dean of students for 1 year. This principal was very strong on building and sustaining a school culture that had been greatly needed—supporting faculty and making sure they feel really appreciated, knowing every single student by name and story, and developing programs such as advisory. Some of the issues that we worked on in partnership were raising expectations for the leadership team (in math, science, and humanities) and building capacity so that it was not so leader-dependent. We knew that at some point the school would need to survive a principal transition. We got partly there, supporting the environment to be prepared for the transition to the following principal (2012–present) who was to take distributed leadership to another level. The hiring process for the new principal was an incredible collaborative experience with participation by teachers, parents, and UC Berkeley. Maybe the folks on the UC Berkeley end were worried that we would go ahead without them, but I cannot imagine making a decision about who leads that school without our partners at the table.

At that time, CAL Prep had stronger and weaker teachers, so that the students were getting an inconsistent experience. We worked hard on hiring but also on instructional leadership, leveraging what this principal had started as a sophisticated and differentiated model of observation of teachers where once a teacher passed out of one domain (culture, lesson plan execution, and discourse), he or she moved to the next one. She rose to that expectation, once she had more of the tools. And then Aspire garnered the Bill & Melinda Gates Foundation grant to implement the Effective Teaching Research Project focused on teacher assessment. We learned by trying things out and by making mistakes—and then learning from them.

One key to our success has been internal hiring for critical positions. Our most successful principals are the principals who have been teachers or administrators with us—the one exception being an individual who came from an aligned organization. Principals who come from outside our network really struggle. They struggle because they have to learn so much about Aspire and the Bay area. They have to figure out all the inner workings of the school, and they do not have any established relationships. Our transition to the new principal was smooth in part because of the school's strong leadership team and in part because he had been a teacher with us. He knew what it meant to be working in a small school and understood that we do whatever it takes. There is no point in complaining about facility constraints, because someone else is working with more constraints. The situation we face is not as dire because of the community of students and families and because we know we can do this. Whereas someone from a traditional district or from another program would perceive the inevitable obstacles as running into walls, an internal hire would say "OK" and "jump over the wall."

An internal hire also gets automatic credibility from folks on the team because they know that this individual appreciates what it is like to be a teacher with Aspire Public Schools and a leader in some of our other schools. It is how I earned credibility, too. There are people who work at Aspire who knew me when I was a teacher, a lead teacher, and a beginning principal. It helps when someone can say, "I know this is why she's good, and I know that this is what she believes about kids." That's invaluable. It should be noted also that the new principal was drawn to CAL Prep because of its partnership with an institution of higher learning. He is a huge reader and thinker. He gets a lot out of the fact that there are many people out there, who with one small e-mail could provide an incredible amount of information. That feels very supportive to him.

Internal hiring has led to better and easier transitions. Of course, it is coupled with a unity of purpose and a focus on affiliation with Aspire. For us this means that we do not fight only for our own schools. It is not just about my four walls. We need to take into account that we are a part of a larger context. And so where the principal at CAL Prep has UC Berkeley to lean on, the principal at another school has this amazing building. Instead of anger about the differences, we promote the sharing of resources. Where we can, we ask how we can help everybody improve.

CAL Prep easily could rest on its laurels. We have been outperforming the other high schools in the Bay Area for a long time. But we are going to keep on running. We are all working on equity now, so we are going to have our staffs cross-collaborate and we are going to look at student ratings. Also, our high school teachers are going to get a better idea of what our elementary school students are doing, so that they understand why students come to ninth grade writing as they do. In addition, as has happened with the high school faculty and the UC Berkeley faculty, we are trying to do that with the lower and upper grades. We are wired at Aspire to just keep moving forward.


## Challenges for the Partnership

A challenge for us is reviving the early college model. We definitely have moved away but see it as a temporary move. When we started talking about early college with UC Berkeley, it was a time when students younger than 18 could take community college classes for a very low per-unit enrollment fee. So the incurred cost was not large. Instead, it was this amazing opportunity. All we had to do is get our students there or get a teacher to come to us. Since then, we have experienced a deep recession, and now the cost of community college classes has risen sharply. Earlier, we required 30 college units, and we kept lowering it and lowering it and lowering it, because 30 units were too expensive for us to sustain. This reduced requirement was always talked about as temporary; when the economy recovered, we were going to move it back up. We are beginning again; we are going to "grandfather" some of our older classes in, but next year's freshmen will have to complete 15 units.

The biggest challenge is a building. Everything depends on buildings. Staying at our current school (St. Joseph the Worker) is not a long-term plan. At this size, CAL Prep is a school that is in the red, which Aspire is floating; there is a bit less floating because of some of the monies that come in through UC Berkeley. One day we will get a new building, but I do not know when. Then, finally, we will be able to make several kinds of important decisions. We will decide whether we will remain a Grade 9–12 school and just expand it by a section in every grade. Or will we make it a Grade 6–12 or a 7–12 school, with an added section so the school can be more financially sustained? CAL Prep is our only Grade 9–12 school. Our model still is K–5 and 6–12, which UC Berkeley wanted as well. But in reality, in the Bay Area, out of 10 schools, we only have 2 schools that are Grade 6–12 and 3 schools that are Grade K–5. All the other configurations (K–6, 7–12, K–8, and 9–12) were decisions made because of building size. We have had to go off-model because of inadequate buildings. When I first started and we were talking about being new principals, we were all amazed that we spent so much time talking about buildings. But as a charter and especially in a place such as the Bay Area, we are very building-dependent.

Whatever the move is, it is going to feel like the school is going in reverse for a time, because there will be much new work to do. It is easy to underestimate what it might be like to take on a middle school, for example. It is probably less challenging to take on new sections in the same grades already served, especially if we can grow it out, so that we take in an extra 9th grade and then the next year, 9th and 10th, and the third year, 9th and 11th. I think the partnership will have to be open to all the different scenarios that might be. Right now it is comfortable. CAL Prep is a Grade 9–12 school, all the students are getting accepted to college, three or four of them every year are going to UC Berkeley, and others are going to other UC campuses. CAL Prep has been successful because of its small size and because of its design. The small size has helped it to be successful quickly, as has the fact that CAL Prep was able to groom its own students in sixth grade. The first group of students started as sixth graders and grew up the school. These students helped the culture gel. When I think of our larger high schools (still small; less than 500 students), it took them twice as long to achieve at the level of CAL

Prep, but they got there. So it is not a matter of whether it is possible or not. It is absolutely possible.

Taking on more students is going to require some sort of shifting and more growing pains again. It can be jarring for students already in the community, and it really can be jarring for the adults in the community, because they are so used to what exists. It is going to require a lot of open-mindedness and reflection back to, "Well, what did we do last time when this was an issue, or how can we think about it differently?" The key to success moving forward is being open to some small failures in order to get back to a place that sustains success.

## Dividends from the Partnership

**For the University of California, Berkeley.** I would hope that the professors who attend the CAL Prep faculty meetings (Early College Initiative) better understand the students who will be coming to them than they might have if they were not part of these conversations. Not just those students coming from CAL Prep but the sort of student that CAL Prep represents—an underserved demographic in the state. I would hope that it gives them insight into the barriers that these students surmount in order to be at UC Berkeley or at any institution of higher learning. Not that folks will make excuses for our students, but faculty will have a little more empathy or thoughtfulness when they are interacting with students who look like and have histories like some of our CAL Prep students. Also, I would hope that the fact that we are all working together keeps people grounded in why they are researching what they are researching and in why they are teaching. We are all working toward the same goal—bigger than just a university or just a high school.

**For Aspire.** One very tangible gain from the partnership is the College Week. I love that we do it because it allows our students to have a tiny glimpse of college life that they do not get by simply going on college trips. Another example is becoming more aware of opportunities that we can then spread to other Aspire schools. With Phyllis Goldsmith's work on college writing, we now have teachers, not just from CAL Prep, but from other schools who have the opportunity to collaborate with the university. I would not have known about that if I did not sit at the table with Phyllis some of the time. This is the same with access to social work interns (Susan Stone in Social Welfare) and to family engagement and college readiness programs (Gail Kaufman in the Center for Educational Partnerships). It is also good for us at the high school and elementary school level to hear about what is being discussed at the higher education level. Somebody will reference an article, I will ask for it, and I will have it in my inbox the next day. That article ends up being shared across Aspire.

Another place where the partnership really helps is in recruitment of staff. Some people gravitate toward CAL Prep because it is connected to a university that is as renowned as UC Berkeley, and that is really enticing for some people. This connection makes possible opportunities for CAL Prep teachers, especially in math and science, to work with professors that teachers at our other schools do not have. For example, Tatiana Lim-Breitbart (Chapter 12) did a significant amount of work on the science standards; this opportunity came to her as a result of where she was teaching and her exposure to faculty at UC Berkeley. She sat with a myriad of different science experts to write the Next Generation Science Standards for California. It is really meaningful to have someone who can explain the "why" behind all the various standards that were adopted. She is now an expert for us in science and that is a huge gift to our organization.

Lastly, I do not want to overlook how much of what is so strong about CAL Prep is brought to other schools within the Aspire system through the movement of staff. CAL Prep's Wrap-Around Services Coordinator, Michelle Cortez (Chapter 13), is now a principal at another Aspire high school. What she understands about school culture and student supports, learned through the partnership, is now being utilized elsewhere. Another example is Stacy Thomas (Chapter 11), who brought knowledge from another school to CAL Prep to help it get stronger and now has moved to another school that needs his expertise. His beliefs about student capability grew from what he saw at CAL Prep and because of the nurturing that he received, not only from people in the partnership but also from the other adults in the building. He is now a dean and helping lead a school that is not experiencing the same degree of success *yet*. I think that this results from the fact that there are many smart people working at CAL Prep on these multiple levels. This is where the power of the partnership comes in; we have not yet felt it all the way, because this movement of individuals takes place over time, at points where the school is strong enough to survive the change.

# Conclusion

CAL Prep is unlike any other Aspire school because of the remarkable partnership that has built this amazing school that continues to evolve and inform the work with our students. This uniqueness is great for the students. They get an additional group of smart, talented individuals focusing on serving them in the best possible way. The school receives rigorous caring, deep questioning, and additional resources including tutors, college experiences and thought partners that none of our other schools get. Aspire gets another set of eyes on our practices and plans. We are exposed to renowned university experts and thoughtful researchers to help us think through hard problems such as supporting our students' social emotional growth. Although the process sometimes involves attending a labyrinth of meetings with different committees at UC Berkeley, and Berkeley being patient with our urgency to get things done, we ultimately are better for having partnered because of the relationships we have built: student to faculty member, Aspire teachers to UCB professors, Aspire home office staff to UCB staff.

Educating underserved students is not for the faint of heart: to do this work you need a team of people working alongside with whom you can laugh at the absurd situations, celebrate the big and small victories, and keep asking the questions that push our work forward. You need people who can pick you up on a hard day or provide an answer when you cannot find one. You need a team of caring individuals who want what you do. This is what we have found in our partnership with UC Berkeley.

# 17 | Conclusion—The Power of a University–District Partnership

**RHONA S. WEINSTEIN, FRANK C. WORRELL, GAIL KAUFMAN, AND GIBOR BASRI**

*"The creators [of new settings] were crystal clear . . . that vigilance about values and goals has to be constant and never ending because it is the price paid for the opportunity to remain free from stifling tradition."* (Sarason, 1998, p. 94)

HERE ARE MILLIONS OF CHILDREN and youth in our nation who do not have access to excellent and equitable schools (1) where their intellect, character, and interests are nurtured and (2) where they are prepared for productive lives. Although many debate the capacity of schools to serve as an engine of social mobility amid problems of poverty and discrimination, the evidence is resoundingly clear that good schools make a critical difference. In a tide of ever rising expectations where "college is for the masses," evidence is growing about the positive benefit of enrollment in and graduation from a 4-year college, especially so for students who have had marginal histories in school (Leonhardt, 2015, p. 1).

Yet on the other side, backlash against these higher expectations is also increasing, as reflected in the title ("How college prep is killing high school") of a *Boston Globe* article by Rumberger (2011). Here, Rumberger warned against the "college ready for all mantra . . . pushing for a tougher and more competitive high school education," which, in narrowing the focus of high school curricula, may result in even more dropouts. And indeed, the possibility of failure is very real. Note this headline in the *Los Angeles Times*: "LAUSD college prep rule puts nearly 75% of 10th graders' diplomas at risk" (Blume, 2015). Are we again at the cusp of having raised standards but failing to meet them because we have not *done enough* to change the inherently unequal conditions of secondary schools? Furthermore, is tough, competitive, and narrow the only road ahead in secondary school reform? Finally, although college-going may not be the best path for all students, must we not ensure that the door to college, if needed or chosen, is open to all? These children are our economic and civic future and deserve our very best efforts.

The partnership between a research university and a charter management organization was our method of building a secondary school that delivered the goods—a college-preparatory education for students who have been underserved. As co-creators of this new setting, we worked hard to remain free from what Sarason (1998) called "stifling tradition" and to innovate in our efforts to eradicate entrenched educational disparities that constrain the development of too many children and youth.

California College Preparatory Academy (CAL Prep) did not *begin* as a life-altering school, but rather it *became* one. Together, we succeeded in turning the normative tumult of the early years into a positive and coherent college-preparatory school culture with the capacity to change the academic trajectory of first-generation college youth. As each chapter made clear, the significant features of school design and our bridging efforts across the secondary–tertiary education divide were progressively built, as was staff capacity to implement these programs and practices. Importantly, these chapters also gave voice to the experiences of a diversity of partners at multiple levels, including working across institutional cultures with mutual respect; engaging in formative research endeavors that served the school's development first; and learning from teachers, administrators, students, and parents about unmet needs, best practices, and conditions necessary for growth. We hope that readers caught a glimpse of themselves somewhere in these pages and drew a dose of optimism about the enterprise.

In this concluding chapter, we return to the three questions framed in Chapter 1. What are the advantages of a sustained partnership between a research university and a charter school district in eliminating achievement gaps and the leaky pipeline? What can we learn from the school creation process that can inform theories about settings and action as well as about the capacity for innovation? What kind of high school provides a fair chance to enable all students, but especially first-generation college students, to meet the highest expectations of college readiness and college success? As partnership, school creation, and a fair chance reflect intertwined aspects of our method, we address these questions in interwoven ways, first, in the identification of six cross-cutting lessons learned, and second, in our assessment of the successes achieved and challenges faced in this collaborative journey. Finally, we explore the implications of this work, examining the generalizability of these lessons to other contexts and the significance of such lessons for practice, policy, and research.

## On Lessons Learned

### Engaging Hearts and Minds

What reflects excellence and equity in a high school education? We learned early on that we must pay close attention to the development of the whole student and to engagement in learning. Engaging the hearts and minds of students leads to deeper, more meaningful, and sustained learning— critical for college readiness and for a productive life journey.

In the research reported here on advisories, students boldly told us what they needed from their secondary school. In response, we targeted holistic development over academic development alone and prioritized engagement over compliance, while nesting students within a caring school-centered rather than subject matter–centered culture (e.g., Fredericks, Blumenfeld, & Paris, 2004). We overcame a narrowed curriculum prevalent under high-stakes testing and closed the opportunity gap in access to enrichment, thus embracing a broadened view of learning and more differentiated expectations. By youth development, we meant *more than* the inclusion of social-emotional skills or character development. We also invested in the cultivation of talents, college and career preparation, the development of coping skills for transitions (such as self-controlled success), and the forging of collaboration with families around college-going. Opportunities across these domains sparked student interest, fueled the hard work required and the development of multiple competencies, and enabled the emergence of an academic identity, respectful of ethnocultural heritage.

### An Aligned and Responsive Pathway to College Readiness

An aligned and responsive pathway ensures that all students had access to and could *thrive* in an educational program that prepares them for college eligibility and college success. Prescribed for all, this transparent pathway is far more indicative of an elite independent school than of the typical comprehensive "shopping mall" high school (Powell, Farrar, & Cohen,

1985), where variety, student interest, and neutrality about program choice are underlying themes. Whether intended or not, in such school settings, curricular tracking, differential social capital (such as past performance and college knowledge), and counselor or teacher recommendation determine inherently unequal programs.

A pathway model, both universal and accommodative, required organizing our high school differently to build in a coherent, challenging and aligned, and developmentally responsive and supportive program that addresses the domains of youth development noted above. This meant preparing teachers both to teach for rigor (the complex cognitive skills critical to inquiry learning) and also to meet the needs of adolescents for engagement, connection, competence–development, and autonomy. Also, this meant creating a positive and inclusive culture with strong and trusting relationships (teacher–student, peer, and parents) and respect for diverse cultures. Although these setting features are important for all adolescents, they are especially important to students of poverty and color who face challenging life circumstances and for whom trust in schools is uncertain.

CAL Prep experimented with new ways of organizing the school year, schedules, and the work of teachers and resource personnel. The goals were to engage and reengage students (defusing disciplinary problems); provide instruction interwoven with acceleration, remediation, enrichment, and support (with second chances that kept students on the college track); minimize transitions between educational levels; and address as well as monitor college preparedness. Reflective of one-stop shopping, these features were programmed at the starting gate, rather than delivered through add-on opportunities that might compete and cancel each other out. Both these features require front-end and integrative work in promoting youth development—universally targeted—with the goal of reducing the need for more individualized interventions. With support integrated into design, curriculum, and instruction, everyone became a support provider. This reality was poignantly described by CAL Prep senior JN, who said, "It's not like you have to go see a specialized person to help you, because they've [principal, teachers] become like your own family" (Chapter 15, p. 000).

## A Boundary-Crossing Partnership

A partnership between postsecondary and secondary education opens doors across the divide and leads to mutual benefits not only for the school and its students but also for the University of California (UC) Berkeley and Aspire Public Schools. This boundary-crossing partnership became a powerful engine for rich college experiences for high school students, with new resources and formative opportunities in research and professional training. The open boundary freed students from encapsulated classrooms and neighborhoods, teachers from the confines of schools, and university faculty from their ivory tower, enlarging world views. College was made vivid and within reach for high school students, with career interests awakened and some transition challenges reduced. Working relationships between teachers and faculty deepened disciplinary understanding and pedagogy, with greater alignment of expectations and teaching across the divide, for example, in the teaching of writing. Problems of practice stimulated opportunities in community-engaged scholarship for faculty and graduate students. And district–university conversations challenged thinking about many issues, including inquiry learning, integrative supports, actionable research, silo-driven professional training, and scaling-up for new schools.

Examples of mutual benefit include the collaborative work of Stacy and Lim-Breitbart (Chapter 12), which led to adaptations in the *Living by Chemistry* high school curriculum, a vertical team for professional development in science, professional opportunities for teachers (in national meetings and on the Next Generation Science Standards Board), and a proposal at UC Berkeley for a more inclusive and responsive Introductory Chemistry course. Similar benefits accrued from our investments in an integrative support system at CAL Prep, which was disseminated to Aspire schools (Chapters 13 and 14). This work also stimulated a UC Berkeley team of Angelica Stacy, Gail Kaufman, and Alix Schwartz to examine the transition challenges and available supports in our own house, as experienced by UC Berkeley–enrolled Aspire students. These university players held monthly dinners to learn from these first-generation college students about obstacles encountered and made individual interventions to help the students resolve their problems. With their guidance, the students made presentations about transition difficulties to financial aid, housing, advising, and the Educational Opportunity Program. Advocacy by these students was part of the groundswell for the new Cal Student Central, instituted to provide a more comprehensive one-stop shopping for financial aid, billing, and course enrollments. These examples reflect the original vision of David Pearson that "our work is not only to make students college-ready but also to prepare universities to become student-ready" (Chapter 1, p. 3).

## A Culture-Challenging Mindset

Holding a culture-challenging mindset helps us identify where, what, and how we need to innovate in practice. Any vision for a new setting emerges in contrast to the prevailing status quo, with the goal of better addressing a perceived need. It was not surprising that many of us around the table, but not all, were first-generation college or postgraduate students and/or members of demographic groups that had encountered inequality or discrimination due to race, gender, or socioeconomic class. Our critical mindset, whether earned or learned as history teacher Ryan Grow noted in Chapter 10, began with the recognition that schools too often fail to create a fair and equally rigorous playing field—a reality we were determined to change. In designing our school, we railed against deficit theories about students and families, opportunity-limiting practices such as curricular tracking and disciplinary exclusion, separate professional silos for student support, and layers of uncoordinated programs.

In contrast, we embraced a collective accountability for the learning of all students; an emphasis on strengths; a belief that support is needed by all; and a partnership that spanned school, district, and university levels where authority, resources, and a coordinated focus were brought to the table. We insisted that problem diagnosis be swiftly tied to specific interventions and evaluated. We invested in promotion, evidence-based and data-driven practice, and integrative programming. We were open to expanded roles and different schedules, doing whatever it took to overcome student struggles. This culture-challenging mindset disrupted business as usual.

School creation, in contrast to school transformation, confronts designers of settings with a dizzying array of choice points all at once. However, awareness of component parts, their structural fit, and consequences are vividly heightened in the creation process, more so perhaps than in existing settings where perceptions of the whole may hide the separate institutional drivers of behavior and where the cost, both fiscal and human, is perceived as too prohibitive for change. Although open boundaries and a critical mindset shaped both goals and vision, our deliberative planning process, occurring within a learning community, helped us make strategic and integrative choices, which were evaluated and refined, again and again.

## Multilayered Learning Communities

The creation of multilayered learning communities from students to superintendent provides the enabling context for evidence-based and data-driven practice. At every level, we were immersed in dynamic learning communities.

In advisories, teachers and students appraised student progress, which was brought to quarterly student-led family–school conferences. In research studies and Aspire surveys, students and parents reported on their satisfaction and appraised qualities of teacher practices. Teachers engaged in regularized cycles of inquiry in subject-matter teams, analyzing benchmark data on student performance, making revisions in teaching practices, and reviewing results. This collegial collaboration was vividly illustrated by two mathematics (math) teachers in Chapter 11 as a critical factor in their professional growth. Teams for supports and school leadership met weekly for analysis and quick action. Our partnership meetings kept us at the table—analyzing, compromising, prioritizing, and aligning—to deepen the development of the school and strengthen the Aspire network. A growth mindset (Dweck, 2006), shared by all, encouraged challenge-seeking, persistence in the face of struggle, a capacity to learn from criticism, and inspiration from the success of others. An examination of data obtained at multiple levels shaped the direction for capacity building to strengthen individuals, programs, and systems. In these interlayered ways, we deepened our reach every year in addressing rigor, support, progressive challenge, and increased student autonomy as well as the comprehensiveness, alignment, and coherence of our programs.

## A Time-Intensive and Tightly Focused Planning Process

A time-intensive and tightly focused planning process—deliberative, strategic, and integrative—is at the core of moving cohorts of underprepared students to college eligibility and college success and of increasing the number of high-quality schools. This planning took a serious investment of time thoughtfully spent—far more time than the policy world typically allows in its orientation toward simple solutions and quick results. There was no single magic bullet or easy fix that could do the job, and the pacing was more akin to a marathon than a sprint. With eyes focused on our goals, we balanced open boundaries with tight management. We made sure that our program choices (such as a single curricular track, eighth-period support option, and credit recovery) upended the unequal status quo. We made sure that these program choices could be aligned with staffing (such as a position of dean for positive discipline and student supports) and professional development (such as strengthening teacher capacity for both rigor and support in instruction). Ongoing improvement of the school, including its instructional and supportive capacity, was progressive.

So what is the theory of action here? Our capacity to erase educational disparities rests on engaging students in an aligned and responsive pathway to a fuller youth development that included college-preparatory work. Our capacity to create a clear pathway is fueled by strategic choices, which when aligned, reduced structural misfit between subsystems of schools and enabled a more powerful setting effect, within and across classrooms (Schlechty, 2005). These aligned choices are likely behind what Larry Cuban (2013) described as some *unexpected* innovations of charter schools, seen in the greater coherence of purpose and practices observed across classrooms. Furthermore, our embrace of a culture-challenging mindset, creation of novel opportunities for students and teachers, and investment in community and capacity-building both sparks and sustains innovation (Maton, 1999). Finally, our linked reforms, strengthened by aligned professional development, deeply affects the social regularities of the school—in the culture and the quality of interactions between teachers and students—ultimately shaping student attainment (Seidman, 2012). The design work described here speaks to a parallelism of conditions—of challenge and support—among multiple levels of this cross-sector partnership.

## Striking Successes and Thorny Challenges

### The School and Student Attainment

Despite tumultuous beginnings, CAL Prep students were successful, as evident in an upward trajectory of achievement and in the results of the first two graduating classes. These results exceeded the average state and national rates as well as the comparable rates for this demographic group of largely low-income and first-generation college students of color—closing the achievement gap and plugging leaks in the pipeline from high school to college. Not all students succeeded, however. Even after controlling for school maturity (when attrition was reduced) and only measured through Years 1 to 4, African American students left the school at higher rates than did Latino students. During these early years, "leavers" perceived disrespect from teachers, pressed for a greater awareness of racism, and railed against the enormous work demands. Yet learning from these data, the school more systematically responded to these issues of equity, efforts so vividly described by Ryan Grow in the teaching of history (Chapter 10) and by Sarah Salazar and Stacy Thomas in math (Chapter 11).

As an early college high school, CAL Prep did not reach the high bar of 60 units or 2 years of college completion as envisioned by the Bill & Melinda Gates Foundation initiative. We were skeptical about this high bar in the face of enormous student underpreparedness, both academically and developmentally, and there were difficulties in providing, funding, and integrating these courses. Because of the high cost of UC Berkeley courses, access necessarily involved another layer of partnerships with several community colleges, which during the recession were in great flux. In California, community colleges faced greater course demand in the context of massive cuts in classes and higher course costs. The cost of a single unit rose from $18 in 2003–2004 to $46 in 2012, making more than five college courses per high school student financially difficult (California Community Colleges Chancellors Office, 2015). Furthermore, we also found course quality to be uneven and the scheduling of both remedial interventions and college courses difficult.

CAL Prep students did, however, achieve consistency in the successful completion of 12 to 15 college units, a graduation requirement. Also, CAL Prep was able to offer students rich opportunities at UC Berkeley beyond credit-bearing coursework, such as access to summer programs, freshman seminars, and College Week, as some examples. In our view, it was not the number of college courses completed, but the opportunities to experience college and be successful there, course by course, and to interact with faculty and college students at CAL Prep or on the campus, that became such a powerful motivator. The prospect of college was made real and attainable.

Achieving full size and fiscal viability of the school—in the context of a highly dense and expensive geographical area and with space constraints on the campus—proved to be a huge challenge. Our charter status carried uncertainty in access to a physical space as well as the costs of renting, buying, or building a school facility, making Aspire and UC Berkeley heavily dependent upon fundraising. On the UC Berkeley side, we identified donors and wrote grants that funded science laboratories, a literacy intervention program, summer and extracurricular programs as well as college visits, a dean of students position, and research studies. Although these contributions of more than a million dollars proved helpful to a small school that grew in stages, we were unable to find a significant benefactor to secure a large enough school site on or close to the Berkeley campus with space for more than 225 students. This major obstacle thwarted the original Grade 6–12 design, required one geographical move with another on the horizon, and delayed full enrollment as a secondary school. This meant that Aspire carried the financial burden for CAL Prep, as an enrollment of 450 students was needed for self-sufficiency. Securing a permanent home continued to be our highest priority—a dream finally realized in 2015 (see Epilogue).

## The Partnership

The early structures we developed, such as a memorandum of understanding (MOU) with distinct roles and responsibilities, regularized meetings (the Early College Initiative [ECI] at UC Berkeley and working partnership at CAL Prep), and records kept of meetings with feedback loops, proved resilient in handling the challenges over the long term. These collaborative mechanisms, the multidisciplinary nature of our membership, institutional growth on both sides, and the intellectual challenge of the issues kept us at the table.

On the UC Berkeley side, the ECI began as a partnership between the Division of Undergraduate Affairs (where the Center for Educational Partnerships [CEP] was housed) and the Graduate School of Education (GSE). This partnership reported to the Chancellor. When the Division of Equity and Inclusion was established in 2007, an ECI member, astronomy professor Gibor Basri, served as its first Vice Chancellor, CEP was moved to this new unit, and the Division of Equity and Inclusion joined forces with the GSE as cosponsors for the ECI. Our ECI committee had considerable administrative clout, diverse perspectives (across multiple disciplines, undergraduate, and outreach programs), and relatively stable membership—features that increased the capital we brought to the table. Unlike Preuss School at UC San Diego and UCLA Community School, we were not embedded within a research center but, instead, we had the full support of our CEP.

UC Berkeley not only got its hands "dirty" in secondary school reform in a very public way but also provided significant and continuing fiscal support for campus planning and release time or research assistant help to those with the most intensive roles, such as Gail Kaufman, Frank Worrell, and Rhona Weinstein. In addition, developments both systemwide and on the UC Berkeley campus also proved encouraging to our work, where departments might not have been. As noted earlier, a systemwide change in faculty appraisal criteria recognized contributions to equity and diversity in research, teaching, and service (University of California, 2005). The

Chancellor's Award for Advancing Institutional Excellence (University of California, Berkeley, n.d.) was instituted to recognize the work of reducing disparities, given for "providing leadership to advance equitable access to education, address the needs of California's diverse populations through public service or highlight inequities through rigorous scholarship." Furthermore, building on Chancellor Birgeneau's 2007 investment in a Division of Equity and Inclusion on the UC Berkeley campus, a $16-million gift from the Evelyn and Walter Haas, Jr. Fund brought an array of resources to the campus, including *campuswide* hiring of endowed chairs focused on disparities and diversity, which were housed ultimately in the Haas Institute for a Fair and Inclusive Society (Rodriquez, 2010). These developments institutionalized a deeper commitment to equity and diversity, and they also positioned the campus for national leadership on these issues.

On the Aspire side, at the start of the collaboration in 2003, Aspire operated 12 schools across California, with student achievement results on state tests that outperformed district schools, particularly at the elementary level. It was an auspicious time for our partnership, as Aspire's secondary model was just evolving, reflected in two secondary schools (Grade 6–12) that preceded the opening of CAL Prep. At this writing, Aspire is the largest and among the highest performing charter school operators in California, with 35 schools in California serving 13,600 students in 10 cities. With a federal grant to seed charter school growth outside California, Aspire will ultimately open 10 new charter schools (with 3 schools currently operative) in Memphis, Tennessee (Fensterwald, 2014). Among many innovative programs, Aspire developed student performance data analytic tools that are now distributed through a spin-off company called Schoolzilla (Cavanagh, 2012), invested in intensive teacher performance evaluations (Tucker, 2013), and created an alternative teacher residency professional training program (Rich, 2014).

There were enormous challenges in bringing together two disparate cultures. At the district–university level, there were complexities in the hybrid structure (one partner with legal responsibility and the other with brand responsibility) and tensions over differing priorities. As examples of these tensions, Aspire valued a replicable model, one that could be funded within the average daily allowance provided by state funds, and UC Berkeley pressed for an optimal model, which could demonstrate what it costs to accelerate and prepare underserved students to become ready for college. Aspire aimed for parity among its schools, and UC Berkeley pushed for privileging the partnered school. Finally, not surprisingly, given that as a district-level partnership, Aspire prioritized the growing of greater numbers of excellent schools, achieved in part through staff changes to spread innovation, and UC Berkeley had its eye on building a single exemplar school, with stability of staff that could serve as a training model.

At the school–university level, there were tensions between conflicting calendars (11-month vs. a 9-month academic calendar), differing priorities (big-picture issues vs. fewer focused improvement efforts), and clashing timelines (quick turnaround vs. measured reflection). The principal carried the extra burden but also seized the opportunity to become a strong as well as a collaborative leader, expected to apply research findings, be open to evaluation, and meet the expectations of both Aspire and UC Berkeley. Finally, within the university, this partnership required the building of a campus infrastructure to engage faculty, staff, and students, and also work through the obstacles presented by different cultural expectations. Among these obstacles were securing a longer-term commitment from undergraduate or graduate students in service delivery and reducing the bureaucracy so that the university could provide a speedier response to research and other requests. Also, despite campus recognition of public scholarship to address issues of equity, it remained difficult for non-tenured faculty to become engaged in such an intensive and long-term project without a clear and quick pathway to publications. As a result, we also faced a governance challenge of an aging leadership for this partnership, with the need to replenish our ranks over time and in response to different phases of school development and dissemination.

We persisted in resolving many of these challenges, including smooth transitions of personnel, we fine-tuned our differentiated but co-equal roles, and we built respect and trust, resulting in the remarkable staying power of the partners with little need to return to the MOU. Most unusually, our partnership has survived more than a decade, witnessing both flux but also stability in the players around the table. In starting a school that carries our name, we held its sustainability dear, not wanting to promise an educational opportunity but then withdraw it in a retreat back to our ivory tower. On the UC Berkeley side, we overcame many of the constraints that interfere with such sustained community-engaged scholarship and social action around reducing educational disparities (Harkavy, Hartley, Hodges, & Weeks, 2013). We worked across disciplines, departments, and professional schools, as well as staff and faculty lines, bringing programmatic, administrative, and research-based strengths to bear on what was an inherently interdisciplinary endeavor. In the eyes of Aspire, we were successful in turning what began as parallel play into intertwined efforts, a judgment with which we at UC Berkeley concurred.

## A Test Bed: From Lighthouse School to Lighthouse District

CAL Prep did become an innovative test bed for practice, research, and training (e.g., teacher preparation and professional development) but not wholly in the ways originally envisioned. A confluence of factors shaped the emerging nature of this test bed, including the school's small size (also its changing grade configuration and slow growth), our commitment to privilege the needs of our school, culture clashes between our respective institutions, and overstretched university partners. Two principles framed the identification and use of the resources (fiscal, personnel, programmatic, and intellectual) that UC Berkeley and Aspire brought to the table. First, we planned for opportunities from large to small, making room for greater participation but in less intensive ways, such as an exhibition judge or College Week faculty or workshop leader or a student inspirational visit to a faculty laboratory. Second, we held firm to our mandate of bringing resources to bear only in ways that could further the development, in an integrative way, of the school, its teachers, and its students.

What did *not* happen, at least to date, was a deep connection between CAL Prep and the GSE, despite the hiring of a number of GSE graduates and the vital role of the GSE Deans, first David Pearson and later, Judith Warren Little. This reality is reflected in the evaluation of former Dean Pearson, Co–Principal Investigator for the ECI:

> Of the four goals that were implicit in my value system—privileging students' futures, serving as a test bed, teacher preparation, and professional development—I'd give us an A+ on the first, a B+ on the second, and incompletes on the third and fourth. No question about it. CAL Prep has demonstrated in its first few graduating classes that it can help serious students of poverty and color achieve their goals for matriculating at serious institutions of higher education . . . But CAL Prep is not at the heart of our teacher education programs, nor is it the "city on the hill" for professional development. And that is not a bad outcome at all. Rather it is a reflection of CAL Prep's commitment to be, above all, a school that serves its students and their families—and serves them very well.

The less favorable but accurate evaluation of CAL Prep's relationship to GSE research and professional training programs—beyond its success as a school—reflects underlying tensions between different cultures and between different goals. The partnered creation of a high school from scratch rested on collaborative and integrative work, whereas academic norms more typically favored individual entrepreneurship and separate program silos (e.g., three separate teacher preparation programs in the GSE). Putting students first meant harnessing those resources that best fit the needs of this college-preparatory school for underprepared students, as well as the needs of the charter district. Unlike the laboratory schools of old where faculty could gain access to research subjects, children, or teachers to test hypotheses, independently derived, CAL Prep provided a welcoming test bed for a different kind of research, described in Part II of this book, and a different kind of teacher preparation and professional development.

The joint commitment to community-engaged and public scholarship—of immediate use to the school—did not match the research opportunities that many faculty members sought. In the pursuit of tests of theory, publication, and promotion, different conditions were needed for the research enterprise (e.g., a narrower focus, greater control, comparison groups, larger samples). A lack of fit also limited the placement of student teachers and principals as well as interns (from clinical and school psychology, social welfare)—in part because placement hours were not immersive enough for the needs of CAL Prep, in part because of differing emphases for professional preparation. As a campuswide initiative, we sought partners across the university, where fit could be maximized. One example was the strong link built between CAL Prep and Cal Teach, a source of undergraduates in training as teachers in the science, technology, engineering, and math fields, who first served as classroom apprentices and were ultimately hired in Aspire schools. A second example, emerging from partnership discussions and currently under development, is a reenvisioned pathway for the joint training of social welfare interns and teacher trainees in schools, toward integrative services.

Thus, CAL Prep became a test bed for innovation in research, practice, and training, with innovations flowing from Aspire and from the university. Not surprisingly, there were tensions between a program focus (particular curricula or assessments) versus a school focus (an integrative mission) and traditional versus charter practices. For Aspire, serving these students well required the resolution of long-standing problems—underprepared teachers, especially for urban classrooms; a limited pool of principal leadership; and piecemeal professional development. Meeting these goals necessitated investments in what might be called alternative or disruptive practices. These innovations included the development of Aspire's own *practice-based* teacher education program (with 1 year as an apprentice teacher and coursework credited through the University of the Pacific), a 1-year apprentice principal program, and the use of a teacher ladder (allowing part-time work, coaching, and administrative contributions). Innovations were also evident in contractual arrangements such as hiring at will without union contracts, and in an integrative professional development. Professional development focused on formative assessment, instructional differentiation, and teaching quality, with salary enhancements tied to observed teaching quality, ratings by students and parents, and the academic performance of students.

UC Berkeley's choice to partner at a district level carried with it a commitment beyond our single lighthouse school to disseminate this knowledge to many lighthouse schools. What we first perceived as a stumbling block, clinging as we did to the model school concept, became a critical lesson about scaling up and spreading innovation districtwide, by helping everyone and every school get better. Of course, there were trade-offs to be made. On the UC Berkeley side, we lost the opportunity to build an entirely stable staff with increasing proficiency in every program that the school offered. Instead, we had exceptional talent in place, many on a long-term basis, with newcomers being brought up the ranks through the teacher and principal residency program. Yet sitting at the table, we watched how Aspire grew their own talent, used internal hires, and moved expertise to other sites in order to spread exemplary practice. These practices are what Elmore (1996) described as a cell division or reproduction model of getting to scale, used by the Central Park East Elementary School (Meier, 1995) in New York to seed more schools like it. We saw the benefits of a district that succeeded in scaling up and the critical task of succession, seamlessly transitioning to new professional staff, principals, and area superintendents, without negative consequences to the culture of the school or loss of the overarching mission. These outcomes were achieved in part because of tight management, inclusive participation in the selection and training of new staff, and transparency of communication. Our eyes were opened to these possibilities of growing more high quality schools because we were at the table.

# Implications

## This Case Study in Context

We speak in this book from the vantage point of a single case study of new school creation for low-income and underrepresented minority youth— one type of university–charter district partnership, one small early college high school, and its first two graduating classes. In this tale of both success and challenge, our students have achieved college dreams. Lessons fueled by our partnership have influenced other Aspire schools as well as programs at our university. Yet, it is clear that we have also struggled, especially with the growing pains of new-start schools, building problems, and understaffing of faculty. Solving the governance issue (the need for new, younger faculty blood and greater fiscal resources) is needed to take this work to another level of public scholarship (e.g., reenvisioned training programs and dissemination efforts across charter and traditional districts).

Nonetheless, this case stands with a growing number of such university– district collaborations to open new schools and scaled-up educational opportunity. It is buttressed by rigorous evidence that redesigns of high schools have impacts on the attainment of underserved students. The value of this single case, in our view, lies in its longitudinal lens and a diversity of perspectives, as well as the rich details of partnership, collaborative research, and reflections on practice. Together, these features make vivid what the interweaving of rigor and support might look like, how such integration might be achieved at a school level, and how these innovations fuel the development of academic scholars.

We live in a highly polarized education climate—the so-called education wars—with a deep chasm between charters and other public school settings as well as tensions growing among the drivers of reform, be it federal and state governments, unions, philanthropy, or the public. We do not wish to minimize the concerns that underlie these differing positions nor the larger questions of serving all children well. But given that "low-income and minority students in urban school districts face a particularly bleak educational landscape," it is critical to move beyond the "tired and often charged school type debates" and search for the commonalities beneath the "urban education that works" (Bangser et al., 2012, p. 1).

But as Bangser and colleagues (2012) underscored, no single type of school (traditional, small, magnet, or charter) consistently succeeds or fails. Rather, the real story lies beneath the averages, in the exemplars, and over time, in the success of implementation. These authors also reveal disparate opportunities and challenges faced in the creation of new schools as compared to the transformation of existing schools—change strategies that require different types of principal leadership, as Duke (2010) has suggested. Accordingly, implementation has been the focus in this case study of new school creation. As such, it provides varied but complimentary insights into factors that stimulate innovation in new school development, propel underprepared students toward college eligibility and college readiness, and create deep cross-sector partnerships.

## Generalizability to and Collaboration with Other School Settings

We believe that the lessons outlined here—from a critical mindset, to a boundary-crossing partnership, to the strategic design of a pathway to college—can be generalized to other new-start schools and to school transformation, in traditional school districts as well as cross-national contexts, while respecting differences in governance and organization. In our view, what we achieved here was not simply the result of small school size, charter status, or the intense gaze and leveraged resources of a cross-sector partnership, although these features were helpful. Rather, the accomplishments grew from bold goals, strong design, thoughtful implementation, much support, and a sustained focus on refinement of the work. The use of evidence-based and data-driven planning, the development of teacher quality, and the building of a strong and trusting community are well-known features of school improvement that have garnered empirical support (e.g., Bryk, Bender Sebring, Allensworth, Luppescu, & Easton, 2010).

But in sharp contrast to what has been characterized as the tough, competitive, and narrow emphasis of the college-for-all mandate, we chose an alternative vision by embracing a warmly demanding, cooperative, and holistic approach. We committed to the development of the *whole* student, long understood to be a critical element of a powerful education. This whole-student perspective was evident in the vision of John Dewey and many models since, such as the Comer School Development Program, Zigler's 21st Century Schools, and Talent Development Schools (see Fleischman & Heppen, 2009; Moore, 2014), as well as in policy recommendations for closing the opportunity gap (e.g., Carter & Welner, 2013).

This commitment to *whole-student development* was not achieved simply through the addition of separate programs but rather through an aligned and responsive pathway to college readiness provided for all students. The detracked program enabled the interweaving of acceleration, remediation, and enrichment in challenging, supportive, non-stigmatizing, and inclusive ways. What Rosenbaum and Becker (2011) have called the package-deal curriculum and Edmunds and colleagues (2013) have described as mandated engagement are key features of the capacity of this early college high school, and others, to both support and accelerate learning.

Although these efforts may have been facilitated by the alternative governance pathways illustrated earlier, change in practices *can* be achieved in other ways. In *Big-City Reforms*, Fullan and Boyle (2014) characterized the dual strategies of push (challenging the status quo) and pull (building ownership) that bold district leaders in contexts such as New York, Toronto, and London have used to improve student achievement. Ferguson and colleagues (2009, p. i) described how the actions of leadership teams, in the use of formal as well as earned authority, garnered in collaborative capacity-building, helped 15 public high schools "become exemplary" in raising the achievement of students and reducing gaps. Similarly, in *Improbable Scholars*, Kirp (2013, p. 9) told a tale of "evolution, not revolution . . . just hard and steady work" that depicts the improvement efforts of one great American school district, framed around challenge and caring, curricular coordination, data analysis, and help. Although we side with Kirp about the evolution of school improvement, we part ways about the need for revolutionary actions. Many deeply entrenched and defeating practices, such as curricular tracking, disciplinary exclusion, and assessment without intervention, must be eliminated in favor of more effective and inclusionary approaches (Alvarez & Mehan, 2006; Carter, Skiba, Arrendondo, & Pollock, 2014; Fletcher & Vaughn, 2009). Also, there is much to be learned about practices that do not kick students off the college track, such as teaching for both rigor and support, building meaningful advisories, strengthening family and school collaboration, meeting the needs of culturally diverse students, and implementing an integrative support system.

In efforts to seed more high-quality and equitable secondary schools, collaboration across the traditional district–charter divide, as well as across high- and low-performing districts and schools, is an important step forward. As examples, Mehan and colleagues (2012) are working with the San Diego Unified School District to take lessons learned from the Preuss School to other high schools. Furthermore, the Gates Foundation has funded a District–Charter Collaboration Compact in 16 US cities (Yatsko, Nelson, & Lake, 2013), a controversial initiative, with the hope that sharing will become a two-way street.

## Investing in an *Integrative* Youth Development

We need to invest in the promotion or seeding of a broader youth development, beyond preparing students for subject matter proficiencies and college eligibility alone. Adolescence is a critical period for the development of identity, critical competencies, and a life plan. Experiences in the arts and sports, opportunities for social-emotional learning and choice in electives, preparation for college and career, and the availability of help for obstacles in their way are essential in fueling student engagement in their education, self-improvement, and attainment. The provision of challenge without support or challenge without enrichment is a nonstarter, doomed for failure.

This broader focus of schooling requires financial investment in enrichment through support programs (such as after-school, extracurricular, and summer activities) and in youth development work by support providers (such as college counseling, special education, health, and mental health), but most importantly, in a different way. The provision of such opportunities—decidedly unequal and viewed by some to be outside the academic enterprise of schools—has been severely cut in the economic recession and in the growing zeitgeist for reducing governmental contributions to education and social programs. If not found in schools, these are the opportunities that wealthier families purchase for their own children, furthering an unacceptable economic divide. As Adelman and Taylor (2010, 2015) have consistently argued, to our detriment, we have underinvested in the enabling function of schools.

But, as we described in this book, these investments in whole-student development and in supports must be deeply integrated with the academic mission. They are best placed in first-chance institutions such as schools and placed not simply as add-ons but aligned toward articulated outcomes. Funding must require this kind of integration and must shape new support roles, moving beyond coordinated or wraparound services toward a coherent and synergistic program.

## Investing in Pathways: Planning, Capacity-Building, and Training Programs

We must also make serious investments in the provision of planning time and capacity-building for teachers, principals, and support providers—an important mechanism for creating pathways to college. Finland, known for its tremendous success in international comparisons of student achievement, has invested heavily in collaborative planning by teachers, nurturing them do whatever it takes to help students succeed (e.g., Hancock, 2011). The development of an aligned and responsive pathway to college—a defining feature of our work—required strategic program and professional development choices, innovative use of supports, and monitoring of student progress. Aligned program features reduced transition challenges. Also, teachers who were responsive—to adolescent needs, learning challenges, cultural, and equity issues—kept students on the college track. In the United States and in other nations, there are rich examples of the kinds of cultural understandings teachers need in order to be responsive to underperforming minority students (e.g., Bishop & Berryman, 2006; Delpit, 2006; Fine & Weiss, 2003; Noguera, 2008). In addition, we recognize the need for different kinds of pathways, which while embracing college preparation also link students to work-related education and technical skill development, such as in career academies (e.g., Stern, 2015). The articulation of a transparent pathway is a vital tool.

Creating such pathways requires building an integrative program up front, and professional training for broader and integrative, not "siloed" roles. Teacher education programs must include not only content knowledge but also knowledge about youth development, cultural literacy, preparation for higher education, and collaboration with support professionals. In addition, the training of support providers must address teamwork and schoolwide programming tied to the school mission, as well as individual and group interventions.

This direction spells change in professional training programs, for teachers (for rigorous, supportive, and differentiated instruction), support providers (for curriculum delivery such as in college preparation, tiered interventions, and social-emotional learning), and principals (for integrative resource use). Although the improvement of teacher quality receives the lion share of attention in school reform, and importantly so, the critical role of principals and districts in blending these conditions needed for student growth too often receives short shrift. Also, there is the danger of overcrowding the educational agenda and not keeping an eye out for a streamlined but coherent program—attainable for schools to mount and students to complete.

Among the advances are efforts to detrack secondary schools (e.g., Burris & Garrity, 2008: Mehan, 2012), instructional practices that are both rigorous and supportive (e.g., Allen, Pianta, Gregory, Mikami, & Lin, 2011), student supports that are aligned with achievement goals (e.g., Seashore Louis & Gordon, 2005), and training teachers and principals to lead learning as well as change efforts (e.g., Grubb & Tredway, 2010).

Both teachers and principals are "being asked to develop new competencies largely centered around data, curriculum, pedagogy, and human capital development" in order to promote higher achievement for all students (Alvoid & Black, 2014). These more integrative investments will likely reap benefits—a testable question—in a greater number of high school graduates prepared for college, while served universally as a cohort and within less specialized educational contexts.

There is also a shift in mindset here, in making a college pathway *transparent* to all. Reflecting a talent-development rather than talent-selection emphasis (Weinstein, 2002), the invitation to take the path is inclusive, the steps to get there are clearly marked, and the opportunities for help as well as second chances are made explicit. There are lessons for universities as well. As one example, faced with low transfer rates, the UC system is creating an explicit pathway, major by major through aligned coursework, from community colleges to the University of California campuses, to improve transfer rates between these levels of the system (Maitre, 2015). As a second and far earlier example, in the face of largely male and white faculty at UC Berkeley, Weinstein and Ervin Tripp, members of the Academic Senate Committee on the Status of Women and Ethnic Minorities, wrote an anonymous document in 1983 to provide a transparent pathway to tenure for those marginalized groups without access to what was a hidden curriculum. Considered heresy then, this document entitled *Advancement and Promotion of Junior Faculty at UC Berkeley* has now become an important part of faculty professional development and can be found on the web—a harbinger of social change (University of California, Berkeley, 2005).

## Investing in Cross-sector Partnerships: Deep and Long

The building of strong connections from kindergarten through the senior year of college has long been seen as critical to achieving educational equity, albeit with multiple goals—through alignment of standards, improvement of teacher preparation, access to college classes in early college models, extra resources for schools reflecting our civic responsibility, and the research–practice interface. The reality is that although collaboration between higher education and K–12 is rampant, it is also variable as to its depth and accomplishments (e.g., Domina & Ruzek, 2012). In a recent report, Coburn and colleagues (2013) pressed for such partnerships to move beyond outreach and the addition of resources, to actual impact on teaching. They underscored that "these after-school, weekend, or summer extras are seldom enough to compensate for watered down instruction the rest of the school day and year" (p. 15). Coburn and colleagues also noted that "at their best, these partnerships facilitate the development of more relevant, actionable research and its use within the practice community (p. ii)."

Our partnership, at the university–charter district level and bridging the divide between secondary and postsecondary education, brought bidirectional effects, as described earlier. Whereas many town–gown partnerships turn out to be narrowly targeted (single programs), short-term (fleeting), and one-sided (unequal in power), with leadership absent at the table, this partnership was different—deep and lasting around a shared mission. It rested on clearly defined but complementary roles and regularized meetings set in stone. One can see the joint impact on the character and quality of the school.

But beyond that, the importance of this collaboration lay in rich learning opportunities for those at a research university, seen in other early college partnerships (Matthews, 2009). Most used to a laser-thin focus on the component parts of complex systems, we expanded our understanding of the interrelationship between part and whole, in the design of a high quality and equity school and its scale-up, with a deepened understanding of how our training programs needed to change (e.g., Worrell et al., 2014), as well as changing the type and responsiveness of our research activities. For those in the district, grappling with the weaving of component parts into an effective whole, opportunities to learn from experts (open about specialized knowledge but committed to integrative solutions), and to reflect on consequences of choices made, proved invaluable. Our success in eradicating disparities, rampant in all our major institutions, requires such an interdisciplinary and systemic view, made possible when universities, writ large, collaborate at a systems level. Our capacity to train visionary 21st-century practitioners and research scholars requires this kind of on-the-ground knowledge, interdisciplinary perspective, and systemic view.

## Promoting Mutuality in Translational Research

Despite the call for the application of scientific research in the No Child Left Behind legislation (2002), we face problems in the underuse of evidence-based practices in schools, severely limiting the impact of our research and the reach of educational improvement. Furthermore, the thrust of translational research continues to flow largely from bench to bedside as in the medical metaphor, but too rarely from bedside to bench. As represented in this book, community-engaged scholarship and reflection by practitioners elevated the problems of practice in the context of creating and refining a new school. As Gutiérrez and Penuel (2014, p. 19) have argued, relevance to practice must become a new criterion for research rigor:

> Consequential research on meaningful and equitable educational change requires a focus on persistent problems of practice, examined in the context of development, with attention to ecological resources and constraints, including why, how, and under what conditions programs and policies work.

New definitions of research rigor within the academy—carrying with it financial support and greater institutional reward—will enable the growth of a bidirectional translational research. This bidirectionality will be oriented toward practitioner as well as researcher knowledge, implementation challenges, and contextual fit, critical to our improvement of schools.

The community-engaged scholarship described in this book illustrates the persisting gap in understanding between expectancy processes or self-fulfilling prophecies as they play out in the world of schools and as operationalized in the far too narrow lens of both research and policy. Researchers are skeptical in debates about the accuracy of expectations and small effects (e.g., Jussim, 2012), and policy-makers are committed to the use of expectations as a lever (e.g., the standards movement); however, the reality is far more complex than typically understood. Beliefs about the capacity to learn (e.g., "CAL Prep believed in me before I did"; Ness, 2012) and to what level (college-ready) are vital, but the communication of such expectations is nuanced as well as multilayered, as transmitted in classrooms, schools, districts, and families. Expectancy effects are also necessarily driven by mediating mechanisms (e.g., in an aligned and responsive pathways to college), and longitudinal in nature (moving us from a focus on short-term achievement gains toward attainment outcomes). Research needs to capture this ecological complexity, looking beneath the averages to examples where, when both message and mediating mechanism are aligned, expectancy effects are most powerful (e.g., McKown & Weinstein, 2008; Rubie-Davies, 2014). Furthermore, in the policy world, expectations are reflected too simply in content standards and too punitively in a negative accountability for outcomes, failing to nurture a genuine and steadfast belief that *all* can learn (the moral obligation of schooling) and failing to invest in the conditions needed to actualize beliefs into desired outcomes.

Another lesson grew from our efforts to implement evidence-based curricula in advisories and in our support system, where we saw very clearly the gap between the high demands of evidence-based modules and the needs of the school for simpler practices, tightly aligned with their mission. To advance use of research findings in mental health settings, Rotheram-Borus and colleagues (2012) advocated for disruptive innovations that reengineer evidence-based practices into briefer and less complex alternatives, serving more at less cost. Empirically validated approaches are not easily taken up in schools, because they must fit within a complex set of systems. To create conditions for evidence use, researchers need to develop briefer assessments of important constructs that allow monitoring of student growth, and to integrate elements together in coherent designs, such as classroom practices that knit together academic challenge and social-emotional learning (e.g., Jones, Brown, & Aber, 2011).

## In Conclusion

At this time of heightened academic expectations—to and through college for all—we cannot afford to let down the ever-increasing number of youth who lack the opportunity to reach these goals, either by lowering our standards or by failing to challenge and support these students. In the face of a rapidly changing world order, retreat or defeat threatens the welfare of our increasingly diverse and economically unequal nation. The stakes are high, not only because of legal accountability but also a moral obligation to right an egregious wrong—the unequal playing field we provide to children of poverty and color. These are *our* children, too.

Even after more than a decade of collaboration, the interest of both UC Berkeley and Aspire in this partnership continues, with issues still to be addressed, especially concerning (1) districtwide and cross-district dissemination of exemplary practices and (2) how universities might better support the success of low-income and first-generation college students in higher education. There is much to learn as we turn our lens on college, shifting from *access to* college to *success in* college.

In his book about complications and the imperfect science of medicine, the surgeon Atul Gwande (2002) described what he calls an uncomfortable truth about teaching: we all aspire to perfection in ourselves and in our students but without an understanding of the importance of practice. Noting studies of elite performers, Gwande suggested that "the process of learning turns out to extend longer than most people know" (p. 25) and that "the most important talent may be the talent for practice itself" (p. 20). Together, we created CAL Prep to herald this process of learning, to be a safe and "can do" setting, where we, including the authors in this book, persisted, learned from our mistakes, and indeed became more effective in our actions. Our time frame was necessarily long and our aim was deep—a message to policy makers that investments must not be short and superficial. On this journey, we were humbled by the scope of our shared enterprise, seeing clearly that although theory and research might guide practice, practice has its own critical lessons to impart.

## References

Adelman, H. S., & Taylor, L. (2010). *Mental health in schools: Engaging learners, preventing problems, and improving schools.* Thousand Oaks, CA: Corwin.

Adelman, H. S., & Taylor, L. (2015, January). Developing a unified, comprehensive, and equitable system. Retrieved from http://smhp.psych.ucla.edu/

Allen, J. P., Pianta, R. C., Gregory, A., Mikami, A. Y., & Lin, J. (2011). An interaction-based approach to enhancing secondary school instruction and achievement. *Science, 333,* 1034–1037. doi:10.1126/science.1207998

Alvarez, D., & Mehan, H. (2006). Whole-school detracking: A strategy for equity and excellence *Theory into Practice, 45,* 82–89. doi:10.1207/s15430421tip4501_11.

Alvoid, L, & Black, W. L. Jr. (2014, July 1). *The changing role of the principal: How high-achieving districts are recalibrating school leadership.* Center for American Progress. Retrieved from https://www.americanprogress.org/issues/education/report/2014/07/01/93015/the-changing-role-of-the-principal/

Bangser, G., Burgess, C., Chalhoub, T., Cohen, E., Disalvo, K., Haugen, D.,. ...Smith, K. (January 2012). *Urban education that works: Moving past school type debates and embracing choice.* Princeton, NJ: The Woodrow Wilson School. Retrieved from http://civilsocietyinitiative.org/media/princeton-Urban-Education-that-Works_email.pdf

Bishop, R., & Berryman, M. (2006). *Culture speaks: Cultural relationships & classroom learning.* Wellington, New Zealand: Huia Publishers.

Blume, H. (2015, May 6). LAUSD college prep rule puts nearly 75% of 10th graders' diplomas at risk. *Los Angeles Times.* Retrieved from http://www.latimes.com/local/la-me-cc-slash-enrollment-classes-20120924-m-story.html

Burris, C. C., & Garrity, D. T. (2008). *Detracking for excellence and equity.* Alexandria, VA: Association for Supervision and Curriculum Development.

Bryk, A. S., Bender Sebring, P., Allensworth, E., Luppescu, S., & Easton, J. Q. (2010). *Organizing schools for improvement: Lessons from Chicago.* Chicago, IL: The University of Chicago Press.

California Community Colleges Chancellors Office. (2015, January 16). *Key facts about California Community Colleges*. Retrieved from http://californiacommunitycolleges.cccco.edu/PolicyInAction/KeyFacts.aspx

Carter, P., Skiba, R., Arrendondo, M., & Pollock, M. (2014, December). *You can't fix what you don't look at: Acknowledging race in addressing racial discipline disparities*. Retrieved from http://www.indiana.edu/~atlantic/wp-content/uploads/2014/12/Acknowledging-Race_121514.pdf

Carter, P. L., & Welner, K. F. (2013). *Closing the opportunity gap: What America must do to give every child an even chance*. New York, NY: Oxford University Press.

Cavanagh, S. (2012, August 7). Charter school to share analytic tools nationwide. *Education Week blogs*. Retrieved from http://blogs.edweek.org/edweek/charter-schoice/2012/08/charter_school_to_share_analytical_tools_nationwide.html

Coburn, C. E., Penuel, W. R., & Geil, K. (2013). *Research-practice partnerships: A strategy for leveraging research for educational improvement in school districts*. New York, NY: William T. Grant Foundation.

Cuban, L. (2013). *Inside the black box of classroom practice: Change without reform in American Education*. Cambridge, MA: Harvard Education Press.

Cucciara. M. (2010, Summer). New goals, familiar challenges?: A brief history of university-run schools. *Perspectives on Urban Education*, 96–108. Retrieved from http://www.urbanedjournal.org/sites/urbanedjournal.org/files/pdf_archive/PUE-Summer2010-V7I1-pp96-108.pdf

Delpit, L. (2006). *Other people's children: Cultural conflict in the classroom*. New York, NY: The New Press.

Domina, T., & Ruzek, R. (2012). Paving the way: K–16 partnerships for higher education diversity and high school reform. *Educational Policy*, *26*, 243–267. doi:10.1177/0895904810386586

Duke, D. L. (2010). *Differentiating school leadership: Facing the challenges of practice*. Thousand Oaks, CA: Corwin.

Dweck, C. S. (2006). *Mindset: The psychology of success*. New York, NY: Random House.

Edmunds, J. A., Willse, J., Arshavsky, N., & Dallas, A. (2013). Mandated engagement: The impact of early college high schools. *Teachers College Record*, *115*, 1–31.

Elmore, R. F. (1996). Getting to scale with good educational practice. *Harvard Educational Review*, *66*, 1–26.

Fensterwald, J. (2014, October 23). Charters plan for future growth outside state. *EdSource*. Retrieved from http://edsource.org/2014/charters-plan-for-future-growth-outside-state/68819

Ferguson, R., Hackman, S., Hanna, R., & Ballantine, A. (2009). *How high schools become exemplary: Ways that leadership raises achievement and narrows gaps by improving instruction*. Report on the 2009 Annual Conference of the Achievement Gap Initiative at Harvard University. Retrieved from http://www.agi.harvard.edu/events/2009Conference/2009AGIConferenceReport6-30-2010web.pdf

Fine, M., & Weis, L. (Eds.) (2003). *Silenced voices and extraordinary conversations: Re-imagining schools*. New York, NY: Teachers College Press.

Fleischman, S., & Heppen, J. (2009). Improving low-performing high schools: Searching for evidence of promise. *The Future of Children*, *19*(1), 105–134.

Fletcher, J. M., & Vaughn, S. (2009). Response to intervention: Preventing and remediating academic difficulties. *Child Development Perspectives*, *3*, 30–37. doi:10.1111/j.1750-8606.2008.00072.x

Fredericks, J. A., Blumenfeld, P. C., & Paris, A. H. (2004). School engagement: Potential of the concept, state of the evidence. *Review of Educational Research*, *74*, 59–109. doi:10.3102/00346543074001059

Fullan, M., & Boyle, A. (2014). *Big-city school reforms: Lessons from New York, Toronto, and London*. New York, NY: Teachers College Press and Ontario's Principals' Council.

Gawande, A. (2002) *Complications: A surgeon's notes on an imperfect science*. New York, NY: Metropolitan Books.

Grubb, N. W., & Tredway, L. (2010). *Leading from the inside out: Expanded roles for teachers in equitable schools*. Boulder, CO: Paradigm.

Gutiérrez, K. D., & Penuel, W. R. (2014). Relevance to practice as a criterion for rigor. *Educational Researcher*, *43*, 19–23. doi:10.3102/0013189X13520289

Hancock, L. (2011, September). Why are Finland's schools so successful? *Smithsonian Magazine*. Retrieved from http://www.smithsonianmag.com/innovation/why-are-finlands-schools-successful-49859555/?no-ist

Harkavy, I., Hartley, M., Axelroth Hodges, R., & Weeks, J. (2013). The promise of University-Assisted Community Schools to transform American schooling: A report from the field, 1985-2012. *Peabody Journal of Education*, *88*, 525–540, doi:10.1080/0161956X.2013.834789

Jussim, L. (2012). *Social belief and social reality: Why accuracy dominates bias and self fulfilling prophecies*. New York, NY: Oxford University Press.

Jones, S. M., Brown, J. L., & Aber, J. L. (2011). Two year impacts of a universal school-based social-emotional and literacy intervention: An experiment in translational research. *Child Development*, *82*, 533–554. doi:10.1111/j.1467-8624.2010.01560.x

Kirp, D. L. (2013). *Improbable scholars: The rebirth of a great American school system and a strategy for American's schools*. New York, NY: Oxford University Press.

Leonhardt, D. (2015, April 26). College for the masses. *The New York Times*. Retrieved from http://www.nytimes.com/2015/04/26/upshot/college-for-the-masses.html?abt=0002&abg=1

Louis, K. S., & Gordon, M. F. (2005). *Aligning student support with achievement goals: The secondary principal's guide*. Newbury Park, CA: Corwin.

Maitre, M. (2015, May 31). UC moving to simplify student transfer requirements. *EdSource*. Retrieved from http://edsource.org/2015/uc-moving-to-simplify-student-transfer-requirements/80636

McKown, C., & Weinstein, R. S. (2008). Teacher expectations, classroom context, and the achievement gap. *Journal of School Psychology*, *46*, 235–261. doi:10.1016/j.jsp.2007.05.001

Meier, D. (1995). *The power of their ideas: Lessons for American from a small school in Harlem*. Boston, MA: Beacon Press.

Mathews, R. S. (2009, May). *The power of partnership: How early college creates rich contexts for engaging faculty*. Princeton, NJ: The Woodrow Wilson National Fellowship Foundation.

Maton, K. I. (1999). Making a difference: The social ecology of social transformation. *American Journal of Community Psychology, 28,* 25–57. doi:10.1023/A:1005190312887

Mehan, H. (2012). *In college's front door: Creating a college bound culture of learning in high schools.* Boulder, CO: Paradigm Publishers.

Mehan, H., Kaufman, G., Lytle, C., Quartz, K. H., & Weinstein, R. S. (2010). Building educational field stations to promote diversity and access in higher education. In E. Grodsky & M. Kurlaender (Eds.) *Equal opportunity in high education: The past and future of California's Proposition 209* (pp. 173–193). Cambridge, MA: Harvard Education Press.

Moore, K. A. (2014). Making the grade: Assessing the evidence for integrated student supports. *Child Trends.* Retrieved from http://www.childtrends.org/?publications=making-the-grade-assessing-the-evidence-for-integrated-student-supports

Ness, C. (2012, May). *Against formidable odds, four from CAL Prep are entering Berkeley this fall.* Retrieved from http://newscenter.berkeley.edu/2012/06/04/31377/

No Child Left Behind (NCLB) Act of 2001, Pub. L. No. 107-110, § 115, Stat. 1425 (2002).

Noguera, P. A. (2008). *The trouble with black boys:... And other reflections on race, equity, and the future of public education.* San Francisco, CA: Jossey-Bass.

Powell, A. G., Farrar, E., & Cohen, D. K. (1985). *The shopping mall high school: Winners and losers in the educational marketplace.* Boston, MA: Houghton Mifflin.

Public Affairs. (2012, June). *Alana Banks: 'Cal Prep believed in me before I did.'* Retrieved from http://newscenter.berkeley.edu/2012/06/04/alana-banks/

Rich, M. (2014, October 10). As apprentices in classroom, teachers learn what works. *The New York Times.* Retrieved from http://www.nytimes.com/2014/10/11/us/as-apprentices-in-classroom-teachers-learn-what-works.html

Rodriguez, J. (2010, February 18). *Pioneering initiative launched on equity, diversity and inclusion, backed by Evelyn and Walter Hass, Jr. Fund.* Retrieved from https://news.berkeley.edu/2010/02/18/haas_jr_fund/

Rotheram-Borus, M. J., Swendeman, D., & Chorpita, B. F. (2012). Disruptive innovations for designing and diffusing evidence-based interventions. *American Psychologist, 67,* 463–476. doi:10.1037/a0028180

Rosenbaum, J. E., & Becker, K. I. (2011). The early college challenge: Navigating disadvantaged students' transition to college. *American Educator, 35,* 14–20.

Rubie-Davies, C. (2014). *Becoming a high expectation teacher: Raising the bar.* London, UK: Routledge.

Rumberger, R. W. (2011, November 20). How college prep is killing high school. *Boston Globe.* Retrieved from https://www.bostonglobe.com/ideas/2011/11/20/how-college-prep-killing-high-school/94mGUe6o9InIEuO9oMhnzJ/story.html

Sarason, S. B. (1972). *The creation of settings and the future societies.* San Francisco, CA: Jossey-Bass.

Schlechty, P. C. (2005). *Creating great schools: Six systems at the heart of educational innovation.* San Francisco, CA: Jossey-Bass.

Seidman, E. (2012). An emerging action science of social settings. *American Journal of Community Psychology, 50*, 1–16. doi:10.1007/s10464-011-9469-3

Stern, D. (2015). *Pathways or pipelines: Keeping high school students' future options open while developing technical skills and knowledge.* Background paper for the Committee on The Supply Chain for Middle-Skill Jobs: Education, training, and certification pathways. Retrieved from http://sites.nationalacademies.org/cs/groups/pgasite/documents/webpage/pga_167702.pdf

Tucker, J. (2013, December 6). Aspire teachers at the center of a fierce national debate. *San Francisco Chronicle.* Retrieved from http://www.sfgate.com/education/article/Aspire-teachers-at-center-of-fierce-national-5039678.php

University of California. (2005). Diversity criteria. In *Administrative policy manual, Section 210* (p. 5). Retrieved from http://www.ucop.edu/academic-personnel-programs/_files/apm/apm-210.pdf

University of California, Berkeley (2005). *Advancement and promotion of junior faculty at UC Berkeley.* Retrieved from http://academic-senate.berkeley.edu/committees/acfr/advancement-and-promotion-junior-faculty-uc-berkeley

University of California, Berkeley. (n.d.). Chancellor's Award for Advancing Institutional Excellence. Retrieved from http://diversity.berkeley.edu/caaie

Weinstein, R. S. (2002). *Reaching higher: The power of expectations in schooling.* Cambridge, MA: Harvard University Press.

Worrell, F. C., Brabeck, M. M., Dwyer, C. A., Geisinger, K., Marx, R. W., Noell, G. H., & Pianta, R. C. (2014). *Assessing and evaluating teacher preparation programs.* Washington, DC: American Psychological Association. Retrieved from http://www.apa.org/ed/schools/cpse/teacher-preparation-programs.pdf

Yatsko, S., Cooley Nelson, E., & Lake, R. (2013). *District/charter collaboration compact: Interim report.* Seattle, WA: Center on Reinventing Public Education. Retrieved from http://www.crpe.org/publications/district-charter-collaboration-compact-interim-report

# EPILOGUE

FRANK C. WORRELL AND RHONA S. WEINSTEIN

TEN YEARS AFTER THE CALIFORNIA College Preparatory Academy (CAL Prep) first opened its doors in 2005, there is still change in the air. In August of 2015, CAL Prep moved into a beautiful new building, one large enough to allow the school to eventually become a full Grade 6–12 secondary school as it was originally conceptualized, rather than a high school serving only Grades 9 to 12. The current principal—CAL Prep's fourth—joined us in 2012–2013 and began his fourth year in the fall of 2015, and the current Aspire superintendent for the Bay Area began her second year. The University of California (UC) Berkeley has its third chancellor since the letter arrived in 2002 soliciting UC Berkeley's participation in the Early College Initiative and both the Graduate School of Education and Division of Equity and Inclusion will soon have new leaders. Change continues to be a constant in the CAL Prep story.

Yet, despite change, there is continuity evident in curiosity about and the commitment to "get it better next time"—as expressed by our newest member (see Chapter 16). This commitment to improving educational opportunity also extends to our own students, with the gratifying result that a 2011 CAL Prep graduate, who just completed her undergraduate degree at UC Santa Cruz, has joined the CAL Prep staff as a teacher resident through Aspire's teacher training program.

By the time this book is published, CAL Prep will have graduated five classes of seniors. The data in this book indicate that CAL Prep is outperforming schools with similar demographic profiles in the Bay Area and in the rest of California, and by the metrics of high school graduation and college enrollment, CAL Prep is a success story. But the CAL Prep story does not end here, and although CAL Prep has achieved much, there is much more to be done. In this Epilogue, we briefly highlight the work ahead of us and conclude with a glimpse into the future.

## Work to be Done: College-Successful Students

Although we have succeeded, by and large, in enrolling students in college, there is another great challenge: doing well in college. Cal Prep has not yet had sufficient numbers of students who have completed college to know whether the school's college completion rates match its high school graduation rates. However, we know that college completion rates continue to be low for underrepresented youth with strong high school performance. For example, the KIPP schools report an 82% college enrollment rate for their 2013 graduates, paralleling the college enrollment rate for high-income students (KIPP, n.d.). However, KIPP's college graduation rate of 44%, although substantially above the 8% graduation rate for low-income students from other schools, is also substantially below the 71% graduation rate for high-income students. What are the reasons for these disparate college outcomes?

In December of 2012, DeParle reported on the story of three Latinas from low-income families in Galveston, Texas. All three were doing very well in high school, and enrolled in college upon high school graduation: one at Emory, one at Texas State, and one at a community college. As DeParle stated (2012),

> Four years later, their story seems less like a tribute to upward mobility than a study of obstacles in an age of soaring economic inequality. Not one of them has a 4-year degree. Only one is still studying full time, and two have crushing debts.

Whether it is a feeling of responsibility for supporting the family, a failure to understand how and why to engage with the university in the process of working out financial aid, or simply being afraid to move too far from home, the end result was the same: an inability to achieve educational goals (DeParle, 2012). Tough (2014) reported,

To put it in blunt terms: rich kids graduate; poor and working class kids don't. Or to put it more statistically: about a quarter of college freshmen born into the bottom half of the income distribution will manage to collect a bachelor's degree by age 24, while almost 90 percent of freshmen born into the top income quartile will go on to finish their degree.

In addressing this disparity in college completion, we are challenged to learn about the problems that underrepresented students face and where the solutions may lie. What more can we do in high school preparation to improve the possibility that these students will *graduate* from 4-year colleges? And looking at our own house, how can we change the climate of colleges and universities to become more receptive, respectful, and safe learning communities where students of poverty and color can thrive and succeed? Finally, how can we ensure that there are affordable spaces to meet the increased demand for college—a demand that we are driving?

**High School Preparation.** Clearly, there are issues related to underrepresented students successfully matriculating into and completing college that go beyond academic preparation. Dwayne Anderson, a 2012 CAL Prep graduate, indicated that he "had to face and overcome many obstacles in order to reach my ultimate goal: going to college" (Ness, 2012). Tough (2014) pointed out that helping low-income—and we would add first-generation and ethnic minority—students succeed in college requires addressing "their doubts and misconceptions and fears," echoing a sentiment of Aronson and Steele's (2005, p. 436) a decade before, who commented that "competence is much more fragile—and malleable—than we tend to think."

Given that our college courses were in community colleges, allowing CAL Prep students to audit freshman seminars and having the seniors participate in College Week offered opportunities for them to orient to the UC Berkeley campus, and by extension, to other large, selective institutions. These opportunities worked well for some students, as Natassija Jordan has reported (Ness, 2011):

I took a freshman seminar about Supreme Court cases. You come in and you're surrounded by all these other kids who are already in college listening to me about why I agree or disagree with a decision, and they look at you like you're just another student there learning. It's open and welcoming.

Yet, this exposure did not help all students choose more selective institutions. Although all CAL Prep graduates have been accepted into 4-year institutions—it is a graduation requirement—some students still choose to attend community colleges rather than a UC campus or another 4-year school, because these students feel safer in the smaller, less-selective environment. Sometimes, negative and less-than-welcoming experiences of siblings or relatives at 4-year colleges help cement these decisions. What measures can be put in place to increase students' comfort levels in 4-year university settings? To the extent that the students who choose to begin at a community college transfer into and graduate from a 4-year institution, they will have met our stated goal, but these are some of the issues that need to be examined in future studies.

**Making Changes in Our Own House**. As we prepared CAL Prep students for UC Berkeley, we considered how best to prepare UC Berkeley for CAL Prep students. We have witnessed how apparently simple issues can derail students who come from families without histories of college-going and how these students' concerns can be invisible to the university bureaucracy. Despite monthly support meetings, Aspire students enrolled at UC Berkeley continued to experience difficulties. We learned, for example, that some students were not aware of the binding nature of the housing contract or that the amount of financial aid one receives changes if there is a change in living situation. Other issues that students faced included proving that their parents were citizens and navigating the various offices required to resolve issues. As noted in Chapter 17, these situations contributed to the development of Cal Student Central, the "one-stop shop" for interfacing with the university on a variety of common student concerns. Based on this uneven knowledge about financial aid and housing contracts, we added a financial seminar to College Week. But there is still much to be done to make underrepresented students more prepared for the university and to make it a more *comfortable* setting for them.

Indeed, it is incumbent upon tertiary education institutions to provide instruction and supports that allow underrepresented students to succeed, an issue now beginning to garner attention from researchers and policy makers in higher education (William T. Grant Foundation, Spencer Foundation, & Bill & Melinda Gates Foundation, 2014). Some universities are doing better than others in providing a welcoming climate and supports for completion (The Education Trust, 2014). Moreover, knowledge about the most recent literature in an academic discipline and the ability to conduct research are not *sufficient* for effective teaching at the university. In addition to clarity, enthusiasm, organization, and interaction on the part of the instructor, effective university teaching requires instructors to have high and equitable expectations for all students, while also recognizing that the messages they convey can be detrimental to students with histories of disenfranchisement if not carefully calibrated (Cohen, Steele, & Ross, 1999). Effective teaching requires curricula that are *relevant* not just to the discipline but also to the societal concerns and social consciousness of the students being taught (Ladson-Billings, 1995). Effective teaching requires introductory courses that develop students' passions and skills, rather than "weed out" as many students as possible.

**Ensuring College Spaces**. Another critical challenge that we as a nation must address is increasing the affordability and accessibility of college. At the same time that society is stressing the importance of a college education and the number of traditionally underrepresented students that are applying to 4-year institutions is increasing astronomically, (1) the cost of going to college has increased at almost five times the rate of inflation, (2) financial aid for low-income students has reached historic lows, and (3) California and other states are disinvesting in public higher education (The Education Trust, 2014). Moreover, the available spaces in selective public 4-year colleges can accommodate only a fraction of the students who can be successful. How do we increase the number of affordable tertiary education opportunities for the traditionally underrepresented groups that we are steering toward college?

## Looking Ahead

What does the future hold for CAL Prep, as the school moves into a new facility? Whereas our most recently used, too-small building was around a mile from the UC Berkeley campus, facilitating easy student and faculty involvement on both sides, the new building is 11 miles away in the city of Richmond. The distance will make it more difficult for partners to get to the school as well as to the university. Also, it may affect the regional character of CAL Prep's current student body, narrowing the geographic footprint of the student body as the city of Berkeley was a more central and accessible location. We have already made a commitment to help with transportation costs for all current enrollees until they graduate.

There are also interesting opportunities in the move. By returning to a Grade 6–12 configuration, we face the challenge of building a coherent program that incorporates middle and high school, and we have a natural experiment that will allows us to compare outcomes for students who came to us in Grade 9 to those that the school will begin to serve in Grade 6. The principal is investing in project-based learning as a vehicle for helping students prepare for college and looks forward to being able to work with students on developing academic identities beginning in the sixth grade. In addition, discussions about the move have broadened the view of the partnership from a singular focus on CAL Prep to a broader focus on Aspire Public Schools. Projects being discussed include (1) conducting longitudinal studies of college persistence using data collected in the elementary, middle, and high schools as predictors; (2) developing and disseminating innovative teaching practices in keeping with our new focus on 21st-century skills; and (3) creating integrated internships at Aspire schools for UC Berkeley graduate students in social work and school psychology.

This is also a time for the renewal of the Early College Initiative committee, which oversees CAL Prep's relationship with the university. Although more than half of the original representatives are still at the table, several members have retired, and it is time to reinvigorate the committee so it can meet the new set of challenges. How do we encourage younger faculty to commit to a long-standing project with limited opportunities for the kind of research that will support promotion and tenure? How do we convince mid-career and senior faculty to devote time to an initiative that they may support philosophically but do not feel that they own? Involvement at different phases of CAL Prep's development evokes different kinds of commitments, but the new challenges on our plate, especially at a district level, will bring new talent to the table.

## Conclusion

It is clear to us that CAL Prep and what it represents—as a school, as a model, as a symbol—will continue to be important for years to come. A United States, where each generation was able to achieve more than its forebears in terms of education and income, is no more. Indeed, this nation, which used to be referred to as "the land of opportunity," has become the country with the third highest level of income inequality according to the Organization for Economic Cooperation and Development (The Education Trust, 2014). In 2012, the top 5% of the population took home more than 20% of the nation's income, whereas the bottom 20% took home only 3% of the nation's income. The reality is that income inequality in the United States is *creating* more students that will need schools such as CAL Prep to help them achieve their college dreams, and this need will only increase in subsequent years.

CAL Prep's success is not due to technology or a focus on the science, technology, engineering, and mathematics disciplines, or any other singular trend in education. Rather, CAL Prep's outcomes come from a *true* district–university partnership based on mutual respect for the expertise that the partners bring, a joint recognition that complex problems require multivariate solutions, and a commitment to the ongoing, sometimes tedious, and ever-evolving tasks by all of the partners—sweat equity if you will—to do what must be done. It is about boldness of vision and the willingness to work on translating the vision into intentional, focused, and committed actions, all the while keeping the mission in mind. As the CAL Prep motto declares—*Graduate from college? Yes we can!*

## References

Aronson, J., & Steele, C. M. (2005). Stereotypes and the fragility of academic competence, motivation, and self-concept. In A. J. Elliott & C. S. Dweck (Eds.), *Handbook of competence and motivation* (pp. 436–456). New York, NY: The Guilford Press.

Cohen, G. L., Steele, C. M., & Ross, L. D. (1999). The mentor's dilemma: Providing critical feedback across the racial divide. *Personality and Social Psychology Bulletin, 25*, 1302–1318. doi:10.1177/0146167299258011

DeParle, J. (2012, December 22). For poor, leap to college often ends in a hard fall. *New York Times*. Retrieved from http://www.nytimes.com/2012/12/23/education/poor-students-struggle-as-class-plays-a-greater-role-in-success.html?pagewanted=all

KIPP. (n.d.). *The promise of college completion: 2013 alumni update.* Retrieved from http://www.kipp.org/results/college-completion-report/2013-alumni-data-update

Ladson-Billings, G. (1995). But that's just good teaching! The case for culturally relevant pedagogy. *Theory into Practice, 34*, 159–165. doi:10.1080/00405849509543675

Ness, C. (2011, May). *CAL Prep's first graduates—all of them—get into college.* Retrieved from http://newscenter.berkeley.edu/2011/05/06/cal-preps-first-graduating-class/

Ness, C. (2012, May). *Against formidable odds, four from CAL Prep are entering Berkeley this fall.* Retrieved from http://newscenter.berkeley.edu/2012/06/04/31377/

The Education Trust. (2014). *Access and success in higher education: Can we do more?* Paper presented at the annual conference of the Northeast Association for Institutional Research, Philadelphia, PA.

Tough, P. (2014, May 15). Who gets to graduate? *New York Times Magazine.* Retrieved from http://www.nytimes.com/2014/05/18/magazine/who-gets-to-graduate.html?_r=0

William T. Grant Foundation, Spencer Foundation, & Bill & Melinda Gates Foundation. (2014). *Measuring instruction in higher education: Summary of a convening.* Retrieved from http://blog.wtgrantfoundation.org/post/116473657707/measuring-instruction-in-higher-education

# ACKNOWLEDGMENTS

This collaborative journey would never have happened without Gail Kaufman, former Deputy Director of the Center for Educational Partnerships, and Genaro Padilla, former Vice Chancellor for Student Affairs at University of California, Berkeley. It was their imagination and gumption that propelled our campus into making a commitment to start an early college secondary school for first-generation college students. We are indebted to them for this transformative opportunity to work together across so many divides—multiple disciplines, research-practice, and secondary-tertiary education systems—around new school development for underserved youth.

We are grateful to those in campus administrative roles who wholeheartedly supported this venture since this work began in 2002, including former Chancellors Robert Berdahl and Robert Birgeneau, and former Executive Vice Chancellor and Provosts Paul Grey and George Breslauer. We are appreciative of the systemic efforts of former Chancellor Birgeneau to strengthen the commitment of our campus to diversity, equity, and inclusion. We were also extraordinarily lucky to have the sustained investment of the subsequent Vice Chancellor for Student Affairs Harry Le Grande, the inaugural Vice Chancellor for Equity and Inclusion Gibor Basri, two Deans of the Graduate School of Education (David Pearson and Judith Warren Little), the Director of the Center for Educational Partnerships Marsha Jaeger, and Development Officers Marguerite Judson, Division of Equity and Inclusion, and Teresa McGuire, Graduate School of Education.

We were also rewarded by the rich contributions of those faculty, staff, and students who served on our Early College Initiative (ECI) committee and/or in many other ways, such as in teaching, mentoring, and research. Although too many to name, we note the deep involvement of the inaugural ECI co-chairs Professors Mark Wilson and Angelica Stacy (still going strong), David Stern, Rory Bled, Phyllis Goldsmith, Alix Schwartz, Meg Conkey, Susan Stone, Ron Gronsky, and the late Norton Grubb. Wise administrative leadership, provided by Gail Kaufman and Bob Jorgensen, kept us on task and documented the history of California College Preparatory Academy (CAL Prep) in exquisitely detailed records of meetings. For critical technical and research support, we thank Marcy McGaugh, Ted Crum, Eric Eichorn, Bobbi Ann Barnowsky, Keira Chu, Jessica Weiss, Jesse Erwin, Cyrell Roberson, and Hila Peretz.

We learned mightily from our enduring partnership with Aspire Public Schools—an opportunity first seized upon by Don Shalvey, supported by James Wilcox, and actualized throughout these many years by the dedicated investment of Elise Darwish, now Chief Academic Officer and subsequent Bay Area Superintendents (Gloria Lee, Tatiana Epanchin-Troyan, and Kimi Kean). In addition, we express gratitude for the support from the Aspire Home Office staff to facilitate research about CAL Prep.

The work described in this book was enabled by generous financial support for which we are deeply grateful. Grants from the Woodrow Wilson National Fellowship Foundation (funded by the Bill & Melinda Gates Foundation) supported campus planning around the Early College Initiative, dissemination to other Aspire Schools, and research on student supports. UC Berkeley provided support in the form of release time for staff and faculty and research assistance, through the central administration, divisions, programs, and departments. Generous donors to CAL Prep (for gifts totaling $10,000 or more obtained through the efforts of UC Berkeley and/ or Aspire Public Schools) included Agilent Technology Foundation, The Honorable Frank and Kathy Baxter, the K& F Baxter Family Foundation, S.D. Bechtel, Jr. Foundation, William K. Bowes Foundation, The Michael and Susan Dell Foundation, Dodge & Cox Investments, Dreyer's Grand Ice Cream Foundation, The Sidney E. Frank Foundation, Gary and Donna Freedman, and the San Francisco Foundation.

This work was inspired by the example set by Hugh Mehan and Cecil Lytle in the creation of The Preuss School, the pioneer in our UC Network of University-Partnered College-Going Schools. It also benefitted from the intellectual and technical support provided by Rob Baird and Kristen Vogt from the Woodrow Wilson National Fellowship Foundation. We are grateful to Gail Kaufman, Elise Darwish, Judith Warren Little, and Christine Rubie-Davis for their thoughtful and valuable feedback on the manuscript, in part or in whole. And we acknowledge the pivotal contributions of Harvey Weinstein—from technical expert to substantive critic, from mainstay cook to book-widower—but mostly for his enduring belief in the importance of this work.

Appreciation is also due to the excellent staff at Oxford University Press, who guided this book to publication. We offer our thanks to the editorial team of Abby Gross and Courtney McCarroll, the production team of Devasena Vedamurthi, Martha Cushman, and Carol Reed, designer Jeanette Levy, and the marketing team of Daniel Petraglia, Emily Gorney, and Greg Bussy. We also benefitted from the incisive feedback of anonymous reviewers.

Finally, to the students and families and to the principals and teachers at CAL Prep, we salute your accomplishments!

# CONTRIBUTOR BIOGRAPHIES

**Gibor Basri** is professor of astronomy at the University of California, Berkeley and served as the founding vice chancellor for equity and inclusion from 2007 to 2015. He is also a founding member of the Early College Initiative committee, which oversees the California College Preparatory Academy. Long involved in encouraging the participation of minorities in science, Basri was honored with the Chancellor's Award for Advancing Institutional Excellence in 2006. Recognized as a Fellow of the California Academy of Sciences, Basri leads a research program focused on the study of brown dwarfs, star formation, and stellar activity.

**Lionel H. Bialis-White** is a graduate of the PhD program in school psychology in the Graduate School of Education at the University of California (UC) Berkeley. He served as graduate student researcher for the California College Preparatory Academy and an instructor for the seniors' College Week at UC Berkeley. He is a research analyst at Schoolzilla, an education technology firm that was founded by Aspire Public Schools to provide real-time, actionable data to teachers and principals across the country.

**Robert J. Birgeneau** is the Arnold and Barbara Silverman Distinguished Professor of Physics, Materials Science and Engineering, and Public Policy at the University of California (UC) Berkeley. He served as the ninth chancellor of UC Berkeley (2004–2013). Birgeneau is internationally known for his leadership in higher education and for his commitment to academic excellence, diversity, and equity. Before his arrival at UC Berkeley, he was president of the University of Toronto and dean of the School of Science at the Massachusetts Institute of Technology, after 25 years as a faculty member. A renowned physicist, Birgeneau is the recipient of many awards in teaching and research for his work on the fundamental properties of matter.

**Michelle Y. Cortez** is principal of Aspire Lionel Wilson Preparatory Academy in Oakland, California, and she served as a teacher, wrap-around services coordinator, interim principal, and dean of students at the California College Preparatory Academy from 2007 to 2012. Cortez was also appointed as secondary supports specialist for Aspire, where she trained high school leaders, created action plans, and consulted with other schools. She received her bachelor of arts in English from Sonoma State University in Rohnert Park, California, and her single-subject credential from National University, San Diego, California.

**Elise Darwish,** a former teacher, principal, and regional superinten-dent, is the chief academic officer for Aspire Public Schools, where she has been on the leadership team since its founding in 1998. Darwish oversaw the opening of the California College Preparatory Academy, shaped its partnership with the University of California, Berkeley, and supported the academy as it grew. She holds a bachelor of science degree in early childhood education from the University of Illinois and a master's degree in educational administration from San Francisco State University.

**Tatiana Epanchin-Troyan** is a senior vice president of regional operations at Teach For America and served as Bay Area superintendent for Aspire Public Schools from 2010 to 2014. She began her teaching career with Teach For America. Under her leadership as principal, Aspire's Monarch Academy in East Oakland garnered a National Title I Distinguished School Award for closing the achievement gap. Epanchin-Troyan holds a bachelor's degree in sociology and master's degrees in both social work and educational leadership.

**Marjorie (Susie) Goodin** completed her PhD in language and literacy in the Graduate School of Education at the University of California, Berkeley. She served as the graduate student representative on the Early College Initiative committee for the California College Preparatory Academy as well as a graduate student researcher. She is a literacy and library consul-tant and volunteer in public school libraries and classrooms.

**Ryan Grow** is a teacher of history and government at the California College Preparatory Academy, where he has taught since 2006, and he has also coached cross-country and track and field. He received a bachelor's degree in English and history from the University of California Davis and a teaching credential from California State University, Chico.

**Shyra Gums** is a writer, poet, and hip-hop artist, also known by her performance monicker, Shy'An G. A 2013 graduate of California College Preparatory Academy, she is a student at the California State University, East Bay, where she is studying philosophy and aspiring to be a journalism major.

**Robert E. Jorgensen** served as director of the Bay Area Consortium for Urban Education and director of school relations for the Graduate School of Education (GSE) at the University of California (UC) Berkeley. He took a lead role over 5 years in the conception and start-up of the California College Preparatory Academy, representing the GSE. After retiring from UC Berkeley, he took an administrative position at Stanford University for undergraduate education programs. Jorgensen has a bachelor's degree in history from UC Riverside and a master's degree in city and regional planning from UC Berkeley.

**Gail Kaufman**, a former teacher of social studies, was deputy director of the Center for Educational Partnerships (CEP) at the University of California (UC) Berkeley, where she led the CEP's work on building college- and career-going culture in Grades K–12 and community college. She is currently serving as senior advisor to the executive director of CEP and continues to be primarily responsible for coordinating and managing the partnership with the California College Preparatory Academy. Kaufman was the recipient of the Chancellor's Outstanding Staff Award in 2012 at UC Berkeley. She earned a bachelor's degree in history at Hunter College and master's degrees from Brooklyn College and the University of Massachusetts, Amherst.

**Tatiana Lim-Breitbart** began teaching chemistry and physics at the California College Preparatory Academy in the 2009–2010 year and has been the lead science teacher since fall 2010. She earned a bachelor's degree in chemistry and a master's degree in education, both at the University of California (UC) San Diego, and a second master's degree in chemistry at UC Berkeley, having come to work with Professor Stacy on the *Living By Chemistry* high school curriculum. Lim-Breitbart serves as a member of the State Expert Panel for Next Generation Science Standards, California Department of Education.

**Justin F. Martin** received his PhD in human development and education from the Graduate School of Education at the University of California (UC) Berkeley, and he is currently a visiting assistant professor of psychology at Whitworth University in Washington State. While at UC Berkeley, he served as graduate student researcher for the California College Preparatory Academy and as instructor for the seniors' College Week at UC Berkeley. He also directed UC Berkeley Scholars to Cal II, providing academic supports for underrepresented students with strong college aspirations.

**Zena R. Mello** is assistant professor of psychology at San Francisco State University. She was a postdoctoral fellow in the Graduate School of Education at the University of California, Berkeley from 2005 to 2009. Mello's research examines time perspective and other psychological factors that facilitate the well-being of ethnic minority and low-income adolescents. She received an Outstanding Dissertation Award in Human Development from the American Educational Research Association in recognition of her work.

**Genaro M. Padilla** is professor of English at the University of California, Berkeley, and he served as vice chancellor for student affairs there from 1995 to 2006. In this role, he facilitated discussion of a precollege charter that would become the California College Preparatory Academy (CAL Prep) and was co–principal investigator for the grant that was used to establish CAL Prep. Padilla has published widely on Chicano/Latino literature and culture. He was also the recipient of the Berkeley Citation (2007) and the Leon Henkin Award for Distinguished Service on behalf of students underrepresented in the academy (2012).

**P. David Pearson** is professor in the Language and Literacy and Human Development programs at the Graduate School of Education at University of California, Berkeley, where he served as dean from 2001 to 2010. He was co–principal investigator for the grant that was used to establish the California College Preparatory Academy. His current research focuses on using reading, writing, and language as tools to foster the development of knowledge and inquiry in science. He has received numerous awards for his research, including the Oscar Causey Award (1989) from the National Research Council for contributions to reading research and the Distinguished Contributions to Research in Education Award (2010) from the American Educational Research Association.

**Megan Reed** is director of school support for the Boston-based Achievement Network (ANet). After 7 years as a teacher in Aspire Public schools, Reed joined California College Preparatory Academy (CAL Prep) as dean in 2007 and served as principal from 2008 to 2011, taking the first cohort of CAL Prep students to graduation. She completed a bachelor's degree in American studies from Yale University and a master's degree in educational leadership from San Jose State University, and she earned her National Board Certification in early adolescent literacy.

**Sarah Salazar** has been teaching mathematics at the California College Preparatory Academy (CAL Prep) since 2006. She earned a bachelor's degree from the University of California (UC) Santa Barbara and a master's degree in mathematics education from the UC Berkeley, where her research focused on issues of diversity and equity in local middle school mathematics classes. She also serves as dean of student life at CAL Prep, in addition to teaching.

**Nilofar Sami** completed her PhD in clinical–community psychology at the University of California, Berkeley and was involved with the California College Preparatory Academy as a graduate student researcher. Her investment in civic engagement in the schools, mental health programs, and with the Afghan community garnered the Chancellor's Award for Public Service in 2009. She works as a clinical psychologist at Youth and Family Services for the City of Fremont, California.

**Angelica Stacy** is professor of chemistry and associate vice provost for the faculty (since 2001) at the University of California (UC) Berkeley. She serves as co-chair of the Early College Initiative committee, which oversees the California College Preparatory Academy. In her administrative role, she addresses issues of recruitment and retention of women and underrepresented minorities. Stacy's research focuses on the synthesis and characterization of new solid-state materials with novel electronic and magnetic properties. Stacy has earned numerous awards for science and teaching, including the Francis P. Garvan-John M. Olin Award from the American Chemical Society (1994). At UC Berkeley, she has been recognized by a Distinguished Teaching Award (1991) and the Chancellor's Award for Advancing Institutional Excellence (2013).

**Stacy Thomas** is dean of academics at Aspire Public School's Golden State College Preparatory Academy in Oakland. After 7 years of teaching, Thomas joined the California College Preparatory Academy as a mathematics teacher and served there from 2006 to 2011. He earned his bachelor's degree at the University of California, Riverside and his teaching credential at the University of San Francisco.

**Rhona S. Weinstein** is professor of the Graduate School and professor emerita of psychology at the University of California, Berkeley. She was founding co-director of research and development for the California College Preparatory Academy and former director of the clinical psychology program. Weinstein's research focuses on expectations and educational equity. Author of *Reaching Higher: The Power of Expectations in Schooling* (2002), she is the recipient of numerous awards in science and teaching, among them the Division K Book Award for Exemplary Research on Teaching and Teacher Education from the American Educational Research Association (2003), as well as the Distinguished Contributions to Theory and Research in Community Psychology (2001) and the Seymour B. Sarason Award for Community Research and Action (2005) from the American Psychological Association. Weinstein was also honored with a University Distinguished Teaching Award (1996), the Chancellor's Award for Advancing Institutional Excellence (2006), and the Berkeley Citation (2007).

**Frank C. Worrell** is a professor in the Graduate School of Education and affiliate professor in the Department of Psychology at the University of California, Berkeley He was founding co-director of research and development for the California College Preparatory Academy and serves as co-chair of the Early College Initiative committee. Worrell also directs the school psychology program and the Academic Talent Development program. Prior to obtaining his doctorate, he worked as a teacher and counselor and was also a principal of a secondary school serving at-risk youth. His areas of expertise include academic talent development and the translation of psychological research findings into school-based practice. Honors include awards for distinguished scholarly contributions from the National Association for Gifted Children (2013) and the Society for the Psychological Study of Culture, Ethnicity, and Race (2015) of the American Psychological Association, as well as the Chancellor's Award for Advancing Institutional Excellence (2011).

# INDEX

Note: Page numbers in italics represent chapters authored or coauthored by a specific person. Page numbers with "*n,*" "*t,*" "*f,*" and "*b*" denote notes, tables, figures, and boxes, respectively.

facilities and sites
  Berkeley site, 188–89
  building challenges, 354
  current, 389, 393–94
  Golden Gate site, 66–67, 84–85, 188
families
  barriers to learning in, 126, 126*t*,
    133, 135
  educational opportunities provided
    by, 320
  support for, 281–82
Ferguson, R., 376
field trips, 307
Finland, collaborative planning in, 377–78
Fleischman, S., 14–15
Forster, G., 11
Fruitvale Central, student recruitment
  from, 67–68, 71
Fryer, R. G., Jr., 295
Fullan, M., 376
Fuller, Bruce, 58
funding
  by Aspire Public Schools, 52, 354, 368
  cost of SMART supports, 309
  by UC Berkeley, 367, 368

Galassi, J. P., 97–98, 100, 294
Garcia, Maribel, 267, 333
Gates Foundation
  District–Charter Collaboration
    Compact, 376
  Early College Initiative, 17, 34, 56 (*See
    also* Early College Initiative)
  expectations for early college
    courses, 69–70
  high school–college blending policy, 63
Geil, K., 16
gender, library use and, 168, 169, 170–71
Gladwell, M., 320
Golden Gate site, 66–68, 84–85, 188
Goldsmith, Phyllis, 355
Goodin, Marjorie (Susie), *163*
  blue notebook/red cart benefits, 171
  book access improvements, 169
  collaboration with teachers, 175
  introduction to CAL Prep, 163

as participant observer, 179
READ 180 implementation, 85
Graduate School of Education (GSE)
  collaboration with Student Affairs, 44–50
  relationship with CAL Prep, 372–73
  vision for Early College
    Initiative, 39–44
graduation rates, high school
  at CAL Prep, 198–200, 199*t*
  in U.S., 11–12
Gray, Paul, 41, 49
Greene, J. P., 11
Gregory, A., 204, 308
Gronsky, Ron, 50
Grow, Ryan, 7, *211*
growth mindset, 303
Grubb, W. N., 295
Gums, Shyra, xi–xii, 7
Gutiérrez, K. D., 381
Gwande, Atul, 382–83

Hale, R. L., 321
Harlem Children's Zone, 294, 295
Harrison, K., 122
Hastings, Reed, 45
health services, 97, 294, 296
hearing, sense of, 218
Henig, J. R., 186–87
Heppen, J., 14–15
high school. *See* secondary school
history. *See* equity in teaching of history
Hoffman, J. L., 16
home–school communication
  challenges, 153–54
  early emphasis on, 144
  parent engagement and feedback,
    148–49, 149*t*, 158–59
home–school divide
  efforts to address, 158–59
  factors in, 146, 149–50, 157–58
  parent involvement and, 82–83, 146,
    149–50, 156
  student transition into CAL Prep
    and, 128, 130, 132–33, 132*f*,
    136, 137
hybrid model of school design, 66–68

Weinstein, Rhona (*Cont.*)
  on developmental progression in support programs, 310
  Early College Initiative involvement, 40
  liaison role, 63, 80
  on organizational culture in higher education, 347
  overview of CAL Prep involvement, 5–6
  student support development, 268
Whiting, G. W., 321
whole-school compact, 89
whole-student development, 271–73, 361, 375–76, 377
Wilkinson, R., 12
Wilson, Mark, 41, 48, 50, 51
Woodrow Wilson National Fellowship Foundation (WWNFF)
  on challenges of boundary crossing, 56
  curriculum expectations, 87

funding for student support development, 268
network of early college secondary schools, 63–64, 81, 289–90
research studies, 90
role in Early College High School Initiative, 56
UC Berkeley grant submission, 50–53
Worrell, Frank, *3, 143, 317, 359, 389*
  on academic identity characteristics, 321
  CAL Prep Chorus, 86
  chemistry department interviews, 250
  liaison role, 63, 80
  overview of CAL Prep involvement, 6–7
Wrap-Around Services Coordinator, 271–73
WWNFF. *See* Woodrow Wilson National Fellowship Foundation